Copyright © 2013 by D. W. Burdick

UNEDITED EDITION

All rights reserved, including the right to reproduce this manuscript or portions thereof in any form whatsoever without permission from the author, D. W. Burdick, in writing, except by a reviewer who wishes to quote brief passages in connection with a review in a magazine, newspaper, email broadcast or online.

Published by: D. W. Burdick

For information please contact D. W. Burdick by email at:
americayouvebeenhustled@gmail.com

ISBN-10: 099108960X (Paperback)

ISBN-13: 978-0-9910896-0-4 (Paperback)

ISBN-13: 978-0-9910896-1-1 (Kindle)

DEDICATION

First, to the Creator of Heaven and earth; Almighty God the Father, God the Son and God the Holy Spirit…

Second, to all of the courageous God fearing, Constitutional Conservative leaders and everyday American citizens who are rising up to stop the insidious march of radical atheism, progressivism, statism, socialism, communism and other secular idealism that is bankrupting the morals and finances of the United States of America…

Third, to our Nation's military and all the other front-line first-responders, especially the police who are under assault by liberal progressives and who protect us and our freedoms everyday…

Last, to my friends Don, Raymond and Jerry who have stood by me and prayed for me when I needed it most. Without them, this book would not have been possible. Thanks to my sister Michelle and my brothers Alan and Don for their love and support along with their valuable feedback and cursory review of the manuscript. And finally, all my love and appreciation to my children, Natalie, David and Christopher, who along with all of our children and grandchildren in this great Nation are the very reasons to write this book…

I pray that God will bless the United States of America, a shining light on the hill; hopefully, guiding the entire World to the true meaning of "The Pursuit of Happiness." May we remain the beacon of hope for the poor and the disadvantaged in the next 2,000 years, or until Jesus returns to establish His Kingdom on earth "as it is in Heaven." Until then, Christians are to bring a little Heaven to earth through our Love and Charity to the poor and the disadvantaged who are suffering from lack or tragedy…

TABLE OF CONTENTS

BLANK PAGE

Letter to Conservative Republican Leaders:

Date: Perpetual

My fellow Conservative Americans,

I have written a provocative, wake-up America, book called ***"America You've Been Hustled!"*** I feel highly confident the main theme in the book has the highest probability of successfully changing the voting trends in America from voting for liberal democrats to voting for conservative republicans.

First, there is no chance whatsoever that this book will be read by a democrat; this book is a Sun Tzu "The Art of Conservative Political Warfare" treatise to be used against our arch enemies, the liberal socialist democrats. Does this sound too harsh coming from a God fearing Christian? Possibly! But, Christian democrats need to come to the realization that many in their party, especially their leadership, are responsible for radical atheism, socialism and most importantly, the abortion of 55+ million American babies.

Every God fearing constitutional conservative republican should be in a battle with liberal socialist democrats; our weapons are words and our battlefield is everywhere. The reason America is currently so polarized politically is the liberal socialist democrats are winning this war. They know how close they are to the permanent tipping point where voters are one or more of these: 1. ignorant to their destructive goals; 2. permanently poor; 3. lack the education to get ahead; or 4. believe the lies of the left. That said the silent majority, who are conservative God fearing Americans, are waking up from their hectic lives and are pushing back. These modern day patriots are called The Tea Party.

Second, how have the **Liberal Socialist Democrats ("LSD")** increased their voting bloc with the disenfranchised, the poor, and the otherwise "made-up" disadvantaged groups like women, races, youth, seniors and gays? **They have used highly successful, but common marketing sound bites.** As I explain in detail (many times) in my book, we must do the same thing. I believe it is the only way we can change the minds of liberal constituents along with the undereducated and those who have no idea of the consequences of socialism. I don't spend too much time calling them progressives, statists, collectivists, big-government liberals, etc., because not everyone understands these labels.

Third, I used to think that everyone understood what socialism means; I no longer do. Most young people have no idea what socialism is or how it leads to corruption from those in charge of the money and other resources. Therefore, summarize clearly and succinctly what socialism is and how it has never worked and will never work no matter which set of con men are in charge. Socialism enslaves the poor in return for crumbs; they are the pawns of the rich liberal socialist democrats and they are blind to the con. Their leadership is addicted to their drugs of choice – power, money, control and fame. These master deceivers turn every crisis (that they cause) to their advantage.

Finally, get the uninformed to envision the pain and suffering waiting for them at the end of the socialist road we are currently on. Then lay their future pain and suffering at the feet of the **LSD Party** and the "enabling" Moderate Republicans. Remember the TV ad of a young republican politician throwing grandma over the cliff? That should have been our commercial because that's exactly what the **LSD Party** will eventually do to the very groups they claim to protect – seniors, the poor, women, minorities like Latino and Black Americans, Gays, and even the middle class…

This strategy must be forceful, relentless and perpetual if the Founder's America is to survive the relentless and insidious encroachment of socialism and the radical atheist's removal of God and morality from our society.

Please give this book your thoughtful consideration. Not everyone will have the courage to personally say the brutally honest and provocative statements in this book. But, I believe promoting it will go a long way to successfully and permanently gaining control of both houses of congress and the presidency.

Remember, this highly successful strategy is/has been used **against** conservative republicans by the democrats and their slobbering sycophants in the drive-by media, Hollywood and Madison Avenue for decades.

The leaders in the democrat party, like all successful hustlers, routinely lie with such boldness and conviction that only the brightest and most skeptical voter will see through their con. Additionally, the main stream media, Hollywood, Madison Avenue and other liberal strongholds routinely acts as a propaganda machine for these hustlers in LSD Party. They cover up any LSD scandal and create or amplify Republican scandals. CALL THEM OUT DAILY…

We are in a battle for America's future, and our weapons are "words!" Therefore, the LSD's casting of Conservative Republicans as "terrorists, extremists, arsonists, murderers, extortionists… well you get the point – must be countered with the language in this book. If they can call us terrorists (which the president is killing) then surely it's OK to call them "HUSTLERS." What do you think? **It is paramount we win this war of words, and I am highly confident we will win with a much stronger offense – from every corner of America.** It's no longer effective just to say, "There you go again," implying they are lying. **Call them socialist hustlers…** Let's face it – if lying was an Olympic sport the White House would be renamed Fort Knox!

My book is just a small, but essential, part of an overall "marketing campaign" to convince the public, especially the ill-informed, that: 1. Freedom and wealth are by-products of "true" free-market capitalism, especially entrepreneurial capitalism within a Judeo-Christian God fearing society; and, 2. Tyranny and poverty are the by-products of a coercive socialist or crony-capitalist society where God is considered the opiate of the ignorant. Do we need a PhD in economics to understand the differences between "true" free-market economies vs. crony capitalism, socialist or government run economies? Absolutely not! Just compare the hugely successful country of South Korea to the misery in North Korea, or Texas to California, or Dallas to Detroit. These comparisons are factual and undeniable…

Our "marketing campaign" or the "war-of-words" needs both the carrot and the stick. **The carrot is** all of our positive speaking conservatives who, like Ronald Reagan, are unflappable in their skillfulness to make us believe in America's ability to achieve greatness under the worst of circumstances. **The stick is** exactly what has been so successful for the **L**iberal **S**ocialist **D**emocrats to scare the public about Conservative Republicans. They have been using the stick to scare our weakest Americans for more than a hundred years. I hope "our stick" becomes successful immediately. **We have facts on our side; let's use them…**

When confronted with their made-up wars on women, the poor, Black Americans, Hispanics or any other group, **just say this**: Women, Blacks, Hispanics and especially the poor are the PAWNs of the LSD Party. They trade crumbs and a failed education department, which keeps them poor, for votes!!!

These master hypocrites are in bed with the FAT CATS in Wall Street, Hollywood and Madison Avenue, but then cleverly feign indignation. I REPEAT: They are USING these groups as PAWNS. Their socialist policies are crushing cities like Detroit and states like California. They don't care who suffers as long as they can get more power, control, money and fame – their drugs of choice! **The LSD Party has hallucinated long enough; vote them out!**

LSD leaders like President Obama and uber liberal Senator Elizabeth Warren love to say to business owners something like: You didn't build that business by yourself – you had the public roads, education system and other government supplied factors that helped you. How stupid are their believers? All those government supplied factors were available to everyone – how come only a few succeeded? To use their reasoning we would have to take away every championship or MVP trophy from the winners because those stadiums, and the roads to get there, were supplied by governments and others. Wow…

The difference between what they're doing and what I'm suggesting is quite simple – THE TRUTH… **They are lying like all con men and hustlers do and my book simply points it out!**

This may be the most important point: **This strategy must be relentless and permanent because socialist hustlers, like all criminals, will never stop their insidious quest for more power, money, control and fame…**

Do you want the Hispanic vote? Start using these tactics and start teaching the fundamental information in this book? Hispanic voters want the same standard of living as everyone else. The Pursuit of Happiness is a philosophy while its attainment is clearly a result of education and/or hard work.

What do democratic leaders, hustlers, thieves, rioters, looters and even ISIS have in common? They would rather TAKE than CREATE…

Here are similar sound bites every republican should be repeating daily:

A Capitalist Creates – A Socialist Takes

The LSD Party, like all Hustlers would rather Take than Create!

Too harsh? Not as harsh as a bankrupt America. "Sound bite" education of these "FACTS," along with fervent prayers, may be our only hope…

D. W. Burdick – americayouvebeenhustled@gmail.com

Introduction

Don't mind criticism. If it is untrue, disregard it. If it is unfair, keep from irritation. If it is ignorant, smile. If it is justified it is not criticism, learn from it. – Unknown source

A democracy cannot exist as a permanent form of government. It can only exist until the voters discover that they can vote themselves largesse from the public treasury. From that moment on, the majority always votes for the candidates promising the most benefits from the public treasury with the result that a democracy always collapses over loose fiscal policy, always followed by a dictatorship. The average age of the world's greatest civilizations has been 200 years. Great nations rise and fall. The people go from bondage to spiritual truth, to great courage, from courage to liberty, from liberty to abundance, from abundance to selfishness, from selfishness to complacency, from complacency to apathy, from apathy to dependence, from dependence back again to bondage.

Alexander Fraser Tytler: (1747 – 1813) was a Scottish advocate, judge and historian who served as a Professor of Universal History including Greek and Roman Antiquities at the University of Edinburgh, United Kingdom.

People will vote politicians into power if politicians promise them money and benefits; and amazingly, crooked politicians don't even have to give voters their own money; they give them other people's money. That's how democrats win elections… Even more disturbing is the massive amount of political and bureaucratic cronyism that is funneling (stealing) billions from the federal government and finding its way to friends of politicians and bureaucrats everyday all over America, especially in and around Washington, DC.

Every politician knows, or should know, the above quote by Alexander Tytler. The ones that couldn't care less about it are the liberal socialist democrats and some of the moderate republicans. Why, because the above truth is their pathway to power, money, control and fame – their drugs of choice… How can I say this with any certainty? The obvious reason is because they, the democrats and moderate republicans, are the group of politicians who are "promising the most benefits from the treasury." They want more taxes, more spending, more job and economy killing regulations and a more expensive, bureaucratically burdened government. Tea Party Patriots and God fearing constitutionally conservative republicans want fewer taxes, less spending, less job killing regulations and a smaller, less expensive government where freedom reigns. **Yes, it's really that simple…**

The very difficult balancing act is to help the poor and the disadvantaged while simultaneously restricting fraud. Jesus said to feed and care for the widows and orphans, the poor, the sick, and the disadvantaged. Holy Scripture also says that if you refuse to work, you don't eat. Meaning if you are able bodied and refuse to work you can forget welfare benefits.

I believe we are in Tytler's apathy to dependence stage now, and will be back to the bondage stage in the next generation if free-market, constitutional conservative republicans can't figure out how to educate our poor, our youth, every race, gender and other "groups" of voters on the destructive consequences of socialism that has been operating inside the Democratic Party for more than a hundred years.

Milton Friedman said:

> Political freedom means the absence of coercion of a man by his fellow men. The fundamental threat to freedom is power to coerce, be it in the hands of a monarch, a dictator, an oligarchy, **or a momentary majority.** The preservation of freedom requires the elimination of such concentration of power to the fullest possible extent and the dispersal and distribution of whatever power cannot be eliminated – **a system of checks and balances**.

George Washington is considered by most to be the greatest president in American history. He was also one of the richest men in America in his time and led this country to freedom from unjust taxation and tyrannical rule by the ruling political powers in England. Few people realize how deeply religious he was and how much he relied on prayer and Christian scriptures to guide his life and everyday decisions.

Historians laud Washington for his selection and supervision of his generals, encouragement of morale and ability to hold together the army, coordination with the state governors and state militia units, relations with Congress and attention to supplies, logistics, and training.

After victory had been finalized in 1783, Washington resigned rather than seize power, proving his opposition to kings or dictatorship and his commitment to American republicanism. He returned home until he was called upon again to preside over the convention that drafted the United States Constitution.

Washington was elected the first president by unanimous choice in 1788, and he served two terms in office. He oversaw the creation of a strong, well-financed national government that maintained neutrality in the wars raging in Europe, suppressed rebellion, and won acceptance among Americans of all types. His leadership style established many forms and rituals of our government that have been used since – such as using a cabinet system and delivering an inaugural address. Washington is universally regarded as the "Father of this Country."

Washington's "*Farewell Address*" was an influential primer on republican virtue and a warning against partisanship, sectionalism, and involvement in foreign wars. He retired from the presidency in 1797 and returned to his home, Mount Vernon, and his domestic life where he managed a variety of enterprises. He freed all his slaves by his final 1799 will.

http://en.wikipedia.org/wiki/George_Washington

We have in office today a president with none of these character traits or management and leadership abilities. And certainly a president that clearly believes it would be better if he were king so he could rule as he sees fit without interference from modern day conservative patriots that believe and act like George Washington.

This book will attempt to show and possibly prove the following:

- America has been taken over by the big-government liberal socialist left and the only resistance over time has come from conservative republicans, most recently the Tea Party movement.
- The liberal left can be labeled as big-government statist or socialist-capitalist or capitalist-socialist or simply socialist. I will use the term ***"Liberal Socialist Democrats"*** or ***"LSD."***
- The "Occupy Wall Street/99 Percenters" had it half right, but their focus should have been on the real crooks, the politicians, that occupy our nation's capital, Washington, DC, not Wall Street. Is Wall Street guilty of crony capitalism and manipulation of economic outcomes? Sometimes, but our leaders in Washington, mostly on the left, are willing accomplices while feigning indignation. Our federal politicians and bureaucrats are in bed with Wall Street, big business, mainstream media and other liberal strongholds to divert/swindle hundreds of billions of the nation's tax dollars into their friends' pockets knowing full well that it will return to them – even while in office. Obama calls them "Fat Cats" – then he golfs, vacations, consorts and gives them insider "crony deals" like $500 million to Solyndra.
- Some of the top 1% may call for higher taxes – but it is just an investment in scamming the next 9% of rich Americans, where the vast majority of "millionaires" exist. The top 1% has the political connections and "tax shelters" that small business owners, the next 9%, don't have. It's these "Fat Cat" political connections that help to create or protect their top 1% incomes. Those supporters in liberal strongholds that don't make millions still get

very comfortable incomes from their connections with liberal power brokers. The liberal socialist democrats, their slobbering sycophants in NYC and Hollywood and some moderate republicans have a vested interest in keeping the status quo.

- After losing the 2012 elections the GOP is planning to showcase their new image by explaining their issues better. Really, is that how the liberal socialist democrats beat you? No, they beat you by demagoguing the rich white straight Christian males in the GOP. They pit race against race, women against men, young and old against middle age, gay against straight, etc. etc… Their war cry is "the rich get richer and the poor get poorer," "the rich don't pay their fair share," "republicans want dirtier air and water," republican this and republican that. They are programing the weak minded or those too busy to notice anything but sound bites (a huge number of voters). Stop playing defense and start playing offense. Every other word should be ***"liberal-socialist-democrat."*** Connect liberal to socialist, socialist to democrat, socialist to failure, socialist to corruption, socialist to bankruptcy, socialist to poverty, socialist to tyranny, socialist to totalitarian control, socialist back to democrat and most importantly socialist to suffering – **the poorest classes always suffer the most in liberal socialist countries.**
- The biggest racists in America today, are the race baiters and race hustlers who have a vested interest in keeping racial tensions alive. If racism ended tomorrow their power would be gone and their careers would be over. Why do these race hustlers belong to the Democrat Party – because of their own unique promise of "something for nothing" fits right in with liberal socialist democrats' narrative?
- Sorry about what I'm saying next, but – A great many democrat voters are too stupid to figure out they're being ***"Hustled."*** Another percentage simply doesn't have the desire or the time to become educated to the truth, so they also accept the sound bites of the left. Fix it with GOP sound bites like "liberal socialist democrats are leading cities, states and countries to bankruptcy." Another percentage are now so dependent, even if they become

convinced America is headed toward socialist destruction they are so addicted to welfare benefits they don't feel equipped to break loose from their dependence on these welfare programs. Start developing conservative designed educational, training and **most importantly motivational programs** that will teach and inspire them to break free from the **LSD crumbs** and do what it takes to achieve financial independence.

- Tell everyone daily – NO, HOURLY – Liberal socialist democrat policies starve capital from the free-market economy with excessive taxes followed by strangling the free-market economy with excessive laws, rules and regulations that are hurting the job market, wealth creation and the upward mobility of the poor from poverty to prosperity. The liberal socialist democrats are creating wealth for themselves and their friends at the expense of the middle class and the poor they are hustling. They expect poor Americans to settle for welfare crumbs in exchange for votes. If the poor realized this they would stop voting for the LSD Party and look to God fearing conservatives for help.

When the liberal socialist democrat's propaganda machine, i.e., the mainstream media, liberal colleges, labor unions, Madison Avenue and Hollywood make a monumental issue out of my suggestions and a **relentless** labeling of the LSD party – just agree and repeat.

DO NOT DEFEND THIS ATTACK – AGREE WITH IT…

If they dare bring it up – gladly and enthusiastically pound it home with agreement. Make them avoid the issue because they know this narrative style works – they have been using this negative attack style for decades ("the rich get richer" and "the rich need to pay their fair share" etc.). Remember your target audience is the same group of the population that the LSD party has used this same tactic on over the last 50 years. This target audience doesn't have the time or the mental capacity to understand complex issues. Keep it short and simple! You may turn off some of our conservative or moderate constitutes if you're not on board by being completely honest and BOLDLY letting everyone know the purpose of this offensive. SAVING AMERICA!

Moderate republicans and more importantly the republican establishment will decry this attack style as negative and self-destructive. Don't pay any attention to them – they are socialist enablers at best and certainly part of the problem. They may have good intentions but this country is being destroyed by good intentions that have led to crushing debt and economy strangling taxes, laws, rules and regulations.

Tell everyone that conservatives are sick of the lies of the left and we are going to be **brutally honest without reservations.** We simply must counter the sound bites of liberal socialist democrats and educate the masses that socialism, in any form, destroys countries, states, cities, families and individual lives. **You know it's the truth so man-up and let's get the job done… If everyone is on board – we can't fail…**

The author is not a rich person trying to serve his own self-interests or the interests of the rich. On the contrary, he is currently living just above the poverty level, and never higher than the middle class. Since leaving college in 1977 to start a small manufacturing company with a friend, his experience has included: small business ownership, commercial banking, securities brokerage, mortgage brokerage, commercial construction and real estate development. These entrepreneurial and fortune 500 experiences have given him a great deal of insight into how a free-market economy works and the causes of the housing crisis that nearly destroyed the world's economy in 2008 and what we need to do today to build a robust economy.

His commercial construction and real estate development career came to an end in 2008 because of the housing crisis. He then suffered a disabling accident in 2010 and lost everything he had because he couldn't afford health insurance and couldn't return to work. As a single father he had to rely on food stamps and good Christian friends for his family's survival for 18 months before receiving social security disability in 2011. This last experience also gives him a unique insight into the trials of the needy, and the government programs that provide a safety-net for them vs. friends and family assistance.

You would think he would be a democrat, like his parents were, since the Democrat Party claims to represent the poor, the needy, the disadvantaged and the disabled. If the Democrat Party really cared about and helped the poor and the disadvantaged over the long-term he would be a democrat. They don't! It's a big lie, a scam, a con artists' hustle of the American people. Europeans have believed this con for more than a century and look at how many are nearing financial destruction, or at least suffering economic and job stagnation. It is only the free-market elements of their socialist economies that have kept them afloat this long. A close examination of two 100 percent socialist countries like Cuba and North Korea clearly, and without a doubt, proves my point. Their people are suffering tremendously…

American liberal socialist democrats have set in place an educational system that (like other socialist and communist countries) is brain washing and indoctrinating our children in liberal socialist propaganda. These con artists are now "buying" gullible college students' votes using more federal debt to reduce their loans. Again, the *"something for nothing"* con! Ironically, these same college graduates will end up paying off ALL the public debt in the future – a stagnant future.

What college students need is a robust worldwide economy that provides more opportunities and jobs. Liberal socialist democrats don't know how to create a robust economy, only conservative free-market republicans and libertarians do. Let's see – democrats want to pay-off or pay-down student loans with more federal debt that these same students will end up being taxed to death for the rest of their lives by the IRS. Again, how ironic!

These young suckers are being caught in another one of the democrats' ***"Ponzi Schemes."*** I repeat again, this college educated "group" will, on average, make more money than the non-college educated group. Therefore, they will have to pay-off most, if not all, the federal, state and local debts owed because the poor don't pay income taxes anyway. ***Are any of you intelligent well educated college students getting any of this?***

As of today, the federal debt per family is $138,000; even more depressing is that amount is going up thousands every month – so get ready young suckers; your lifetime share is going to $1,000,000+ if liberal socialist democrats continue to get their way. How are you college graduates going to pay the projected $122 trillion in unfunded federal liabilities/debts? You can't – it's impossible! Hopefully, enough of these young adults will wise-up and make a difference in future voting cycles and stop voting for celebrity politicians like Bill Clinton and Barack Obama. If they don't get wise to the con they deserve to inherit their $1,000,000+ share of the federal public debt. Fortunately, there is a conservative and libertarian movement sweeping campuses all across America and these passionate young adults are becoming wise to the democrats' con game.

CNBC occasionally has a special titled: *"Scams, Scoundrels and Suckers."* They have some very interesting stories about con artists' hustling the public out of millions and sometimes billions of dollars. They should do a documentary about the $18 trillion dollar scam that the liberal socialist democrats and moderates have "hustled" from America's future and its' children since 1912. Who are the central criminal figures in each of these scams – a good looking, glad handing, back slapping, charming man with a big smile and a slick believable story. He/she is someone that everyone likes and wants to be associated with – a guy you want to hang with! Hmm… sounds like a couple of guys we all know who plays the saxophone or sings the blues!

When I was a bank Vice President and a commercial loan officer in the late 1970s and early 80s my brother-in-law approached me with an investment opportunity in the Bahamas. It was a construction project that he was invited to participate in. He was a commercial contractor and did a little due diligence on the project. These guys had a very elaborate proposal that was very convincing but my gut told me to dig deeper. After further investigation, I was sure this investment was a scam. I told my brother-in-law what I had found out, but he still put a small fortune in the deal. After several months, these guys came back to my relative for more money to keep the "deal" afloat. Of course, he didn't listen to me again and gave the hustlers more money. At this point, he felt he had to or he would lose his original investment. I wonder how many other commercial contractors put money into this scam. This is how investment scams work – even investments in education, jobs, roads and bridges by the president and liberal socialist democrats in congress. Their programs will only work if they can get more money. See the scam? I realize these roads, bridges and other critical infrastructures must be rebuilt or repaired soon, but there are better ways than taxing incomes. I will detail these better ways later in this book.

I was a commercial banker, stock broker and investment advisor for several decades. I have seen hundreds of scams and have saved many friends small fortunes in losses to these hustlers. I had a gut for bad loans and bad deals, and developed that gut intuition through experience over many years. If you listen to what people are saying they will always give you a "tell" that they are lying, or at the very least "up-to-something." If you don't pay attention and investigate further, you have no one to blame but yourself. Liberals rely on suckers being gullible...

Listen carefully to what the democrats say every day. Sometimes it is so obvious they are blatantly lying and sometimes they are extremely slick and even someone like me who is very skeptical is inclined to believe what they are "selling." I could fill a book with examples of hustlers selling their scams – but at the center of each scam is a very convincing story and a very persuasive (and likable) con artist trying to get your money; and, if he gets your money on the first pass the second pass is even easier. In government, more money is never enough...

Don't get me wrong – I was scammed by someone I had considered a relatively close friend and an arm's length business associate in 2008 when the housing development industry came to halt. I was offered a partnership if I could help him raise the funds for a business venture and then manage it. This friend had targeted one of my best friends who he thought could fund the business venture and needed me to "put the deal together." I was feeling very uncomfortable so I didn't press the issue with my investor friend who really didn't have the needed resources. To my later extreme regret another one of my best friends became aware of the venture and offered to put up the money for not only the operation but also the real estate.

The vast majority of the investment was used to purchase the real estate required for the operation. At least I had the wisdom to structure the deal to protect my best friend (with the capital investment) in case the operating company failed. It did fail but not before the con artist friend had scammed my investor friend out of about $100,000. Later, a different best friend of over 25 years was offered what seemed to be a "sure thing" investment opportunity. He did not have the cash so I was again offered a one-third partnership if I could raise the money. This time I had my eyes wide open and followed my gut instincts to investigate the "deal" to the fullest extent. At the time, I concluded my best friend's partner, that had the "sure thing" business deal, was without a doubt either an idiot or a con artist. It turned out he was both; he was just another stupid hustler. My point is scams are everywhere – even close to home in a circle of friends.

What are democrats dealing in? Bottom line – power, money and control for themselves! What are the dupes who believe in these scams buying? Some are settling for the crumbs of welfare and some are getting the "good feelings" about the socialist utopia they fantasize about. But others, the LSD associates, are getting lucrative connections, contracts or careers. Essentially, the liberal socialist democrats' goal is more taxes on the rich and spending on anything and everything in such large amounts that it is just too easy for waste, fraud, abuse and "skimming-off-the-top."

The bigger the government, the easier it is to hide their embezzlement of the American tax payer. Who really pays in the end? Our children and grandchildren… Republicans, you better find a way to educate these kids to what the liberal socialist democrats are doing to their future or you too will be held responsible for just standing by and complaining about the obvious. The debt tsunami is building…

Let me make this crystal clear right now: Honest, caring, generous, fair minded, God fearing democrats who believe they must be part of the Democrat Party because the Republican Party doesn't care about civil rights, the underprivileged, women's rights, senior citizens, gay rights, or the environment are just plain wrong and are being duped by those in power and their sycophants in the mainstream media.

Conservative Republicans care far more for the weak, human rights and the underprivileged than the leaders of the liberal socialist democrats do. Republicans freed the slaves in the 1860's and we are desperately trying to free the unwanted unborn babies since the Roe v Wade Supreme Court ruling in the 1970's. I prove this with examples throughout this book.

All of my friends are either very conservative republicans or libertarians. I don't know any one of them that believe women or minorities or seniors or gays should be treated any differently than anyone else. All are God's creations. All deserve to be treated with compassion and equality – no better and no worse.

This grouping of Americans is a major warfare tactic of the Liberal Socialist Democratic Party and their trial lawyer friends. This grouping warfare will prove to be a total failure as more data is widely published by conservatives, libertarians and the only "Fair and Balanced" news program – Fox News. Most of the anti-conservative, anti-God liberal news outlets are going broke anyway, so maybe in another decade or so they will all be gone or further diminished.

Consider this: Do we really need to elect "celebrity politicians" that can play the saxophone or sing the blues, or do we need to elect "statesmen" like George Washington, Abraham Lincoln, Ronald Reagan and Tea Party movement conservatives/libertarians who will make the tough decisions to return America back to the path of prosperity – for all of us. In this modern age we need a "hardnosed" Chief Executive, a CEO, like Jack Welch of GE, Henry Ford or maybe Mitt Romney who turned around many businesses along with the Utah Winter Olympics. Good Lord, he was even a very successful republican governor in a very liberal state run by democrats. He made a fortune, for himself and his investors, running a private equity investment management firm. He may not have been as conservative as Ronald Reagan but his resume was surely as impressive. Who were some of his investor clients – liberal college endowments and labor unions? Go figure!

The future will certainly prove that voters should have given him a chance to see what he could do for America. He may not be the most conservative republican, but he seems to have had a very comprehensive conservative plan. I believe his greatest decision was to choose Paul Ryan as his running mate and his biggest mistake was to throttle him back and go soft on Obama in the final weeks before the Election.

He should have allowed Paul Ryan to bring "saving" Medicare, Medicaid and Social Security to the forefront of the campaign. Everyone knows these programs are not sustainable if changes are not made soon. Even more important is changing regulations and the tax system which will lead to a robust economy and job growth. Liberal socialist democrats are masters at diverting these paramount issues – which they created, to focus on abortion rights, women's rights, homosexual rights, gun control and other lessor issues that will not feed or educate anyone. They are all wedge issues designed to divide Americans and cause deep resentments and, just as important, to divert attention from the serious problems facing our nation – problems that can be laid at the feet of the liberal socialist democrats and moderate republicans…

The purpose of this book is to encourage enough thought provoking ideas to wake up enough people to think for themselves and see the socialist con that the liberal left has been selling to gullible democrats and moderate republicans for over a hundred years – before this great country self-destructs.

Also, enough with political correctness – I'm sick of how one sided it is. It only applies to conservatives. Liberal socialist democrats routinely demonize conservatives and libertarians, especially Tea Party conservatives, and call them every ugly name in the book. Tea Party conservatives and libertarians are the modern day patriots, who like their counterparts of 1776, are sick of the how the liberal elites (King Barack the 1st and his royal Democrat Party) are destroying the America that George Washington and our other Founding Fathers created.

I believe I am providing a different perspective on what conservatives need to focus on to turn this country around through provocative insights, brutal honesty and a no-holds-barred attack narrative. My use of juvenile name calling is certainly no worse than the left's labeling the Tea Party Patriots as "Tea Baggers or conservatives as "right wing extremists" or even terrorists – so they can just get over it. If they whine about the name calling, pile on by calling them slobbering hypocrites…

I use some harsh language in this book. I use some harsh language from time to time with my kids also. I apologize to them when I do and I apologize to those I direct this book's harsh language to. I don't hate my kids when I use harsh language with them and I don't hate the liberal socialist democrats that I refer to in this book. I do, however, hate what they are doing to America. These con artists, who are hustling weak minded Americans, will label this book as hate speech as they always do when the light of truth illuminates their real motives. If liars lie, and hustlers con, then the light of truth is the only offense/defense we have.

First, I don't hate anyone although I may hate their actions.

Second, there is a big difference between hate and disrespect – I have no respect for liberal socialist democrats or go-along, lukewarm, moderate republicans.

Last, no matter how good some of their motives might be, their actions are destroying freedom, liberties, morality, marriage and families, our education system, our health care system, our economy, our military, foreign policy, and most importantly – wealth creation opportunities for the poor and middle class. Fortunately, the rich find ways to invest and therefore spur the economy and production forward even in bad times. Without rich investors we would really be doomed to perpetual depressions and national poverty without any avenue for recovery. When are we going to have a national **"Rich Person Holiday"** to celebrate their contributions to America?

I hope this book shocks, angers, educates and quickens enough people to think for themselves, see the truth about liberal socialist democrats' propaganda, make the necessary changes suggested here and vote for God fearing Constitutional Conservative Tea Party Republicans or Libertarians. Here is how I categorize liberal socialist democrats; the **"LSD"** Party:

- Most nonpolitical everyday middle-class democrats, moderate republicans and independents don't have the time to pay much attention to what the democrat leaders real agenda is – power, control, money and fame, i.e., socialism; and, how destructive progressive liberal socialist policies are. They are too consumed with taking care of their families and trying to make ends meet;
- Some of the democrat voters are locked into voting for democrats because their career, *or welfare,* depends on it and they simply don't understand their short-term benefits are a Ponzi scheme that will eventually destroy their long-term future. Remember the FRAM Oil Filter ad that illustrated you could pay the $5 now for the oil filter or pay the $3,000 later to rebuild your engine. Great commercial and illustration of socialism;
- Some liberals are born with a temperament or brain "wiring" that causes them to believe in some kind of utopian fantasy that lends itself to the liberal socialist democrats' scam;

- Some democrats are self-confessed big-government socialists that are incapable of seeing what is happening to socialist cities, counties, states and countries worldwide. These countries are failing miserably; their citizens are suffering needlessly, and they're too stupid to see it – or they just don't give a damn. They want their money, career, power and fame **right now**, and they don't care about the consequences in the future;
- The leadership in the Democratic Party, along with their sycophants in labor unions, academia, media elites, DC, NYC, California and other democratic strongholds are control freak addicts whose lust for "more" cannot be satisfied. Their pathologies are no different from wife and children beaters! They want total control. They lie with such boldness it is amazing to watch. Even if America is crushed, they believe they will flourish because they belong to the "Club" in power. They chose the Democrat Party instead of the Republican Party because it is the easiest path to power by simply hustling the weak minded masses and promising crumbs for votes. Besides, republicans believe in fewer taxes, less spending and less government. Just the opposite of what they need to get more power, control, money and fame for themselves, their friends and associates.

Republicans fight like boxers, with gloves on and very restrictive and proper rules; democrats fight like MMA cage fighters with the referees (the news media, Hollywood and Madison Avenue) on their side. Under those circumstances, we don't have a chance. This fight is for the survival of the greatest country in history. Therefore, take the gloves off and start kicking the hell out of them! **Using their rules not ours…** Your weapons are not your fists, knees and feet. Your weapons are words! Start PUBLICALLY calling these people exactly what they are; lying, cheating, deceiving, swindling, con artist and "Hustlers!" If they are conservative democrats or moderate republican "nice guys" – then they are enablers at best, which is helping the LSD Party lead America to moral and financial destruction. Remember we have Fox News and the hugely successful talk radio conservatives on our side which will tip the scales in our favor. So get busy and grow a set…

The minority voters and the poor that are being duped by the LSD Party believe the propaganda that these political hustlers have sold them in exchange for voting and keeping the LSD in power. Once the LSDs get a taste of this power and fame, no amount of rehab will help them. Look at the disgraced Congressman Anthony Weiner. He can't help himself – he is so addicted to power and fame he is willing to make a snickering laughing stock of himself and run for mayor of NYC.

He appears to have always been eaten-up with narcissism and can't resist the impulse for more power, control, money and fame. And now look who they voted into office. If this is the best that NYC can do, what does that say about the voters of NYC? When are they going to wake up and stop electing power addicts? In the end that's really all it's about – POWER to control lives, guns, salt, sugar and who knows what is next! Again, these leaders, most notably, President Obama, Senator Majority Leader Harry Reed and Congresswomen Nancy Pelosi are the exact opposite of our first leader, George Washington.

I wish Barack Obama was a God fearing constitutional conservative because he is "somewhat" intelligent and extremely charming and likeable; traits that serve the successful con artist! He is a liberal "big-government" democrat who is hostile to free-enterprise, small businesses and the American way that our founders established over 200 years ago. He has been associated in the past, during his youth and then as a young adult, with communist sympathizers and radicals. He attended a church for 20 years where the pastor made the most radical and seemingly hateful statements about America.

The President is intimately involved in details that reflect favorably for him like the killing of Osama bin Laden, but he was uninvolved with saving our diplomatic mission personnel at Benghazi, Libya on the night of September 11, 2011. WHY? What was he doing that night? Was he afraid to "Send in the Marines" to save our people? We have specialized military forces whose motto is "to never leave a fallen soldier behind." Did he give the stand-down order, or Hillary Rodham Clinton, or one of their political hacks, so that the situation would not get any worse just before Election Day? We'll never know because "The Buck Doesn't Stop at his White House!"

The great Ronald Reagan said it best **"Government is the problem, not the solution."** I believe a "We the People" government can be...

I don't think we should just blame the "Hustlers" in the power centers of DC, the northeast, the great lake states, the west coast, the mainstream media, academia, labor unions, Madison Avenue and Hollywood. We will always have socialist hustlers. No, I blame the republicans for not relentlessly educating Americans on the socialist direction the democrats are taking us and the destructive consequences we are about to endure. **America, we live in a sound bite society where repetition is the mother of all skill – get with the program...**

This book isn't necessarily about the current leadership working hard against free-market capitalism, freedom and liberty – Barrack Hussein Obama, Hillary Rodham Clinton, "Dirty" Harry Reed and "We've got to pass it before we can read it" Nancy Pelosi. No, it's about every democrat and moderate republican VOTER who has ever aided and abated liberal social democrats since 1912. That's right – in 1912 our first LSD president, Woodrow Wilson, gave us the Sixteenth Amendment, Federal Income Taxes and the IRS. Of course the liberal socialist democrat, Woodrow Wilson, could not have done this without the help of the two previous moderate republican (progressive) presidents.

Must we wait until America is suffering another depression before we wake up to stop the insidious advance of this political cronyism and outright socialism? ObamaCare is a noble ideal, like all socialist ideals, but it will never work. It is far too complicated with too many opportunities for waste, fraud, abuse and "crony-capitalism." Crony-capitalism is the only capitalism the Liberal Socialist Democratic Party believes in. These idiots will never understand simple free-market principles. I predict that this leviathan bureaucratic blunder will finally end the fascination with utopianism and socialism. I just hope Americans don't suffer too much before we ALL wake up...

You think you vote for some democrats or moderate republicans, but you're not advancing socialism – Keep Reading!

Chapter 1

What do we mean by "Hustled?"

Liberal socialist democrats ("LSD") are a highly specious group with expertly developed persuasion skills combined with narcissistic motives and behaviors – "Hustlers!" Think about it – if you've ever known a con man, he is usually the most likeable guy in the room. He may be tall, dark and handsome, have a great smile and be very intelligent and charming. He's a glad hander and a back slapper; he hugs and kisses the ladies and can hold an audience spellbound. He can parse words and deflect blame with the best of them. Anyone challenging his motives or character is systematically demonized and destroyed. Can you think of anyone like that in American politics today? I thought so!

What do we mean by hustled? We don't mean "energetic activity or drive" in the positive sense of the word as it would be used in sports or business. No, we use the slang meaning of the word in the negative sense as in: 1. to sell or get by questionable means; 2. an illicit or unethical way of doing business or obtaining money, a fraud or deceit; and, 3. to pressure into buying or doing something in a rushed manner to avoid the necessary research required to make an informed decision that might lead to the rejection of the idea, investment or involvement.

Remember Nancy Pelosi's now famous quote, "We have to pass the bill, ObamaCare, so that you can find out what is in it." Even though the democrats controlled the House, the Senate and the Presidency, several Senators had to be *"bought-off"* to the tune of hundreds of millions of dollars by Harry Reid, the Majority Leader of the Senate, before the law could get enough democrat votes to pass (literally in the middle of the night). Really, this LSD law could not even get enough democrat votes to pass without bribes? If the law survives, and it looks like it will, this multi-trillion dollar hustle will ultimately prove to be the final straw to bankrupt the greatest nation in history. Our politicians are arguing over a "fiscal cliff" the size of an ant hill and this new big-government gigantic mountain will eventually dwarf the fiscal cliff.

What a con job this complex law from the LSD Party is on the American People. It is proving to be a bureaucratic nightmare! Sure, universal health care is a noble cause and in theory who could be against it? Like all well-meaning socialist ideals, the problem is in the unintended consequences. It opens up so many new ways for taxes, costly and abusive regulations, waste, fraud and abuse; not to mention cronyism that is the hallmark of the LSD Party.

For you simpletons who can't figure out who the hustlers in politics are, the liberal democrats or the conservative republicans, consider this: What do hustlers want – more power, control, money and fame. What do liberal socialist democrats want – more power, control and money (taxes, spending and regulations)? What do conservative republicans want – less taxes, spending and regulations (smaller, less expensive and less controlling government)?

It's really just that simple yet 51% of American voters in 2012 were too stupid, too lazy or too self-centered to figure it out. And now everybody and, I mean everybody, is going to suffer the consequences – especially our children and grandchildren. The old proverb "There's no free lunch" is about to be proven once again – on a massive scale… Talk about child abuse; this is grandchild abuse!

Here is a Milton Friedman quote that says it best:

> The ICC [Interstate Commerce Commission] illustrates what might be called the natural history of government intervention. A real or fancied evil leads to demands to do something about it. A political coalition forms consisting of sincere, high-minded reformers and equally sincere interested parties. The incompatible objectives of the members of the coalition (e.g., low prices to consumers and high prices to producers) are glossed over by fine rhetoric about "the public interest," "fair competition," and the like. The coalition succeeds in getting Congress (or a state legislature) to pass a law. The preamble to the law pays lip service to the rhetoric, and the body of the law grants power to government officials to "do something." The high-minded reformers experience a glow of triumph and turn their attention to new causes. **The interested parties go to work to make sure that the power is used for**

their benefit. They generally succeed. Success breeds its problems, which are met by broadening the scope of intervention. Bureaucracy takes its toll so that even the initial special interests no longer benefit. In the end, the effects are precisely the opposite of the objectives of the reformers and generally do not even achieve the objectives of the special interests. Yet the activity is so firmly established and so many vested interests are connected with it that repeal of the initial legislation is nearly inconceivable. Instead, new government legislation is called for to cope with the problems produced by the earlier legislation and a new cycle begins.

Good Lord – that's ObamaCare in a nutshell and it's 1/6th of our nation's economy; the size of France's economy. The federal government is on its way to nationalizing the health care industry. What will be next for these liberal "socialist" democrats? ObamaCare will be the proverbial straw that will break America's back. Liberal socialist democrats and their sycophants keep saying that 60% of all bankruptcies in America are attributable to medical bills. Is that one of their reasons for justifying the socialist takeover of the healthcare industry?

What America needs to realize is the LSDs will bankrupt an entire nation attempting to save a very small percentage of us from personal bankruptcy. Again, good intentions from a group of socialist and crony capitalist idiots will never solve society's problems; only a robust economy built on conservative free-market principles has the best chance of solving social issues. Our economy and job creation is suffering from decades of the socialist policies of democrats and moderate republicans. These people are either too stupid to see what they are doing to America or they just don't care. What do you think?

Another major tactic of the skilled hustler is manipulation. Manipulation is rampant and perverse in legislative politics on both sides and should be outlawed as much as possible. What I'm talking about is legislation that is sent to "kill committees" or laced with "poison pills." Everyone knows what is happening – manipulation – by the powerful members to stop the weaker members of the Senate and the House. It's time these bums start earning their fat incomes and start letting everything come to the floor for an up or down vote in its simplest form without riders or amendments of any kind. Stop adding pet projects or pork amendments. This country is chocking on pet projects and pork.

It appears some of our best "statesmen" are doctors and most of our worst "politicians" are liars, I mean lawyers. We need to somehow limit the number of lawyers elected and start electing more "successful" businessmen and medical doctors. Medical doctors understand the pathology of manipulation and how destructive it is to relationships, families, societies and governments. Again, I refer you to Obama, Reid and Pelosi as the gold medal winners of lying and manipulation.

Getting back to bureaucratic nightmares… Why is modern health care so expensive? Because of health care insurance! Simple supply demand economics proves that "free" health care supplied by employers and insurance companies reduce the selection discretion of patients shopping for the best price. Price shopping is essential to increasing the competitive element which historically results in lower costs or prices. Health insurance coverage for services without some percentage of a cost sharing by patients will *always* result in higher prices for services. Also, with 30 million new customers (ObamaCare) without a proportionate increase in doctors, nurses and other providers will also result in higher prices. Oh! Wait a minute, we could use price controls as we did in the stupid 1970's liberal socialist democrat gas shortage turmoil.

When will liberals learn? NEVER, so get rid of them…

It is simple supply/demand basics – something that seems to elude the liberal socialist democrats' brain functioning. More customers indiscriminately demanding more services without more providers will result in either: higher prices, fewer services or both. Health care costs have risen at a much higher rate than anything else in the economy the last many decades because of the combination of health insurance and lawsuits. Watch what happens now that ObamaCare is the law of the land and when it is fully implemented. Now, in the summer of 2013 the liberal socialist democrats are postponing the most expensive and restrictive elements of ObamaCare until after the 2014 midterm elections. We should have predicted that move by these control freak political criminals long ago! Now, what are we going to do about it?

Proof of the supply/demand equation is Lasik Eye Surgery and elective plastic surgery. **Because these are not covered by common healthcare insurance policies, prices have fallen drastically over the years.** You can't say it's because of technological advances – that is common to most medical services. No, it is simply free-market competitive economics that is so difficult for liberal socialist democrats to understand. Let's say absolutely everything associated with health care is covered by every insurance company, or the government, including drugs, vitamins, aspirin, runny noses, scratched knees and elbows, Kleenex, acne, prophylactics, eye glasses, sunglasses, sunscreen, suntan lotion, regular lotion, health clubs, health foods – well you get the point. Only a sucker believes you get *"something for nothing."*

The result would be that demand for all of these free goods and services would go up. As demand goes up – prices go up. Then insurance premiums go up. Oh, that's right! Universal healthcare would be provided by the government, so it really doesn't cost us anything. **What idiot believes that?** Therein lays the liberal socialist democrat hustle leading to a bankrupt country. Consider this old saying: "Short-term pain leads to long-term gain." The opposite is true also: "Short-term something-for-nothing pleasure (spending) leads to the long-term pain of a bankrupt economy." If America doesn't choose to rid this country of all the socialist laws and big-government bureaucracies soon (short-term pain) then we will be forced through austerity (long-term pain) for decades. Again, just like the old FRAM Oil Filter commercial said; "You can pay me now, $5 for the oil filter, or you can pay me later, $3,000 to rebuild the engine. Clever commercial, but very true!

Healthcare costs, and college education costs for similar reasons, have increased much faster than the rate of inflation because of government intervention and the incentive to price shop or question costs have been insulated from the buyer. This all started with employers (those evil corporations) competing with each other for the best employees by offering ever increasing benefits like "free" health insurance.

Combine this indiscriminate selection of "free" services with the blood sucking trial attorneys' gaming of the legal system and you get the perfect storm of out of control health care costs. Now, the democrats' solution to this problem is to transfer the cost to our national debt – to our children and grandchildren. How can so many old people (I'm 62 so don't have a cow) and women, who vote for democrats, continue to go along with this? Maybe it's the same reason so many seniors and women are targeted by other con artists – ***they're gullible!***

Does this make you angry? Those of us who don't vote for the Liberal Socialist Democratic Party and moderate republicans are the ones who deserve to be angry. We are suffering the same fate for your poor voting decisions. In a "fair and equitable" political system, pulling the voting lever for a big government liberal socialist democrat or a moderate republican should increase those voters' income taxes by an extra 5 to 10 percent. Let them put their own money where their mouths are and see how much they really care. **You and I both know they wouldn't pull the democrat lever under those circumstances!**

Scams and hustlers are everywhere – on TV and the internet, in the mail and all print media. There are billions hustled from gullible Americans every year, but nothing compared to the trillions that the LSD Party have and will continue hustling from future tax payers and the American economy. New laws, regulations and taxes will eventually strangle the economy to the point that tax revenues will drop even more than happened in the great recession. Once we exceed $20+ trillion in debt and have another recession we are doomed. I predict this scenario may occur around the end of Obama's second term if changes are not made soon. Whoever follows Obama will have it much worse if nothing is done before 2016. Once the debt exceeds $20 trillion and if the economy picks up enough the potential higher interest rates will significantly increase the federal debt with zero corresponding benefit.

The only way out of this eventual disaster is to double the economy while holding spending as close to current levels as possible – just the opposite of what the liberal socialist democrats and moderate republicans are doing. Doubling the economy would significantly increase tax revenues and bring down the "real" jobless rate back near the 4% level that America enjoyed during republican control of the presidency and/or congress. If we don't do this, the poor and the middle class will continue to decline resulting in needless suffering… How do we double the economy? The same way Reagan, Clinton (Gingrich) and Bush 43 did except to a much greater extent: Slash regulations and simplify taxes to turn businesses and the economy loose. Add to that the enormous new oil reserves we have discovered (we are the new Middle East). Drill on federal lands with royalties paid directly to our nation debt. The new energy boom will generate enormous tax revenues and new job creation. Reform welfare and ObamaCare and replace them with free-market based and state administered programs. **K**eep **I**t **S**imple **S**tupid should be the guiding principle.

Speaking of taxes – liberal socialist democrats refer to *payroll taxes* in the same category as *income taxes.* Every time a sensible politician (conservative or libertarian) refers to the majority of American households paying no *income taxes* they are demonized and corrected by saying every working American pays taxes – what they mean is *payroll taxes.* Payroll taxes are contributions to our Social Security retirement program, not income taxes. It also makes me sick to see the republicans using this issue to say the democrats raised taxes (the return of the 2% payroll tax reduction that was used to spur the economy) on working Americans after the end of the year 2012 sequestration deal. When you guys pull this kind of crap you're no better than the democrats!

<u>Payroll taxes are not income taxes</u>; it is a workers payroll contribution to our countries' Social Security retirement system. Only dirty politicians or dirty media co-conspirators would try to get away with such a stupid and easily debunked lie that everyone pays income taxes. For the last 2 years, this lie of calling this a tax break to stimulate the economy is a joke. All they are doing is causing social security to go bankrupt sooner. Besides, many economists believe this "stimulus" tax cut does little for the economy anyway. In later chapters, we will discuss tax reform that increases some income taxes while decreasing other taxes which I believe will supercharge the economy and by consequence supercharge treasury income tax collections. At the very least, my suggestions reduce the cronyism built into our completely unfair income tax system by ridding it of loopholes, deductions and tax credits which favors some over others.

Another massive socialist hustle that is being propagated on developed nations is commonly known as **"<u>The "New World Order</u>."** I don't quite get this conspiracy theory. Of course, I don't get socialism either. I'm not saying it isn't true. But, why would the super-rich want to inhibit anyone from rising up the wealth ladder? Wealth isn't like beach front property near population centers, which is limited. The wealth pie can be grown and therefore can be unlimited in size.

Increased commerce worldwide leads to increased wealth creation worldwide. Honest, fair trade between nations also promotes peace. We should be doing everything possible to promote fair trade, especially with poor countries. International socialism between countries produces the same failures and dependencies as it does within countries. It just doesn't work by any measure. What it does do very well is transfer our tax dollars to the crooks running those countries receiving our money. Think about it, our leaders are knowingly sending Americans' money, which we borrow with interest, to the crooked leaders of third world countries. Who are the dupes? We are – for allowing liberal socialist democrat and moderate republican politicians to get away with it!

Free trade is extremely important to worldwide wealth creation. Think about it – the wealthier the population the more commerce and trade occurs. I repeat, increased wealth creates increased commerce, and therefore increased tax receipts. Who benefits? Everyone! Surely the people behind the new world order believe this. Wealth derives from ones hard work, savings, creativity, investment, innovation, productivity, invention and good decisions within a free-market capitalist society. It doesn't come from conquering new lands or redistributing wealth between nations!

The idea that America is imperialistic is absurd. No one in this day and age should believe countries should conquer new lands to get more wealth. And, if America were imperialistic why didn't we keep Germany, Italy, Japan, Iraq and so on. No! We not only didn't keep the spoils of war, but Americans paid for the rebuilding of these countries and encouraged freedom, free-market capitalism and democracy. In fact, defeated countries like Japan and Germany are now two of America's greatest competitors – and allies! You idiots in other countries and even many of you stupid liberals here in this country that believe America is imperialistic are either lying or have a limited depth of understanding the reality of the facts noted above!

I certainly understand the pathology of these *New World Order* elites wanting more power and more control over people and nations; but that's just it – it's a sickness, an addiction, which has destroyed not only nations, but those seeking such power.

Here is what I believe: These super rich and their celebrity sycophants (of the "One World Order") are the ultimate crony capitalists.

They control, or at least highly influence politicians, and in turn their governments, to siphon off (steal) money. With a 2012 USA federal spending budget of $3,800,000,000,000 ($3.8 trillion) how much do you think will be "Hustled" (stolen) by the politically connected? The golden goose is the American taxpayer and their offspring. This "One World Government" and its twin, "Global Warming," is just another way for these liberal socialist democrats to hustle American's wealth.

The connections between the Federal Reserve, the money center banks, the White House, Congress, the International Monetary Fund ("IMF") the United Nations and other international organizations too numerous to list here are where most of the money just disappears. Small business owners, the real targets of liberal socialist democrats, are <u>not</u> where the problem rests – its money center and international banking along with well-connected big businesses! Hey stupid liberals in Washington and Hollywood; Exxon is not the problem. It's "The One World Order International Bankers!"

Of course, you already know it and most of you hypocrites are at the root of the problem. Liberal socialist democrat leadership, labor unions, media elites and their sycophants in New York and Hollywood like to blame the rich and big corporations for the disparity between the rich and the poor. Sure, there are many corrupt CEOs but they pale in comparison to the waste, fraud and abuse that is occurring within the political connections in Washington, DC. Obama likes to disparage the "fat cats." Who is he kidding? He's in bed with a good percentage of them and is rewarding those connected to liberal socialist democrats with "fat" government contracts, tax breaks, and favorable rules and regulations. Hollywood and the media elites look the other way because they belong to the Liberal Socialist Democrat ("LSD") Club. Don't believe me – just look at all the Wall Street insiders in his administration; and Bush's for that matter.

This book will highlight only a tiny fraction of the crony capitalism that goes on between the politically connected rich and powerful, corrupt corporate executives and corrupt politicians. I don't care if they are republicans, democrats or independents; we should investigate, expose and prosecute those guilty of these insidious crimes. Crony capitalism should be a severe crime because it involves those in power – the politically connected, big business, big labor unions and big government (congress, bureaucrats and the executive branch); some of the very people we entrust to protect the weak and the rest of us from crooks.

The hypocrisy of the democrats to demonize all corporate America and all of the rich for the injustices and inequalities between the classes is amazingly absurd. What about their many billionaire donors, such as the radical liberal activist leader, George Soros.

It is part of the misdirection these liberal socialist democrat con-artists use to get you looking at their right hand while their left hand is stealing the wallets of the non-connected rich and the middle-class; dooming the poor to perpetual suffering.

Most of America's millionaires own small businesses and live in middle class neighborhoods. They have nothing to do with the government. They pay the vast majority of this country's income taxes and hire the majority of America's employees. They far outnumber the very rich and well-connected rich that live off their connections. These self-made millionaires are the real targets of the liberal socialist democrats, labor unions and the media elite. Why – because they are competitors of those with connections and they are expendable…

Think about it – the small business with less than 100 employees that "nets" $3 million before taxes needs that money for "working capital" to expand operations. Let me repeat: **WORKING CAPITAL…** But this small business owner is the target of President Obama and the rest of the liberal socialist democrats' class warfare machine. These hustlers say; "the rich needs to pay their fair share." They want to take as much of that $3 million in **working capital** out of that business and into Washington as they can. Not only do they want his money, but they want to take control of his operation, as well. Between federal, state and local rules, regulations and bureaucracies that hinder him, it's a wonder the business can make any money at all. Next step, nationalize as many businesses as possible – say the entire health care system which is 1/6th of our nation's economy! **Sounds like socialism to me…**

These same liberal socialist democrat crooks are the con artists' that "use" women, minorities, seniors, college students and the poor as pawns to scam America. Sure, they do some good for these groups – but at what cost to everyone's future? Who will be hurt the most when we turn into Greece? Not the ruling class liberal socialist democrats, the media elites or the politically connected rich but the middle class and the poor! Like P.T. Barnum said, **"There's a sucker born every minute."**

Here's how you beat these con artist's at their own game – but take it to the next level and be ready for all-out war. Start calling every democrat a "liberal socialist democrat" and a "hustler," and every voter of a democrat candidate a "duped sucker." Take the near-term heat and say it over and over again. **Start programming everyone in American that the socialists have taken over the Democrat Party and the socialists are now taking over America.**

Conservative democrats (are there any left?) and moderate republicans are the enablers – enabling the destruction of America that is! When the mainstream media tries to demonize you for this relentless name calling, remind them they are either a slobbering sycophant or an enabler (ask them which one?). When they laugh and make fun of you, and they will, tell them it's not a laughing matter, or they're part of the problem, not part of the solution. If they become indignant or offended or defensive that's even better. **Give it right back to them like Newt Gingrich did during the debates or Chris Christie does every day.**

If you believe what I am saying but don't have the stomach to withstand the counterattacks from the left and the socialist media propaganda machine then just pray every day for the kind of courage that founded America over two hundred years ago. Those groups that vote in large percentages for liberal socialist democrats – blacks, Hispanics, women, seniors, gays and young adults don't want socialism; and, if they naively do, they certainly don't want to destroy America. Therefore, what the republicans have been doing is not getting through to these groups who want more but will end up with far less. If these groups can see the suffering that citizens are experiencing in Greece, North Korea, Detroit, California and other socialist strong holds, they will be much more likely to vote for constitutional conservative republicans – maybe even Tea Party movement candidates…

That's how we will save America, not trying to defund ObamaCare and risk shutting down the government. This is especially true if we see moderate republican senators not only surrendering before the battle begins but actually switching sides and joining the LSD in demonizing our conservative Tea Party leaders. If these senators disagree with Ted Cruz and Mike Lee; that's ok, but they need to keep their big liberal mouths shut in public. See what I mean when I say, "moderate republicans can be worse than the LSD Party." Moderate republican senators sabotaged the conservative cause and within weeks the ObamaCare website proved Senators Ted Cruz and Mike Lee right. I consider myself very conservative, and I completely disagreed with shutting down the government for more than 1 minute, but I would have never publically expressed my disagreement; but, in private I would have "pounded the table" to try and get my Tea Party brothers to avoid a shut-down.

Without the ObamaCare website disaster we would have given the LSD an easy victory with the budget and debt ceiling battle. We will win this war at the polls with words of truth, not attempted legislation that has near zero chance of passing the senate and the president. It is paramount that we win the senate in 2014 so any "fumbles or penalties" must be avoided. Sometimes trying the unlikely is important on principle and sometimes it is too costly. Again, our political generals must be experts in the teachings of Sun Tzu in ***"The Art of War."*** Had two of my favorites, Senators Ted Cruz and Mike Lee studied his strategies and tactics, the GOP would have avoided very negative controversy and be better off today. These guys along with Rand Paul and all the other constitutional God fearing conservatives are not only the future of the GOP but the future of America.

For those of us who believe in God: **Jesus said, "He who is not with me [us] is against me [us]," and, "I would rather you be hot or cold for if you are lukewarm I will spit you out of my mouth."** Thank you Ted Cruz, Mike Lee and all the other God fearing Tea Party movement conservatives for being "hot" in the way Jesus said. For you moderate republicans, you might consider turning up the heat and joining the "right" team before history leaves you out in the cold with the other pukes in the LSD Party…

**WAKE UP AMERICA AND STOP BEING HUSTLED.
THE FINANCIAL SURVIVAL OF AMERICA IS AT STAKE…**

Chapter 2

Marxism, Socialism, Idealistic Utopianism & Keynesian Economics

There are three kinds of men: The ones that learn by reading; the few who learn by observation; the rest of them have to pee on the electric fence for themselves. – Will Rogers

Let me get this out of the way right now! Communism doesn't work; socialism doesn't work, has never worked and will never work! It sounds like a noble idea. No more poverty, no one disadvantaged, no one going without healthcare, or food, or housing, or clothes, or child care, or money, or – you get the point! How did we take care of these needs before the 1930's? And if one's family, friends, church and neighbors were the helping hands before the 1930's; then how many of them were swindled and/or for how long were they swindled, by the able bodied bums looking for "something for nothing?"

Now, compare that scenario with the invisible bureaucrat's hand in Washington, DC and it becomes obvious how waste, fraud and abuse have become so easy. I contend that liberal socialist democrats don't really care about how many people are abusing the system. They only care that they can get enough votes to gain and maintain power. Everything else is just a shiny object meant to divert attention away from their power, money, fame grab. If I had to use a single word to describe the LSD leadership and their slobbering sycophants it would be **arrogance…** Career socialists are simply con artists!

Liberal socialist democrat politicians and their sycophants in the media and academia is a "Members Only Country Club" for power addicts and control freaks. If you want to have success on Madison Avenue, Hollywood, the mainstream media including the TV networks and other liberal strongholds you must be a loyal democrat to be in the "Club." Liberal socialist democrats don't appreciate competition; in fact they detest and decry it. What they appreciate and excel at are connections. And, just like all socialist organizations they will crush their opposition every chance they get – using every dirty means to their ends.

To succeed in a socialist society you better have connections!

Here is an interesting observation and quote from CNBC on May 22, 2013: Michelle Caruso-Cabrera had a segment titled *"Chinese Investing Big in US."* The segment was on why Chinese companies were locating in America – the typical answer was; "because of the rule of law and lack of corruption." During the segment, she interviewed a Chinese executive with International Vitamin Corporation on why they opened a new factory in New Jersey. He said; "you can focus on what you're doing… you're hard work will be rewarded… you don't have to deal with many other things like **connections or relationships**"…

Think about it, these Chinese businessmen are opening factories in the US to avoid the corruption that is inherent in communist or socialist countries even as those countries are becoming more capitalist. Why – because of the rule of law and lack of corruption in America? What are we doing nationalizing 1/6th of our economy (ObamaCare) and restricting Boeing from opening a new factory in the "right-to-work" state of South Carolina? The National Labor Relations Board ("NLRB"), a federal agency reporting to the White House, fought to stop Boeing from opening a new plant unless that plant was unionized. I won't get into the details here (you can Google the story) but this appears to be a pattern of the NLRB, since Obama took office, to help stop the losses of union membership of the last several decades. Unions had a definite purpose in the early days of the industrial revolution, and would be much more relevant and popular today, if they were more of a free-market capitalist organization and less of a socialist organization. With unions, it's not what you know; it's who you know, i.e., connections and relationships. Connections are paramount in socialist societies, countries and organizations.

That's why President Obama says to small business owners; "You didn't build that business by yourself – you had help." My response is – those roads and bridges were available to everyone; those teachers were available to everyone, everything he attributed to the business owner's success was available to everyone! Why was that small business owner on that street successful? I believe for most of them, it was because they were willing to risk their "capital" working extremely long hours, sometimes at less than minimum wage, and apply everything they knew to succeed. Most fail, but the successful never give up and may try several times before they succeed. Of course, the more they succeed the more our government, the small business owner's hostile partner, will take his ever larger "fair share" (*a term that makes me want to puke*) – "to spread the wealth around" as President Obama said to Joe the plumber!

Have you noticed that President Obama has stopped saying the rich need to "pay their fair share" and has started saying the rich need to "pay a little more?" You can bet he will never slip again and say "spread the wealth around" because that is a basic tenant of socialism. Very shrewd! Watch for the rest of the liberal socialist democrats to follow his lead. The one promise he is definitely keeping is: **"To Fundamentally Transform America."** Barack Hussein Obama's presidency may very well be an epoch in American history – the time when the insidious march of socialism peaked and began to decline or, when the socialist cancer advanced too far to save the patient – America…

Saul Alinsky's "*Rule's for Radicals,"* is a must read for all of us who fear the socialist/communist/progressive take-over of America. Many believe that Barack Hussein Obama and Hillary Rodham Clinton are disciples of this early 1900's radical agitator who kept company with the likes of Al Capone and believed many of the tenants of communism, socialism, progressivism and totalitarian societies. This primer for community organizers, agitators and socialists, teaches how to destroy American free-market capitalism from within, and set a new course for an idealistic socialist style nation.

Let's face it; socialism is alive and well in America and throughout the world. The problem is wherever it is strongest; those cities, counties, states and nations are stagnant at best, or going broke and are heading for bankruptcy and/or depression. In all of these economies, the poor and middle class are suffering the most and have almost no chance whatever to become financially independent. Why then are so many of these groups voting for the LSD leaders who caused this mess in the first place? Are they so addicted or down-trodden that it seems hopeless to break the habit? Is that the goal of the liberal socialist democrat? I believe, just like a drug dealer, they get as many poor people hooked on socialist crumbs as possible, so their "royalty" train is set…

America has been sliding insidiously into socialism ever since President Woodrow Wilson was elected in 1912, and we are just a few more elections away from total financial collapse if radical changes are not made soon. How many poor and disadvantaged citizens will we be able to help if we fail to make the necessary changes to save America?

Liberal socialist democrats like to blame capitalism for the financial collapse of 2008. Really! What about the meddling of congress in who gets a home mortgage and the pressure on the mortgage industry to lower credit standards? Once the lower standards "Genie" was let out of the bottle, only a crisis could put him back in. Congressman Barney Frank was a prime mover for the growth of government backed Fannie Mae and Freddie Mac, the multi-trillion dollar packagers of standard and sub-prime mortgages, which was the key element of the crisis. Rumors exist concerning Barney's corrupt ties to these quasi government agencies. He then followed that big-government socialist act with legislation, Dodd-Frank, that further crippled free-markets. Sure, free-market capitalism was at fault – what gullible idiot believes that? The non-connected, ignorant, gullible voters – that's who!

It wasn't *"free-market capitalism"* that was to blame; it was *"crony-capitalism"* and *"socialist capitalism."* We haven't been a true free-market capitalist country in the modern age, if ever! There have always been big government central planners who think they know better than free-markets on what will and will not work or which industry is favored over another industry.

This book doesn't use gentle words like liberals, or progressives, or reformist, or statist because it doesn't lead the average person's focus to where the democrats are leading this nation – socialism.

Therefore, I use the term *"Liberal Socialist Democrat"* or *"LSD"* or the *"Club"* to describe every democrat. Why, because you can't be a member of a group (the democrats) that for over a century has moved this country insidiously closer to total socialism and away for God, and not be so naive as to believe you're not part of the problem. If you feel just a little bit of socialism is ok then you have not done your homework. A little bit is never enough with liberal socialist democrats.

Every election adds just a little more socialistic ideals, rules and regulations, i.e., wealth redistribution and controls on commerce. America is nearing total financial destruction because of just a little bit more big-government socialism brought to us by "all" democrats and go-along moderate republicans.

This book makes the case that no matter how much a liberal socialist democrat politician pretends to be for the poor, they are really out for themselves and their friends in the *"Club."* They use class warfare to seduce the weak minded for votes. If you are not politically connected with the elites in DC, NYC, Chicago, San Francisco, Hollywood, and the other liberal socialist democrat strongholds like labor unions, academia, news media and trial lawyers – you must rely on free-market capitalism to rise above poverty or the middle class in America.

Democrats are made up of two primary groups:

The first group, "the hustlers" are masters of the second group, "the hustled." The first group is the elite classes who are self-professed intellectuals and who seek to control and dominate individuals, families, cultures and societies for their own personal gain or because of their ignorant grandiose delusional beliefs. They have a sick notion that they are smarter and better than the average person, and they deserve to rule over them and control everyone's lives.

To gain and maintain power they need as many poor people voting as possible. The best way to ensure a maximum poor population is to dumb-down our children through a unionized (socialist) public education system. This will lead to getting as many of the poor as possible addicted to the LSD crumbs from public welfare programs. It's the same philosophy that the slave owners had to keep the slaves ignorant and downtrodden. It's working – isn't it? Also, the liberal socialist democrats want to brain wash as many of our children as possible and as young as possible.

That's why Hillary Rodham Clinton said; "it takes a village to raise a child" or the latest propaganda by Melissa Harris-Perry on April 9, 2013; "children don't belong to their parents; they belong to whole communities," i.e., society or the state. Communism anyone…

What they really mean is they belong to the liberal socialist democrat propaganda machine. Sure, why not – just look how great it has worked in Cuba or North Korea or any of the Soviet bloc countries! Wake up stupid voters, the poor in these countries are suffering massively, and the middle class is not much better off. The only classes of people who are thriving in these countries are the ruling socialist elites. Now, consider the massive wealth creation that is going on in China since their move towards a more free-market capitalist system. They have a long way to go, but the point is still crystal clear for anyone with an ounce of intelligence and honesty.

The second group, the hustled or the delusional utopians, have very good intentions and wants the best for society but they simply don't understand how free-market capitalism really works, that it is the best and the only hope for helping all Americans, especially the poor, to achieve the financial freedoms we all dream of. This group has a distrust of corporations, past and present, which have abused its employees (workers). There will always be abusive humans even in civilized societies. Socialism is not the answer. Socialism is much more coercive and corruptible than a completely free-market capitalist system of companies competing for customers and employees, to not only survive but to thrive and grow. A company that is well managed and a great place to work will at some point put its abusive competitor, which mistreats its employees, out of business. Even if the lousy company doesn't go out of business, its employees can leave for better opportunities. In a full blown socialist country, the "worker" is trapped.

Look around the world (using Google!) at the countries that are the most socialist vs. the countries that are the most free-market capitalist. Actually, one can look at American states or cities which are the most socialist like California or Detroit and Stockton vs. the most conservative or free-market like Texas or Provo, to see how destructive liberal socialist democrats are to these states and cities. It doesn't take much research, for a wise person with an open mind, to understand what these hustlers' real motive is, or to sort out the con. These wise people are called constitutional conservatives or libertarians. They believe what the founders established in the *"Declaration of Independence," "The Constitution of the United States," "The Bill of Rights"* and the phrase *"Pursuit of Happiness."*

Want more examples? Is China becoming an economic super power because they are more free-market capitalist than they used to be? The obvious answer is yes! Are North Koreans starving because of their unyielding communism and socialism? Of course! Is Greece suffering because of the capitalist or socialist elements of their economy? How about the beautiful Caribbean island nation of Cuba? Can you imagine the prosperity Cuba would enjoy if they became a free-enterprise capitalist nation? I predict they will be in less than one generation and will experience a tremendous explosion of wealth and prosperity. Cuba will become a worldwide vacation destination in just a few years by returning to their pre-communist Caribbean island culture!

The list goes on and on but somehow it escapes the voters' attention in American and we continue to elect liberal socialist democrats, or moderate republicans, to guide our country further away from conservative ideals and towards liberal, progressive, socialist ideals. Constitutional conservatives, and especially the Tea Party movement, energized after the democrat controlled congress and presidency over reached with their socialist agenda after the 2008 elections, returned republican control to the house in 2010. The LSD and their sycophants' masterful propaganda campaign from 2010 to 2012 resulted in casting conservatives, primarily in the house as extremists. IT WORKED! Why can't you republicans take the gloves off and do the same thing? The only difference is that the LSDs <u>are</u> actually the real extremists wreaking America.

Labor unions are the twin brothers of socialism – especially in the public sector. Corporate abuses of its workers gave birth to labor unions in the early days of the industrial revolution, but they went way too far in the opposite direction. Public sector employees enjoy complete job security plus salaries and benefits that far exceed a comparable job in the private sector. They should be limited to 20% above the income and benefits of the private sector, and their retirements should be converted to a defined contribution 401k, not defined benefits. The only choice should be when we make these changes, not if we make these changes. We can make them now, or we can wait until the country is totally bankrupt with no hope of recovery. What makes more sense?

First of all, the country can't afford these public sector union premium benefits and secondly, it's not right or fair to bleed the tax payers to death and keep them perpetually down to benefit public "servants." What irony; the public ends up being the servant of government employees. As far as the military is concerned they should also be converted to defined contribution retirement programs just like a 401k program. Most of the military are in support positions and yet they can retire after only twenty years and make much more, in retirement, than their private sector counterparts who are still working full-time. The rest of America must work another 20 to 25 years before they can retire. This is insane – a 40 year old retired military person without a college degree collecting $3 to $5,000 a month for the rest of his/her life at the expensbuck1952

e of the rest of us who have to work until we are 60 to 70 years old. The exception to this would be gun carrying soldiers who rely on the strength of a young person for war or battle readiness. They can't be expected to work at that position much further than age 40. And, as far as our veterans who return from war with "real" permanent disabilities, they should be praised and completely taken care of for the rest of their lives.

Because America is still a democratically controlled nation, socialists need votes to achieve their power. How do they get enough votes? They promise benefits and entitlements to the masses. This ***"something for nothing"*** is the age old scam that gets the attention of the gullible.

I realize that many social programs are funded by contributions like the Social Security system and Medicare, but these programs will go broke in a generation and have become a Ponzi scheme with out of control future deficits if changes are not made soon. The Ponzi scam was named after Charles Ponzi, who became notorious for cheating investors out of their money in 1920. The scam is so simple; it promises significant returns and pays out a small portion of those claimed returns from newly conned investors. He wasn't the first, and certainly not the last, to use the scam, but it was so successful and took in so much money that the scam was named after him.

The latest and greatest of these con artists is Bernie Madoff, another Jewish democrat that hustled billions from unsuspecting investors. He allegedly paid some $400,000 over his last decade in business to a lobbying firm to keep him in good standing with politicians and regulators. He also paid hundreds of thousands to individual politicians and political action committees – mostly democrats, but some republicans. This is the only explanation of how he could have gotten this fraudulent scheme by the regulators and bankers for so long. Another twist to the relationship between crony capitalism, money center banks and our politicians!

America, there are no trust accounts that hold our social security and Medicare *contributions,* or payments, to these retirement and medical insurance programs – new suckers are needed every day to pay the promised returns to senior citizens. If we don't make some changes to these programs soon, future generations will be left holding the proverbial Ponzi bag. There are several constitutional conservatives with plans to save these programs, but again, the liberal socialist democrats are masterfully demagoguing and subverting these plans…

Democrats and liberal media elites say; "President Obama is not responsible for the *"Great Recession,"* it was Bush's fault. They're half right! They're both at fault – along with every other democrat and moderate republican elected since the 1850s. That's right, the 1850's when socialism and communism began taking hold around the world and centralized big government planning began to replace the free-markets that are so much more efficient in creating innovating products, lowering prices and creating greater wealth for the masses.

Who dreamed up these socialist ideas? Radical atheistic philosophical intellectual Jews! Don't believe it – research it on Google. Socialism spread like wild fire among these pointy headed self-professed intellectuals. Intellectuals my ass! None of their theses was backed by research data. They just made claims and all of these immoral creeps agreed with each other. A little research reveals this bunch of morons and other radical atheist do-gooders have no real understanding of mans' desire to not only succeed, but to be champions, *"to be number one"* and hoist the winner's trophy over his/her head!

The real trophy of a free-market capitalists' life is to accomplish something great, to build a big business and maybe to use one's vast wealth to help mankind. Nobody is more generous than a conservative, free-market capitalist in contributing to charities and society as a whole.

Most liberal socialist democrats are the stingiest people in the world. Look at the tax returns of Joe Biden and other democratic leaders, compared to someone like Mitt Romney who has given tens of millions to noble causes. Sure these LSD millionaires are willing to tax the hell out of successful small businesses and individuals to fund their socialist programs, but remember those socialist programs are the source of their power and "royalty." **Power is their drug of choice, but none of them ever go to rehab! Remember that…**

Estate taxes are immoral: After taxing the successful person for his entire lifetime, a liberal socialist democrat wants to take more than 50% of what is left when he dies. The children are given 2½ seconds to come up with the money, that a bureaucrat determines, or the assets are liquidated for pennies on the dollar. This is socialist government sanctioned stealing by any measure but these con artists never go to prison.

The greatest danger to the American way of life: If Lehman Brothers and Bear Stearns, two big investment banks, nearly brought down the world's economy in 2008, and Greece, Spain, Portugal, Italy and other European countries are causing periodic financial crises around the world – what will the coming debt tsunami of America do to the world's economy?

Who will bail us out? China? Japan? Germany? The European Union? Give me a break – we're all going down if drastic changes are not made very soon. Remember how Speaker Newt Gingrich and the newly elected republicans' *"Contract with America"* (welfare reform) was going to slow down the economy and cause wide spread suffering of the poor in the mid-1990s. It didn't happen! It did just the opposite and led to a balanced budget for several years – along with a big percentage of folks getting off welfare, going to work, feeling better about themselves and even prospering. Who took the credit? Bill Clinton? What a joke! And stupid republicans just go along with that lie. Bill Clinton was dragged kicking and screaming, after he tried to stop it with vetoes, into signing the legislation into law. And now Obama is doing his best to undo the work requirement elements of welfare to work. Go figure!

Liberal socialist democrats like to refer to themselves as progressives. Here is what a progressive really stands for:

- Progressively more job killing, suffocating regulations;
- Progressively less liberty and freedom;
- Progressively more socialism and crony capitalism;
- Progressively less free-enterprise;
- Progressively more taxes; and,
- Progressively more bureaucrats enjoying progressively better incomes & benefits than ***"we the people,"*** by making progres-

sively more rules, regulations, controls, and restrictions that progressively strangles jobs, commerce and wealth creation – especially for the poor and the middle class.

What is socialism? Better yet – what is socialism in America? Well, depending on who you're talking to you'll get hundreds of definitions. In my opinion, it's like defining salt water vs. fresh water. What is the amount of salt needed to be added to fresh water to make it saltwater? Trace amounts may not be detectable to humans, but at some point more of it becomes deadly. We're getting close to that now! My simple definition of socialism is: 1. Redistribution of wealth from the "haves" to the "have-nots" (instead of teaching wealth building strategies to the poor); and, 2. Government owned and/or controlled means of production or trade (ObamaCare and the millions of needless commerce crippling laws, rules and regulations). Is that too simple for democrat voters to understand – I hope and pray they get it before we lose too many jobs and experience more needless suffering…

Here is what the web site U-S-History.com lists as **"Socialism in America:" Ideas and Movements, 1850-Present**

Roots of socialism in America - The roots of socialism in America can be traced to the arrival of German immigrants in the 1850s when Marxian socialist unions began, such as the National Typographic Union in 1852, United Hatters of 1856, and Iron Moulders' Union of North America in 1859. Theodore H. White, author of *Fire in the Ashes: Europe in Mid-Century* (1953) wrote, "Socialism is the belief and the hope that by proper use of government power, men can be rescued from their helplessness in the wild cycling cruelty of depression and boom."

Progress of socialism – The Socialist Party in America was born and grew dramatically between 1900 and 1912. Under the charismatic leadership of Eugene V. Debs in 1912, 160 councilmen, 145 aldermen, one congressman, and 56 mayors, including Milwaukee, Wisconsin, Berkeley, California, and Schenectady, New York, were elected as Socialists. At the time, Socialists published

300 newspapers, including the *Appeal of Reason*, which was a Kansas-based publication with 700,000 subscribers. Membership in the Socialist Party totaled 125,000.

Debs converted to socialism while serving jail time for his part in the Pullman Strike in 1897, and began to edit the *Appeal to Reason* publication. From 1900 to 1920, he ran for president on the Socialist ticket while increasing membership to the Socialist Party tenfold. Although Debs insisted he was a Marxist, he spoke more about poverty and injustice than typical socialist concerns about the class struggle and the dictatorship of the proletariat (Marx).

In 1912, Debs received 900,000 votes, which was six percent of the presidential votes cast that year, principally for his stand against America's involvement in World War I. Debs appealed to blue collar workers hungry for improved working conditions and higher wages, but also such intellectuals as authors Jack London and Upton Sinclair.

Prominently with President Theodore Roosevelt and through the 20th century's first years, the Progressive Movement came into view with its belief in "the perfectibility of man, and in an open society where mankind was neither chained to the past nor condemned to a deterministic future; one which people were capable of changing their condition for better or worse." [Sounds reasonable, but so do most cons!]

The Socialist Party was included within the Progressive Movement. The party dealt with American problems in an American manner. Unlike the Communist Party, the Socialist Party at that time felt no obligation to adhere to an international party line. For example, socialists and other progressives campaigned at the local level for municipal ownership of waterworks, gas and electric plants, and made good progress in such endeavors. In 1911, there were 18 Socialist candidates for mayor, and they nearly won the Cleveland, Ohio, and Los Angeles, California, mayoral races.

In 1905, Upton Sinclair founded the Intercollegiate Socialist Society, which soon had chapters in the leading universities. Lively young men and women discussed the "New Gospel according to St. Marx." Universities were considered to be favorable ground for progressive thought.

Following the election of 1912, Socialist Party membership began to decline as some members cast their vote for Woodrow Wilson. Others were expelled, such as the Industrial Workers of the World (IWW), of which Debs and labor organizer "Mother" Mary Harris Jones had once been members. The IWW had been organized in 1905, grew into a radical, direct-action wing of American socialism by 1910, and had up to 100,000 workers by 1915.

By 1917, Socialist Party membership had slipped to 80,000. Nevertheless, by 1920 Debs managed to garner 919,800 votes for his presidential candidacy, the most a socialist has ever received in America, albeit making up only 3.4 percent of the popular vote. Those votes were representative of Americans' disillusionment with World War I, and of Debs himself, who spoke passionately against our involvement in the war.

The Espionage Act of 1917 was crafted to jail "anyone who interfered with the draft or encouraged disloyalty [to America]" and provided for jail sentences of 10 to 20 years. The Sedition Act of 1918 extended further penalties to those found obstructing the sale of U.S. war bonds, discouraging recruitment, uttering "disloyal or abusive language" about the government, the Constitution, the American flag, or even the U.S. military uniform. Under those acts, the government arrested more than 1,500 people, including Eugene Debs. [An un-American loss of freedoms]

The Socialist Party's strength was further sapped by 1920, because of government suppression and public disapproval during World War I. Such anti-socialist hysteria as the Red Scare, and internal factionalism aggravated by the presence of Communists, took their toll. Fears associated with the Bolsheviks' seizure of power in Russia, bombings in the United States, along with a series of labor strikes, led to the Red Scare in 1919. Suspected socialists and Communists were arrested and thrown into jail. In the end, of the 5,000 people who were given arrest warrants, only slightly more than 600 aliens were actually deported.

In addition, the party's failure during the 1920s was due to its inability to appeal to the upwardly mobile worker who yearned to be part of the middle class. The party also was divided along racial and ethnic lines. **Their broadest appeal was to the well-educated members of society.** In 1928, the Socialist presidential candidate, Norman Thomas, received only 267,835 votes. Thomas was a Princeton graduate and Presbyterian minister in New York. He succeeded Debs after the latter's death as the perennial presidential candidate in the 1928, 1932 and 1936 elections. Thomas stood as more indicative of the Socialist Party member, which was made up of mostly intellectuals and the middle class, rather than a worker's party that Debs had basically represented.

Socialists were also plagued by extreme doubt on the part of most progressives, who were leading the charge to free America from the economic woes of the Great Depression and were weathering deep hostility from conservatives. By the mid-Twenties, the party was deeply divided and failed to revive itself during the depression years of the 1930s.

During the election of 1932, the Socialist and Communist parties, who had insisted that capitalism had collapsed, pulled less than one million votes combined. American voters had grown weary of Republican policies and therefore Democrats won big in both the Senate and the House of Representatives, illustrating that Americans had faith in their country and its institutions. In that election, Norman Thomas received only 892,000 votes.

"Creeping socialism," an expression used in modern times to describe America's so-called drift towards a socialistic society, was coined by author F.A. Hayek in his book *The Road to Serfdom.* Published in 1944, Hayek's book warned of the dangers of state control over the means of production, which he perceived to be occurring, especially in regards to the Tennessee Valley Authority (TVA), during the New Deal and the Fair Deal administrations of presidents Franklin Roosevelt and Harry Truman, respectively.

Hayek believed that excessive governmental controls on society did not deliver on their promises and that their ideology actually delivered dismal economic results. But more importantly, he averred, it produces a psychological change in the character of the people in that man's desire to better himself is what drives him to succeed and also improves the way of life for those around him.

According to F. A. Hayek; "Socialism strips man of his desire to succeed."

Because of the Cold War, McCarthyism, and dominance of the "Middle American" values, the Communist and Socialist parties virtually disappeared in the 1950s, when membership fell to below 2,000 members. **Many Socialists left the party because it was seen that more progressive reform could be achieved through membership in the Democratic Party.** Among those who departed were: Walter Reuther, Philip Randolph, and Bayard Rustin. Life was good for the average American, who worked fewer than 40 hours per week. Most received annual two-week vacations and had twice the income to spend as they had during the nation's previous economic boom time in the late Twenties.

During the 1960s and '70s, the Socialist Party exerted little influence on American society because of intra-party conflict, as well as a refusal to support the anti-Vietnam War movement that was sweeping across America. **In 1968 at the Socialist Party convention, members passed a resolution to support Democrat Hubert Humphrey for president, instead of nominating their own candidate.**

And in 1972, the body chose to support democrat George McGovern for president. But then for the first time in 20 years, in 1976, the Socialist Party decided to run its own presidential campaign with former Milwaukee mayor Frank Zeidler (1948-1960) for president and J. Quinn Brisben, a Chicago teacher, for vice president. Since that time, others have been nominated, including Willa Kenoyer (1988), J. Quinn Brisben (1992) and Mary Cal Hollis in 1996.

Modern socialist movements and organizations – In American society today, socialist groups range in political views from the extreme right to the extreme left. The extreme right wing groups comprise neo-Nazi, anti-Semitic and fascist groups such as the National Socialist Movement or NSM, whose purpose is to "purify" American society through violent and non-violent means. The NSM is said to wear the uniforms and paraphernalia of the Third

Reich. According to their website, the NSM is an organization that is "dedicated to the preservation of our Proud Aryan Heritage, and the creation of a National Socialist Society in America and around the world.

Representing the far left wing are such groups as the Socialist Party U.S.A. **That party believes in what is called "Democratic Socialism,"** defined as "a political and economic system with freedom and equality for all, so that people may develop to their fullest potential in harmony with others." The party further states that it is "committed to full freedom of speech, assembly, press, religion, and to a multi-party system" and that **the ownership and control of the production and distribution of goods "should be democratically controlled public agencies, cooperatives, or other collective groups."** [Another con job – they're lying about freedom of religion if it's Christianity] Other socialist groups include the Democratic Socialists of America, National Alliance, Young Democrat Socialist, and the Democratic Progressive Party.

Utopianism has been around for thousands of years and is central to all the anti-God and anti-capitalist belief systems like communism and socialism. At its root is arrogance…

Virtually every form of utopianism, especially communism, in history eventually led to mass killings and/or bankruptcy; yet some form or variation of these fantasies exists today in the elitist intellectual Liberal Socialist Democratic Party. Their promise is *"equality for all"* and cars that don't need gasoline, power companies that don't use fossil fuels and run off of the sun and wind, subsidized housing, free medical care, guaranteed union jobs with high incomes and free education – including college.

Wow! Who doesn't want that? If only free lunches were really free. Get back to reality America. Not every team can win the Super Bowl – only the team with superior preparation and performance all season and then in the playoffs. That's life and reality. If hard work, diligence and excellence are essential to be successful in sports why do utopians think it's any different in life? **Guaranteed outcomes for some, eventually guarantees misery for all!**

Guess who will eventually replace fossil fuel energy with renewable energy? The free-enterprise, free-market capitalist system of inventors and investors, from the unknown individual in his or her garage at home, to the biggest corporations in existence today – that's who! Hydrogen is virtually unlimited and produces zero pollution. This technology is a generation away from common use in powering our vehicles.

Global warming is another scare tactic of the liberal socialist democrats. Get some common sense environmental wackos – there used to be glaciers as far south as Yosemite Valley in the Sierra Nevada Mountains in central California. Which industry can you blame their disappearances on? They have been gone for more than 10,000 years. Global warming from industry – my ass! The globe has been warming, and the ice caps have been melting and receding long before Cornelius Vanderbilt and Henry Ford were even born. Actually before Jesus was even born! Contrary to the lies of the LDS crowd (**L**iberal **S**ocialist **D**emocrats in case you forgot), republicans want clean air and water – we just don't want to destroy economies and lives to get there in 2½ seconds or the EPA shuts down businesses everywhere and everyone goes to jail. That's right – jail! The EPA, the Injustice Department and the IRS have become the Obama Departments of Tyranny!

Conservative God-fearing republican statesmen will also solve the needs of the poor and underprivileged who are willing to help themselves. America just needs all of you liberal socialist democrats and big-government moderate republicans to get out of the way of conservative Senators like Tom Colburn, Rand Paul, Marco Rubio, Mike Lee, Ted Cruz, among others and Congressmen like Paul Ryan, Jason Chaffetz, Michelle Bachmann, Justin Amash, David Schweizer and others. It was a shame Allen West and Mia Love lost in their congressional election contests. They are exactly the kind of "statesmen" this country needs to save us from socialist destruction.

There are many "anti-socialist" groups, which includes the Future of Freedom Foundation, Heritage Foundation, and the Cato Institute. They express various beliefs regarding anti-socialism in America and the rights of the American public. These organizations along with many other anti-socialist groups can be found on the web.

Here are some of the beliefs of socialist organizations that can also be Googled on the web:

<u>The Democratic Socialists of America</u> – They believe that both the economy and society should be run democratically to meet public needs, not to make profits for a few. What a socialist con! **Let's break down the above statement,** "believe that both the economy and society should be run democratically – to meet public needs, not to make profits for a few." Who are the few? They must mean the owners of companies. But, in a public company anyone can be a stockholder or owner. If you have a retirement plan, you probably own mutual funds which invest in these public companies.

What about employees of these companies – do they benefit from company profits that are used to expand operations, hire new employees, buy new equipment and build new plants? Who builds the new equipment and new plants – the few owners? No, the employees of other companies!

Also, what about employees that learn the business operations, have great ideas for improvements, and have the freedom to start their own companies. In a socialist society, one could never do this – rise from the bottom to the top. To rise from the bottom to the top in a socialist society, you must have political connections. Anyone can rise from the bottom to the top in a free-market capitalist society.

Additionally, in a free-enterprise capitalist system one can go from the top to the bottom if the wrong decisions are made. In a socialist society, the well-connected people at the top are protected from their mistakes so long as they remain loyal to those in power of the *"Party."* Just look at the many failures of senior people in the Obama administration – they never get fired.

In a socialist system, the underlying belief is that the pie is only so big, so to get a bigger piece of the pie you must be part of the politically connected "*Club.*" In a free-market capitalist society, the pie can be multiplied, and those who invest "at risk" to grow the pie usually get a bigger piece of a bigger pie they helped to grow. See Chapter 20 "The Rich get Richer and the Poor get Poorer – Liberals are you Smarter than a 5th Grader" for some inspiring examples of *"Rags to Riches"* success stories.

Please study, in detail, the Democratic Socialists of America website, dsausa.org, to learn more about their beliefs and goals for "Fundamentally Transforming the United States of America" into

a socialist country. It is predictably full of idealistic clichés about worker's pay, women's and minority's rights and other noble causes that no reasonable American could disagree with. A socialist loves to talk about philosophy while totally ignoring facts or the results of their failed policies. They don't dare talk about the most socialist cities like Detroit or states like California that are being crushed by decades of liberal socialist democrat rule. The point is these idiots still think in terms of ideas as if they have never been tried. THEY HAVE! And the verdict is in; socialism leads to massive suffering – mostly for the poorest families, the very people these con artists profess to help.

A good example of centralized big-government socialist planning vs. the free-markets is the public education system. Make no mistake – our public educational system is a monopolistic socialist system that is ruining our chances to provide the very best education for our children to compete with the world, to invent and innovate, to solve complex problems, and to create greater wealth for themselves and America. Our public education system and especially our liberal universities have become a socialist propaganda machine for the liberal socialist democrats. Sounds like the former Soviet Union and the current North Korean regime to me! Get to the kids while they are most impressionable (gullible)...

We have some of the worst performing schools, when measures are based on what students actually know and understand, of any advanced nation. Schools are not run for students; they are run for the employees, administrators, bureaucrats and especially the labor unions. Labor unions could care less about the education of America's children. They only care about increasing their power and protecting union dues. In fact, I believe they purposely dumb-down our poor children to ensure America has the largest poverty class possible – a class of democrat voters that is!

The Website "Teachers Union Exposed" should be studied by every politician, teacher, parent and voter in America. Here is one of their better exposes:

"Bargaining Away Quality" The Union Contract: Wrapping Schools in Red Tape – Modeled after labor arrangements in factories, the typical teachers' union contract is loaded with provisions that do not promote education. These provisions drive away good teachers, protect bad teachers, raise costs, and tie principals' hands.

Paying Teachers to Do Nothing – New York City was once home to the infamous rubber room – a place where teachers awaiting disciplinary measures were sent to twiddle their thumbs while still receiving full pay as their grievances went through the system – but now it has an even bigger problem on its hands: The city spends more than $100 million every year paying teachers who have been excessed but have yet to find jobs.

The ironclad union contract requires that any teacher with tenure be paid their full salary and benefits if they are sent to the "Absent Teacher Reserve pool," according to *The Wall Street Journal.* **The average pay of a teacher in that pool is $82,000 a year.** Some of the teachers have been in the pool since 2006. According to the *Journal*, the majority of teachers in the pool had "neither applied for another job in the system nor attended any recruitment fairs in recent months.

This is what the union wants: To keep teachers on the payroll regardless of whether or not they are doing any work or needed by the school district. Why? As long as they are on the payroll, they keep paying union dues. The union doesn't care about the children who will be hurt by this misallocation of funds — think of all the new textbooks $100 million (each year!) would buy. All union leaders care about is protecting their members and, by extension, their coffers.

Thinning the Talent Pool – One problem related to the destructive transfer system is a hiring process that takes too long and/or starts too late, thanks in part to union contracts. Would-be teachers typically cannot be hired until senior teachers have had their pick of the vacancies, and the transfer process makes principals reluctant to post vacancies at all for fear of having a bad teacher fill it instead of a promising new hire.

In the study *Missed Opportunities*, The New Teacher Project found that these staffing hurdles help push urban districts' hiring timelines later to the point that "anywhere from 31 percent to almost 60 percent of applicants withdrew from the hiring process, often to accept jobs with districts that made offers earlier." Of those who withdrew, the TNTP report continues, the majority (50 percent to 70 percent) cited the late hiring timeline as a major reason they took other jobs.

The kicker is that it's the better applicants who are driven away: "Applicants who withdrew from the hiring process had significantly higher undergraduate GPAs, were 40 percent more likely to have a degree in their teaching field, and were significantly more likely to have completed educational coursework" than the teachers who ended up staying around to finally receive job offers.

One Principal's Story, as told to The New Teacher Project – If you are smart enough, you hide your vacancies. You say to the HR staffing liaison, "I don't anticipate that I will need another English teacher." At the same time, you have already identified the teacher you want for the position. You say to the teacher, "If you can hang in there and not start officially teaching until late September, but remain as a substitute until then, I will do everything to try to hire you." Then, you call the liaison back when you know all of the excessed teachers have been placed someplace else, and say, "Oh I actually do need someone." You say, "I have some resumes" and pretend to just find someone for the slot even though I had them all along. If you are a smart principal, you do this all of the time. But it is very hard to do this where there are a lot of excess teachers, like in social studies.

Keeping Experienced Teachers from Poor Children – Another common problem with the union contract is a "bumping" policy that fills schools which are more needy (but less desirable to teach in) with greater numbers of inexperienced teachers. In its report *Teaching Inequality*, the Education Trust wrote: "Children in the highest-poverty schools are assigned to novice teachers almost twice as often as children in low-poverty schools. Similarly, students in high-minority schools are assigned to novice teachers at twice the rate as students in schools without many minority students.

Taking Money from Good Teachers to Give to Bad Teachers – During the expansion of teacher collective bargaining in the mid-twentieth century, economists from Harvard and the Australian National University found, the average, inflation-adjusted salary for U.S. teachers rose modestly – while "the range of the [pay] scale narrowed sharply." Measuring aptitude by the quality of the college a teacher attended, the researchers found that the advent of the collectively bargained union contract for teachers meant that more talented teachers were getting less, while <u>less</u> talented teachers were getting more.

The earnings of teachers in the lowest aptitude group (those from the bottom-tier colleges) rose dramatically relative to the average, so that teachers who in 1963 earned 73 percent of the average salary for teachers could expect to earn exactly the average by 2000. Meanwhile, the ratio of the earnings of teachers in the highest-aptitude group (from the highly selective colleges) to earnings of average teachers fell dramatically. In states where they began with an earnings ratio of 157 percent, they ended with a ratio of 98 percent.

Data from the National Center for Education Statistics (NCES), as reported by *Education Week*, add further evidence to the compressed-pay claim. NCES stats indicate that the average maximum teacher pay nationwide is only 1.85 times greater than the nationwide average salary for new teachers.

Locking Up Education Dollars – Much of the money commanded by teachers' union contracts is not being used well, at least from the perspective of parents or reformers. Several provisions commonly found in union contracts that cost serious money have been shown to do little to improve education quality.

In a 2007 report, the nonprofit Education Sector found that nearly 19 percent of all public education spending in America goes towards things like seniority-based pay increases and outsized benefits – things that don't go unappreciated, but don't do much to improve teaching quality. If these provisions were done away with, the report found, $77 billion in education money would be freed up for initiatives that could actually improve learning, like paying high-performing teachers more money. That's $77 billion with a "B."

The Bottom Line – Too many schools are failing too many children. Americans should not remain complacent about how districts staff, assign, and compensate teachers. And too many teachers' union contracts preserve archaic employment rules that have nothing to do with serving children.

Source: http://teachersunionexposed.com/bargaining.cfm

The poorest Americans are the most dependent on public schools for preparing their children to achieve the American dream. Any comparison between private or charter schools and government unionized schools illustrate how destructive unions are to educating our children and preparing them to thrive in the future. These union leaders could care less about the poor – especially intercity minorities. The irony is these same minorities vote predominately for liberal socialist democrats who back the teachers' unions who keep their children in perpetual poverty.

Tell me and I forget. Teach me and I remember. Involve me and I learn. Life's tragedy is that we get old too soon and wise too late. – Ben Franklin

He who dares to teach must never cease to learn.
– Unknown Source

He, who opens a school door, closes a prison.
– Victor Hugo

Teachers open the door, but you must walk through it yourself. – Chinese Proverb

WAKE UP minority voters – your kids' futures and the future of America, your America, is at stake!

The well-off or even the middle class who live in good neighborhoods have the best public schools or send their children to private or charter schools. Private schools tend to hire the best teachers, have the best teaching methods and produce the best educated students or they go out of business. That is the essential difference – government schools can't go out of business. Or can they? We'll see…

Without a good education, our children and especially poor students are doomed. We spend more per child on education than any other advanced country, but we rank in the last quartile on student knowledge and proficiency. **Money is not the problem, liberal socialist democrats, and the labor unions are!**

This country was not founded to be a democracy; it was founded to be a republic. **A democracy leads to mob rule. A republic follows the established constitution and the rule of law.**

Keynesian Economics: This theory is the typical economic belief of the liberal socialist democrat. It states that active government intervention in the marketplace and monetary policy is the best method of ensuring economic growth and stability. A supporter of Keynesianism believes it is the big-central-planning federal government's job to smooth out the bumps in business cycles.

Intervention would come in the form of increased government spending and tax cuts in order to stimulate the economy during recessions, and government spending cuts and tax hikes in good times, in order to curb inflation. Really! What the hell happened to the government spending cuts in good times and tax cuts to stimulate the economy in bad times?

Here we after the 2012 elections with a poor economy and all President Obama and the democrats can talk about are more taxes on rich small business job creators. When was the last time we had spending cuts? That's right – when Newt Gingrich was Speaker of the House and dragged President Bill Clinton kicking and screaming all the way to welfare reform! Seriously, when has a liberal socialist democrat ever supported spending cuts except for military spending which is the primary responsibility of the federal government?

Think about it – just about everything the federal government does, with the exception of military defense, can be done closer to the citizens' home by their respective states. Then the states that waste the most, and tax the most will lose the most citizens. Actually, that is happening today! Just compare the most socialist state, California, to a state with no income tax and tort reform like Texas. It's no comparison… If Texas had the weather, the ocean, the mountains and the beauty of California – Californians would be moving even faster to Texas.

Most Keynesians advocate an active stabilization policy to reduce the amplitude of the business cycle, which they rank among the most serious of economic problems. According to the theory, government spending can be used to increase what is known as aggregate demand, thus increasing economic activity, reducing unemployment and deflation. For example, when the unemployment rate is very high, government can use a greater dose of expansionary monetary policy. We will discuss an opposing economic theory, *the "Austrian School,"* later that will illustrate the negative unintended consequences of this expansionary Keynesian monetary policy (Like the Great Depression!).

In fact, very few people know we had a severe depression in 1920; the government responded with what would be considered the Austrian School of economic theory and did absolutely nothing? The reason so few know of this extremely sharp deflationary recession is it lasted months – not years. Which economic theory did we use during the Great Depression which lasted from the early 1930s to the early 1940s? The big-government socialist Keynesian economic theory was used, of course. Which economic theory are we using to recover from the great recession of 2008 – again, the big-government socialist Keynesian economic theory? Why, because the electorate is too ignorant to know the difference and republicans are too stupid, or lazy, or afraid to educate this country on the differences between socialist Keynesian and free-market Austrian economics in the simplest terms.

Keynes argued that the solution to the Great Depression was to stimulate the economy through some combination of the following two approaches: 1. A reduction in interest rates; and, 2: government investment in infrastructure. The theory says, "This in turn stimulates more production and investment involving still more income and spending and so forth. The initial stimulation starts a cascade of events, whose total increase in economic activity is a multiple of the original investment." Sounds good, doesn't it?" Did it work? No! Are they working today? Hell no! Do these failed approaches sound familiar? Yes, the big-government command-and-control LSD Party are fighting conservative republicans today to keep applying these failed fiscal policies (Congress & Obama) and monetary policies (Federal Reserve) in spite of the obvious failures to get the economy revving in high gear.

The republicans, especially the cleverly demonized Tea Party republicans, are trying their best to stop the failed Keynesian policies and initiate the free-market Austrian economic policies. This fight is called gridlock – hang in there conservative republicans and libertarians! The economy is currently limping along because of Keynesian economics policies. When will we learn?

Free-market Austrian School conservatives see the socialist consequences of this stimulus planning. They believe the effect, or consequence, of every form of Keynesian economic intervention is to make society less prosperous, and even more importantly less free, than it would otherwise be under a completely free-market society.

A popular story by Frederic Bastiat to put Keynesian economics into a simple perspective for the non-economist avoiding some of the confusing theoretical discussions. Bastiat pointed to one of the fallacies of Keynesian economic artificial stimulus spending: The belief that the destruction of wealth (property) fuels more wealth creation. He explains this by means of an allegory that has come to be known as the story of the broken window. It was retold as the opening of Henry Hazlitt's *"Economics in One Lesson,"* which is one of the bestselling economic books of all time. Here's the story:

A kid throws a rock at a window and breaks it, and everyone standing around regrets the unfortunate state of affairs. But then up walks a man who purports to be wise and all-knowing. He points out that this is not a bad thing after all. The man fixing the window will get money for doing so. This will then be spent on a new suit, and the tailor too will get money. The tailor will spend money on other items and the circle of rising prosperity will expand without end.

What's wrong with this scenario? As Bastiat put it: "It is not seen that as our shopkeeper has spent six francs upon one thing, he cannot spend them upon another. It is not seen that if he had not had a window to replace, he would, perhaps, have replaced his old shoes, or added another book to his library. In short, he would have employed his six francs in some other way which this accident has prevented."

You can see the absurdity of the position of the wise commentator when you take it to absurd extremes. If the broken window really produces wealth, why not break all windows up and down the whole city block? Indeed, why not break doors and walls? Why not tear down all houses so that they can be rebuilt? Why not bomb whole cities so construction firms can get busy rebuilding? It is not a good thing to destroy wealth. Bastiat puts it this way: "Society loses the value of things which are uselessly destroyed."

It sounds like an unexceptional claim. But herein rests the core case against everything the government does. Perhaps, then, we can see why the allegory is not better known. If we took it seriously, we would dismantle the whole apparatus of American economic intervention. If you agree with this point, perhaps you have a hard time believing that anyone really believes that wealth destruction is actually a good thing. Let me try to show that the fallacy is as pervasive as ever.

After every natural disaster, the Mises Institute, an Austrian School, starts what they call the Broken Window Watch.

After Hurricane Katrina, the Labor Secretary said: "What will happen – and I have seen this in previous catastrophes and hurricanes – there is a bright spot in that those new jobs do get created."

As I point out elsewhere in this book, big-government liberal socialist democrats clamor for massive infrastructure spending on decaying roads and bridges all over America. They said, after the 2008 recession, "This would put the [home] construction workers back to work."

How stupid did they think we are? First of all, it takes a long time to do the engineering on these massive projects. So how "shovel ready" were/are they? Second, how many framers, roofers, window and door installers, painters, plumbers, electricians, heating and A/C techs, landscapers, cabinet makers, appliance and carpet installers, etc., do you think would/will be hired for these road and bridge projects? You got it! NONE… In fact, the construction companies that will get hired for most of these "road and bridge jobs" are the well-connected huge democrat corporations that the liberal socialist democrats pretend to battle against. Why do I believe these heavy equipment large construction companies are owned by democrats? Because if they were not, I suspect they would not likely get very many big government road and bridge contracts. These same construction companies are some of the biggest campaign contributors to the Liberal Socialist Democratic Party machine. That's right those evil rich people and their evil corporations that the left use as a "shiny object" to hustle the poor into thinking the left is on their side.

What a joke! Of course we need thousands of roads and bridges repaired. As I repeat elsewhere in this book, why don't we just sell municipal tax-free revenue bonds to "rich" investors to be repaid out of gasoline and diesel fuel taxes collected in those geographical areas?

Hmm, let's see – rich people providing the up-front construction funding with repayment collections from the drivers, including big transportation trucks, using those particular roads and bridges. Seems fair to me… Why should retired Americans, or anyone for that matter, who seldom drives, or lives in the rural west, pay for the road and bridge repairs for the cities of the northeast and mid-west? Do you ever hear this logic from any of our politicians in Washington, even conservative republicans? Why? I have no idea…

This is why we have so many problems in America – all of these liberal socialist democrat and moderate republican politicians are stupid. No! Scratch that – they're con artists; the gullible suckers who vote for them are stupid. Wait a minute – I may have the answer! The northeast and the mid-west have some of the biggest concentrations of democrat voters in the nation. That makes sense; they want the rest of the nation to pay their bills, i.e., liberal democrat socialism… See how this LSD hustle of the American taxpayer works.

Look around the world, big-government socialism is killing economies and crushing the inspiration, motivation and hard work ethic of many of the poor. Socialism should have never been tried in the first place. The Olympics don't give gold medals to all the athletes, only those who have worked the hardest and beat the competition on the day of the contest. California and many of their counties and cities are going broke, and it's only the beginning. Then look at the states where conservative Governors have rid their governments of socialist programs and have instituted conservative Austrian School of Economics programs.

These states have turned around economically and have attracted new businesses and commerce, which is leading to more taxes and growth for those states and its populations. Given more time these changes from Keynesian socialist policies to Austrian School free-market policies may be enough to influence future elections. I certainly pray they will…

I repeat – President Obama and all his sycophants think small business owners should not take credit for their success because the country and everyone else contributed in some way. Really, then why are there so few successful businessmen? This logic is so easily dismissed; otherwise, everyone starting a new business would succeed and become a millionaire. Doesn't everyone have the same access to the same education, roads and bridges? What are the differences between the successful small businesses and the rest? These guys are so stupid I want to puke!

How do you stop this utopian socialist economic cancer now that it has spread everywhere? Constitutional conservatives had better figure it out so America can completely and entirely destroy any notions or societal attractions to socialism. It should be easy to point to the most socialist countries in history and prove how they have destroyed those countries and their citizens' wealth and freedoms. Talk about China and their move towards capitalism in the last several decades and how much wealth and the increase in the standard of living capitalism has created for hundreds of millions of China's poor. **IT'S THE CAPITALIST COMPONENT OF THEIR ECONOMY… STUPID…**

Don't give reams of data that proves our point – that will only bore the voters to death. Keep it simple stupid! Relentless sound bites and demonization of conservatives have worked for the liberal socialist democrats so just use their playbook narrative against them. When they cry about it, proudly state that "the liberal socialist democrats are ruining Europe, California and cities like Detroit and we conservatives are going to put a stop to it in America." Get busy now, before the next elections and it's too late…

Eventually, the rest of the world will learn from us and also rid itself of this corrosive political and philosophical cancer…

What is the best catalyst to effect a total change in someone's addictive behavior? Massive suffering… – D. W. Burdick

Let's pray that America can avoid this fate and make the necessary changes before the socialist tipping point occurs here.

Those changes will be to educate "all" minority groups who vote predominately for democrats and therefore are partly responsible for the worst recovery since the great depression – ironically, a recovery that has hurt the poor more than any other group of the American population. "That" education must lead to changes in minority voting trends from liberal big government ***politicians*** to constitutional, conservative, small-government, ***Statesmen.*** Look to the Tea Party Patriot movement for many of them…

In closing, it is incredibly puzzling to me how a God fearing Christian, who should be sensitive to the promptings of the Holy Spirit, can belong to the Democrat Party; an organization hell bent on removing God from America and most responsible for the government approved murder of more than 55 million babies. The Democrat Party is home to the Democratic Socialists of America (www.dsausa.org) and has become the enemy of God the Father, God the Son (Jesus Christ) and God the Holy Spirit. They passionately rejected any mention of God in their national platform during the democrat presidential convention of 2012 and, they work tirelessly to remove Christian symbols and any mention of our

God in any public place. If anyone who claims to be a God fearing Christian can justify belonging to the Democrat Party after reading this book – I would like to know their rationalizations…

I am so tired of the LSD's drum beat of "the rich get richer and the poor get poorer." It is precisely the LSD's laws, rules and regulations that work to strangle the economy that make it harder each year for the poor and the middle class to get ahead. If we took all the money from the rich, the country would collapse economically because of the lack of capital being expertly directed into investments of all types. What if we only took ½ the money of the rich? See my point! When will we learn that LSD policies only serve to guarantee the poor stay poor?

Only a robust economy that is best enabled by a truly free market, as defined by Adam Smith in his 1776 book, *The Wealth of Nations,* will provide higher wages and the best opportunity for the poor to achieve financial prosperity. That's right, a book about free-market capitalism written and published at the birth of the most blessed and prosperous nation in history. Had we not enslaved Africans maybe we would not have grown as fast in the first few centuries but maybe we would also not have brought a curse upon America. If we return to God and repent our collective sins as a nation maybe we can survive the socialist crush we appear to be destined for…

If you are a kind hearted, well-meaning democrat, some serious "soul searching" may be in order!

Chapter 3

Saul Alinsky – Mentor of Hillary Rodham Clinton & Barack Hussein Obama's ACORN goal to "Fundamentally Transform the United States of America" into an Anti-Capitalist, Socialist Nation

Barack prophesied 5 days before he was elected president in the fall of 2008 that he would "Fundamentally Transform the United States of America" and he was right! America has become more divisive, more racist, more hateful, more socialist, and sadly, less moral and less Godly. He has helped to gin up reverse racism instead of what should have occurred with the election of a black president. Barack Obama's corrupt administration has created more "real" scandals in less time than any other presidency in history. "The buck" never stops with him. He is as protected by his underlings as any mob boss could ever expect or hope to be. Billions of federal dollars (borrowed) are funneled annually to his loyal cronies, and now billions more are being spent on advertising his socialist agenda – spending that goes to "his" media elites cronies. Who ever said: "crime does not pay," had no idea…

Instead of "spreading the wealth around," why can't Obama have the nation's schools and universities teach the entrepreneurial skills it takes to create wealth? Or, instead of nationalizing 1/6th of America's economy, why can't Obama pursue the proven free-market elements of the Austrian School of Economics to reduce medical care costs for everyone? The obvious answer – he is a closet socialist or as the LSDs preferred label – a progressive. Who cares what we call them? They are destroying the American dream! Why doesn't he just admit it? Is he ashamed to be a socialist, or is it that he knows gullible Americans would side against him if he were honest about it? The Alinsky doctrine taught him to sell socialism as "social justice" and/or "progressivism." That is how you dupe a gullible nation…

I believe, at the root of all the communist, socialist, leftist, progressive, statist believers is a hatred of free-market capitalism. What they fail to grasp is – American free-enterprise capitalism, especially entrepreneurialism is not a European Aristocracy social order. You don't have to be born with privilege in America to rise up the "ladder." In America, you can be born black, in the ghetto, without a father, and become a world renowned brain surgeon where millions of the white population prays that you will become their next president – Dr. Ben Carson. Or, a black woman, born under similar circumstance, can become the richest self-made woman in the world – Oprah Winfrey

In historical Europe, there were haves and have-not, the oppressors and the oppressed, but Americans died in a revolution to create a "New" Nation where "anyone" could become whatever they wanted to be. All they had to do was "pursue" what made them "happy" with hard work and a determined "spirit."

CAPITALISM IS NOT EUROPEAN ARISTOCRACY...

Barack's strategy of deception comes right off the pages of Saul Alinsky's 1971 book ***"Rules for Radicals."*** You can find this book online or you can download a number of PDF files by Googling it.

Barack Hussein Obama, and before him Hillary Rodham Clinton, were disciples of the radical progressive/socialist community organizer, Saul Alinsky. Barack was raised and trained to be an anti-American communist/socialist, but Hillary was not. She came from a church going, middle-class, republican family but somehow became polluted by the 60's counter-culture revolution. Her 1969 college thesis is a good place to begin to know the "real" Hillary Rodham Clinton. Here are some of the main principles taught by Alinsky, and advanced by Obama and Clinton:

- Organize the masses to amass power.
- Deceive and distract: The issue is never the issue – it's always the revolution! Women, blacks, Mexicans, climate and poverty causes are just the means to the end; which is power, money and total control of resources and everything else.
- Infiltrate the institutions of American society like labor unions, academia and media elites, and leftist government programs, like LBJ's War on Poverty, and then direct federal funds into their

pockets, programs and causes, e.g., ACORN. Imagine getting billions from America and using those funds to destroy it; rebuilding it in the image of the idealistic, utopian state. Of course the leaders of this utopian state would live like kings and eventually, like history reveals, would turn on the poor because they would eventually become expendable.

- Alinsky helped create the race hustling and extortion practices of today's civil rights leaders like Jesse Jackson and Al Sharpton, who are nothing like the great Dr. Martin Luther King, Jr.
- Saul and his disciples made their way into the inner circles of the Democratic Party including the Kennedys.
- Organize inner-city populations and voter registrations to stack the deck in their favor. Voter laws are of no consequence and any attempt to stop voter fraud would be met with massive demonization and charges of racism. Predictable behavior from hypocritical "hustlers."
- Work within the system until you can accumulate enough power to destroy it.
- The "ends justifies the means." Nothing is too dirty to use to get what they want – a socialist society; a society where they are in charge of the money! They are the ultimate "HUSTLERS!"
- Take from the haves and give to the have-nots. [It's just a con!]
- Social justice is just a stepping stone to tyranny and a totalitarian state. Once the LSD crowd is firmly in power, and the constitution is torn down, social justice will be kicked to the curb!
- Make the conservatives live up to their own rules and then use those rules against them.
- Demonize and "completely' destroy your enemy – God fearing free-market, constitutional conservatives; Especially the Tea Party movement conservatives.

Remember, Hitler used the democratic ballot box to gain power in the 1930's and once in power everything changed. Once the voting tipping point is firmly reached in America, everything will change here too. The art of deceptive communication, or the con, has not only been used by the common hustler, but also Lenin, Stalin, Hitler and every other Machiavellian monster in history.

Well trained Alinsky radical organizers are like brick masons building a tower to the sky – one insidious brick at a time.

It will be absolutely amazing, and a testament to the success of Saul Alinsky's "Rules for Radicals," if Hillary Rodham Clinton follows Barack Hussein Obama to the White house. They may have started out with totally different roots but, due in large part to their radical mentor, Saul Alinsky, they both will have arrived at the most powerful political position in the world – if she is elected president. The warfare tactic of demonizing voter registration laws as "racist" is central to their goal.

I think it is highly unlikely she will become the next president because the last four years of Obama will be a disaster for America. If the republicans again nominate another moderate instead of a Reaganite Conservative anything is possible. It is imperative that republicans stop nominating all these socialist enabling, establishment, moderate republicans. We have so many young, constitutional conservative republicans to choose from this time it would be ridiculously stupid to nominate another moderate.

If you really care about America's future, please Google the following PDF documents; share them and what you learn with everyone:

- David Horowitz's ***"Barack Obama's Rules for Radicals"***
- Saul Alinsky's ***"Rules for Radicals"***
- Hillary Rodham Clinton's 1969 Thesis ***"THERE IS ONLY THE FIGHT..." An Analysis of the Alinsky Model***

Read them in that order and be frightened – there are millions of these Alinsky disciples and their unwitting sycophants in public and private labor unions, academia, News Media, Madison Avenue, Hollywood and other liberal socialist strongholds across America. I would venture to say that 70 to 90 percent of those voting for democrats and moderate republicans would change their minds if they really understood the eventual suffering waiting at the end of Saul Alinsky's road.

All we, or any halfway intelligent person, have to do is listen very closely to what leaders like Barack Hussein Obama or Hillary Rodham Clinton say in unscripted interviews. They or their spokesmen are constantly walking back or parsing what they really intended to say when controversy erupts from their off handed comments. Is it because they live in a fabricated world created by lies, deceitfulness and popularity polls? Hustlers have to remember not only what they have to say but everything they have already said. Honest people don't have to remember anything except the truth and reality.

That's why I call them the LSD party – they live in an alternate state of reality full of socialist hallucinations where they hold all the power and the purse strings.

Honest statesmen like Ronald Reagan, Paul Ryan and Rand Paul or God fearing citizens like Dr. Ben Carson don't have to remember what to say or the talking points generated by polls because they simply live the truth and it flows out of them naturally without the need of a teleprompter.

When will America wake up and see these HUSTLERs who are leading America to destruction, or at the very least mediocrity?

Bill and Hillary are worth hundreds of millions and Barack will be the first billionaire ex-president. EXTREME FAT CATS!!! "And the little people (suckers) can eat cake (crumbs)." Again, WAKE UP…

If Hillary Rodham Clinton is somehow elected president in 2016, after 8 years of Obama, America is surely DOOMED…

> **Freedom is never more than one generation away from extinction. We didn't pass it to our children in the bloodstream. It must be fought for, protected, and handed on for them to do the same. – Ronald Reagan**

Chapter 4

STUDIES: Code for "Socialist Indoctrination" and the Cultural Breakdown of Free Speech, Religious Freedom, Morality, the Family, Community, Society, Western Civilization and the big prize – America!

A society that puts equality before freedom will get neither. A society that puts freedom before equality will get a high degree of both. – Milton Friedman

Political Correctness: Charlton Heston said: "Political correctness is tyranny with manners." PC has become the favorite weapon of the left to stop conservative free speech in America. This term may have started out with good intentions but has evolved into a weapon of the left to batter the right. Any attempt of conservatives to use worthwhile and honest data to bring the facts into public debate – like how to really help the poor, or why guns should be removed from criminals, especially gangs, instead of law abiding citizens, or abortion is murder of the unborn human baby, or traditional marriage should be reserved to a man's and a women's relationship, or the injustice of reverse racial discrimination. The real, indisputable facts are always kicked to the curb and the term politically correct (or incorrect) is used to attack conservatives. "Just (ignore) the facts mam" has replaced "Just the facts mam!"

Sexual Revolution and Psycho Analysis: I believe the goal of these strategies is to break down the family structure. If the left can destroy the family structure, then control of the country is much easier. A study by the Brookings Institute concludes that a marriage is the best anti-poverty program there is. If we value the short-term thrill over the long-term happiness of a stable family unit, suffering will result. Just look at results of the family structure breakdown that started with removing God from public schools and the sexual revolution of the 60's: Greater welfare burden, families without fathers or multiply fathers, increased teen pregnancies, disregard of human life resulting 55+ million abortions, increased teen suicides, gang and drive by murders.

Anti-Christian and Atheists' Rights: Why is it that the rights of the radical atheist supersede the rights of Christians to enjoy public expressions of a Christian's faith? Our judicial system is based on the Old Testament, which is the Hebrew or Jewish Torah. The Ten Commandments should be posted in every public building and as many other public places as possible. Why are radical atheists so bothered by Christians or even morality in general? How does it harm them? On the contrary, they benefit from a moral society which has rules and standards to live by. Many of these radical atheists are of Jewish heritage so why are they against the Jewish Ten Commandments. I discuss this fully in Chapter 34 near the end of ***"America: You've Been Hustled."***

I realize they think religious people are either simple minded or gullible, but what if there is a Creator of the universe? They think they think logically, but is it really possible that the giant blue whale came from the same organism as the hummingbird, or the giant redwood sequoia tree and the tomato? Even given a billion years to evolve, some brilliant mathematicians don't think it is remotely possible. I believe humans are immortal "spiritual beings" living in mortal bodies. Even if you're not religious, it might be a good idea on your part to get curious and do some research on the subject of religion before your mortal body dies. There are many religions, why not begin with the one that founded the greatest country in history and is still the most wide-spread spiritual belief on the planet – Christianity!

Union's Super Rights: The National Labor Relations Board (NLRB) has become the coercive tyrannical Federal Government arm of the labor unions. A close examination of the new Boeing plant built in South Carolina and the ruling against it by the NLRB proves my point. The Barack Administration isn't just pro-union – it "in bed" with the unions and entertains union leadership far more than any other group. He is probably the most anti-business, pro-union, socialist president ever. History is unavoidable and will validate my statements.

<u>Equal Opportunity:</u> Equal opportunity is a great thing if it doesn't have destructive unintended consequences. These rules, laws and regulations are being used to further the break-down of free-enterprise in America today and to generate billions in trial lawyers' fees. Race and gender groups can use our injustice system to coerce a business into giving into pressure or being sued. I'm 100% for racial, gender, sexual preference and other previously discriminated groups enjoying equality. What I'm 100% against is the use of these laws as a reverse discrimination weapon to grab money, power and control, i.e., socialism

<u>Equal Pay:</u> Again, I'm 100% for equal pay. One thing I like about 100% commission sales is that it does not care about race or gender – it only cares about production. If there is a provable condition where discrimination exists, it must be corrected. If these rules, regulations and laws are being used to coerce businesses where no discrimination exists then that is also a crime in my opinion and should suffer consequences.

<u>Minimum Wage:</u> I will keep this brief because it is discussed elsewhere and in Dr. Williams' book ***"The State Against Black"*** in Chapter 22. Minimum wage laws have the unintended consequences of high unemployment for high school students and entry level employees. High minimum wages would allow, and maybe even force, employers to hire employees with greater experience and skill levels – leaving high school students and other entry-level or inexperienced employees without the opportunity to get the necessary experience to get ahead…

<u>Women's Studies:</u> Women's studies, also known as feminist studies, is an interdisciplinary academic field that explores politics, society, media, and history from women's and/or feminist perspectives. Women's studies were first born as an academic rubric apart from other departments in the late 1960s, as the second wave of feminism gained political influence in the academy through student and faculty activism. As an academic discipline, it was modeled on the American studies and ethnic studies (such as Afro-American studies) and Chicano Studies programs that had arisen shortly before it. Again, I'm 100% behind women's equal rights – but so many of these worthwhile accomplishments have been co-opted by the socialist movement to drive a wedge between Americans wanting the same thing: "The Pursuit of Happiness" without restrictions or discrimination. Source: Wikipedia.org/

Youth Studies: In a recent study conducted by young republicans about why so many college age voters voted for Obama and other democrats, many of their findings echoed the propaganda of the democrats – that republicans are old, ridged, uncaring, bigoted white men. On the Bill O'Reilly Factor, he implied; "why would anyone pay attention to stupid young people?" He missed the point – they helped win the election for Obama. He should have focused on the fact that these young people are being educated with LSD propaganda "sound bites!" They are being hustled… Again, as I say throughout this book, we must educate these impressionable young Americans with truthful sound bites about socialism and the LSD. Youth lends itself to non-conformity and rebelliousness but in reality most of those claiming to be non-conformist are really super-conformists. The real non-conformist is a young republican…

Learning is the Paramount Excellence Element for America

No! I'm not talking about reading, writing and arithmetic… I'm talking about morality, culture, expectations, career aspirations and success modeling in general.

Are our children learning the above from highly successful parents, relatives, friends and even their friend's parents; or, are they learning from undereducated and unmotivated parents that struggle to get a job and don't instill a higher education career path?

We've all heard about success stories of those individuals whose parents (married or single) pushed their kids to be the first in their family tree to get a college degree. This is the best way to break generational poverty. Generational poverty is a curse in some inner cities and some rural areas in America. Even more destructive are the poor kids, who by birth, are stuck learning from career criminals, gangs and a music culture that teaches to feed our most primitive impulses.

Instead of focusing on these poverty breaking principles the LSD Party focuses on more money! Why? The hidden answer is because they are in the money loop. In fact, some of these psychopaths want to keep these poor people down so they will continue to get the votes to stay in power. Again, just enough crumbs to survive – for votes! I'm not going to elaborate further here because I cover this issue in more detail several times throughout this book.

The main point is how can we teach success achievement through morality, culture, expectations, career aspirations and success modeling? Morality is the key issue here because if we measure success by wealth then those poor kids will simply chose a criminal career.

The last point along this issue is the indoctrination of our children by the LSD education system and the LSD media outlets, both mainstream and online social media. How we fix this is going to be extremely difficult but must begin by replacing our LSD and moderate republican leaders with leaders like Abraham Lincoln, Ronald Regan, Dr. Ben Carson and others who are guided by a power higher than mortal men.

Do I believe all democrats are socialists? No! But, I do believe if they read, and carefully studied, the book "The Naked Communist" their eyes might be opened and they would stop their superficial analysis of cause and effect. They might even look at the real causes of poverty, especially inner city poverty.

It's not money – it's hope and faith followed by education, inspiration, motivation, success modeling and hard work. Instead of liberal "Hustlers" spending trillions on inner city housing projects (money to LSD owned construction companies) they should have spent that money on helping those poor people leave those decaying neighborhoods and go to the suburbs, trade schools and community colleges.

The LSD Party has hallucinated long enough; send them to permanent rehab; vote them out forever and never give them their drugs of choice again – power, control, money and fame.

Chapter 5

Free-Market Capitalism, *The Wealth of Nations* & The Chicago and Austrian Schools of Economics

Most of the energy of political work is devoted to correcting the effects of [previous] mismanagement of government.

The great virtue of a free-market system is that it does not care what color people are; it does not care what their religion is; it only cares whether they can produce something you want to buy.

Milton Friedman – 1912 to 2006 Nobel Prize winning Economist

My addition to the above quote is: It doesn't matter what one's sexual preference is, male or female, old or young, or any other group that liberal socialist democrats can create to divide us. If that individual or group supplies you with the best product or service at the best price and in the most professional and courteous manner, you will gladly give them your business. If your brother or sister or best friend doesn't – they'll not likely get your business (more than a few times)!

If companies and economies are left alone to win or lose without government help or interference it's classified as free-market capitalism. It is the only proven socioeconomic system to build wealth for a free society and anyone in that society who is willing to invest the time and/or money to achieve financial freedom. Also, this country was not founded to be a democracy; it was founded to be a republic. A democracy leads to mob rule. A republic follows our established Constitution and our "Rule of Law." **America is not a democracy it is a Republic; don't forget it…**

Milton Friedman was, in my opinion, one of the greatest economists and socioeconomic debaters of all time. He was a free-market economist and a key advisor to the greatest president since Abraham Lincoln, Ronald Reagan. Many Austrian School economists disagree with his views on the role of the Federal Reserve and monetary policy during the great depression, but we'll leave that debate to others.

Before I get to the definition of "Free-Market Capitalism" and the differences between the "Austrian" school and the "Chicago" school of economics here are some additional **Milton Friedman quotes** that plainly illustrate the differences between pure free-market capitalism and libertarianism vs. socialism, crony capitalism, socialist capitalism and other socialist means to ends:

> The existence of a free-market does not of course eliminate the need for government. On the contrary, government is essential both as a forum for determining the "rules of the game" and as an umpire to interpret and enforce the rules decided on.
>
> One of the great mistakes is to judge policies and programs by their intentions rather than their results.
>
> When unions get higher wages for their members by restricting entry into an occupation, those higher wages are at the expense of other workers who find their opportunities reduced. When government pays its employees higher wages, those higher wages are at the expense of the taxpayer. But when workers get higher wages and better working conditions through the free-market, when they get raises by firms competing with one another for the best workers, by workers competing with one another for the best jobs, those higher wages are at nobody's expense. They can only come from higher productivity, greater capital investment, more widely diffused skills. The whole pie is bigger, there's more for the worker, but there's also more for the employer, the investor, the consumer, and even the tax collector. That's the way the free-market system distributes the fruits of economic progress among all people. That's the secret of the enormous improvements in the conditions of the working person over the past two centuries.

Minimum wage laws are another socialist policy that hurts entry level jobs for students and low skilled workers. The best minimum wage policies are robust economies and full employment; leading to greater demand for everyone, especially high school students and entry-level low-skilled workers. A socialist leaning America may never again experience a robust economy and full employment if significant changes are not made soon. But why would the LSD Party care – their leaders will always live like the rich and famous as long as they can continue hustling votes from the poor and ignorant who vote for them in return for crumbs.

More Milton Freidman quotes:

> Nothing is so permanent as a temporary government program.
>
> Underlying most arguments against the free-market is a lack of belief in freedom itself.
>
> I am in favor of cutting taxes under any circumstances and for any excuse, for any reason, whenever it's possible.
>
> Well first of all, tell me: Is there some society you know that doesn't run on greed? You think Russia doesn't run on greed? You think China doesn't run on greed? What is greed? Of course, none of us are greedy; it's only the other fellow who's greedy. The world runs on individuals pursuing their separate interests. The great achievements of civilization have not come from government bureaus. Einstein didn't construct his theory under order from a bureaucrat. Henry Ford didn't revolutionize the automobile industry that way. In the only cases in which the masses have escaped from the kind of grinding poverty you're talking about, the only cases in recorded history are where they have had capitalism and largely free trade. If you want to know where the masses are worse off, it's exactly in the kinds of societies that depart from that. So that the record of history is absolutely crystal clear, that there is no alternative way so far discovered of improving the lot of the ordinary people that can hold a candle to the productive activities that are unleashed by the free-enterprise system.
>
> Education spending will be most effective if it relies on parental choice & private initiative – the building blocks of success throughout our society.
>
> Governments never learn. Only people learn.

The Great Depression, like most other periods of severe unemployment, was produced by government mismanagement rather than by any inherent instability of the private economy.

I think that nothing is so important for freedom as recognizing in the law each individual's natural right to property, and giving individuals a sense that they own something that they're responsible for, that they have control over, and that they can dispose of.

There is one and only one social responsibility of business – to use its resources and engage in activities designed to increase its profits so long as it stays within the rules of the game, which is to say, engages in open and free competition without deception or fraud.

In a much quoted passage in his inaugural address, President Kennedy said, "Ask not what your country can do for you – ask what you can do for your country." It is a striking sign of the temper of our times that the controversy about this passage centered on its origin and not on its content. Neither half of the statement expresses a relation between the citizen and his government that is worthy of the ideals of free men in a free society. The paternalistic "what your country can do for you" implies that government is the patron, the citizen the ward, a view that is at odds with the free man's belief in his own responsibility for his own destiny. The organismic, "what you can do for your country" implies that government is the master or the deity, the citizen, the servant or the votary. To the free man, the country [government] is the collection of individuals who compose it, not something over and above them. He is proud of a common heritage and loyal to common traditions. But he regards government as a means, an instrumentality, neither a grantor of favors and gifts, nor a master or god to be blindly worshiped and served. He recognizes no national goal except as it is the consensus of the goals that the citizens severally serve. He recognizes no national purpose except as it is the consensus of the purposes for which the citizens severally strive.

Only a crisis, actual or perceived, produces real change. When that crisis occurs, the actions that are taken depend on the ideas that are lying around. That, I believe, is our basic function: to develop alternatives to existing policies, to keep them alive and available until the politically impossible becomes the politically inevitable.

I contend that liberal socialist democrats use this philosophy to their advantage every chance they get. Remember the statement by President Obama's Chief of Staff, Rahm Emanuel; "You never want a serious crisis to go to waste," as told to the Wall Street Journal conference of top corporate chief executives in November 2008 during the greatest financial crisis in America since the Great Depression. The WSJ article essentially says the Obama Administration has a greater chance of driving its long-term agenda through congress and public opinion much faster because of the severity of the crisis.

Let's see – the liberal socialist democrats' mismanagement of our nation for decades produces the greatest financial crisis since the great depression and we resort to more liberal socialist democrat policies. Is this a joke? Go figure!

When will conservative republicans learn to stop defending themselves against LSD's sound bites, and start reframing the LSD narratives to reflect the real world truth? Change the narrative to the **"Rich get Richer and the Poor also get the best opportunity to get Rich!"** Why, because that pushback of the LSD propaganda message is the absolute truth! Correct the idiots that say "The Poor get Poorer." The liberals are distorting and manipulating the truth in the most negative way and have been getting away with it because of spineless moderate republicans.

In Chapter 20 we outline how dishonest the Liberal Socialist Democratic Party has been in perverting their popular war cry of "The Rich get Richer." Of course, the rich get richer, and then invest in production that will result in a better economy, that results in more jobs, and that results in more opportunities for the poor to get ahead. I point out in simple terms that it's just basic arithmetic and nothing else that leads to a wider gap between the rich and the poor each year. The rich have more money left over after living expenses to invest and then those investments grow and compound over time. Nothing evil about that! We need to slam the intelligence of any LSD or sycophant whenever they are stupid enough to repeat it in the future. Do you see what I am getting at?

After a while they will be afraid to use their sound bite because we will slam their intelligence with our sound bite…

Why aren't we (Americans) teaching this simple principle to the poor at every opportunity?

The only logical answer is: because the poor are the pawns of the liberal socialist democrats who need them to stay poor and settle for the crumbs that these LSD maggots give them in return for votes…

Like I said, we republicans better learn how to get this point across every minute, every day and to everybody possible. Repeat it so often the liberal socialist democrat propaganda machine, the news media, get so sick of hearing it they complain constantly and make fun of us for saying it. Narrative repetition is the best offence/defense to their narrative repetition and is the mother of all skill. Our relentless countering to their "Rich get Richer" with our "Socialism makes the Poor Poorer" and "Free-Market Capitalism allows the Poor to become Rich" will work – **just give it time…**

More Milton Friedman quotes:

> Even the most ardent environmentalist doesn't really want to stop pollution. If he thinks about it, and doesn't just talk about it, he wants to have the *right amount* of pollution. We can't really *afford* to eliminate it – not without abandoning all the benefits of technology that we not only enjoy but on which we depend [for advancement and survival].

> Many people want the government to protect the consumer. A much more urgent problem is to protect the consumer from the government.

> For example, the supporters of tariffs treat it as self-evident that the creation of jobs is a desirable end, in and of itself, regardless of what the persons employed do. That is clearly wrong. If all we want are jobs, we can create any number – for example, have people dig holes and then fill them up again, or perform other useless tasks.

Work is sometimes its own reward. Mostly, however, it is the price we pay to get the things we want. **Our real objective is not just jobs but productive jobs – jobs that will mean more goods and services to consume.**

Our minds tell us, and history confirms that the great threat to freedom is the concentration of power. Government is necessary to preserve our freedom, it is an instrument through which we can exercise our freedom; yet by concentrating power in political hands, it is also a threat to freedom. Even though the men who wield this power initially be of good will and even though they are not corrupted by the power they exercise, the power will both attract and form men of a different stamp.

Because we live in a largely free society, we tend to forget how limited is the span of time and the part of the globe for which there has ever been anything like political freedom: the typical state of mankind is tyranny, servitude, and misery. The nineteenth century and early twentieth century in the Western world stand out as striking exceptions to the general trend of historical development. Political freedom in this instance clearly came along with the free-market and the development of capitalist institutions. So also did political freedom in the golden age of Greece and in the early days of the Roman era.

Referring to congressional two year terms with term limits of six years: "Because from an economic point of view, one of the worst features of our system is that you have a new tax law every year or every two years. However bad the tax law is, if you didn't change it for five years it would do less harm. Why do you keep changing it? Because that's the most effective way to raise campaign funds. Lobbyists will pay you to put loopholes in; they will pay you to take them out.

Most of the energy of political work is devoted to correcting the effects of mismanagement of government.

Hell hath no fury like a bureaucrat scorned.

The unions might be good for the people who are in the unions but it doesn't do a thing for the people who are unemployed. Because the union keeps down the number of jobs, it doesn't do a thing for them.

Was Keynes was a great economist? In every discipline, progress comes from people who make hypotheses, most of which turn out to be wrong, but all of which ultimately point to the right answer. Now Keynes, in *The General Theory of Employment, Interest and Money,* set forth a hypothesis which was a beautiful one, and it really altered the shape of economics. But it turned out that it was a wrong hypothesis. That doesn't mean that he wasn't a great man!

A major source of objection to a free economy is precisely that it gives people what they want instead of what a particular group thinks they ought to want. Underlying most arguments against the free-market is a lack of belief in freedom itself.

With respect to teachers' salaries: Poor teachers are grossly overpaid and good teachers grossly underpaid. Salary schedules tend to be uniform and determined far more by seniority.

The key insight of Adam Smith's *The Wealth of Nations* is misleadingly simple: If an exchange between two parties is voluntary, it will not take place unless both believe they will benefit from it. Most economic fallacies derive from the neglect of this simple insight, from the tendency to assume that there is a fixed pie – that one party can gain only at the expense of another.

There is no place for government to prohibit consumers from buying products the effect of which will be to harm themselves.

I'm in favor of legalizing drugs. According to my values system, if people want to kill themselves, they have every right to do so. Most of the harm that comes from drugs is because they are illegal.

Now here's somebody who wants to smoke a marijuana cigarette. If he's caught, he goes to jail. Now is that moral? Is that proper? I think it's absolutely disgraceful that our government, supposed to be our government, should be in the position of converting people who are not harming others into criminals, of destroying their lives, putting them in jail. That's the issue to me. The economic issue comes in only for explaining why it has those effects. But the economic reasons are not the reasons.

This plea comes from the bottom of my heart. Every friend of freedom, and I know you are one, must be as revolted as I am by the prospect of turning the United States into an armed camp, by the vision of jails filled with casual drug users and of an army of enforcers empowered to invade the liberty of citizens on slight evidence. A country in which shooting down unidentified planes "on suspicion'" can be seriously considered as a drug-war tactic is not the kind of United States that either you or I want to hand on to future generations.

It is because it's prohibited. See, if you look at the drug war from a purely economic point of view, the role of the government is to protect the drug cartel. That's literally true.

And finally: **A society that puts equality before freedom will get neither. A society that puts freedom before equality will get a high degree of both.**

Milton Friedman has written or been part of dozens of books. I have read several of them and highly recommend: *Capitalism and Freedom* along with *Money Mischief: Episodes in Monetary History, Free to Choose* and *The Tyranny of the Status Quo.* His books along with the great works of black economists Dr. Walter E. Williams and Dr. Thomas Sowel are valuable reading for any patriotic American wanting a better understanding of free-market vs. socialist economics. All of their books are available from Amazon.com at very reasonable "free-market" prices. Pun intended!

In 1988, just before the Soviet Union collapsed, Nobel Prize winning libertarian economist Friedrich Hayek wrote in *"The Fatal Conceit"* that "the curious task of economics is to demonstrate to men how little they really know about what they imagine they can design."

What is "Free-market Capitalism"?

Free-market Capitalism is first and foremost about private property rights and personal decisions and freedom. Adam Smith's seminal work, *The Wealth of Nations (1776)*, created a new understanding of economics; where the study of individual decisions, not the coercive dictates of governments or the collective, are paramount to the well-being of societies. Smith wrote mainly against the mercantile system that existed at the time and gave a complicated but brilliant account of an economic system based in human nature and deeply rooted social dynamics. His writings became a cornerstone of America's foundation…

What about the Founders? What did they think about free-market capitalism?

> Although the term *capitalism* was scarcely in use at the time of the founding, the Founders supported the principle of economic liberty underlying it. The Founders understood that property rights and free-markets were constitutive elements of what it means to be free. They therefore believed that government has a responsibility to protect the rights of all to participate in the economy by upholding contracts, lifting artificial trade barriers, and protecting the right to acquire, possess, freely use, and dispose of property.
>
> The Founders did not, however, advocate a completely "laissez-faire" economic policy, since they understood that the government had a role to play – a limited role – in regulating the economy. For example, at the time of the Founding, the government inspected goods that were imported into the United States and created licensing systems for certain professions – such as medicine – that were essential to public health and safety. Such regulations strengthen a free-market economy by protecting consumers from fraud and by expanding the opportunity for all to participate in the market by ensuring the reliability of goods and services.
>
> The Founders' defense of limited regulations enacted by elected representatives is a far cry from the Progressives' [liberal socialist democrats] embrace of far-reaching regulations made by unelected and unaccountable bureaucrats.
>
> Source: freemarketcapitalism.net/

Another definition of Free-Market Capitalism is: A system of economics that minimizes government intervention and maximizes the role of free-markets. According to the theory of the free-market, rational economic participants acting in their own self-interest deal with information to price goods and services the most efficient way possible. Government regulations, trade barriers, and labor laws are generally thought to distort markets. Proponents of free-markets argue that it provides increased opportunities for both consumers and producers by creating more jobs and allowing competition to decide which businesses are successful.

Critics maintain that an unfettered free-market concentrates wealth in the hands of a few, which is unsustainable in the long term. If this were true IBM would not have replaced the older bigger NCR and Microsoft would not have replaced the older bigger IBM and Apple would not have replaced the bigger more established Microsoft as the leading technology companies of their day. The economy transformed from agricultural to industrial to technology and now to information largely because of free-market capitalism. AOL gives way to Yahoo; Yahoo gives way to Google and I suspect someone is currently developing the successor to Google.

In practice, no country or jurisdiction has a completely free-market; but the most free-market economies like Singapore are providing its society with the most freedoms and wealth creation opportunities in the world today. Those economies ruled by the collectives like labor unions, both private and public sectors; are doomed to failure, bankruptcy and suffering – just look at Detroit, again both private and public unions and the LSD party have destroyed a great city.

The defenders of Detroit blamed automation for and foreign competitors for Detroit's demise. Really, then how do you explain all of the foreign auto companies that have built factories elsewhere in America; companies like Honda, Toyota, Nissan, Subaru, Mazda, Mitsubishi, VW, Hyundai, Kia, BMW and Mercedes Benz. In 2011, Honda built more cars at its Alabama, Indiana and Ohio facilities than it did in Japan — 826,440 versus 710,621, according to data from Automotive News and the Japan Automobile Manufacturers Association.

It's the first time Honda's U.S. production topped production in its home country. All of these American cities, where these factories are located, used competitive free-market principles to get these foreign companies to open factories here. What has the liberal socialist democrats or the defenders of Detroit have to say about that? Crickets… "Just ignore the facts mam!"

Comparison of free-market jobs vs. stimulus or government jobs: When the free-enterprise employer hires an employee that employer must consider how that expense component, i.e., the wages, will be paid for. If that employee is in sales, service or manufacturing then the employer can calculate directly the sales or services or widgets built that that employee must "create" to justify the new hire expense.

If the salesman is paid 100% of his income from commissions and works out of his car with no office expenses then it doesn't really matter how good, or bad, his success. There is no lost expense component that has to be added to the product or service relative to a non-productive salaried employee.

If the salesman gets paid a salary and works out of an office with a support staff, then he must meet production quotas to pay for his salary and support expenses. Above and beyond a minimum sales quota he creates a greater profit for the company. The same applies to the widget manufacturing employee or the service provider employee (carpet cleaner, mechanic, doctor, CPA, attorney, etc.).

All of the indirect support staff needed to run the company is also an added expense to the final price of the widget or service. Another widget or service expense component includes all of the plant, equipment, quality control, advertising, accounting, legal, transportation, financing and other associated costs needed to produce and deliver the company's products or services. All of these elements and many others are combined and compared to all of the company's competitors in the market to see who "wins." Companies thrive or go out of business based on how well they execute the above and whether or not their product or service is desired and in sufficient demand.

Now compare the government employer and whether they have to meet any profit demands to stay in business or how much they can charge for their services before competition drives them out of business. Who are the government's competitors, who are their customers, who are the owners and how do they fire management? The federal government operates with total monopoly powers without any consequences, but interestingly enough, cities and states must compete with each other to keep its citizens and companies, i.e., tax payers, from moving away.

That's why "The People's Republic of California" and many of its cities will continue seeing an exodus of companies and tax payers to places like Texas and Arizona if they don't stop their liberal socialist democrat trends. Now, why would anyone want to leave the most beautiful state in America; with all if its magnificent coastlines, mountains, weather and natural beauty to live anywhere else? The answer is: tax and regulatory tyranny! The same reason the Founders declared our independence from England and fought the revolutionary war (1776 – 1783).

The only checks and balances to complete tyranny in America are our periodic elections. But this last presidential election (2012) seems to be an approval of more government, more taxes, more regulations and controls which will lead to less freedom, less wealth and more tyranny. Why would America, with such a rich history of freedom and prosperity, choose more government, more taxes, more regulatory controls, more tyranny, and less freedom and prosperity? The answer is really very simple – the country is finally at the tipping point where the population on some form of government assistance votes for the liberal socialist democrat who will to continue the march towards total socialism and redistribution of wealth. Add to that the LSD propaganda machine of media and entertainment elites along with the LSD universities polluting gullible minds and we get Obama! Lastly, honest republicans have no chance when matched against the expertly developed "Hustling" skills of the liberal socialist democrats and their slobbering sycophants in the mainstream media and Hollywood.

The republicans – especially moderate republicans and the republican establishment have done a dismal job in "teaching" the public the failures of socialism and drawing very clear distinctions between free-market constitutional conservative principles and the liberal socialist principles of the Democrat Party. Correcting this failure is paramount to saving America from the insidious effects of the liberal socialist democrats' polities and propaganda!

The Austrian School of Economics was founded in 1871 with the publication of Carl Menger's "*Principles of Economics.*"

Different Schools of Economics:

There are three main schools of economics that fight for mainstream attention: **the Keynesian school** (most identified with John Maynard Keynes and Paul Krugman), **the Chicago school** (most identified with Milton Friedman), and **the Austrian school** (most identified with Friedrich Hayek and Ludwig von Mises). This article will proceed with the intent of giving you some basic resources for learning about Austrian economics. Although this will be the focus of the article, a general – albeit imperfect – distinction should be drawn between the three schools.

Although no school of economics is infallible, the Austrian school of economics generally is the most rational and realistic. It is premised upon the notion of studying economics as a part of the axiom of human action.

For the Austrian economist, economic growth and prosperity are based on sound money, real savings, and production. The value of goods and services is subjective, thus the best way to ration goods and services is through a free and flexible price system that constantly adapts to the changing realities [human preferential decisions] of the market. Generally, currency should be the result of market competition and not be a fiat paper currency that is printed by the central bank.

In contrast, the **Keynesian school** of economics is much more mathematically based, although it too has prior assumptions that inform its methodology. Keynesian economists believe that markets are generally decent, but that they also need significant amounts of restraint and regulation in order to produce an optimal result.

Wealth is generally measured by cumulative macroeconomic totals, such as a nation's GDP, among other things. Depressions and recessions result from failures in the market that need to be corrected and stimulated by government spending. Money should be a matter of fiat paper currency that is controlled and regulated by a central bank. [This discipline has brought us both The Great Depression of the 1930s and now The Great Recession of today, or at least the most limp recovery ever to follow a deep recession].

The **Chicago school** generally agrees with much of the Austrian analysis regarding competition, flexible pricing, and reduced regulation, however, it agrees with the Keynesian school on monetary policy. The Chicago school economist generally is more prone to allowing the government the authority to regulate the money supply by the use of paper fiat currency. Furthermore, the Chicago school favors the scientific approach to economics. They simply believe their models can, on the whole, defend free-market concepts while refuting Keynesian models.

The reason I tend to side with the Austrian school is because I believe they are the most methodologically rigorous and practically realistic. Additionally, Austrian economists understand that much of modern economics has turned into a math contest rather than a legitimate study of human action. Thus, one does not have to be a whiz at calculus in order to understand and defend Austrian economics. This does not imply that the Austrian school is lazy or unacademic. Rather, it is more grounded in common sense and philosophical rigidity than its counterparts.

Yet, despite the clear and simple nature of Austrian economic principles, one still needs to be able to defend them in this day and age. To do that requires more in-depth knowledge than being able to recognize the name, "Hayek." Therefore, what resources can we look to provide the cornerstone of a good education in proper economic methodology?
Source: capitalisminstitute.org/economics-101/

One of the greatest wealth creations from commerce innovators of the 21st Century are the works of the late Dr. Edwards Deming and how his methods and theories completely changed the Japanese manufacturing industry after World War II. How is it that an academic with a PhD in mathematics, physics and statistics from America was responsible for Japan's post-war manufacturing excellence and the 2nd greatest economic power of the world for more than 30 years? The rebirth and acceleration of Japanese manufacturing excellence was due to free-market capitalist strategies, not socialist ideas. It took only one generation in which, "Made in Japan" went from a critical joke to "Made in Japan" became a badge of value and excellence.

A review of Dr. Edwards Deming last book:

"The New Economics for Industry, Government and Education" is a horizon expanding book because it talks about a completely different approach to management of people. Even though many believe he had a somewhat utopian labor view or style of management; nevertheless, Dr. Deming worked within a very free-market capitalist industry of competition of the fittest company to produce the highest quality product at the lowest cost. It did not matter if the product was a car, a service or an education. Unions, as they are today, certainly don't fit within his principles.

Dr. Deming's 14 Principles in full may seem to have some minor socialist philosophies, and therefore may appear somewhat contradictory in that the results of these principles increase market share and profits. I believe in a noble free-market goal that leads to more jobs and wealth creation. His methods accomplished those goals. Keep in mind his audience was Japanize senior management several decades ago:

1. <u>Constancy of purpose:</u> Create constancy of purpose for continual improvement of products and service to society, allocating resources to provide for long range needs rather than only short term profitability, with a plan to become competitive, to stay in business, and to provide jobs;

2. <u>The new philosophy:</u> Adopt the new philosophy. We are in a new economic age, created in Japan. We can no longer live with commonly accepted levels of delays, mistakes, defective materials and defective workmanship. Transformation of Western management style is necessary to halt the continued decline of business and industry.

3. <u>Cease dependence on mass inspection:</u> Eliminate the need for mass inspection as the way of life to achieve quality by building quality into the product in the first place. Require statistical evidence of built in quality in both manufacturing and purchasing functions.

4. <u>End lowest tender contracts:</u> End the practice of awarding business solely on the basis of price tag. Instead require meaningful measures

of quality along with price. Reduce the number of suppliers for the same item by eliminating those that do not qualify with statistical and other evidence of quality. The aim is to minimize total cost, not merely initial cost, by minimizing variation. This may be achieved by moving toward a single supplier for any one item, on a long term relationship of loyalty and trust. Purchasing managers have a new job, and must learn it.

5. Improve every process: Improve constantly and forever every process for planning, production, and service. Search continually for problems in order to improve every activity in the company, to improve quality and productivity, and thus to constantly decrease costs. Institute innovation and constant improvement of product, service, and process. It is management's job to work continually on the system (design, incoming materials, maintenance, improvement of machines, supervision, training, retraining).

6. Institute training on the job: Institute modern methods of training on the job for all, including management, to make better use of every employee. New skills are required to keep up with changes in materials, methods, product and service design, machinery, techniques, and service.

7. Institute leadership: Adopt and institute leadership aimed at helping people do a better job. The responsibility of managers and supervisors must be changed from sheer numbers to quality. Improvement of quality will automatically improve productivity. Management must ensure that immediate action is taken on reports of inherited defects, maintenance requirements, poor tools, fuzzy operational definitions, and all conditions detrimental to quality.

8. Drive out fear: Encourage effective two way communication and other means to drive out fear throughout the organization so that everybody may work effectively and more productively for the company.

9. Break down barriers: Break down barriers between departments and staff areas. People in different areas, such as Leasing, Maintenance

and Administration, must work in teams to tackle problems that may be encountered with products or service.

10. <u>Eliminate exhortations:</u> Eliminate the use of slogans, posters and exhortations for the work force, demanding Zero Defects and new levels of productivity, without providing methods. Such exhortations only create adversarial relationships; the bulk of the causes of low quality and low productivity belong to the system, and thus lie beyond the power of the work force.

11. <u>Eliminate arbitrary numerical targets:</u> Eliminate work standards that prescribe quotas for the work force and numerical goals for people in management. Substitute aids and helpful leadership in order to achieve continual improvement of quality and productivity.

12. <u>Permit pride of workmanship:</u> Remove the barriers that rob hourly workers, and people in management, of their right to pride of workmanship. This implies, among other things, abolition of the annual merit rating (appraisal of performance) and of Management by Objective. Again, the responsibility of managers, supervisors, foremen must be changed from sheer numbers to quality.

13. <u>Encourage education:</u> Institute a vigorous program of education, and encourage self-improvement for everyone. What an organization needs is not just good people; it needs people that are improving with education. Advances in competitive position will have their roots in knowledge.

14. <u>Top management commitment and action:</u> Clearly define top management's permanent commitment to ever improving quality and productivity, and their obligation to implement all of these principles. Indeed, it is not enough that top management commit themselves for life to quality and productivity. They must know what it is that they are committed to – that is, what they must do. Create a structure in top management that will push every day on the preceding 13 Points, and take action in order to accomplish the transformation. Support is not enough: action is required!

One might ask why the author ended a chapter on Free-Market Capitalism with a treatise about manufacturing excellence. The reason is this man, Dr. Deming, invented "Total Quality Management" and is practically worshiped in Japan because of his methods and teachings. Again, these methods can be applied to any endeavor – including government.

Why can't the Executive Branch, Congress, the Legislative Branch, State, County, City governments and bureaucrats at all levels make these 14 Principles mandatory for every department and public servant?

I firmly believe that if our government implemented these 14 Principles, we really could win the war on poverty and public debt. Our nation would be a better place for everyone…

If creativity, productivity and hard work builds wealth why would anyone chose socialism which stifles creativity, productivity and hard work?

The answer: Because hustlers would rather take (steal) someone else's money or property instead of taking the time and effort to create it themselves. Carl Marx was too mediocre and lazy to achieve wealth and prominence through creating jobs and industry so he turned to philosophy, deciding to justify his laziness to work hard and/or invest capital, and his jealousy of those who did – he decided to hustle instead…

Summation of Capitalism vs. Socialism

Capitalism equals high creativity and productivity that is rewarded. Socialism equals low creativity and productivity – that diminishes reward.

Capitalism Creates & Socialism Takes

100% free market capitalism is the best wealth creator the world has ever known. It is the best means of allowing the poorest among the population to become the richest. Socialism traps the poor in mediocracy. It saps the greatest dreams a person can have and therefore steals what could be – from him/her and even societies' benefits of those dreams come true.

How does something so obvious and verifiable still exist in an information enriched WORLD? The answer is why I wrote this book…

Hustlers Would Rather Take Than Create

How do they do that? By lying with such skill and audacity that they can take the above statement, **"Hustlers Would Rather Take Than Create,"** and claim it for their own propaganda. They claim rich people steal from poor people to gain riches.

The best examples I can think of to debunk this con is Sam Walton. He created Walmart to bring "everything" to the masses far cheaper than anyone else in the market place. Let me repeat: he helped the poor buy more stuff with their limited income. Again, he helped the poor, and in the process he became the richest person in the world. How about Apple, Google, Facebook – did they do it to help the poor or themelves?

Who cares! That's the point the socialists refuse to understand and why I say, they're either stupid or they're lying con artists and hustlers… Get it – **"America You've Been Hustled!"**

Chapter 6

Crony Capitalism, Corporate Welfare, Private/Government Coercion and Corruption… Just another money grab!

News Flash: On CNBC June 8th 2012 a guest commentator, Peter Cecchini, from the investment banking firm Cantor Fitzgerald, had the following quote written on the screen: "Eurozone does not have the same mechanisms to transfer debt to the public sector from banks, as the U.S. does!" The comment adds, "This is beginning to impact rest of the world."

They're talking about private bank debt in countries like Greece, Spain, Portugal and Italy being transferred to public tax payers (like in the US). It's incredible how flippantly these guys on CNBC talk about bailing out European and American banking sectors with American tax payers' money. This is not free-market capitalism; it is crony capitalism (corruption), and it goes on every day somewhere in the world.

And here we sit in our living rooms and bitch about Exxon who is charging us about half what the rest of the world pays for a gallon of gas and is directly or indirectly responsible for millions of great paying jobs. And, if liberal socialist democrats like President Obama will get out of their way, the oil industry will create hundreds of thousands new great paying jobs that will help energize the economy, create millions more indirect jobs, untold increases in tax collections and an improved trade deficit. Go figure! But isn't that what control freak liberal socialist democrats do best – demagogue free-market capitalism and business? They especially like to target the oil industry as money grubbing environmental polluters yet they conveniently ignore the millions of great paying jobs, the billions in taxes paid and most importantly, the fact that America pays about one-half the average price for fuel energy paid elsewhere in the world.

Crony capitalism is a term describing an economy in which success in business depends on close relationships between business people and government officials. It may be exhibited by favoritism in the distribution of legal permits, government grants, special tax breaks, and so forth. Crony capitalism is believed to arise when political cronyism spills over into the business world; self-serving friendships and family ties between businessmen and the government influence the economy and society to the extent that it corrupts public-serving economic and political ideals.

In its lightest form, crony capitalism consists of collusion among market players. While perhaps lightly competing against each other, they will present a unified front to the government in requesting subsidies or aid (sometimes called a trade association or industry trade group). Newcomers to a market may find it difficult to find loans or acquire shelf space to sell their product; in technological fields, they may be accused of infringing on patents that the established competitors never assert against each other.

Distribution networks will refuse to aid the entrant. That said, there will still be competitors who "crack" the system when the legal barriers are light, especially where the old guard has become inefficient and is failing to meet the needs of the market. Of course, some of these upstarts may then join with the established networks to help deter any other new competitors. Examples of this have been argued to include the *keiretsu* of post-war Japan, the print media in India, the *chaebol* of South Korea, and the powerful families who control much of the investment in Latin America.

Crony capitalism is generally associated with more virulent government intervention, however. Intentionally ambiguous laws and regulations are common in such systems. Taken strictly, such laws would greatly impede practically all business; in practice, they are only erratically enforced. The specter of having such laws suddenly brought down upon a business provides incentive to stay in the good graces of political officials. Troublesome rivals who have overstepped their bounds can have the laws suddenly enforced against them, leading to fines or even jail time.

Here is a story that illustrates this point exactly. The feds cracked down on Gibson Guitar because of their use of a special wood from India called "East Indian Rosewood." One of Gibson's leading competitors is C.F. Martin & Company. The C.E.O., Chris

Martin IV, is a long-time Democratic supporter, with $35,400 in contributions to Democratic candidates and the DNC over the past couple of election cycles. According to C.F. Martin's catalog, several of their guitars contain "East Indian Rosewood." In case you were wondering, that is the exact same wood in at least ten of Gibson's guitars. Did the feds storm Martin's company? NO! Why Not? Democrat connections…

As for Gibson's political support, Henry E. Juszkiewicz, Gibson's Chief Executive Officer, is a donor to a couple of Republican politicians. According to the Open Secrets database, Juszkiewicz donated $2,000 to Rep. Marsha Blackburn (R-TN07) last year, as well as $1,500 each to Sen. Lamar Alexander (R-TN). Juszkiewicz also has donated $10,000 to the Consumer Electronics Association, a PAC that contributed $92.5k to Republican candidates last year, as opposed to $72k to Democrats.

The raid served no legitimate purpose. Gibson was not even accused of violating any American law, but was shut down by armed storm troopers, of Obama's Justice Department, for allegedly violating picayune procedures India wants people to follow regarding the nationality of those who work with certain wood. Indian officials have better things to do than to prosecute such cases, but not our Injustice Department, which is heeding Comrade Obama's call to "punish our enemies." Now we know why the Obama Regime put its "boot on the neck" of Gibson Guitar. It isn't about building guitars from oppressed wood; it's about politics:

The bigger government gets, the more inevitable this sort of tyranny becomes.

Source:http://www.rightwingnews.com/freedom/fed-crackdown-on-gibson-guitar-explained/

Wu Jinglian, one of China's leading economists and a longtime champion of its transition to free-markets, says that it faces two starkly contrasting futures: a market economy under the rule of law or crony capitalism.

More direct government involvement can lead to specific areas of crony capitalism, even if the economy as a whole may be healthy. Governments will, often in good faith, establish government agencies to regulate an industry. However, the members of an industry have a very strong interest in the actions of a regulatory body, while the rest of the citizenry are only lightly affected. As a result, it is not uncommon for current industry players to gain control of the "watchdog" and use it against competitors. This phenomenon is known as regulatory capture.

A famous early example in the United States would be the Interstate Commerce Commission, which was established in 1887 to regulate the railroad "robber barons;" instead, it quickly became controlled by the railroads, which set up a permit system that was used to deny access to new entrants and functionally legalized price fixing.

The military-industrial complex in the United States is often described as an example of crony capitalism in an industry. Connections with the Pentagon and lobbyists in Washington are described by critics as more important than actual competition, due to the political and secretive nature of defense contracts. In the Airbus-Boeing WTO dispute, Airbus (which receives outright subsidies from European governments) has stated Boeing receives similar subsidies, which are hidden as inefficient defense contracts. In another example, Bechtel, claiming that it should have had a chance to bid for certain contracts, said Halliburton had received no-bid contracts due to having cronies in the Bush administration.

Gerald P. O'Driscoll, former vice president at the Federal Reserve Bank of Dallas, stated that Fannie Mae and Freddie Mac became examples of crony capitalism. Government backing let Fannie and Freddie dominate mortgage underwriting. The politicians created the mortgage giants, which then returned some of the profits to the politicians – sometimes directly, as campaign funds; sometimes as "contributions" to favored constituents.

Critics of capitalism including socialists and other anti-capitalists often assert that crony capitalism is the inevitable result of *any* capitalist system. Jane Jacobs described it as a natural consequence of collusion between those managing power and trade, while

Noam Chomsky has argued that the word "crony" is superfluous when describing capitalism. Since businesses make money and money leads to political power, business will inevitably use their power to influence governments. Much of the impetus behind campaign finance reform in the United States and in other countries is an attempt to prevent economic power being used to take political power.

Source: www.wikipedia.org/wiki/Crony_capitalism

Let me make it crystal clear at this point: The millions of small businesses that are taxed at the individual owner level (LLC or "S Corp") and not as a "C Corp" like the big corporations discussed above don't have any crony capitalism powers. That's why President Obama is going after them. They, unlike the big boys, are the biggest group of millionaires to tax. The problem with more tax collections and regulations (ObamaCare) on small business owners is that it leaves less working capital for their businesses to expand operations and therefore hire more employees. Why aren't they using more of their working capital now to hire and expand? Could it be that they're scared to death of Obama and his administration? I think so…

What do you do when you're fearful or unsure of the future? Hold on to your safety net – cash… The really stupid thing about taxing these job creators is the resulting drain on commerce and economic expansion that has a multiplier effect on American's economy, i.e., more social welfare expenditures and less tax collections to pay for them over the long term, resulting in bigger deficits.

Stupid democrats? No, stupid voters!

Corporate welfare is a pejorative term describing a government's bestowal of money grants, tax breaks, or other special favorable treatment on corporations or selected corporations. The term compares corporate subsidies and welfare payments to the poor, and implies that corporations are much less needy of such treatment than the poor. The Canadian New Democratic Party picked up the term as a major theme in its 1972 federal election campaign. Ralph Nader, an American critic of corporate welfare, is often credited with coining the term.

Subsidies considered excessive, unwarranted, wasteful, unfair, inefficient, or bought by lobbying are often called corporate welfare. The label of corporate welfare is often used to decry projects advertised as benefiting the general welfare that spend a disproportionate amount of funds on large corporations, and often in uncompetitive, or anti-competitive ways. For instance, in the United States, agricultural subsidies are usually portrayed as helping honest, hardworking independent farmers stay afloat. However, the majority of income gained from commodity support programs actually goes to large agribusiness corporations such as Archer Daniels Midland, as they own a considerably larger percentage of production.

According to the Cato Institute, the U.S. federal government spent $92 billion on corporate welfare during fiscal year 2006. Recipients included Boeing, Xerox, IBM, Motorola, Dow Chemical, and General Electric.

Alan Peters and Peter Fisher have estimated that state and local governments provide $40–50 billion annually in economic development incentives, which many critics characterize as corporate welfare.

Some economists consider the recent bank bailouts in the United States to be corporate welfare. U.S. politicians have also contended that zero-interest loans from the Federal Reserve System to financial institutions during the global financial crisis were a hidden, backdoor form of corporate welfare.

Source: http://en.wikipedia.org/wiki/Corporate_welfare

Private Coercion: A corporation which successfully engages in coercion to the extent that it eliminates the possibility of competition operates a coercive monopoly. A firm may use illegal or non-economic methods, such as extortion, to achieve and retain a coercive monopoly position. A company which has become the sole supplier of a commodity through non-coercive means (such as by simply outcompeting all other firms), may theoretically then go on to become a coercive monopoly if it maintains its position by engaging in coercive "barriers to entry."

The most famous historical examples of this type of coercive monopoly began in 1920, when the Eighteenth Amendment to the United States Constitution went into effect. This period, called Prohibition, presented lucrative opportunities for organized crime to take over the importation ("bootlegging"), manufacture, and distribution of alcoholic beverages. Al Capone, one of the most famous bootleggers of them all, built his criminal empire largely on profits from illegal alcohol, and effectively used coercion (including murder) to impose barriers to entry to his competitors.

However, it may be relevant to take into account the fact that government was intervening in the alcohol industry by making manufacture and sales illegal and arresting those in the business, thereby enabling unnaturally high profits, and was not providing the usual service of enforcing trade contracts; likewise, some corrupt public officials derived rent-like profit from bribes that ensured that Capone would receive preferential treatment against potential competitors.

Government Monopolies: Undisputed examples of coercive monopolies are those that are enforced by law. In a government monopoly, an agency under the direct authority of the government itself holds the monopoly, and the coercive monopoly status is sustained by the enforcement of laws or regulations that ban competition, or reserve exclusive control over factors of production for the government. The state-owned petroleum companies that are common in oil-rich developing countries (such as Aramco in Saudi Arabia or PDVSA in Venezuela) are examples of government monopolies created through nationalization of resources and existing firms; the United States Postal Service is an example of a coercive monopoly created through laws that ban potential competitors such as UPS or FedEx from offering competing services (in this case, first-class and standard mail).

Government-granted monopolies often closely resemble government monopolies in many respects, but the two are distinguished by the decision-making structure of the monopolist. In government monopoly, the holder of the monopoly is formally the government itself and the group of people who make business decisions is an agency under the government's direct authority. In government-granted monopoly, on the other hand, the coercive monopoly is enforced through law, but the holder of the monopoly is formally a private firm, or a subsidiary division of a private firm, which makes its own business decisions.

Examples of government-granted monopolies include cable television and water providers in many municipalities in the United States, exclusive petroleum exploration grants to companies such as Standard Oil in many countries, and historically, lucrative colonial "joint stock" companies such as the Dutch East India Company, which were granted exclusive trading privileges with colonial possessions under mercantilist economic policy. Intellectual property such as copyrights and patents are government-granted monopolies. Another example is the thirty-year government-granted monopoly that was granted to Robert Fulton by the State of New York in steamboat traffic, but was later ruled by the U.S. Supreme Court to be unconstitutional because of a conflicting inter-state grant to Thomas Gibbons by the federal Congress.

Economist Lawrence W. Reed says that a government can cause a coercive monopoly without explicitly banning competition but by "simply [bestowing] privileges, immunities, or subsidies on one firm while imposing costly requirements on all others." For example, Alan Greenspan, in his essay *Antitrust* argues that land subsidies to railroad companies in the western portion of the U.S. in 19th century created a coercive monopoly position. He says that "with the aid of the federal government, a segment of the railroad industry was able to 'break free' from the competitive bounds which had prevailed in the East." In addition, some claim that regulations can be established that place burdens on smaller firms that attempt to compete with an industry leader.

Source: http://en.wikipedia.org/wiki/Coercive_monopoly

Congressional Insider Trading: Insider trading is illegal – except for members of Congress. A Wall Street executive who buys or sells stock based on insider information would face a Securities and Exchange Commission investigation and quite possibly a federal prosecutor and jail time. But senators and congressmen are free to legally trade stock based on nonpublic information they have obtained through their official positions as elected officials – and they do so on a regular basis.

On Sunday night, CBS News' *60 Minutes* looked into this form of "lawful graft." The 60 Minutes story exposed, among others, then House Speaker Nancy Pelosi for participating in a lucrative initial public offering from Visa in 2008 that was not available to the general public, just as a troublesome piece of legislation that would have hurt credit card companies began making its way through the House (the bill never made it to the floor). And it showed how during the 2008 financial crisis, Rep. Spencer Bachus (R-Ala.) then ranking Republican on the House Financial Services Committee aggressively bought stock options based on apocalyptic briefings he had received the day before from Federal Reserve Chairman Ben Bernanke and Treasury Secretary Hank Paulson.

The report was based on an explosive new book by Peter Schweizer titled *"Throw Them All Out: How Politicians and Their Friends Get Rich off Insider Stock Tips, Land Deals, and Cronyism That Would Send the Rest of Us to Prison."* (Full disclosure: Schweizer is a close friend of Marc Thiessen (the author of this article), a former White House colleague and my business partner in a speechwriting firm, Oval Office Writers.

The 60 Minutes story only scratches the surface of what Schweizer has uncovered. For example, Bachus was not the only member of Congress trading on nonpublic information during the financial crisis. On Sept. 16, 2008, Schweizer writes, Paulson and Bernanke held a "terrifying" closed-door meeting with congressional leaders. "The next day Congressman Jim Moran, Democrat of Virginia, a member of the Appropriations Committee, dumped his shares in ninety different companies; [his] most active trading day of the year."

Rep. Shelley Capito (R-W.Va.) and her husband dumped between $100,000 and $250,000 in Citigroup stock the day after the briefing, Schweizer writes, and "at least ten U.S. Senators, including John Kerry, Sheldon Whitehouse, and Dick Durbin, traded stock or mutual funds related to the financial industry the following day." Durbin, Schweizer says, "attended that September 16 briefing with Paulson and Bernanke. He sold off $73,715 in stock funds the next day. Following the next terrifying closed-door briefing, on September 18, he dumped another $42,000 in stock. By doing so, Durbin joined some colleagues in saving themselves from the sizable losses that less-connected investors would experience." Some members even made gains on their trades, at a time when ordinary Americans without insider knowledge were seeing their life savings evaporate.

Schweizer also documents numerous examples of how members of Congress of both parties – including Pelosi, Senate Majority Leader Harry Reid and former House speaker Dennis Hastert – have used federal earmarks to enhance the value of their own real estate holdings. They have done so, Schweizer shows, by extending a light-rail mass transit line near their property, expanding an airport, cleaning up a nearby shoreline, building roads and bridges, and beautifying land and neighborhoods nearby – in each case "substantially increasing values and the net worth of our elected officials, courtesy of taxpayer money."

Perhaps the most disturbing revelations come from Schweizer's investigation into the Obama Energy Department and its infamous "green energy" loan guarantee and grant programs, a program Schweizer calls "the greatest and most expensive example of crony capitalism in American history." The scandal surrounding Solyndra, the now-bankrupt, Obama-connected solar power company that received a federally guaranteed loan of $573 million is well known. But Solyndra, Schweizer says, is only the tip of the iceberg.

According to his research, at least 10 members of President Obama's campaign finance committee and more than a dozen of his campaign bundlers were big winners in getting tax dollars from these programs. One chart in the book details how the 10 finance committee members collectively raised $457,834, and were in turn approved for grants or loans of nearly $11.4 billion – quite a return on their investment.

In the loan-guarantee program alone, Schweizer writes, "$16.4 billion of the $20.5 billion in loans granted went to companies either run by or primarily owned by Obama financial backers – individuals who were bundlers, members of Obama's National Finance Committee, or large donors to the Democratic Party." That is a staggering 71 percent of the loan money.

Schweizer cites example after example of companies that received grants or loans and documents their financial connections to the Obama campaign and the Democratic Party. And he shows how "the [Energy] department's loan and grant programs are run by partisans who were responsible for raising money during the Obama campaign from the same people who later came to seek government loans and grants."

There is much, much more, which means that when Schweizer's book hits stores Tuesday, heads in Washington are going to explode.

http://www.aei.org/article/crony-capitalism-exposed/ Marc A. Thiessen, The Washington Post, November 14, 2011 *Marc A. Thiessen is a visiting fellow at AEI*

Since this article was written the 112th Congress passed the Stock Act of 2012 which should have outlawed government employee insider trading. I said should have! As one might expect from these DC pigs, the legislation was watered down and some believe it lacks enforcement teeth. Anyone surprised?

Chapter 7

If you're a Democrat – you're either a Socialist or an enabler! You don't get credit for "Good Intentions..."

Rarely do we find men who willingly engage in hard, solid thinking. There is an almost universal quest for easy answers and half-baked solutions. Nothing pains some people more than having to think.
– Martin Luther King, Jr.

Here is the essence of Marxism, communism or socialism in America: If a person has liberal socialist democrat (LSD) political "connections" he can live like royalty, but it depends entirely on giving crumbs and other advantages or benefits in a democracy in return for votes from the poor and the gullible. And that's exactly what has been happening in America since 1912. The liberal socialist democrats have "progressively" moved this country away from self-reliance towards dependence, from achievement to who cares, from hard work to hardly working, from integrity to deceit and from excellence towards mediocrity. All you need to win in this political game is the talent to lie, cheat, steal and hustle for the "Party." And, the smoothest talking, back slapping, glad handing hustlers can even become presidents! It certainly helps to be a good looking celebrity politician who can play the saxophone or sing the blues. Let's face it, if you're cool, who cares if you're an incompetent "Hustler" leading America to bankruptcy.

Imagine that – "Hustlers" in the White house...

There are primarily five (5) groups that comprise the Liberal Socialist Democratic Party:

1. <u>The elites or the royalty class</u> – Those that depend on political or liberal connections for their livelihoods, i.e., politicians and bureaucrats, the mainstream media, Madison Avenue, Hollywood, academia, political organizations and businesses or industries that depend on government contracts. This group considers itself the "Ruling Class" and some enjoy the trapping of royalty enjoyed by Kings and the friends of Kings. They feel they are entitled to power, wealth and fame;

2. **The utopian believers or enablers** – Again, some are hard-working good-hearted next door neighbors that truly want to help their fellow citizens. Before the liberal socialist democrats created the "welfare state" these people were the first to help their family, friends and even strangers in times of need. Again, some in this group are just not capable of discerning the con man's "hustle" and simply don't understand that liberal socialist democrats are amplifying poverty and suffering – not solving it. The 50 year "war on poverty" has been a losing disaster, creating a culture that actually increases poverty and suffering;

3. **The suckers** – Average everyday good hearted citizens that don't have the time or the inclination to learn the political issues and the different solutions to the problems facing our nation. Some are lazy; some don't care; some are great people just trying to cope with the pressures of life and raising children; and, some don't have healthy functioning brains and are incapable of distinguishing when they are being used or conned by liars and hustlers. They are trusting and gullible – a bad combination for themselves and our nation. Recent medical research studies reveal how some people or even groups, like some seniors, are consistent targets of swindlers who take advantage of them. This group simply doesn't understand the differences between true free-market capitalism, crony-capitalism and capitalist socialism.

They know that pure socialism is bad, but they don't think some socialism is bad. They don't really know the difference between an expensive and inefficient, big-centralized, command and control federal government and a small, inexpensive and efficient decentralized federal government. These are the true believers in "Something for Nothing." They believe the rich can afford to pay "their excessive fair share" without any understanding of how investment and working capital in a free-enterprise system provides the most jobs and wealth for everyone; even more importantly it provides the greatest opportunity for the industrious poor to become prosperous;

4. **The dependent class,** for whatever reason, will settle for crumbs doled out by the elites who only pretend to care about them; in reality they are using them; they can barely tolerate the poor. This is because we live in a democracy where the majority rules and democrats

need their votes to win power. Don't believe it? Look who promises "free" benefits to so many groups. Who pays? That's the catch – everyone in the end; including and especially the poor and uneducated. But, in the meantime the liberal socialist democrat elites will get rich and live like royalty off everyone else in America; and

5. **<u>The crooks</u>** who steal from the welfare system. Most are just getting food stamps for their family by lying about their true situation, and some are working elaborate schemes to take hundreds of thousands or even millions from the government. Collectively, this group is getting away with billions, if not hundreds of billions. Pretty soon those hundreds of billions add up to trillions…

Here is a hypothesis that has been studied recently by several scientific researchers: Scientists from Harvard and the University of California San Diego have discovered what they're calling the "Liberal gene." Some people are born with a liberal ideology gene similar to a person who is born with an alcoholic or homosexual gene. Think about it, each of us knows someone who after drinking alcohol for just a few months or years – watched their personality's change and they had clearly become addicted to alcohol. These people are genetically predisposed to alcoholism.

Also, most of us know some boys that at a very young age exhibited very feminine traits and later became gay. Here is a genetic reality that may begin to explain why some men feel they were born to be a female and some women feel they were born to be a male:

> Men have nipples because we all were conceived gender neutral. Somewhere during fetal development we develop into a female or a male. You may notice male and female have all the same "bits"' but they differ in size and function. The clitoris for example is the female counterpart to the penis, ovaries to gonads and nipples either sit on a pair of breasts or for the male are just there. Also, early embryonic tissue that turns into the uterus in females turns into the prostate gland in males.

Source: http://wiki.answers.com/Q/Why_do_men_have_nipples

Not only the extreme genetic development differences above but we seem to be born with temperament and personality predispositions. Why are some people hot-tempered while some are so even-tempered, why are some so competitive while some could care less, why do some seek to be the center of attention and others are scared to death to be center stage?

Some humans appear to be firmly alcoholic or homosexual and very little can influence their behavior even if they wanted to be influenced. I have believed these hypotheses for several decades simply through observations within my friends and family. It is not my intention here to scientifically prove the liberal vs. conservative ideology gene hypothesis but to open the debate of its possibility. If this is, in fact, true, it might help to explain why some people hold fast to their utopian beliefs even in the face of mountains of data proving socialism doesn't work and is actually destructive to society, families and individuals.

Every year we are learning more about the functioning, or malfunctioning, of the human brain. Remember the movie Rainman with Dustin Huffman and Tom Cruise? What a great illustration of the complexities of the human brain. On one hand the savant, played by Hoffman, had no understanding of emotional connections or relationships but was an absolute genius in mathematical calculations and memorization. How could this be, someone who at the same moment could be considered mentally challenged and a genius? This may describe some of our neighbors who are very smart and hardworking, who derive no benefits from a socialist society, but vote for a Democratic Party because they "believe" the democrats help the poor and disadvantaged more than the republicans. The purpose of this book is to dispel that notion and "persuade" them to see the "truth" based on reality and mountains of facts; facts the LSD and their sycophants in academia and media conveniently ignore.

I'm neither condemning nor excusing these groups in anyway. I'm only hypothesizing a genetic predisposition to liberalism in the same way medical professionals have hypothesized the alcoholic or homosexual predisposition. We all know some people that are either very liberal or very conservative. Most have been that way all of their lives and their beliefs are very concrete and not easily influenced.

Let's suppose that approximately 40 percent of the American adult population is liberal, and another 40 percent is conservative; the remaining 20 percent are independent or "moderate." Some of these 40 percent groups may be explained by the above hypothesis; the rest can be explained by social environment and cultural influences. The latter, social and cultural, may explain why almost 90 percent of blacks and most women, Jews, seniors, Mexicans and other Latinos, and young adults vote for democrats predominately. It may also explain why Hillary Rodham Clinton left the Republican Party after being exposed to the 60's liberal revolution and became an LSD radical.

Look at the similarities in the words and symbols that democrats, socialists and communists use to hustle gullible, weak minded people. "Workers, the working class, the people's party, the raised fist, greedy corporations, evil capitalist, the greedy rich, the rich get richer and the poor get poorer, and requiring corporations and the rich to use *their own property* in the national interest to *pay their fair share*."

Their fair share is a total socialist lie! Who are the biggest hustlers promoting these con artists' lies? President Obama, democratic leaders, labor union leaders and the liberal socialist media elites! The rich pays the vast majority of income taxes collected by the IRS. Don't give me that bull about every working American pays payroll taxes. That's a payment to the Social Security retirement system. I repeat – retirement payments!

Look at the facts: According to the Office of Tax Analysis, the U.S. individual income tax is "highly progressive," with a small group of higher-income taxpayers paying most of the individual income taxes each year. I'm not against progressive income taxes, just the current overly complicated tax system with all of the built in favors to the powerful and connected elites; especially millionaire and billionaire democrats. And, I'm really tired of the class warfare of President Obama and the rest of the liberal socialist democrats who are never satisfied with more taxes and spending. The only time they are concerned with the US deficit is when they cry for more taxes. Once they get more taxes they spend it immediately on new programs and the money finds its way into the pockets of those with connections! Remember the bigger the annual budget the easier it is to steal from the tax payer and give federal money to their cronies. In a later chapter, I suggest a simplified tax overhaul that is still progressive, but far simpler and has everyone paying something in *income taxes* – even if it's only 1 or 2%.

In 2002, the top 5 percent of taxpayers paid more than one-half (53.8 percent) of all individual income taxes, but reported roughly one-third (30.6 percent) of income. The top 1 percent of taxpayers paid 33.7 percent of all individual income taxes in 2002. This group of taxpayers has paid more than 30 percent of individual income taxes since 1995. Moreover, since 1990 this group's tax share has grown faster than their income share.

Taxpayers who rank in the top 50 percent of taxpayers by income pay virtually all individual income taxes. In all years since 1990, taxpayers in this group have paid over 94 percent of all individual income taxes. In 2000, 2001, and 2002, this group paid over 96 percent of the total. Treasury Department analysts credit President Bush's tax cuts with shifting a larger share of the individual income taxes paid to higher income taxpayers. In 2005, says the Treasury, when most of the tax cut provisions were fully in effect (e.g., lower tax rates, the $1,000 child credit, the marriage penalty relief), the projected tax share for lower-income taxpayers fell, while the tax share for higher-income taxpayers increased.

The share of taxes paid by the bottom 50 percent of taxpayers fell from 4.1 percent to 3.6 percent, and the share of taxes paid by the top 1 percent of taxpayers increased from 32.3 percent to 33.7 percent. The average tax rate for the bottom 50 percent of taxpayers decreased by 27 percent; compared to a 13 percent decline for taxpayers in the top 1 percent. These 2002 figures are after the Bush tax cuts that the liberal socialist democrats demonize as a tax cut for the rich. Since these 2002 data revelations the poor and middle class are paying a smaller portion of the total taxes collected and the rich are paying a higher percentage of all taxes collected!

As a reminder, the author is currently poor and has never achieved better than the middle class. He is writing this book because he believes the socialist class warfare and policies of the democrats lead to laws and regulations that will result in the financial destruction of America and much greater suffering for those of us in the poor and middle class.

"The rich get richer and the poor get poorer." This makes sense to the poor, and the uneducated (a polite way of saying the ignorant), but it's still just a socialist propaganda con that will end in a bankrupt country unable to care for the needy they profess to represent. What a joke! After the coming financial collapse, the poor will include those currently in the middle class and government workers who will lose their jobs and can't find any other; or suffer pay and benefit cuts because of drastic austerity measures. Look at the riots in Greece by citizens who have allowed themselves to become dependent on government socialism. **Wake up LSD voters you're making a big mistake!**

This could all be avoided if the new legislative (2012-2013) measures of the conservative leaders in congress could get their legislation pass the liberal socialist democrat leaders in the senate and President Obama.

Hey poor and middle class suckers of the elite controlled Liberal Socialist Democratic Party – do you think these elites are going to suffer when this country crashes and can't recover for decades? Look at the people rioting in the streets of Greece. The elites in Greece are living like kings while their non-connected "subjects" are suffering. You don't need a degree in economics or social science to see what is happening to European big-government socialist countries like Greece, Spain, Portugal, Italy, France and others – they are going broke, and their people are suffering! What about Detroit or Stockton?

Don't you get it yet? Again, socialism doesn't work; it has never worked, and it will never work – for anybody except those cronies in power (the Club) that collect the money and spend a "share" of it on themselves and their friends.

How do you think all of these career politicians became rich? Crony capitalism… They certainly didn't risk their own money on an idea or venture and then hire employees to grow the company. I had a small manufacturing company with 7 employees in the 70's after college. I worked 90 hours a week to pay their salaries. These political or bureaucratic con artists' get careers in government and then think of new ways to collect taxes from the rest of us. Who do they have to compete against to stay in business? No one! Do they have to be price or cost conscience? Hell no! They're spending other people's money…

Sure, for a while most of the money makes its way into social programs but eventually there's such a drain on investment and production, and such a demand for more social program monies that, either the country wakes up and makes the necessary changes or we collapse into chaos and riots. Just like Greece and the Soviet Union, this is where the big-government Liberal Socialist Democratic Party is leading our nation. We may continue to limp along in a "stagnant" economy for a while, but if changes are not made, heart break and massive suffering will be experienced by all of us who are poor or in the middle class.

The most accomplished of these con artists (liars) reach the highest positions in the Democratic Party. Remember President Clinton's assertion that he "did not have sex with that women" or his famous statement, "it depends on what is, is." Who didn't laugh out loud when they saw him make these statements on national TV? Liberal socialist democrats – that's who! History has been very kind to Bill Clinton – mainly because of the economy Ronald Reagan and Gingrich & Co. set in motion in the 1980s and 90s. Sure, he signed the bills after much resistance and revisions, but ***"The Contract with America"*** was the blueprint, and the architect was the newly elected republican majority in congress lead by the brilliant Newt Gingrich. Republicans make me sick for allowing history to be rewritten in favor of Bill Clinton instead of the house republicans. Why? Is it because they're trying to get Obama to be more like Clinton and cooperate with the newly elected republican majority in the house (2010)? Don't bother – Obama is much too clever and much too liberal (socialist ideologue) to fall for your naïve attempts to get him to do what you want him to.

Back to the subject of lying: Howard Dean may be the best democrat con artist not to reach the presidency. This master hypocrite can look right into the camera and call his truthful opponent in an interview a liar in such a way and with such conviction he should have already received an Oscar from his socialist buddies in "The People's Republic of California." How often do you hear him say; "that's a lie" to his opponent's facts, and "that's a fact" when he states his bold face lies?

The polite and chicken hearted republicans just sit there, trying to maintain their composure; letting these liars get away with it. Screw dignity; we're getting our butts kicked – fight back using the LSD rules, which is: anything goes… This is a fight for the survival of America for our children and grandchildren. Stop being composed and dignified – let your passion show. **"Righteous indignation"** is our goal and our battle cry. Republicans must realize they will receive a nationwide standing ovation in living rooms all across America every time they call these liars – a liar!

Lets' practice – You're a liar Howard Dean, you're a liar Nancy Pelosi, you're a "dirty" liar Senate Majority Leader "Hairy Slug," you're a gross liar Barney Frank, you're a liar's liar Debbie Whopperlies-Schultz, you're a stupid liar Joe Biden, you're a racist liar Maxine Waters, you're a smooth talking liar Dick Durban and Chris Van Hollen – well you get the point! You don't like my unprofessional juvenile name calling of Harry Reid and Debbie Wasserman-Shultz? Get over it! They set the standard for juvenile unprofessionalism. If they are going to act juvenile on national TV lying about and slandering the Tea Party Patriots and other republicans, then they deserve these new juvenile names. That's their political tactic so "what comes around goes around!"

If "Hairy Slug" is the best the senate democrats can produce to be their leader, how pathetic are they? And, how the democrats can justify using Debbie for their national spokesman during the campaign of 2012 after telling so many easily provable lies, or "whoppers," as Obama puts it, is really stupid on their part. I realize lying is a sport in Washington so maybe the players don't care about such ridiculous dishonesty. "We The People" do care and we're sick and tired of it…

If brave Americans will call these parasites – liars, especially on national TV, maybe it will get through to a few more of the gullible suckers and they will vote these hustlers out of office before it's too late. And, if you're a lying republican, you should be called a liar too and voted out of office also.

Don't worry about the debate devolving into a tit-for-tat, "you're a liar, no you're liar" mess. Just change the argument to: LSDs are socialists and socialism always leads to suffering – especially among the poor and middle class citizens who don't have the means to survive the coming debt tsunami that will bankrupt America. Socialism is wealth redistribution and state run industries!!!

Republican politicians probably shouldn't (I'm not real sure at this point) call the President of the United States a liar – that language is just too harsh and we should show respect for the "Office of the Presidency," regardless of the man or woman who might be diminishing the office like Clinton or Obama.

Remember the congressman calling Obama a liar during the State of the Union address (I think it was 2011). I thought it was accurate and deserved, but wrong. Any kind of shout-out during the address is probably (still not sure) inappropriate no matter how much it is deserved. I would just continue with polite "bull-crap" words like: "you're not accurate, not truthful, disingenuous, etc.," for the President. For the rest of them – call them liars!

Some of the best scandals in our history have been provided by liberal socialist democrats. During the democrats majority rule in the house for over 40 years from 1954 to 1994 they thought an agency of the federal government, the Congressional division of US Post Office, was their personal piggy bank.

Remember the **Congressional Post Office scandal** in the early 1990's that refers to the discovery of corruption among various Congressional Post Office employees and members of the United States House of Representatives, climaxing in the conviction of the powerful House Ways and Means Committee Chairman Dan Rostenkowski.

> Initially this investigation by the United States Capitol Police moved from a single embezzlement charge against a single employee within the Post Office to wide spread corruption that included congress. Evidence rapidly led to the inclusion of several other employees, **before top Democrats in the House of Representatives moved to shut down the whole line of inquiry, i.e., a cover-up,** despite protests from Frank Kerrigan, chief of the Capitol Police.
>
> A new investigation was started by the United States Postal Service eventually submitted a report which was held in silence by the third in line to the Presidency, Speaker Thomas Foley (D-WA). It wasn't until media reports of embezzlement and money laundering leaked out in 1992 that the public became aware of this scandal. Following public outcry, the Democratic leaders of the House were forced to refer the matter to the Committee on House Administration, which started its own investigation. That committee broke into two parts along party lines, the Democrats issuing a report saying the matter was closed, but the Republicans issuing a

dissenting report including a number of unanswered questions and problems with the investigation.

The Republican charges were largely ignored until July 1993, when the Congressional Postmaster Robert Rota pleaded guilty to three criminal charges and implicated Representatives Dan Rostenkowski (D-IL) and Joe Kolter (D-PA). They were accused of heading a conspiracy to launder Post Office money through stamps and postal vouchers.

Rostenkowski was convicted and sentenced to 18 months in prison but President Bill Clinton, a democrat, pardoned him. The Republicans took control of the House in 1995, under the leadership of Speaker Newt Gingrich. Gingrich attempted to pass a major legislative program, the "Contract with America" on which the House Republicans had been elected, and made major reforms of the House, notably reducing the tenure of committee chairs to three two-year terms. Many elements of the Contract did not pass Congress, were vetoed by President Bill Clinton, or were substantially altered in negotiations with Clinton.

An earlier scandal: In 1988 Wright became the target of an inquiry by the House Ethics Committee. Their report in early 1989 implied that he had used bulk purchases of his book, *Reflections of a Public Man*, to earn speaking fees in excess of the allowed maximum, and that his wife, Betty, was given a job and perks to avoid the limit on gifts. Faced with an increasing loss of effectiveness, Wright tendered his resignation as Speaker on May 31, 1989, the resignation to become effective on the selection of a successor. He was the first Speaker to ever resign because of a scandal. On June 6, the Democratic Caucus brought Wright's speakership to an end by selecting his replacement, Tom Foley of Washington, and on June 30 Wright resigned his seat in Congress.

The incident itself was controversial and was a part of the increasing partisan infighting that has plagued the Congress ever since. The original charges were filed by Newt Gingrich in 1988 and their effect propelled Gingrich's own career advancement to the Speaker's chair itself.

In 1989, controversy arose from media reports that Jim Wright's main aide, John Mack, had violently attacked Pamela

Small sixteen years earlier. Small was attempting to replace blinds in a store Mack managed, and he took her to the storeroom where he then asked her to lie down. When she refused, he repeatedly hit her in the head with a hammer, stabbed her with a steak knife, and slashed her throat, before putting her body in his car and going to see a movie.

Pamela Small survived the attack, and reported it to the police. John Mack pled guilty to malicious wounding "with the intent to maim, disfigure, disable and kill" and was sentenced to fifteen years in prison. However, after repeated correspondence with Rep. Wright, whose daughter was married to his brother, Mack was paroled after serving less than 27 months and given a job working for Wright on Capitol Hill. Critics, including feminist activist Andrea Dworkin, alleged that Wright manipulated the legal system to get Mack off and, subsequently, protected him from media scrutiny. The story later broke in 1989, when Pamela Small gave an interview about her ordeal with the Washington Post. Amid media criticism, John Mack resigned from his post.

Source: www.wikipedia.org/Congressional_Post_Office_scandal

In case this story is not obvious, the democrats, who were in power since 1954, were stealing cash and lying about it to investigators and the public. Shortly after that, in 1995, the bums were thrown out and replaced by a republican majority.

Democrats protect their friends no matter what they do. Anything goes – even brutal attacks and attempted murder of women. And women vote for these dirt bags because they believe the Democrat Party stands for women's rights – come on women, this book is replete with how democrats use and abuse women. When are you going to wake up and stop lusting over the likes of Bill Clinton? Don't you see the hypocrisy of the Godless left?

Gingrich was repaid for his aggressive pursuit of Jim Wright and the "Republican Revolution" of 1994. The democrats filed 84 ethics charges against Gingrich during his term as Speaker. All were eventually dropped except for one: claiming tax-exempt status for a college course run for political purposes. Gingrich, unlike any democrat in the history of the world, fell on his sword and resigned his Speakership and congress. Regarding the situation, Gingrich said in January 1997, "I did not manage the effort intensely enough to thoroughly direct or review information being submitted to the committee on my behalf. In my name and over my signature, inaccurate, incomplete and unreliable statements were given to the committee, but I did not intend to mislead the committee. I brought down on the people's house a controversy which could weaken the faith people have in their government." In 1999, the IRS cleared the organizations connected with the "Renewing American Civilization" courses under investigation for possible tax violations.

I lived in Atlanta at the time of these classes being aired on TV and watched most of Newt's college classes. They were completely non-partisan. He was far more gracious and two-sided towards democrats than I expected and any democrat would have been. How anyone could interpret them as politically biased is ridiculous.

The Republicans held on to the House until the 2006 Congressional elections, during which the Democrats won control and Nancy Pelosi was as the first female Speaker in history. In the 2010 House elections, Republicans retook the House in the largest shift of power since the 1930s. Republicans won in a landslide, primarily because ObamaCare was rammed through congress in the middle of the night, under special rules, without a single republican vote. "Law of the land" my ass! It was as unconstitutional as any law ever passed.

The socialist liberal media likes to demonize the republicans for Washington gridlock and shutting down the federal government. They say, **"Republicans refuse to compromise with democrats." Well, God bless every one of those brave souls! Without them, we would already be a full blown socialist nation** with a name change to the "People's Republic of America." Why would any true conservative compromise with a big-government liberal socialist democrat's agenda?

Chapter 8

Being a Democrat is the easy path to power – why would anybody chose to be a Republican? Maybe the same reason Abraham Lincoln chose to be a Republican?

Here's how easy it is to be a liberal socialist democrat:

- You can buy votes with promises of money and benefits.
- You don't even have to use your own money.
- You can use other people's money – without their permission!

Think about it – the LSD candidate can promise to tax the rich and give to the poor money and benefits. **How hard is that?** There are far more poor people than rich people. It should be easy to get elected and stay in power. Just think about all the benefits of being in the "Club." Some would say it's like taking candy from a baby or shooting fish in a barrel. You'll be in the Club! And, here's the best part – you can get rich liberal democrat businessmen, rich liberal media elites, rich Hollywood stars, rich college professors, rich union leaders, rich Black leaders, rich women's activists, youth activists and some senior citizen groups to completely agree with "soak the rich" policies and reelect you every 2, 4, or 6 years. And, the benefits are absolutely amazing; these guys get free health care, great retirement programs after only a few years of service, the ability to make millions from deals that non-politically connected citizens could never access, enjoy all-expense paid vacations all over the world, and living the life of the "rich and famous." Young girls (power groupies) are plentiful for powerful politicians, and there is always a lobbyist hanging around to pick up the tab.

This countries' problem, and the reason we may suffer another depression, is not just the politically connected con men or women in positions of power; society will always have criminals, crooks and con men or women that feed off of societies' producers. No, it's the dupes and suckers who believe this ***"Hustle"*** can go on much longer without severe economic consequences. The non-connected voters that believe this

LSD con are pathetically uninformed or too stupid for words! What I mean by non-connected is this:

- They're not on welfare or some other form of government help, so these voters don't feel insecure about losing any of those benefits if those evil conservative republicans are elected. **Conservatives will actually save** the long-term future of these programs through practical financial budget reforms;
- These voters don't have federal jobs, so they don't fear losing those jobs and benefits if those evil Tea Party Republicans win. Again, conservatives will strengthen the financial future of our government, like so many republican governors have done recently thereby securing the future of "warranted" federal jobs;
- Their power and entire careers don't depend on towing the line of the liberal socialist democrats' *"Club,"* or they will get kicked out of those Hollywood, the news media, or labor union careers (in other words the vast majority of us); and,
- They're not big-businesses that have a stake in keeping complex regulations in place that favor them over small businesses that don't have any political connections. Small business owners make up the vast majority of the rich in this country; they have no political connections, so they are the targets of LSDs.

If you're a republican and certainly a Constitutional Conservative or Tea Party Republican, you will be demonized by the Liberal Socialist Democratic Party and their slobbering sycophants in the liberal strongholds of society. Here are the biggest republican targets to be destroyed by an "all-out war" from this dirty LSD party:

- All Conservatives especially Tea Party Conservatives;
- Conservative women and especially black women (thank God their numbers are growing);
- Conservative black men (again, thank God their numbers are growing too);
- Wealthy conservatives (those evil rich guys – liberals only value rich liberal socialist democrat politicians like John Kerry, Ted Kennedy, Nancy Pelosi and hundreds more);

How do liberal socialist democrats wage war on conservatives, especially on God fearing Constitutional Conservative Tea Party Republicans and Libertarians?

- Mainly through the liberal mainstream media, Hollywood, Madison Avenue and other liberal media outlets' relentless spinning and twisting of the news to champion the left and demonize the right, especially the Tea Party Patriots and their movement;
- Indoctrination of our children starting in 1st grade. Remember the communist like chants that were being taught to those elementary students early in Obama's first term. Good Lord folks, this was clearly a communist indoctrination tactic. It's common knowledge that our university system is totally polluted with liberal socialist democrat leaning professors. Try to be a conservative republican on many of these campuses if you are a student and especially if you're a professor – you will be minimized and/or punished;
- Millions of overlapping laws, rules and regulations that strangle the success and limit creation of small businesses;
- Now (May 2013) conservatives, especially Tea Party Conservatives, have been vindicated for their belief that the IRS targets them using the tyrannical powers of the agency; and,
- The relentless demonization of the rich and non-rich conservative, especially the Tea Party, by the liberal socialist democrats in congress and the White House. They are routinely called tea baggers, terrorists, extortionists, anarchists, arsonists, suicide bombers, ransom criminals, racists, old lady killers, homophobes, against the poor, against the Latinos, against college students and the young, against seniors – you name it and the lying slandering propaganda machine of liberal socialist democrats are always at work praising the left and demonizing the conservative right as extremists.

When will they stop? NEVER – so let's use their tactics against them!

Sound bites are the only thing that works with most of America's "clueless" voters that can't seem to distinguish fact from fiction or

the truth from the lying con that the "Hustlers" in Washington, DC, NYC, Chicago and LA are feeding them.

Educating this 10 to 30% group of Americans to the consequences (suffering) that is coming because of the Liberal Socialist Democrat "Ruling Class" **is the only hope we have to turn this country around.** Then we can launch the long-term policy changes that will create a robust economy with more high paid jobs because we will have the presidency and both majorities in congress.

The primary point I'm trying to make with this book is again: Socialism doesn't work, has never worked, and will never work. We must educate our youth and any other ignorant groups of Americans to the insidious elements of socialism and is destroying nations, states and cities.

To quote Ralph Peters, **"History is vengeful toward the ignorant. And we're historically illiterate."**

The God fearing constitutional conservatives, libertarians and the Tea Party must be stronger than the enablers called "moderate republicans" else we fail…

In closing, I leave you with this profound quote from Ann Coulter: "The definition of 'liberal' is quickly becoming: people who believe their fantasies should be facts."

The LSD Party is doomed to fail. I only hope we don't suffer too much before that prediction is realized!

Chapter 9

Scandals, Abuse of Power and "The Buck Doesn't Stop Here Anymore!"

First, I want to make a very important point before I comment on the many scandals of the liberal socialist democrats and their leadership since 2010. That point is this – who is really effected by these scandals? The poor and those on public benefits could care less about IRS or Justice Department tyranny because they don't pay taxes anyway and are too insignificant to be targets… The stupid can't understand… The ignorant don't care enough to learn the facts… The too busy don't have the time to even notice…

How are any of these scandals really affecting the percentage of democrat voters who are most at risk of suffering during the next economic down-turn? These scandals don't really affect them so don't expect any change in voting behaviors from this voting bloc. Also, the die-hard liberal socialist democrats are just laughing because they know we are at the socialist tipping point anyway as predicted in the opening paragraph of this book by Alexander Tytler.

Do you think Latinos, as a group, care about the democrat leadership scandals we discuss below? Do you think Black Americans as a group care? Do you think the average woman cares? Do you think the average homosexual cares? Do you think the average senior citizen cares? Do you think the average young person cares? **These scandals will have very little effect on voting behaviors**, which is the ONLY solution to resolving our long-term insidious slide into a socialist state, a hamstrung economy and the mass suffering when our economy collapses again as it did in 2008 and the 1930's.

The only solutions, in my opinion, are sound bites that educate the gullible public who believe the LSD's promise of "Something for Nothing." **We must get the voters most at risk of the coming suffering to "feel," I REPEAT "FEEL" the inevitable "SUFFERING" that socialism causes and contrast that with the wealth creation results of**

free-enterprise capitalism. It should be so easy to "teach" the differences in simple and rapid sound bites that will keep the LSD party on their heels, and slowly, I repeat, slowly change the minds of the poor and other minorities who have continuously voted LSDs into office in the past. Remember, successful socialist "hustlers" think in terms of generations not election cycles. They use propaganda, especially in our elementary and university school systems, to "educate" and "train" the next generation on what is right or politically correct.

CONSERVATIVES MUST DO THE SAME THING...

Back to the scandals in which nobody in the Obama Administration knows anything. Plausible deniability is the hallmark of organized corruption! Protecting the head of a corrupt organization by insulating him/her from knowing any of the details of a crime or wrong doing is paramount – especially for a liberal socialist democrat loyalist. Remember what brought down the brilliant but tyrannical Richard Nixon? He thought he was above the law too. It wasn't his loyal "right hand men" that turned on him – it was the presidential tapes that eventually did him in. Don't count on that happening again! And, with Bill Clinton, it was his word against others, until the DNA stained dress did him in! In other words, Barrack Obama is here to stay so forget about removing him from office – it will never happen. Besides, he's too cool and charming – everybody loves him!

Here's a question to ponder... How much of the IRS scandal is attributable to the IRS employee union? This was my first thought when this scandal broke. Unions function like a communist or socialist organization, spread the wealth around and take their cut off the top – tyranny and abuse of power has been used by unions for a hundred years! Again, how much did the IRS union play in targeting the Tea Party using the powers of the IRS. Did anyone at the top of the LSD really have to do anything but express distain and contempt for the Tea Party, and then discuss how influential they had become in the 2010 elections and that they needed to be quieted before the 2012 elections?

This is how it's done in most corrupt organizations – a wink and a nod is all that is needed to destroy one's opponents! Congressional investigations need to continue until they have exhausted all witnesses and then turn it over to a special investigator appointed by Obama's loyalists. Of course, any new revelations will be buried, and nothing will be done until after the 2016 presidential elections – and then only if a strong constitutional conservative is elected president along with a republican controlled house and senate. If America does indeed finally turn the country over to constitutional conservative Tea Party republicans (please: no moderates!) they better not drop their investigation into the tyranny we suffered under the Obama "Regime" or else it happen again and will not benefit history. What I mean by that is:

It is paramount that American history is totally accurate and we understand the depth of corruption that can permeate our government if America elects the "slicksters" and "hustlers" of the power addicted Liberal Socialist Democrat Party…

Federal Reserve Bank Qualitative Easing ("QE") Scandals – Some may not consider what I'm going to outline as a scandal, but I'm including it because the Fed has been meddling with the free-market allocation of capital and interests rates at the expense of the American (and world) economy for way too long. Free-markets have natural business cycles that can and will create imbalances of capital, but these imbalances will be corrected naturally and swiftly by free-markets if left alone. When the Fed gets involved it causes those imbalances to grow larger than they usually would and then once the recession begins the Fed tries to "fix" it causing unnecessary delays in rebalancing malinvested assets.

Here is why I believe the Fed and all these QE or attempts to pump money into the economy are scandals: 1. Artificially lowering interest rates help money center banks and the nation's largest corporations at the expense of senior citizen's interest or CD earnings. Senior's earnings have been crushed causing them to look for higher paying investments that may not be suitable for them. Sure lowering interest rates help everyone with a mortgage, but at what expense – a long-term stagnant economy with far fewer jobs that a true free-market recovery would have created. What good is it to have a low interest rate mortgage if you don't have a job, or the higher paying job you once had? 2. The Fed is buying long-term treasuries and mortgage-backed securities at huge premiums from money center banks, and they will likely unwind them in the future at huge losses. Again, the big winners are money center banks to the tune of hundreds of billions. Who is the Fed working for, the money center banks or the average American? If this isn't a scandal than what is…

<u>Buying Senate votes for ObamaCare</u> – to the tune of hundreds of millions in pork further exposes just how corrupt the liberal socialist democrats can be. If republicans do this, they should get the boot also! Literally, in the middle of the night, democrats rammed socialism (ObamaCare) down the throats of the American people. Not one republican in either house voted for this hugely historic law! There was no statesmanship here; it was heavy handed backroom deals and bribes in the senate that led to this future train wreck disaster. Again, I believe this crowning achievement by liberal socialist democrats and their supreme leader President Barack Hussein Obama will back-fire on them and become the beginning of the end of socialism in America.

<u>NLRB</u> – On April 20, 2011 the National Labor Relations Board filed a 10-page complaint against Boeing alleging the company's decision in 2009 to locate its second 787 Dreamliner assembly plant in South Carolina represented illegal retaliation against employees belonging to the International Association of Machinists & Aerospace Workers (IAM). As a remedy, the NLRB sought a judicial order for the company to shift all production of its planned 787 Dreamliner commercial jet back to its main facility in Washington State. The IAM, predictably, was delighted. Equally to the point, Boeing and South Carolina officials were furious. South Carolina is a Right to Work state and the primary reason for the fight. Did the NLRB care about South Carolina's worker? Hell no!

Back on March 26, 2010, the Machinists filed a complaint against Boeing with the National Labor Relations Board. The union claimed the Chicago-based company, in moving its final assembly plant for its 787 Dreamliner wide-body, twin-engine jet aircraft to a facility near Charleston, South Carolina, illegally had "retaliated" against the IAM for four separate strikes the union conducted over the course of 1989-2008. Instead of expanding its existing production facility in Everett, Washington, located about 25 miles north of Seattle, Boeing instead chose a site at Charleston Airport near Charleston, S.C. Boeing settled with the NLRB and the union by "paying" penalties and other benefits to them.

Any fair study of this situation would conclude that the NLRB is just as corrupt as the unions. This isn't about labor relations; it's about labor corruption and Obama Administration coercion. Tell me why the citizens of South Carolina can't compete for "NEW" Boeing jobs – why are they denied high paying jobs by the liberal socialist democrat controlled NLRB? No one at the Boeing plants in Seattle Washington was losing their job; on the contrary thousands of jobs were being added to the Washington state plants. I believe this was a really stupid move by the NLRB because the vast majority of Americans could now see just how socialistic the Obama Administration and their sycophants in this nation's unions really are.

Fast & Furious – Selling assault weapon to Mexican drug gangs? Who in the world would have thought of such a thing? Some think it may have had something to do with gun control propaganda, but that doesn't make any sense either. This is one of the stupidest things the Obama InJustice Department has ever done. They say it originated in the Bush administration – maybe, but they came to their senses. We may never get to the bottom of this because how does the InJustice Department investigate itself? We might have gotten to the truth if we had elected Mitt Romney and a majority of republicans in the senate.

Benghazi – Conservatives need to stop saying America wants to know what really happened. Most of them could care less. **Start admitting that it is your job (responsibility) to get to the bottom of this scandal no matter who cares.** Any reasonably honest, non-biased investigator would conclude that the Obama "reelection generals" would want to hide the fact that for months Ambassador Christopher Stevens had warned that his facility in Libya would likely be attacked. His facility was in fact attacked prior to the attack that killed him and three others. The CIA and the Libyan President said immediately after the attack that killed Stevens and three other heroes was a coordinated terrorist attack on the anniversary of 9/11/2001. Why was that ignored?

Also, a call for help was denied apparently because it was thought that the military was too far away and not enough was known to risk more casualties. That makes since until you ask a Marine or a Special Forces soldier what he would do; which is "never leave a fallen soldier behind." I suppose a "reelection general" has the power to override a "military general," just weeks before a presidential election. Then to cover up their extreme negligence and the electioneering narrative that "Osama bin Laden is dead; General Motors is alive; and Al-Qaeda has been decimated" they sacrificed one of their rising stars, Susan Rice, to blitz the Sunday morning news programs to "spin lies" about the facts.

Let's face it – this attack had better be covered up or they could have lost the election in just a few weeks. Some conservative talking heads said Susan Rice was given talking points, by the CIA, to spread the word that the attack was cause by a video that had originated earlier in Egypt. Do you really think this LSD loyalist needed talking points to say what she said?

Do you really think the CIA changed the talking points without the help of the reelection generals in the White House or that Susan was that stupid? I didn't think so! And then Romney just laid down in the last debate and gave Obama the election. Stupid handlers…

IRS vs. The Tea Party, AP & Fox targeting, National cell phone, email and internet drag-net of American citizens – "I don't know, I can't remember, It wasn't me…" President Obama was giving a speech to students at the University of Ohio on May 5, 2013 and made a prophetic slip that has turned out to be comical. He said; "They'll warn (I assume he is referring to conservatives) that tyranny is lurking just around the corner. You should reject these voices."

How ironic that within days scandals started surfacing everywhere about the federal government trampling on the constitutional rights of the press and the IRS targeting and intimidating conservatives, especially Tea Party Patriots. I don't know about you, but I would put all these scandals under the "tyranny" label. Now, my question is – did the president know about any of these abuses and was trying to dispel any rumors, not realizing they were about to be exposed nationally, or is he really that unaware of what is happening within "HIS" administration? Did you read Michelle Malkin's book *Culture of Corruption*? I think maybe her book reveals the answer to my questions…

On June 7, 2013 President Obama gave a news conference that I watched on CNBC. His most amazing statement was something to the effect that "after he leaves office he would likely be at the top of any surveillance list so he wants to make sure there are no abuses of power." **What! Why would he suspect that? Is President Bush being surveilled by the Obama administration? Is President Clinton?** President Bush is considered part of the republican establishment and there are rumors by many that Bill Clinton and Barack Obama can't stand each other. Is this why Obama is concerned? Hmm, makes one wonder…

I'm not a conspiracy type; I just watch these politicians and their slobbering sycophants on TV every day and can discern that something is awry by their words and other even more important communication "tells," which are common to liars hustling their "marks."

When liberal socialist democrats essentially takes control of this nation's healthcare system (1/6th of our economy), and creates more economic strangling taxes and regulations, the personal pain may be tolerable; but, when the IRS, or the injustice department through the EPA, comes after you, it is bone chilling and the very definition of tyranny.

The tremendous attacks by the LSD and their sycophants on the Tea Party is proof of how much they fear these patriotic Americans and the threat they pose to the socialist state. Otherwise they would just ignore them instead of a full-out offensive to demonize them to the American public. I hope and pray the LSD will not be effective and only their most devoted drones will believe their lies and propaganda.

It has never been more critical that this country find or create many more statesmen like George Washington, Abraham Lincoln and Ronald Reagan. I pray that the Tea Party Movement continues growing every day and their communication skills become even better than the great Ronald Reagan.

Chapter 10

If you're a moderate Republican – You're enabling socialism: You're "lukewarm" so you've got to go too!

The reason moderate republicans are so destructive to America is they compromise with big-government liberal socialist democrats. If you believe that socialism doesn't work and that democrats are always looking for ways to advance our nation ever closer towards complete socialism then it becomes obvious why we can NEVER compromise with them – unless they hold all the cards and there is a strategic reason to compromise for a longer-term goal. If we can find an excellent Tea Party Patriot to run against them in the primaries then vote these moderate republicans out of office too.

Again, moderate republicans and conservative democrats may have noble motives to help those who are underprivileged. We just differ on how to help the poor and underprivileged move up the economic ladder. Real conservatives believe in an individual's right to "Pursue Happiness," not the right to happiness. Besides, drowning a country in debt and strangling an economy with too many regulations only leads to bankruptcy. How many poor and needy citizens will we be able to help then?

If intelligent honest liberals really wanted to help the underprivileged and the poor they would completely change the public education system and include in every grade level and every year a study, with examples, of how people climb out of poverty to become financially independent. Instead liberal socialist democrats spend their time and energy demonizing profit-making businesses, success and accomplishment. Just listen to them – it is obvious…

These same liberal jerks call bright conservative women like Sarah Palin stupid. Sarah Palin is one of the brightest and quick thinking people in America. Not to mention she is very attractive, which is a plus for Bill Clinton and Barack Obama among liberals, but a minus for a conservative woman like Sarah Palin – go figure. More importantly, she has the core values and convictions of our founding fathers – the values and convictions that made this country the greatest in world history.

Compared to Obama she's a genius; remember Obama "has been to all 57 states," pronounces Navy Corpsmen with a loud "ps" instead of a silent "ps." My God folks – Obama is over 50, he's the Commander-in-Chief of the Armed Forces and doesn't know how to pronounce "Corpsmen." On several occasions during the summer of 2013 he said that the Ports of Charleston, South Carolina, Savannah, Georgia and Jacksonville, Florida are on the Gulf Coast. Do I think President Obama is stupid? No, and neither is Sarah Palin! Here is what I'm certain of: Sarah Palin is much smarter than Barack Obama. Why do I say that with certainty? Because, she knows socialism leads to massive suffering, especially among the poor, and he does not…

She was thrown into the national political spotlight without much *knowledge* in the fields of foreign policy, world history or world geography. How much knowledge in those areas does a city mayor or a governor of Alaska need? She wasn't chosen to be the Vice Presidential candidate because of that knowledge or lack of knowledge of foreign affairs. She was chosen for her passionate conservative principles and her ability to communicate them unmistakably. These core principles are paramount to a thriving America and exactly what we need to turn our country back to where the "Pursuit of Happiness" is alive and well.

John McCain's staff was completely to blame for not vetting her more thoroughly or bringing her up to speed quicker and then not defining why she was picked in the first place – again, because of her strong conservative core values. Did President Lincoln have the qualifications to be president? Probably not! What he did have was the same core values and spiritual insight that Sarah Palin has. That's right – spiritual insight… George Washington and Abraham were two of the most religious Christian political leaders this country has ever had – they relied on the inspiration of the bible and God to make their decisions.

If anything happened to McCain she was ten times more qualified to become president than Barack Obama. Any president, including Barack Obama needs a huge group of advisors to "lead" the country. Does he rely on the bible, God and Jesus for guidance as did Washington and Lincoln? How could he? He criticized rural Americans for clinging to their bibles and religion. He believes aborting unborn babies is a woman's right! He selects his team from several radical atheistic liberal socialist democrats that share his core values of a socialist America. Sarah

Palin would have selected her team from free-market God fearing constitutional conservatives that share her core values. Again, the same characteristics that made Abraham Lincoln and George Washington the two greatest presidents in history! She had run a city and a state; he had never been an executive or an administrator or run anything of consequence. Again, go figure…

Slobbering sycophants and democrats everywhere called her stupid. Albert Einstein would have not fared any better than Sarah Palin. Would he be called stupid or ignorant? Liberal socialist democrat intellectuals don't know the difference between *knowledge and intelligence.* Ignorance can be fixed, stupid is permanent. Stupid liberal socialist democrats! That includes the greasy haired maggot, Bill Maher and all of his liberal socialist democrat buddies in Hollywood, network and cable TV, and the drive-by lamestream media.

See "The Obama Deception" on YouTube. Although I strongly disagree with many of the conspiracy theories this video submits, I do agree that Bush 41, Bush 43 and Obama have done more for the growth and intrusion of big-government, big-money center banks, socialism, and the loss of our personal liberty and national sovereignty than anyone in power since LBJ and FDR.

Don't get me wrong, the Bush family beginning with Senator Prescott Bush should be renowned for their many great contributions to America. Bush 41 was a World War II hero and was considered the most prepared man ever to become President of America. I hold the entire Bush family, especially First Ladies Barbara and Laura Bush in the highest esteem. I just disagree with the Bush presidents' moderate political actions. Many believe both Bush Presidents were of the One World Order organization – I hope not!

Here's what Henry Kissinger said on the business cable news channel CNBC during the economic collapse of 2008, speaking about Barack Obama: "But he (Obama) can give a new impetus to American foreign policy partly because the perception of him is so extraordinary around the world. I think his task will be to develop an overall strategy for America in this period when really a **New World Order** can be created. It's a great opportunity. It isn't just a crisis."

WOW! Think about what he said – "the perception of him." Not his achievements, or his experience, or his character, or his skills, or his knowledge – but the perception of him. I couldn't have said it any better. He is the consummate con artist hustler achieving great success in politics simply with his charming personality and good looks. Some might add his intelligence – really "57 States!" No, he's just a salesman. But, what's he selling? Big-government, big-labor, socialist redistribution, a stagnant economy and eventually a bankrupt nation…

And, the 2nd telling statement Kissinger said was: "It isn't just a crisis." That statement by Henry Kissinger; along with the same type of statement made by long-time key Obama advisor, Chief of Staff, Rahm Emanuel is very scary! Emanuel said, "You never want a serious crisis to go to waste. And what I mean by that is an opportunity to do things you could not do before." **Like advance the socialist agenda in America more than it has been since LBJ and the Great Society, or FDR and the New Deal!**

Liberal socialist democrats never admit to what their long-term goals are: a complete takeover of the American economy and the destruction of the private free-enterprise or free-market system. i.e., connections not competition – socialism! You don't believe that statement? Just investigate the 10 thousand new rules, regulations and taxes that are being enacted since Obama and his legions of bureaucrats have taken over. And now he has 4 more years. Way to go voters!

Again, Obama had no executive skills, no leadership or legislative achievements, or any other experience that qualified him to be president of anything other than ACORN – the organized criminal equivalent of community organizations that was working to help advance the socialist agenda mainly by getting the recipients of the social welfare state to register and vote as democrats. These people don't vote unless the liberal socialist democratic machine puts an all-out effort into getting them registered and to the polls. Contrast that action with the self-energized Tea Party Conservatives' mobilization after Obama won in 2008. I can only hope they will be even stronger in the 2014 mid-term elections and then again in 2016. If not, America is screwed!

The 2009 scandals brought to this nation's attention on just how corrupt ACORN was, which led to Congressional defunding. President Obama's major experience on his resume to qualify for president of the

United States was the he was a community organizer and ACORN's attorney in Chicago. Let's see – Chicago was the home of Obama, Al Capone, organized crime and one of Obama's mentors, Saul Alinsky.

I'd bet ACORN is now operating under a new name and has probably been renewed their billion dollar congressional funding. Why do I think that? Because the LSDs are currently in charge and this political "grass roots" organization is just too valuable to the democrats to abandon. I believe one of their main purposes is to advance the socialist liberal democrats' agenda and recruit voters that would not usually bother to vote by promising and delivering socialist benefits. They say their goal is to help the poor. Really, the goal of this book is to show how the liberal socialist feed like maggots off the poor and need as many of them as possible to stay poor and accept the crumbs that democrats hand them.

Let's get back to the "One World Order" discussion that includes some of the most prominent moderate republican leaders. I don't fully understand the conspiracy theorists conclusions that the world's elite, old money, super rich, Bilderberg Society, Tri-Lateral Commission, etc., would want a collapse of the world economy so as to gain more power. They're already in power. What also doesn't make any sense is they had the most to lose in what happened in the Great Recession of 2008 and would happen in another financial collapse. It's just too great a financial risk for them to make any sense to me.

The stock market would collapse again, treasury yields are at the lowest levels in generations and real estate was crushed. Remember, the world's financial institutions were on the brink of total collapse. They ("One World Order") had the most to lose. I just don't see how or why they would have orchestrated such a collapse.

<u>Here's what does make sense – they transferred as much of their losses that they could to the American taxpayer.</u> I also clearly see how they used this financial disaster to advance their coercive power and control over the lives of free people (socialism). That's the common evil goals of democrats, socialists, labor unions, bureaucrats, collectivist, statist, dictators, despots, Marxists, communists, terrorists, etc. In the end they're all really the same – destructive to the freedom, safety, prosperity, general welfare and "happiness" of the common man.

Even though history has proven them wrong, socialist are always trying to remove your freedom to succeed and keep the fruits of your own labor or investments. It's their chosen profession – it's what they have learned to do. Just like the criminals learn from their buddies, they pass their socialist beliefs on to the next control freak coming up. It's easier to take from those who made the income or produced the wealth than to earn it themselves. Because America is a democracy, they need the majority to buy into their con so they (or their chosen puppets) can be voted into office. Sooner or later they get enough suckers wanting ***"something for nothing"*** to vote in socialism.

Look how the democrats have compared the dirty, stinking, Occupy Wall Street ("99%) bums to the Tea Party Activists. Are they kidding? If 10,000 Tea Partyers met in a park, the park would be cleaner after they left than before they arrived. The Occupy Wall Street bums would have raped the women, crapped and urinated all over the park, broke into and terrorized neighboring businesses, and generally trashed everything in sight! They are the perfect symbols of the far left and, the Tea Party Activists are the perfect symbol for Conservatives. And, the slobbering LSD sycophants on each coast can't see the distinctions! With that in mind, who looks like the ignorant morons now?

Self-respecting persons, no matter if they do believe in socialism, should not be associated with these 99% scum bags. But no! Even the President and democratic leadership praise these creeps and call Tea Party citizens demons. Can you see the pattern of lies?

Amazing! Any intelligent non-socialist person can see the difference between the Tea Party and the Occupy Wall Street gangs. Any negative comparison of the Tea Party by democratic leaders like President Obama, Senator Reid, Congresswoman Pelosi and all the other liberal socialist democrats are so ridiculous, it's laughable.

Moderate and establishment republicans, no matter how good hearted they are, have been a disaster to the conservative or libertarian cause and may be even more responsible for the advancement of socialism than the far left. At least conservatives and libertarians can see the far left coming. **We get blind-sided by moderate and establishment republicans.** Again, I believe most of these moderate republicans are very similar to conservative democrats in that they are very compassionate to the poor and underprivileged but just don't realize how destructive big-government social engineering is to real long-term success in helping those in poverty to move to the middle class. I'm trying to be kind and ignore their pathologies or their own lust for power, money and fame (in this paragraph!).

Some of these good hearted people just don't understand reality. More government leads to more waste and corruption. The only way to end waste, corruption and unnecessary rules and regulations is to severely limit the size and scope of government. We need to get rid of stupid regulations as much as stupid bureaucrats and ludicrous federal departments like the Department of Interior, Education, Agriculture, Energy, Commerce, Labor, Housing and Urban Development, Health and Human Services and Transportation. None of these departments are necessary at the federal level and only add to waste, fraud, abuse and cronyism. In fact, excess federal lands and buildings should be sold and/or given to the states to raise revenues to pay off federal and state debts. Most states have these same or similar departments and could handle these functions more efficiently and less expensively. If a state mismanages these departments, and corruption or waste crushes a state's budget then citizens can leave; if the federal government does these things we're stuck.

Another troubling observation I have is the republican establishment seems to always back the moderate republican. Who are these republican establishment people? Are they also part of the "One World Order" clan? Why do they seem to always back the moderate republican? Maybe the candidates that the republican establishment and liberal socialist media elite hate the most should be the conservative's candidate. Think about it: Ronald Reagan, Sara Palin, Newt Gingrich all put freedom first and believe big-centralized governments are the main reasons we lose "Life, Liberty and the Pursuit of Happiness." There are many others but Reagan, Palin and Gingrich were the most hated and feared by the liberal socialist democrats and their liberal stooges in the mainstream media – and therefore the most demonized. You can see the liberal socialist democrat's veins begin to bulge when the Palin and Gingrich are discussed. Makes you wonder…

My last and perhaps the most significant point is this: Why is there any difference between a social and a fiscal conservative. If you read the works of free-market economists F. A. Hayek and Milton Friedman you will understand the two are inter-connected and should not be separate in any way. Belief in the Judeo-Christian God and the bible, especially the New Testament, is one of the foundations of the American experiment and should lead to a better person and therefore a better society. The bible said to feed the poor but also said if you don't work you don't eat, meaning if you can work and don't, you're not to be given free food.

A passionately God fearing bible believing person should be more honest, more hardworking, fairer, more generous, more accepting, more forgiving, more devoted, more courageous, more reliable, more humble, more determined, more responsible, more involved, more positive, more self-confident, more respectful, more thrifty, more unpretentious, more friendly, more self-reliant, more selfless, more considerate, more loyal, more faithful, more accountable, more encouraging, more inspired, more brave in the face of evil, and many more positive human traits that leads to a much better society where "Life, Liberty and the Pursuit of Happiness" is a way of life and the foundation of America. Whew! That was a long, but accurate statement…

The radical atheist, who is almost always a liberal socialist democrat, has the biggest problem with the above three paragraphs. Their beliefs have led to the current financial crisis spreading around the world. They should have the freedom to believe anything they want but they don't have the right to remake America into a nation that believes in "Death, Tyranny and the Guarantee of Benefits."

The radical atheist liberal socialist democrat believes in life for the baby seal but death by "choice" for the black baby girl. Again, too harsh! Too bad, it's the truth, so get used to it! You're the ultimate anti-feminist racist if you believe it's ok to kill that unborn black baby girl.

This can't be said by too many people, in too many venues, too many times. The left has their "destroy the right harsh language," why aren't we using "destroy the left harsh language." This is serious business; we better get serious about winning this war of words – right now! Make them feel ashamed of their hypocrisy!

Chapter 11

Government Waste, Fraud and Abuse… A Million here a Billion there – who will even notice? Let's send all the greedy crooks back home to get real jobs!

Before I get into the obvious areas of waste in government I'm going to use a Rush Limbaugh tactic of illustrating a point using absurdity. Why don't we pass legislation to give criminal inmates even more rights to taxpayer supported lawyers than they enjoy now. Here it is: inmates should have the best legal teams available to the richest citizens. Expense is no object – teams of lawyers and investigators could be hired to overturn their convictions and even sue the government for potential large multi-dollar settlements. Think about it – the government would have to spend a fortune not only on the convict's team, but they would have to spend another fortune defending themselves with an opposing team of experts and lawyers. Expect never ending motions and appeals. Let's see – lawyers making laws that create work and billions for their fellow lawyers. This absurdity is not really that far from reality! See why we have so many parasites running for office… Which political party do the Trial Lawyers Association support – that's right the LSD party! How many billions is it costing us? Nobody knows…

The Government Services Administration ("GSA") is an independent agency of the United States government, established in 1949 to help manage and support the basic functioning of federal agencies. The GSA supplies products and communications for U.S. government offices, provides transportation and office space to federal employees, and develops government-wide cost-minimizing policies, and other management tasks. Here is what the GSA says about itself:

> **Their Mission:** The GSA mission is to use expertise to provide innovation solutions for our customers in support of their missions, and by so doing, foster an effective, sustainable, and transparent government for the American people.

Their Vision: The GSA vision is a government that works ever better for the American people. This vision: Insists upon continual improvement in all the GSA does, so that the mission work of our customers is not vulnerable to the stagnating tools, services, and work environments but, instead, is accomplished with the benefit of excellence and forward leaning expertise.

[The GSA] positions the government to be ever adapting its work environments, tools, and processes so as to better serve the public. The GSA uses the notion of "the future workplace" to express and visualize this evolution for its customers.

[The GSA] is fueled by two powerful sparks for change, namely sustainability and transparency. The former is a doctrine for managing resources with the upmost care and an obsession with "no waste." The latter is a doctrine for inviting our collective intelligence and wisdom to our work.

Their Strategic Goals: The three GSA strategic goals align the agency to our mission, setting direction and linking its planning.

Innovation: GSA will model and promote the future workplace, incorporating space use, technologies, practices, and a GSA-goes-first culture. We will be a green proving ground that demonstrates the full value and viability of new green technology and practices. We will generate new ideas through innovative and collaborative technologies. The GSA will test innovative solutions in its own operations and offer those solutions to other agencies through its government-wide contracting and policymaking authorities.

Customer Intimacy: GSA will aggressively integrate with customers. We will communicate better with customers through evolving social technologies; employ enterprise wide, creative, and data-based solutions to meet their increasingly difficult resource constraints, and lead with our expertise to drive the market for high-performance green products, services, and solutions that support our customer agencies' missions and their sustainability goals. The GSA will develop strategic partnerships with industry and with other federal agencies to develop new and innovative tools for more effective government.

Operational Excellence: GSA will deliver support to our customer agencies ever more efficiently. We will particularly draw upon our commitment to a zero environmental footprint in order to pull forward services and solutions that eliminate waste. The GSA will use data, evidence, and analysis to support decisions that wring out inefficiencies in operations.

Source: http://www.gsa.gov/portal/content/100735

They must be joking? But this isn't funny at all. The hypocrisy of the above statements along with the level of corruption, waste, fraud and abuse by the very agency that is responsible for saving tax dollars and ridding the federal government of waste! This in your face "stealing" of tax payers' dollars is sickening. I'm sure there are many great employees at the GSA with the highest level of integrity, but the GSA is the new poster child for government waste, fraud and abuse. In case you haven't seen the news about this out of control agency over the last several years, they have been burning through money like it is heating oil in mid-winter. Why in the hell does the government need to have lavish conferences or training seminars – especially away from town spending money we don't have on airfare and hotel rooms in Hawaii and Las Vegas. This bureaucratic fiefdom is wasting taxpayers' money at such a sickening rate heads should roll and a complete overhaul of the agency should be mandated by congress.

I have a suggestion: No more government conventions of any kind and anywhere. This is the internet age; you can get an MBA through the internet. Any training program should use the internet until the federal debt of nearly $17 trillion is paid off – before anymore all expenses paid conference "vacations" are allowed.

We've all heard about the ridiculous prices paid by the Defense Department for tools and materials. When will all of this insanity stop? Hopefully, it will stop when enough voters wake up, come to their senses and vote for Tea Party candidates to clean-up this mess. And, if they don't get the job done, replace them and start again.

We are borrowing 40 cents of every federal dollar spent and the liberal socialist democrats are foaming at their mouths to raise taxes on small businesses. Give me a break – start with fixing government corruption, waste, fraud and abuse first. Then, we need to unleash the energy industry in creating millions of direct and supporting jobs, reform strangling regulations, reform and simplify the tax code and get rid of all loopholes before we take away the working capital of small businesses. Don't think for a minute that small business working capital cash is not the target of liberal socialist democrats. Owners of small businesses make up the vast majority American millionaires they want to steal from.

Do you care if someone is needlessly costing your family money every month because of a mistake or intentionally? The biggest reason the government is losing money to waste, fraud and abuse is due to the massive size and complexity of the federal government and its massive budget. Then we have an agency, like the GSA, that has the mission to save the government money, is granting their employees massive bonuses and overtime in excess of their already generous salaries, benefits and retirement. If Americans really knew how corrupt some of our government employees are the Tea Party would grow tremendously. One could spend days Googling the GSA and other government agencies' waste, fraud and abuse. This agency is sitting on hundreds of billions of real estate that is not being used and could be sold to help offset the budget deficit. I hope some of the new Tea Party republicans will turn this department upside down and completely overhaul and reorganize it to do their jobs – which should be to maximize resources and save money for the American taxpayer.

Here are some nauseating examples of government corruption from some great websites that help to shine the light of day in these dark areas and educate America:

> May 23, 2012 Richard Billies – We all know that unemployment is the major problem that this country faces now and in the future. So, it stands to reason that the federal government would offer job training for the unemployed. But in true government fashion, we have 47 different job training programs embedded in the federal bureaucracy.

According to a report by the Government Accountability Office (GAO), that's exactly what we're paying for. And it's costing $18 billion in taxpayer money. The 2011 report, commissioned by Senator Tom Coburn (R-OK), gives us a picture of 47 overlapping programs administered by 9 different agencies.

According to Coburn, "The vast majority of money we spend in job training doesn't go to job training; it goes to employ people in those job training federal programs.

The GAO study reported widespread and abuse across the programs.

- Some job training participants spent their days sitting on a bus.
- Some were trained for jobs that didn't exist.
- Others were paid to sit through educational sessions about jobs they already had.
- Funds were misspent to pay a contractor for ghost employees and to purchase video games.
- Job training administrators spent federal funds on extravagant meals and bonuses for themselves.
- In one state, workforce agency employees took more than 100 gambling trips to casinos mostly during work hours.

The GAO report was not the only study done in 2011. The Parthenon Group produced a study for Corinthian Colleges, Inc. In it, they pointed out that of the 26 million people that participated in federal job training programs in 2009, only 4% received classroom-based instruction that led to lifelong income gains.

The job training programs have become a campaign issue. In a recent campaign appearance in Lorain, Ohio, Barack Obama highlighted one such program, saying, "Ninety percent of people who graduate from this program have a job three months later – 90 percent. That's a big deal. Why would we want to cut this program to give folks like me a tax cut that we don't need and the country cannot afford?

The problem with this statement is not only is it not true, and Obama knows it's not true, but just the opposite is true.

Mitt Romney and the Republicans would like to see the programs run by states and localities in order to tailor them to local conditions rather than a one-size-fits-all mandate from Washington. Speaking during a February town meeting, Romney said, "Let's take the money, give it back to the states; let you fashion your own programs so that you can train your own workers for the jobs of tomorrow."

Advocates of federal programs believe that Washington is the best place to create and administer the programs. They believe that the government can allocate resources much better than the private sector. The private sector points out that the inefficient use of tax dollars siphons money out of the general economy.

Source: wastefraudandabuse.org/wasteful-job-training-programs/

If the republicans had done a better jobs of educating voters on the failures of liberal socialist democrats' job training programs it may have helped the independent voters make the right decision and elect Mitt Romney.

July 24, 2012 Richard Billies – Jimmy Durante used the catchphrase, "Everybody wants to get into the act." It seems that just like Hollywood, it also holds true in Washington.

Reports on scandals like the recent GSA conference that spent over $800,000 on everything up to and including clowns can be titillating. But the real waste is in the institutional programs spread across the Federal government. In a recent blockbuster report, the non-partisan Government Accountability Office ("GSA") highlighted billions of dollars in government waste that could be eliminated if Congress had the will to streamline the Federal Government.

Many of the programs were created to service one particular narrow demographic, such as Native Americans, veterans and youth. Once a program is established it builds a constituency that fights to make sure that it remains in operation. Some of the programs are duplications of other programs within the same department with very minor differences.

Agency officials acknowledged that greater efficiencies could be achieved in delivering services through these programs, but said factors such as the number of clients that any one-stop center can serve and one-stop centers' proximity to clients, particularly in rural areas, could warrant having multiple entities provide the same services. In other words, they're saying "Buzz off" because we can marshal support for our particular program.

The report covers the full range of government programs. No department or area escapes the spotlight. Agriculture is criticized for a fragmented food safety system with 15 federal agencies collectively administering at least 30 food related laws. Much of the problem lies between the USDA and the Food and Drug Administration (FDA). USDA is responsible for the safety of meat, poultry, processed egg products, and catfish and FDA is responsible for virtually all other food, including seafood. The question taxpayers need to ask is why. Couldn't these two agencies be merged with the potential savings of billions of dollars? Congress just needs the political will to act. More than likely the majority of taxpayers could care less, as long as their food is safe.

With the current fight over sequestration, the Department of Defense needs to take a hard look at their overall costs. The GAO points out that the DOD has numerous areas of potential savings. One of the biggest issues at DOD is service-specific equipment purchasing. It seems that every service has a friend in the defense contracting industry. What's good for the Marines is often disdained by the Army. Military radios are a good case in point. Until recently, the Marines had different radios than Naval Air. This meant that the grunt on the ground couldn't talk to the pilots overhead. They had to go through the chain of command. In a combat situation, this time lag can mean the difference between life and death. This is just one area at DOD that needs attention.

We all know about the tremendous duplication in the intelligence-gathering area. What is Congress' response to this situation? Rather than confront the issue head on, they added an expensive new layer of bureaucracy that filters information through it. It's costly and slows the response to act on time-sensitive information.

In the area of economic development, there are 80 different programs spread over at least four departments and agencies. The design of each of these fragmented programs appears to overlap with that of at least one other program in terms of the economic development activities that they are authorized to fund. For example, four agencies administer a total of 52 programs that can fund "entrepreneurial efforts," which includes helping businesses to develop business plans and identify funding sources.

This report has an almost endless number of areas that are ripe for improvement. The Federal government is a sprawling, inefficient mess of conflicting, overlapping and duplicative programs that cost the American taxpayers hundreds of billions of dollars every year.

Washington isn't Hollywood. Everybody can't be in the act. It's simply unproductive and wasteful. But without the political will to change the current system, we will continue to fund these programs until the entire house of cards falls down.

Source: http://wastefraudandabuse.org/

A small list government waste fraud and abuse:

$30 million to help Pakistani Mango farmers: This was part of a four-year, $90 million effort to boost hiring and sales among Pakistani businesses funded through the U.S. Agency for International Development.

$765,828 for pancakes: Federal funding went to the Anacostia Economic Development Corp to build an International House of Pancake franchise (and train its workers) in an "underserved community." The underserved community, however, turned out to be a toney area of Washington D.C. - Columbia Heights, which is termed "one of Washington's more wealthiest and desirable neighborhoods."

$120 million in retirement and disability benefits to federal employees who have died: The Inspector General for the U.S. Office of Personnel management found that **"the amount of post-death improper payments is consistently $100 million – $150 million annually, totaling over $601 million in the last five years."**

$652,740 to create an Oklahoma "visitor's center:" The scenic highway that runs from Talihina, Oklahoma to Mena, Arkansas, already has three visitor's centers, but this federal grant would create a fourth. The abandoned rock house that the government proposes to turn into a new visitor's center will cost more than 14 times the median value of a home in the area.

$113,277 for video games: The International Center for the History of Electronic Games got the money to conduct a detailed conservation survey of video games.

$484,000 for pizza: A private developer was given federal grant money to build Mellow Mushroom Pizza Bakers, an Arlington, Texas outlet known for its tongue-in-cheek references to drug and hippie culture.

$100,000 for a celebrity chef show in Indonesia: The Washington State Fruit Commission asked for the grant to help promote their fruit and cooking recipes in an emerging market.

$10 million for Pakistani Sesame Street: We must really love the Pakistanis. We must have a close and trusting relationship with the country that somehow managed to miss the fact that Osama bin Laden was living within spitting distance of a Pakistani military base for years. Because, after funding the Pakistani Mango growers, the government felt it needed to spend some time and money remaking big bird and the other Sesame Street characters into a show called "SimSim Humara" for the Pakistani market.

$550,000 for "Rockin" the Kremlin: A documentary on how rock and roll contributed to the end of the cold war.

$702,558 to bring television to Vietnamese villages: No, it wasn't just for the sitcoms. Researchers at Pennsylvania State University wanted to know how television affects family formation and reproductive health. So where better to study the problem than 14 remote Vietnamese villages, where the government paid to bring the TVs and gas generators; because, of course, these villages also don't have electric power?

Little Green Menus: NASA spends $1 million a year on developing recipes for foods which astronauts could prepare while visiting Mars, even though the agency has no plans to go there any time soon. But just in case NASA changes its mind someday, it wants to ensure that astronauts on Mars don't experience "menu fatigue."

Why Fruit Flies Fall in Love: The National Institutes of Health spent $939,771 on research that has discovered male fruit flies are more sexually attracted to younger female fruit flies. Video of the encounter, the scientists wrote, "Showed that the male was much more attracted to the young fly."

All of these outrageously stupid "pet projects" pale in comparison to the waste, fraud and abuse that is occurring in Medicare, Medicaid and the federal drug support programs. Fraud is so rampant in these programs that organized criminals and Miami drug traffickers are said to be switching careers. The big reason fraud is believed to be so rampant is the government spends too little on enforcement. The FBI is ill-equipped to compete with the con artists. Republicans are going to have to do a better job on prioritizing spending on finding and stamping out, as much as possible, criminal activity in this area. If it means a bigger budget for the FBI then it is money well spent.

Other savings programs that seem so obvious are:

1. **Printing of government documents, especially for storage.** Good Lord people, this is the information and technology age. You can read documents on your phones, tablets, laptops and PCs. I'm not talking about classified documents, although I'm sure many of these documents are already available on many of these devices; no, I'm talking about the millions of single page to major works like ObamaCare that should not be printed in abundance. Some reports have this resource inefficiency at more than $1 billion. Does this estimate including handling, storage and disposal? I doubt it…
2. **Government energy waste.** I will make this brief because this is almost impossible to calculate. How many government buildings have automatic lighting and air conditioning and systems to save energy?
3. **The GSA needs to rent or sell "all" government buildings that are not being used.** By selling or renting these buildings we

would avoid the costs of maintaining them and significantly benefit from the sales or monthly rents.

We need to shut-down several federal agencies at the cabinet level, most notably the Department of Education, and establish a new cabinet level department called the "Department of Government Waste, Fraud and Abuse." Then combine all overlapping duties in this area from other departments into this one.

This agency should have complete criminal and investigating powers; something like a police department's "internal affairs" investigators. This department would be independent of the administration's justice department and would report to a trilateral commission comprised of 1/3rd congress, 1/3rd executive branch and 1/3rd federal courts. Maybe then we could get to the bottom of all these scandals and fraud that gets "swept under the rug" by a justice department investigating their own bosses in the White House or congress, whether democrats or republicans…

Folks, like the IRS, this agency would be a revenue generating department; but, the revenues would come from ending waste, fraud, abuse and needless expenditures.

Chapter 12

Election Reform – America should radically change the election cycles and terms to increase the ratio of leadership and governing to sleazy political campaigning? Here's how!

Freedom reigns supreme in America, therefore we can't restrict free-speech and the right to express that free-speech through donations to "any" particular candidate whether I completely disagree with their beliefs and politics or not. What we can do is change the length of terms between the elections of our political leaders and their length of terms (limits), to help diminish their entrenchment and corruption.

This is one of the most critical ideas/suggestions in this book! Begin the long constitutional process of changing the Congressional and Presidential election cycles to minimize the ratio of sleazy campaigning to governing. Change the Presidential term to 1 five year term. At first this may seem strange or illogical but stay with me for a moment. As it is now, a president doesn't even give America 5 years of executive governing in (2) four year terms. Most of his time is spent campaigning or at least positioning his party for the next campaign. Also, choosing a single 5 year term will mean that only in each tenth year will the presidential and some of the congressional elections coincide. That would be a good thing!

Change Congressional House terms to 4 years with 50% of the House members up for reelection every 2 years and term limits of 16 years. Combined term limits for someone elected to the House and then to the Senate would be 20 years. Enough of these "professional career" politicians – 20 years in DC is actually too much but much better than what we have now. Senator's terms would remain at 6 years with 1/3rd of the Senators up for election every 2 years. Nothing would change for them except for the term limits which would be 18 years or (3) six year terms. We must finally ratify term limits…

If we could ever get this huge endeavor through the Constitutional Amendment process we could better ensure a citizen's mentality in

Washington, DC instead of the "royalty or aristocratic" mentality we currently have. We should restrict the President from campaigning of any kind during his five year term in office. As it is now we are getting a President (Obama) whose major focus is campaigning for himself and his party. We need a president whose "only" focus should be on increasing the safety, freedoms and prosperity of our citizens. He/she is the most powerful person in the world – reducing his stature to sleazy political salesman is demeaning to the office and to America.

How would we determine if an event is a campaign event? It could be as simple as identifying any type of fund raising or promoting a party and/or party candidate… Penalties must be severe – three strikes and you're subject to impeachment. After a non-compliant political hack president is impeached the standard would be firmly set for the future. Again, once elected he works for America, not a party.

Also, let's devise a standard resume/application to vet all politicians. We should never again elect someone as inexperienced and anti-American as Barack Hussein Obama. Who would have ever thought that 7 years after the 2001 suicide attack on the World Trade Center by 19 terrorists from the radical Islamist militant group al-Qaeda, we would elect a little known senator from the corrupt Chicago political machine with a Muslim name that had communist, socialist, radical anarchist and anti-American mentors? If he had been white, we would have never even considered him.

In the future, I hope and predict we will have many conservative black Americans elected to be president, both male and female. Stupid establishment republicans had a black American candidate with the qualities and attributes of George Washington, Abraham Lincoln and Ronald Reagan combined. They stood by and allowed the liberal media to demonize this brilliant man. His name is Alan Keys and he is an outstanding God fearing constitutional conservative. Many in our party think he is too religious to head our party.

What they fail to understand is that he is "exactly" what God ordained in George Washington to free this country from the tyrannical rule of England in 1776, and in Abraham Lincoln, and the Republican Party, to free the slaves in 1865. Abraham Lincoln was assassinated for his strong religious beliefs put into action. Go figure! If this country's best days are behind us it will be the fault of moderate republicans for not adhering to the God fearing constitutional conservatives' ideals in our party and allowing the radical atheists and liberal news media to intimidate them.

Republicans could have had the first black president and America could have had a remarkable and historical man to turn this country back on the path that God planned for it.

The biggest problem with finding qualified conservatives to run for office is the foul nature of politics. What self-respecting successful business leader, who has probably become rich from his hard work, intellect and risk capital, and is highly qualified to lead this country, could stomach the lies and slander from the liberal socialist democrats and their slobbering sycophants in the drive-by media. My previous suggestions would go a long way to reducing the amount of sleaze endured by God fearing conservatives that have too much integrity to work in such a corrupt environment. Also, just like so many of America's outstanding young military soldiers that have volunteered to fight our battles; hopefully, enough of our brave qualified conservatives will sacrifice their lives and careers to rescue America from where the LSD party is taking us… Socialist bankruptcy and massive suffering!

The system of a lobbyist educating America's congressional representatives and their staffs is broken! It must be changed…

I realize this has been talked about in campaigns a million times, but when a new jet fighter program is being considered, congress doesn't get an oil or banking expert (lobbyist) to educate and advise them on the issues of that new fighter jet program. They must rely on industry experts (lobbyists) to advise and educate them. That said the status quo is unacceptable. There must be a solution to this systemic problem that is running our country into the ground. Washington, DC has become the wealthiest city in America – a "Boomtown" that is awash in income tax payers' money and the bill for this scandal is coming due soon.

The primary problem is the built-in compounding debt-building expenditure called "base-line" budgeting. This means it has a built-in automatic increase that <u>is</u> the budget. Then federal departments, bureaucrats and every other entity with its hand in the tax payers' pocket demands another percentage increase. Now, thanks to these liberal socialist democrats we have ObamaCare, which has taken control of our health care industry, which is larger than the entire economy of France.

Here is a prediction if republicans don't win the senate and the presidency in 2014 and 2016:

In the next 5 to 10 years **ObamaCare** will be renamed **YugoCare** after the car built in the former communist nation of Yugoslavia. Introduced in the 1980s the Yugo quickly became known as the worst car in the world; it was a laughing stock of a car compared to autos built in the west and especially Japan. Google Yugo, the "worst car in history" and get a glimpse of what is in store for our health care industry after the LSD have had their way for several years. The problem will not be our great medical doctors, nurses and other health care people; they will still be the best in the world. No, failure will be 100% the fault of ObamaCare. **YugoCare** will also become a laughing stock, except unlike a crappy built car, **YugoCare** will be responsible for bankrupting America and killing patients… Don't believe me? You will!

Liberal socialist democrats, the chest-pounders of a big wasteful government scream: if the federal budget "INCREASE" is "CUT" from 6% to 3% by Constitutional Conservative Tea Party Republicans, people will die! These pigs in congress and the administration, along with their sycophants in the media and Hollywood start their highly successful and proven demonizing campaign of fiscal conservatives wanting to starve children, deprive them of an education, fire (layoff) police officers and fire fighters and of course, "kill" grandma! You would think I'm exaggerating or trying to be funny but we've all seen the commercials of these pigs in action on TV, the internet or in the print media. **One of the primary purposes of this book is to persuade the GOP to fight back and do EXACTLY the same thing. Here is what will be different: Unlike the lying LSD, we will be telling the absolute truth!** This is a long-term process so be patient…

In interviews say something to the effect of: "You think because you're poor and don't pay income taxes anyway, that you will not suffer the consequences of a bankrupt America – think again! Look around the world at other countries where mobs are burning buildings and rioting in the streets. The poor, including poor Blacks and poor Latinos, will suffer the most. And, you democrat voters who have enough wealth to withstand any big recession or depression; will you be able to protect it, and yourself, from the mobs that are suffering and will take your stuff by force? Don't think this scenario is possible? We came close in 2008 with only 10 trillion in debt and the ability to drop interest rates to ZERO, and pumping trillions into the economy. There are limits – and we're getting closer every year. If you don't wake up soon and stop voting for these political "hustlers" and start voting for Conservative Republican "Statesmen" we're all in trouble. Look to the Tea Party Patriot movement for many of these Statesmen/women."

For an enlightening and in depth study of why we owe 17 trillion; get the book *"Throw Them All Out"* by Peter Schweizer. Here is a short quote of Peter from an interview on Fox's Sean Hannity program:

> **At the end of the day, [a corrupt politician] is primarily looking for ways to make money. And you don't make money by shrinking government. You make money by growing government.**

Chapter 13

Was it Clinton or Gingrich & Co. – Who really balanced the federal budget and reformed welfare in the 1990s?

I'm sick of republicans giving President Bill Clinton credit for reforming welfare, ending big-government and balancing the budget. Give me a break – Speaker Newt Gingrich & Company were the architects of the 1994 "Contract with America" that provided great detail on how to reverse the liberal socialist course that the democrats (and moderate republicans) had put the country on since the democrats took control of congress in 1954.

Why are these stupid republicans giving Clinton credit? Do they think drawing a distinction between Clinton's policy change from the far left to the center right after the republicans were elected to the majority in congress for the first time since 1954, vs. Obama's double down on liberal socialist policies after he caused republicans to retake congress in 2010 well help the GOP? Well then, just make the distinction! Don't give him any damn credit! Clinton vetoed most of what Gingrich sent him. Clinton sent it back for revisions. He fought the reforms as best he could while keeping an eye on how to get re-elected.

I believe by giving him credit "all the time," these stupid republicans have lost the opportunity to take the credit that is rightfully theirs. Their assumptions that by giving Clinton credit for moving to the middle, reforming welfare and balancing the federal budget vs. Obama's hardline partisanship somehow benefits republicans is really naive. Something they're good at (being naive)! It only serves to tell the country over and over again that it was a democrat that reformed welfare and balanced the budget. Good job "establishment" republicans. When are you moderates going to get it? This is extremely serious – the future of the country is at stake and you're playing nice. They don't play nice – they play for keeps and will crush you out of existence every chance they get!

Now that the stupid republicans have given Clinton what seems to be sole credit, Obama and the liberal socialist democrats have used these historic reforms against them (the GOP). They have twisted the facts so "artfully" that now it seems only the liberal socialist democrats know how to balance the budget. They say, and their sycophants repeat, "Only the democrats have ever balanced the budget." Again, stupid republicans lobbed the ball to the liberal socialist democrats to smash for game, set and match. **You moderates will be as much to blame for the future suffering of Americans as the liberal socialist democrats!**

We can fix this (see the chart below) if we stop wasting time and start being honest with the country and the direction that the liberal socialist democrats are taking us and the inevitable consequences. Updating the chart below to 2013 brings us back to the 100% debt to GDP level that the great depression and World War II gave us. It will be much harder this time around because we have to dismantle the engrained socialism along with the strangling regulations instead of just growing out of our debts. **We can do it, the sooner we get started, the easier it's going to be!**

Historical Ratio of GDP to Federal Debt

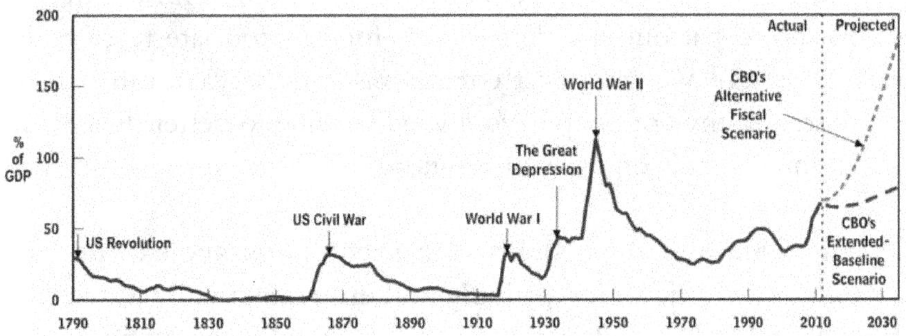

Chapter 14

What is Gridlock? It's the fight against redistributionist big-government central planning – which is socialism: Keep-up the "Good-Fight" Tea Party Patriots!

Gridlock is wonderful! It means the 100+ year old socialist march on the economy and citizens' freedoms is being halted by brave conservatives and libertarians. It should be celebrated when the socialist media elites try to condemn gridlock as a bad thing. Why is compromise considered is a good thing? Do you think a home owner should compromise with a burglar? Should a policeman compromise with a rapist attacking a woman? Hell no! Should a surgeon compromise with cancer? Am I saying liberal democratic socialism is cancer – absolutely! Just look at the destruction of Detroit caused by 50 years of democrat and labor union rule of the auto industry and the city government. Compromise with cancer – hell no; cut it out and destroy it before it's too late to save the patient (America)! We can never compromise on the values that made this country the envy of people worldwide wanting to better their families' lives and certainly on our Constitutional foundations.

When the LSD and their slobbering sycophants accuse the Tea Party Patriots of gridlock – proudly and enthusiastically agree and then repeat what I said above. Stop the weak defense and begin the strong offence. IT WILL WORK…

Here is a crude metaphor to illustrate how the democrats and the president "sets-up" the republicans to vote against their proposed legislation for the sole purpose of labeling them as obstructionists. Let's say someone in a gourmet restaurant wanted to ruin the restaurant's reputation, so they managed to put parts of a week old dead rat somewhere in each meal. No one would eat the meal ("vote for the president's jobs bill") so the reputation of the restaurant would be ruined. Congressional democrats poison pill (dead rat parts) proposed legislation all the time so they can label conservatives as obstructionists. Correct these accusations in the same way I suggested with gridlock – TRUTH…

Why do we need new laws every year? We don't! Think about it – these control freaks in Washington have created millions of overlapping laws and regulations that strangle commerce, productivity and wealth creation. When will it stop? When will enough be enough? How many ways can it be said not to lie, cheat, steal, defraud, coerce, pollute and harm your fellow man? We need a new law that requires 10 old laws and associated regulations be repealed for every new law passed. Additionally, a new law that says no law can be named after narcissistic politicians seeking fame and immortality. Most new laws are simply created by lawyers to create more lawsuits (money) – for lawyers. This strangling of the American economy is costing jobs that we need so badly to grow this economy and collect more tax revenues.

Let's see: more laws stacked on top of similar laws and regulations strangles commerce and job creation which reduces tax revenues which increases the national debt which further strangles the economy. Again, when will enough be enough? Liberal socialist democrats are destroying Americans' lives and the nation's wealth. And, because America is the economic engine of the world, liberal socialist democrats in America are destroying lives all over the world. It's a vicious and deadly cycle – like drug or alcohol addiction. Is anyone getting this?

Why do we need congressmen to live in Washington? This is the age of the internet and computers. We have programs that allow groups of people to collaborate online. Let's keep these public representatives in their home districts close to voters. The more we keep them out of the Washington ***"culture of corruption"*** the more likely they will do the right thing and down size the bureaucratic leviathan that is bleeding the country dry. Also, it would be more difficult for the parasitic lobbyist to get them drunk and buy them expensive dinners if they were spread all of the country. Makes sense to me!

Congress with all its *"royalty"* perks and expense accounts is a huge waste of money. We need to significantly reduce the size and intrusion of government in Washington. Keeping them close to home will go a long way to do this.

The liberal socialist media likes to demonize the republicans for Washington gridlock and shutting down the federal government. They say, **"Republicans refuse to compromise with democrats." Well, God bless every one of those brave souls! Without them, we would already be a full blown socialist nation.** Why would any true conservative compromise with the big-government liberal socialist democrat's agenda?

Earmarks are congressional white collar crimes! It must be ended along with a total package of comprehensive reforms to end waste, fraud and abuse in governments at all levels. Add to that a complete overhaul and simplification of our rules, regulations and tax code.

Do we really need more lawyers than the rest of the world combined? Why are new laws created? I contend the primary reason new laws, rules and regulations are created is because: 1. Liberal socialist democrats (the majority of bureaucrats) are control freaks; 2. Someone is elected or hired to make laws and therefore dream up as many rules and regulations as possible without regard to unintended consequences; and, 3. New laws lead to more lawsuits which lead to more income for lawyers. Again, anybody getting this?

If you or I had a job that required us to do something to continue getting a paycheck, we would probably do something. These elected politicians and hired bureaucrats (public servants) should also have the task of getting rid of stupid laws, rules and regulations that have a negative impact on jobs and wealth creation. Now, that would be money well spent!

The more complex a law or regulation is the more attorneys and accountants are needed to sort them out. This is simply make-work for these two well-connected groups, especially attorneys. Does anyone really know how much attorney fees are paid by the tax payer? That's right; we are paying hundreds of millions, if not billions to attorneys to create complex laws that when challenged in the courts will last for years (paying lawyers on both side of the dispute).

We also pay defense attorneys fees when criminals can't pay. These expenses are endless! Who do you think created these laws of requiring tax payers to pay the bills? Lawyers! I understand the need to help the helpless defend themselves, but who is monitoring these expenses? Do you think democrats, who are the main beneficiaries of trial lawyers' contributions, will work to curb these expenses? Forget it…

I believe about 25 percent of the people defaulting on their mortgages do so because new rules say they can get away with it. They have the money to make the monthly payments, but they read about or talk to friends and neighbors who are underwater and defaulting without consequences. They don't want to miss the "gravy train" so they follow suit and here we go again with out of control federal deficits. Behaviors changed because of government meddlers' ***"promise of something for nothing."***

How many people turn down free money and other stuff when offered by our big government do-gooders? They never seem to figure out these unintended consequences. They are hurting the housing market and prolonging the recession with all of these Keynesian economic programs – just as they did during the Great Depression of the 1930s.

I will use a little absurdity to over-simplify reform of the legal system that would result in an opposite extreme of what we have now.

This new law would replace all existing laws:

- It is against the law to physically hurt, lie, cheat, steal, defraud, force, bribe, coerce, collude and pollute. If someone or organization is caught doing any of these, or knows someone else is doing any of the above and does not report it, they will be fined and/or jailed. Each subsequent occurrence will result in ever increasing fines and/or jail time.
- A one page description for each *"crime"* above should be sufficient to describe each crime and identify the penalty *"that fits the crime."*
- Make whistle-blowing an income option. Instead of worrying about "big-brother" catching you, worry about your neighbors, friends, co-workers and employees catching you. I know this sounds extreme but isn't reporting a crime valuable to society and a form of integrity. Looking the other way should be a crime too. Catch the criminal and put a stop to the hundreds of billions to trillions it is costing all of us. **For those reporting bogus crimes to harm someone, that is a crime and punishable also.**

Again, this over-simplification is about as absurd at one end of the spectrum as we have now at the other end. The securities and banking laws of 1933, 1934 and 1940 were sufficient to protect the financial "system" of this country for seventy plus years and those laws should have never been changed.

I don't care if the changes were the fault of democrats or republicans; both contributed to the "Great Recession" of 2008 and the anemic recovery. The stupid regulations that followed – like Dodd-Frank along with elements of the Sarbanes-Oxley act of 2002 continue to restrict our economy and job creation.

If we don't learn to repeal stupid laws and stop making more economy and job killing laws, rules and regulations, we are doomed…

Chapter 15

The Great Recession – Who's really at fault?

I realize this has been beaten to death by the free-market non-socialist community, but "repetition is the mother of all skill" (or education). So it bears repeating as often as possible.

1. **The Federal Reserves'** manipulation of the money supply in its effort to control inflation, the economy and now to benefit full employment leads to an exaggeration of the natural business cycle. The Federal Reserve should have never been created in the first place. There were other ways to accomplish their purpose without giving away the store. Think about this significant hustle not only on America but the rest of the developed nations globally.

   Our government gave monopoly banking powers to a private organization with little or no government ("We the People") oversight. This is crony-capitalism on steroids or better yet crony-capitalism with super powers. Let's see – we have a private organization with private citizens running it connected both educationally and socially to the biggest banks not only in America, but in Europe and other developed countries globally. They have the authority to print money that is not asset backed (the gold standard)!

   The latest Quantitative Easing, "QE3" announced September 2012, has not worked any better than the previous rounds to increase the money supply or stimulate the economy. It has only worked to increase asset prices of big banks, business and the rich. Go figure! The reason it has not increased the money supply of the economy is because banks have not lent out their increased reserves to small businesses, the life blood of the American economy. Let me explain: when the FED "buys" the treasuries and mortgage backed securities from money center banks, i.e., QE, they simply make a ledger entry on their books to increase the reserves of the particular money center bank that they "bought" those treasuries or mortgages from. Those increased reserves could then be lent out to increase the nation's economy – but they were/are not. Why? I don't know. The probable reasons are that the money center banks could make better and less risky returns elsewhere. So why did the FED keep doing it if it wasn't working. The varied answers to that are beyond the scope of this book, but likely have to do with the cozy relationship between the well-connected "blue-bloods" at the central banks and the well-connected blue-bloods at the money center banks.

Are there any opportunities here for payoffs, quid pro quo, and crony capitalism between all these blue-bloods? Also, could this organization be used for the advancement of socialism – especially between nations? Hmm, I wonder!

2. **Congress and the Presidency:** Congress, the legislative branch, is currently made up of 100 Senators and 435 Congressmen; add to them the substantial influence from the President and his hugely powerful Executive Branch. Over the past 100 years, Congress has passed laws leading to ever increasing idealistic utopian laws, i.e., socialism. As I have pointed out elsewhere, these laws have led to devastating consequences for America with their "stated" goal to help the poor and the disadvantaged. I say stated because I obviously believe they are "hustling" America and actually hurt the poor.

   Again, many of these laws sound great, they promise to protect us from being taken advantage of by the powerful or by making sure everyone is treated equally. How can anyone argue with that? That is precisely what the Founding Fathers of the United States intended in the creation of the Constitution and the Bill of Rights. The reality though, is that most of these laws give advantages to the politically connected and restrict the non-connected. Again, this has led to crony capitalism with big business and friends of politicians.

   Remember all good hustles by any con artists have a great story with great sounding benefits for the suckers…

   Some men and women crave power and the limelight so much they will sell their souls to get it. Liberal socialist democrats as a group crave power. How do they get and keep power? By taxing producers and giving free benefits to "groups" of voters. Once a group gets a benefit, no matter how expensive and damaging it becomes to America, just try taking it away!

Congress created several laws that would make it illegal to redline certain poor areas of communities in making mortgage loans. This sounds very good doesn't it? The problem again is the unintended consequences. See 3 below.

3. **The "Community Reinvestment Act of 1977 ("CRA")** was passed as a result of national pressure to address the deteriorating conditions of American cities – particularly lower-income and minority neighborhoods. Community activists, such as Gale Cincotta of National People's Action in Chicago, had led the national fight to pass, and later to enforce the Act.

   The CRA followed similar laws passed to reduce discrimination in the credit and housing markets including the Fair Housing Act of 1968, the Equal Credit Opportunity Act of 1974 and the Home Mortgage Disclosure Act of 1975 (HMDA). The Fair Housing Act and the Equal Credit Opportunity Act prohibit discrimination on the basis of race, sex, or other personal characteristics. The Home Mortgage Disclosure Act requires that financial institutions publicly disclose mortgage lending and application data. In contrast with those acts, the CRA seeks to ensure the provision of credit to all parts of a community, regardless of the relative wealth or poverty of a neighborhood.

   Before the Act was passed, there were severe shortages of credit available to low and moderate-income neighborhoods. In their 1961 report, the U.S. Commission on Civil Rights found that African-American borrowers were often required to make higher down payments and adopt faster repayment schedules. The commission also documented blanket refusals to lend in particular areas (redlining). The "redlining" of particular neighborhoods originated with the Federal Housing Administration (FHA) in the 1930s. The "residential security maps" created by the Home Owners' Loan Corporation (HOLC) for the FHA were used by private and public entities for years afterwards to withhold mortgage capital from neighborhoods that were deemed "unsafe." Contributory factors in the shortage of direct lending in low and moderate-income communities were: 1. a limited secondary market for mortgages; 2. informational problems to do with the lack of credit evaluations for lower-income borrowers; 3. a lack of coordination among credit agencies.

In Congressional debate on the Act, critics charged that the law would create unnecessary regulatory burdens. Partly in response to these concerns, Congress included little prescriptive detail and simply directs the banking regulatory agencies to ensure that banks and savings associations serve the credit needs of their local communities in a safe and sound manner. Community groups only slowly organized to take advantage of their right under the Act to complain about law enforcement of the regulations. As is usually the case hustlers in and out of government used this law to beat up banks into making loans that would have never been made in a well-run lending company. Banks should make loans in all neighborhoods they serve, but they should protect the bank with accurate asset pricing, neither over nor undervaluing. That's their job…

4. <u>**Fannie Mae and Freddie Mac:**</u> This was another great idea that became perverted by well-meaning and crooked politicians alike. One of the original purposes of these pseudo government agencies or government sponsored enterprises ("GSA") was to fund the buying of mortgage backed securities

5. **The creation of the "Mortgage Backed Securities Market," "Mark-to-Market" asset valuations and the massive leverage of "Credit Default Swaps:"** Initially this new investment "product," **Mortgage Backed Securities**, was a great idea for mortgage companies, borrows and investors. It provided far more money to the mortgage community to lend than was previously available to commercial banks and savings & loan companies from deposits alone. This investment is simply a large "basket" of mortgages packaged and sold to investors both large and small.

The most obvious negative of this new source of mortgage money was the deterioration of credit standardization and documentation. Lenders hire clerical staffs and loan officers commonly known as underwriters. Once loans are approved, packaged into billion dollar blocks and sold as mortgage backed securities investments, the feedback, accountability and responsibility usually charged to the mortgage loan underwriter team was almost completely removed.

In the past, mortgage loans were approved according to underwriting standards set by a direct lender, such as banks and savings & loan companies using depositors' money. If an underwriting staff screwed up and caused too high a delinquency and loan loss rate then heads would roll. In the mortgage backed securities market, this fear of losing one's job is reduced.

It was **"Credit Default Swaps"** and the accounting requirement of **"Mark-to-Market"** that caused the financial avalanche in 2008 to bring down Lehman Brothers investment house and nearly brought down AIG had the federal government and Warren Buffet not stepped in. **Mark-to-Market** accounting is simply a valuation process of an asset. Everyone is familiar with stocks getting hammered, but no one expected home prices to get hammered. Remember home mortgages had been packaged in these "mortgage backed" securities, so it was only natural that they could fall in value – and they did rather quickly. **Credit Default Swaps** was a hugely leveraged insurance like derivative that the Mortgage-Backed-Securities packagers/investors bought from banks or insurance giants like AIG. Once the slide in "market" prices of homes started, the prices in these highly leveraged securities fell even more rapidly and the situation began to get out of control. The rest is history…

6. **Removing the barriers of the Glass-Steagall Act of 1933:** The Banking Act of 1933 is commonly referred to as Glass-Steagall. This Act was the result of bank failures during the Great Depression caused by commercial banks' highly leveraged participation in the securities markets. Sounds a little like 5 above. When will we learn? The Act separated commercial banking and investment banking for 63

years until parts of the Act was repealed by the Gramm-Leach-Bliley Act, also known as the Financial Services Modernization Act of 1999. Specifically, it removed barriers in the markets among banking companies, securities companies and insurance companies that prohibited any one institution from acting as any combination of an investment bank, a commercial bank, and an insurance company.

The year before it passed Citicorp merged with Travelers Group to form the conglomerate Citigroup. Citigroup combined banking, securities and insurance services under a house of brands that included Citibank, Smith Barney, Primerica, and Travelers. Because this merger was a violation of the Glass–Steagall Act and the Bank Holding Company Act of 1956, the Federal Reserve gave Citigroup a temporary waiver in September 1998. (Again, we have blue bloods looking out for each other instead of the rest of us!)

There are many arguments on whether repealing Glass-Steagall was one of the causes for the financial crisis that led to the worst recession since the great depression. It seems obvious to me that it was a contributing factor and now that the Genie is out of the bottle – how do you put him back?

7. **<u>The mortgage interest tax deduction</u>** caused people to borrow too much money on their homes in an effort to save on their taxes. Also, without this incentive to borrow, apartment dwellers might have stayed in their apartments or waited longer to save a prudent down payment. Home owners may not have transferred other debts to second mortgages or refinancing with cash-out money if they could not get that tax deduction. How many CPAs or realtors advised their clients to borrow based on this tax deduction?

In summary: It was the combination of the above 7 items that lead to the perfect storm that almost brought down the world's economy.

Very important – It is only because of conservative republicans and a much more complex economy that we are not in a 1930's era depression in 2013. Obama and the democrats are following the depression era big-government, central-planning policies of FDR only worse. He is taking over healthcare (1/6th) of our nation's economy – next stop global warming taxes to the tune of trillions of dollars going to cronies like Al Gore – the latest quarter billionaire Ex politician. Are any of you poor folks getting a penny of Al's new $100+ million profit? Hell no – he did everything he could to close his sweetheart deal with the Islamic Oil regime's propaganda machine, Al Jazeera, before the end of 2012 so he could save nearly $10 million in additional income taxes.

Can't you "little people," as these elites think of you, see your liberal socialist democrat rulers are only generous with "other peoples" money – successful small business owners' money that is! Sure, Obama talks about him and his rich friends paying "their fair share" but his higher taxes are really just an investment in crony capitalism that will return him and other liberal socialist democrats' huge guaranteed returns in the future. **I predict Barack Obama will become the first billionaire ex-president!** I remember seeing somewhere that $1 spent by a DC lobbyist returns over $200. Why wouldn't they play con games with those returns? Again, the real targets are the millions of small business owners that have no power in Washington, DC.

By the way: I believe Al's cable network was worth maybe 50% of what the Islamic Oil regime paid for it! I wonder what they expect in return for their premium of $50+ million. Someone said Hairy Slug heard that Al Gore tried to rename the new network "Al Gorezeera" but they refused. Just kidding!

Obama has scared honest businesses so much they have been coerced into going along with his socialist programs as did honest businesses in the 1930s by FDR and the liberal socialist democrats of his day. I say "honest" because the dishonest big businesses of then and now are in an unholy alliance with dirty politicians to "skim the cream" off the $3.8 trillion federal budget.

The Fed is following similar monetary policies as the 1930s, and congress and the president are following similar fiscal policies as the 1930s. Therefore, it's only logical today's economy would follow the same patterns as the 1930s. There was even a rumor the LSD wanted to repeal the 20th Amendment so Obama can run for president again. Problem with that is he will not be able to the escape the economic facts, as FDR did, because we are in the information age and the truth can't be hidden as easily as it was in the 1930's and 40's.

Prior to World War II (1941) American businesses were very concerned with the spread of socialism, fascism and communism in Europe and the extreme left leaning FDR Administration – just as American businesses are today with the extreme left leaning Obama Administration. FDR brow beat the Supreme Court to get them to comply with his agenda just as Obama did with the current Supreme Court on ObamaCare.

All we need to do is look at the most liberal socialist countries, states and cities compared to the most conservative free-market countries, states and cities to reveal the HUSTLE – a monumental money/power grab by the liberal socialist democrats. Big government is in bed with big business even though the democrats con the public into believing they are protecting the public from the evils of big business. Everyone should see the Hannity special on Boomtown USA – Washington, DC, a DVD documentary based on the book by Peter Schweizer titled, *"Throw Then All Out."*

President Barack Hussein Obama is the epitome of how a liberal socialist democrat lawyer who has never run a company, big or small, or has otherwise produced and achieved very little beyond education and politics – can by his very personality (one that epitomizes a cleaver hustler's personality) rise to the level of the most important person in the world and live like a King from the taxes of his servants! "Only in America" now has a very negative side to it.

Think about it – he lives in a mansion with hundreds of servants, has two jumbo 747 jets, two big helicopters and many other military support aircraft at his disposal to fly anywhere in the world anytime he or his wife wants and can take as many vacations as he wants with all benefits of royalty. Each of these trips costs America millions and ties up traffic in each city where he visits adding to their frustrations along with the associated costs to local governments and its citizens.

What we need is an extremely rich self-made business man or woman whose only desire and motive is to "right" this country back towards a "Government of the People, for the People and by the People." Maybe Mitt Romney was the perfect person for this time in America? I firmly believe America missed an outstanding opportunity to elect someone with the moral character, integrity and most importantly, the experience to get America back on track to a robust economy and "The Pursuit of Happiness."

Instead of electing a charismatic, tall, dark and handsome man maybe we should have elected a short, light skinned, ugly and unlikeable Newt Gingrich to "fix" our nation's problems like he did in the mid 1990's. Just kidding Newt, millions like you and you're not ugly! Seriously, Newt has an incredible resume and would have been a fantastic president. He is usually referred to as the smartest person in the room. He knows exactly what to do to get this country back on track, but maybe we need to suffer the proverbial gutter before we can really recover from this addiction to big government socialism, removing God from society and the breakdown of the family.

Will someone please explain how we elected a man with the name of Barack Hussein Obama (a distinctly Muslim name) to be our president 7 years after 19 Muslim radicals murdered over 3,000 while trying to kill 50,000 innocent Americans and destroy our financial center, the Pentagon and possibly the Capital Building or the White House? He had no qualifications to be our president other than his ability to be charming and persuasive.

Maybe after the next four years America will be ready for a qualified conservative president. I certainly hope so!

Chapter 16

The Fiscal Cliff – What a Joke!

Conservatives, stop fighting over raising the debt limit – it only serves to give the opposition a winning narrative in public opinion and more importantly, it causes fear and indecision in business and the economy. It's a waste of time, energy and valuable resources. Have any of you republicans read the book *The Art of War* by Sun Tzu? It sure doesn't look like it, because you keep making tactical mistakes in all these budget battles. If you make a blunder and take on the wrong fight, learn to retreat; retreat is a tactical move to conserve valuable resources; the sooner you come to the conclusion that you have blundered, and retreat, the stronger you remain for the next battle. The poor economy belongs 100% to the democrats, but all these budget battles give the LSDs the opportunity to blame republicans, especially Tea Party republicans. How stupid can you guys be?

First, get every republican, every day and at every opportunity, to ask Americans; **"Are you suffering from a job loss, or reduced pay, or reduced hours?"** Then convince them the primary reason for their suffering are the socialist elements of our economy; the reason for the socialist elements of our economy are the liberal socialist democrats' big government economy strangling taxes, laws, rules, regulations and policies; the only way Americans can ever again enjoy full employment and more income is to vote the LSD party out of office. Simultaneously, policy republicans, like Paul Ryan, should focus all their time and energy on reforming and simplifying the tax code and regulations that are choking the US economy. Next, enact a national energy policy that will create millions of jobs and billions of new tax revenues. Then, freeze non-discretionary spending at current levels for several years before allowing very small increases with inflation.

The average federal worker should not be making twice the income with benefits as the average private-sector worker. In fact, because they have superior job security – they should be making less! Freeze their salaries for several years to allow private sector comparisons to catch up.

Change ALL government pensions to defined contributions from defined benefits – including the military. Government retirements with health care benefits should start at age 65. In fact, let them rely on Medicare like the private sector or buy their own health care on the open market.

As it is now the private sector tax payers are the "servants" of the public sector employees. These premium benefits are bankrupting cities, counties and states and will eventually be a major cause of America's financial collapse. The only exceptions might be gun toting soldiers because that job is for the relatively young only. Let them retire after 20 years at 40% of their military base pay and give them free VA medical or Medicare like health insurance for 7 years while they get their college degree or assimilate back into the job market. I realize this will be a major undertaking, but so are the rest of my suggestions in this book. If they were easy, we wouldn't need statesmen like our Founding Fathers.

Payoff the deficit through growth and spending freezes! The republicans did a superb job of tactically winning the fiscal war of 2012 by negotiating a "tax the rich" bracket of $400,000, instead of the lower $200,000, with Obama. Someone in the leadership must know something about winning at poker or the principles taught in the *Art of War.* Obama clearly had the winning hand in the "fiscal battle" of 2012 and these guys shrewdly knew to "fold-them" until the next battle. Here is what I'm concerned about: The spending element of the "sequester" battle win may come back to defeat the republicans if the economy is hurt near-term.

Brave men like Congressman Paul Ryan and Senator Tom Coburn have solutions that will put this country back on a path to solvency and prosperity but the liberal socialist democrats and their propaganda machine, the media elites, are lying about and demagoguing these solutions. Although very complex, these solutions can be summed up by: 1. cleaning up waste, fraud and abuse; 2. Simplifying the tax code to get rid of stupid tax deductions and loop holes, and lowering tax rates to offset the loop hole closing; 3. Getting rid of job strangling laws, rules and regulations; 4. Getting rid of redundant and worthless government agencies, i.e., reducing and limiting the size of government; and, 5. Slowing the rate of growth of spending; better yet – adopt the "Penny Plan" it cut 1% per year till the budget is balanced.

If we can regain the presidency and the senate and we are again successful in reforming government and balancing the budget we better never forget how temporary these successes can be. Liberal socialist democrats will never let up. They can't compete honestly; they must lie to the weak minded about facts and issues, cheat at creating increased democrat voter rolls, and therefore stealing elections. All the while these con artists are accusing the conservative republicans, and especially the Tea Party, of doing these same things. Sure, voter IDs are stealing elections like drivers' licenses are causing people to steal cars. Liberal socialist democrats are always making more laws, rules and regulations unless those laws, rules and regulations inhibit their dishonest "means justify the ends" quest for more power and control over the rest of us.

The leaders in the liberal socialist democrat party have now started a new propaganda fairytale: "If we start an austerity program in America our economy will become just like Europe's economy." Really? You've got to hand it to these slicksters – they've got all the con angles covered! The definition of slickster in the dictionary.com is: "crafty and opportunistic or deceitful person; hustler; swindler." If we don't start some level of austerity in the very near future the forced austerity later will make the fiscal cliff of January 1, 2013 look like an ant hill.

According to the US Debt Clock.org the US National Debt is projected to be nearly $21 trillion in 2017. That's not the scary part – the unfunded Social Security liability is projected to be over $ 16 trillion; the projected unfunded Prescription Drug Liability is over $ 22 trillion; the projected unfunded Medicare Liability is over $ 87 trillion; and, the Total Unfunded Liabilities are projected to be over 126 trillion dollars. That is over $ 1,102,169 per family as of October 28, 2013 per the US Debt Clock.org. This is insanity and yet our President and the other liberal socialist democrats don't have a clue how to avert this future crisis. They talk about the Fiscal Crisis of 2013 as if taxing the rich will solve all these problems. Why can't the public see how evil these pathetic morons are? If the government took all the income of the rich it wouldn't solve problem. The Fiscal Clift of January 1, 2013 is nothing compared to the future financial disaster that is ahead of us if nothing is done to curb the above spending.

The republicans had no real choice but to cave in to the better tactical position of the president and the LSDs in the 2012 fiscal cliff negotiations, which led to raising taxes on the top 1 percent; those earning over $400,000 per year.

Now in the summer of 2013, the constitutional conservatives in congress are preparing to pass a continuing resolution for the next budget year allowing spending for everything except ObamaCare. I am undecided on whether this is a good tactical or public relations battle. If they don't pull it off (so far it has never helped them) then the LSD leaders will beat them to death in the public arena. I feel we should focus all our efforts on what I'm suggesting in this book and pound these socialists with sound bites making them responsible for a crippled economy where too many millions have part-time or low paying jobs.

It's the economy stupid all over again except it's their (the LSD's) economy!

We are in a long-term struggle for the future survival of America. Each battle is critical in winning the struggle, so we need the most conservative candidates with the best talents in communications and battle winning tactics. So far, I'm not very impressed with the political strategies of the Republican Party or even the Tea Party Republicans. Why do these guys always seem to fall into the **"Shut-Down-the-Government"** trap? Why can't they frame the battle into a win-win narrative like this? Republicans want to shut down the **"Economic and Job Killing"** **<u>ObamaCare law</u>; it is the beginning of a complete take-over of the healthcare industry, essentially socializing 1/6th of our economy;** then frame it like this:

The Republican controlled House of Representative and Senate Republicans offers Reid and Obama the following choice:

- SHUT DOWN OBAMACARE; or eventually **"IT"** will
- SHUT DOWN AMERICA (the economy)

Ask the LSD politician: "Why did you shut down the government instead of shutting down ObamaCare?"

Ask the drive-by Obama propaganda media: "Why did you prefer that the LSD shut down the government instead of shutting down ObamaCare?"

Then shut up! Leave it at that! When the sycophants on the left whine and howl about the how dastardly those republicans are – about how they are "Tea Party Anarchists" and other clever name calling; just laugh at them and keep-it-simple-stupid… Respond with something like: ObamaCare is killing jobs and the economy so republicans want to at least delay its implementation until it can be fixed. Don't over explain; don't get pulled into the weeds by trying to defend yourselves against "shutting down the government." Hold each senate democrat responsible for their choice to either shut down ObamaCare or the entire government. The House of Representatives have done their job and passed the spending bill, funding all of the government, except for ObamaCare. It's up to Reid and Obama; it's their choice whether to shut down ObamaCare or the entire government – I repeat; it's their choice… As it is, the GOP keeps falling into the LSD trap.

If the GOP feels this battle is paramount – then do it right. What good does it do to win a budget battle but lose (the war) at the polls? Also, learn that retreat is a battle tactic (to not get wiped out) so you can regroup resources to fight another day. As soon as you see you are losing, retreat! Especially if some of your troops, like moderate republicans, have already surrendered. Don't just maintain your "position" until you get totally annihilated – retreat! I have a question for my conservative friends in the GOP: If you have the guts to shutdown the government and threaten a credit default, then why don't you have the guts to repeat what I'm recommending throughout book; **every republican** should be saying these things – **EVERYDAY!!!**

Think about it – the collective voice of the Democratic Party is divisive and includes: racial, gender, age and especially the poor vs. the rich divisions. They are creating as much hatred between Americans as they possibly can. They don't care who they destroy as long as they can get the money, power, control and fame they crave. Deception and outright lies are the weapons of choice for all "Hustlers…"

Maybe if republicans stop being "gullible" and saying; "my friends on the left," then maybe the voters will stop being "gullible" and voting for the LSD. We are at war for the moral and financial survival of America; our battlefield is the news media and our weapons are words. That said we are woefully outgunned because the president can hold 32 news conferences daily and his LSD propaganda machine will stop everything to broadcast his words; but, **we have the truth on our side... So let's get busy!**

Here is another analogy that might make sense to someone still missing this whole issue of short-term vs. long-term struggling: I was an ocean lifeguard at Cocoa Beach, Florida in 1969 and 1970 while I was in high school. No one taught me this life saving strategy – it just occurred to me when I first encountered the situation. If there was a storm causing big waves to come ashore, it created a situation called rip tides or currents. This occurred when big waves brought a great volume of water onto the beach. The water brought in by the waves had to return to the ocean, so it carried with it sand that created underwater trenches.

Even though we had warnings, some people would get caught in these rip currents and get carried, sometimes very swiftly out to sea. Inevitably these victims would panic and try to swim straight back to shore. To save them, I would enter the rip current and swim directly to them. I first had to calm them down and assure them that I knew how to get them back to shore. I explained my strategy and warned them that as we started back in it was going to get very rough and they would have to hold their breath at times when these big waves passed over us. I would wrap my life saving buoy around them and start swimming sideways to the beach until we were out of the rip current pulling us out to sea. The struggle in to shore was always strenuous because of crashing waves, but I never failed.

We can save this economy, but we have to stop swimming against the current and come up with a strategy to get America's economy, not only back to shore, but better and more robust than ever.

We're Americans – we put men on the moon just 67 years after the Wright Brothers first winged flight and just 8 years after President John F. Kennedy set a national goal to put Americans on the moon.

We can do anything we set our minds and our goals to do... We just need the right Leadership!

By the way, JFK was a pro-business, pro-growth tax cutter.

> **Even today, there is little value in insuring the survival of our nation if our traditions do not survive with it. – JFK**

Chapter 17

Tax Reform should be once and for all – then leave it the hell alone! Taxes and spending should be a reasonable percentage of the economy or GDP on a budgetary basis…

I believe the very rich should pay the largest share of the federal income tax burden and the very poor should pay little to no income taxes at all. The rich should also be thanked every day for their most generous financial contribution to America. God bless these great Americans. They should also be applauded every day for their generous financial contributions to worthy causes like children's hospitals, churches and so many more worthy charities and non-profit organizations that help the poor and the disadvantaged.

Tax reform is not rocket science; it is simple financial ratios between GDP and taxes collected. Income taxes should be directly related to the economy as defined by GPD or any other broadly defined economic measure. As the economy grows so do tax collections and as the economy contracts tax collections contract. During growth times, surpluses should be saved to cover deficits during the bad times. I believe a complete overhaul of the tax code is paramount to the robust growth of our economy and wealth creation of America and everyone in it.

Many believe a value added federal tax or a *national sales tax* is needed to make sure everyone pays federal taxes. The rich buy more so they would pay more and this national sales tax would ensure that everyone pays taxes to support the federal government. THIS IS A BUNCH OF BULL! Who cares if the poor don't pay any income taxes? By making the poor pay taxes we will just end up giving them more benefits to offset the drain on their living resources. So why do it?

I strongly disagree with a "national sales" or "value added" tax and here are several reasons, which should be obvious:

- These would be new "additional" taxes – what naive moron believes income taxes would go down respectively;
- The poor can't afford it – it's regressive;

- We would <u>not</u> get rid of the IRS – it would be expanded to collect this new source of revenues from companies that are required to collect them from the public. As it is now the IRS can look at drug dealers' big homes, expensive cars and other luxury assets and conclude that they made a great deal of money; so why haven't they paid the obvious income taxes. How would we catch tax cheats that are buying from a newly created black market? We would probably have to keep even more records to prove we paid these new sales or value added taxes – another pain;
- We would expand the government with huge new departments and bureaucracies – not reduce it;
- This would greatly expand the underground economy and significantly increase the culture of tax evasion and would create a new black market for goods and services, especially a barter market, all to avoid paying these new taxes;
- It would burden retailers (& wholesalers) with new bookkeeping and administration requirements. This should be obvious even to my "brilliant" friends on the right;
- Those suggesting it (like Herman Cain's 9-9-9 Plan – God love him) say we could reduce individual and corporate income taxes. History suggests just the opposite would happen. It would ultimately lead to more overall taxes collected followed by more spending and a bigger government. Exactly what Herman and others like him are against; and,
- My really naïve friends on the right keep saying this would end the IRS. Put your thinking cap on guys – people will cheat on paying taxes. We need the IRS to keep dishonest people from cheating. Who will make sure these new taxes are collected. The answer is not getting rid of the IRS – the answer is making sure the IRS is fair and not tyrannical. The answer is simplification.

Here are two of many suggestions in this book to simplify a fairer tax code, close loop holes and help the economy:

- Dividends should be a deduction on the corporate books otherwise profits are taxed twice; and,

- Carried interest (specifically earnings of hedge funds and other money managers) should be taxed as ordinary earned income. Taxing this income as a capital gain is one of the most ridiculous tax breaks that exist.

Hedge Funds, Private Equity Managers, Commodity Trading Advisors and their companies are paid a percentage of the investment profits, commonly called incentive fees or "Carried Interest." It is not capital gains and therefore should be taxed as ordinary income on the manager's tax returns. This is a huge loop-hole for hedge funds and other money managers that must be closed. If they don't have any of their own money invested at risk then they should not enjoy a capital gains tax benefit. If they do have investments in the fund, then only profits on that investment would enjoy the capital gains benefit.

Income as a percentage of a customer's net-new-profits is not a capital gain; it is earned income and should be taxed accordingly. Some of these people make hundreds of millions in/on clients' profit incentives. Therefore, closing this preposterous loop-hole would help offset other changes like lowering inheritance taxes and corporate dividend deductions.

I don't have anything against tax accountants but we should completely overhaul and simplify the tax code for the benefit of the overall economy and an increase in the standard of living for the poor and middle class.

Here are additional suggestions for a very simplified but progressive tax reform policy:

- Increase capital gains to 20% after the first $100,000. I realize they were already increased in the beginning of 2013 but this was a mistake. Small investors should not be paying this greater amount. Get rid of the higher "short-term capital gain" taxation as ordinary income. It's stupid to manipulate when a capital gain is held or taken. A short-term investment is still an investment. By doing this <u>more</u> taxes would be collected because trading would occur more often;

- Change corporate (C Corp not LLC) income taxes to 20% above the first $100,000. That first $100,000 should not even be taxed. This is critical for the growth of a small company which is critical for job creation in America. More jobs leads to more overall taxes from commerce. Also, this lower rate would cause small and large manufacturers all over the world to relocate to America resulting in more jobs, greater commerce and therefore more tax collections;
- Stop double taxing profits from foreign made and/or sales on products or services sold overseas by American companies. If products are manufactured in foreign countries and sold outside America then our government shouldn't tax those profits on top of taxes paid to foreign governments. Otherwise we have the situation of double taxation and major corporations holding capital outside the US. Liberal socialist democrats should stop being stupid and greedy because we need this capital here in the USA;
- Get rid of all corporate welfare and subsides of any kind especially and including agriculture. Don't try to steer investments through tax policy – let an investment stand on its own merits. **Anything else leads to political favors which is *crony-capitalism or socialist-capitalism*;**
- Get rid of the individual non-investment mortgage tax deduction. It could be phased out slowly over a 5 to 15 year period. This is one of the reasons for the mortgage banking meltdown because some people reached for this tax deduction (on their CPA's or realtor's advice) when they should have stayed in a less expensive apartment and saved more money for a larger down payment. Or, even more ridiculous, they borrowed on the equity in their homes to take advantage of these tax deductions to buy new cars or other property, make investments or even take vacations. If investment homes have a mortgage it certainly would qualify for the mortgage tax deduction, like any business expense. Millions would have avoided the foreclosure process and the transaction monies lost if they had just stayed in apartments. Apartment living is much more economical in the near term. It is only in the long term where owning a home pays off compared to apartment living. This was one of the elements that caused the speculative

fever that led to the housing crisis. **I'm not saying don't buy a home, I'm saying don't buy a home for the mortgage interest deduction. Why in the world should tax payers subsidize mortgage debt? They shouldn't.** Also, fewer people would borrow on their equity;

- Get rid of all non-investment or non-work related individual expense deductions except for deductions above 10% given to qualified charities. Giving a 10% tithe to your church and then getting a tax refund to help with that tithe is not giving 10%. Anything above 10% should be tax deductible. Example: those in a who are extremely generous to the point of giving nearly 50 to 80% can't because they would have nothing left without the tax break. Some very generous rich people give 50% or more of their income to help the poor through charities. Not giving tax deductions will severely hinder the amount they might give to those charities;
- Loans from "C" corporations to individuals should be taxed at the individual rates in the year granted and those taxes refunded in the year it, or a portion of it, is repaid.

New (replacement) Tax Rates for Individuals

- 1% taxes from 0 to $15,000 in income for an individual, $30,000 for married couples plus $5,000 for each dependent (Taxes due $350 for family of 3 for an effective rate of **<u>1% on $35,000 or $350 for a family of 3</u>;**
- 5% tax for next $15,000, i.e., $22,500 for an individual, $45,000 for a married couple and $50,000 for a family of 3 (Additional taxes due $750 for family of 3 for an effective rate of **<u>2.2% on $50,000 or $1,100 for a family of 3</u>;**
- 15% for next $15,000, i.e., $30,000 for an individual, $60,000 for a married couple and $65,000 for a family of 3 (Additional taxes due $2,250 for a family of 3 for an effective rate of **<u>5.2% on $65,000 or $3,350 for a family of 3</u>;**
- 20% for next $20,000, i.e., $40,000 for an individual, $80,000 for a married couple and $85,000 for a family of 3 (Additional taxes

due $4,000 for a family of 3 for an effective rate of **8.7% on $85,000 or $7,350 for a family of 3;**

- 25% for next $25,000, i.e., $52,500 for an individual, $105,000 for a married couple and $110,000 for a family of 3 (Additional taxes due $6,250 for a family of 3 for an effective rate of **12.4% on $110,000 or $13,600 for a family of 3;**
- 30% for additional earned income in excess of the above categories which will result in the following taxes paid and rates for **a family of 3**:
- **$250,000 earned income; $55,600 in fed taxes;** for an effective rate of **22.2%** on the $250,000;
- **$500,000 earned income; $130,600 in fed taxes;** for an effective rate of **26.1%** on the $500,000;
- **$1,000,000 earned income; $280,600 in fed taxes;** for an effective rate of **28.1%** on the $1 million;
- **$5,000,000 earned income; $1,480,600 in fed taxes;** for an effective rate of **29.6%** on the $5 million; and,
- **Inheritance taxes would be reduced to 10%** above $5 million and due in the year any assets are sold – not the year of the parents' death. The cost basis would be the original cost basis on the books, zero if none could be established. Making children sell businesses, real estate or farms to pay this ridiculous double tax is government theft and should really be permanently eliminated. Of course, the greedy LSD party would never allow that.

Remember, except for charitable giving and business expenses, there would no longer be any deductions or "write-offs." And because capital gains above $100,000 would be taxed at 20% instead of 15% the very rich would still be paying the vast majority of income taxes in America. Mitt Romney's federal taxes paid would have increased nearly 35% under these suggestions.

As you can see from the above examples those with "wage" earnings of $1,000,000 or more per year are effectively paying 30% in taxes. Is the family of 3 earning $5,000,000 and paying $1,480,600 in federal income taxes getting anymore from the federal government than the family of 3 earning $35,000 per year and paying only $350 in federal income taxes? Why should the rich family of 3 pay $1,480,250 (or 4,229 times) more? The answer is – because they can and America needs it to pay for all our government expenses and social programs for the poor! What is this family of 3 getting for all those taxes? Nothing at the federal level because property protection comes from police and fire departments at the local level – where it should be.

The real answer is the rich are being demonized by the LSD Party for not paying their fair share! Are the gullible voters who believe this con really that stupid? APPARENTLY!

Again, THANK GOD for rich tax paying Americans!

We should have an American holiday like a combination of Labor Day and Thanksgiving to celebrate anyone paying more than $100,000 in federal income taxes. Make sure it a mandatory government day off like Thanksgiving and Labor Day. **Call it "Thank the Rich Taxpayer Day."**

I don't have the massive amounts of data needed and the wherewithal to make sure the above ideas are close to revenue neutral or how the economy would be dynamically affected by the changes. The point is, if somebody like me, a regular every day citizen without congressional or government resources, could come up with ideas to simplify the tax code enough to unleash the power of free-market capitalism and create a fairer system for all socioeconomic classes, why can't democrats come up with anything other than the failed **"tax and spend socialist policies of Europe."**

Socialist class warfare only causes hatred and resentment from those who are not wealthy and thanks to the LSD Party the poor believe they never will be wealthy. How pathetic! Democrats want the poor and middle class to blame the rich for their poverty or lack of wealth when just the opposite is so obvious.

Democrats are responsible for the culture of socialism that creates national poverty. Everything they do drags down hope, along with the investment and productivity that this country needs to build wealth, and more importantly, the opportunity to create wealth from innovation and hard work. The LSDs will never teach the poor how to move from poverty to prosperity. They'll lose power if they do.

Democrats always talk about investments in education and infrastructure when what they really mean is simply more taxes collected from all of us and then directed to their cronies in teachers unions and corrupt businesses. If they really cared about our children's education they would do away with socialist teachers' unions and change to a competitive merit based system that would focus on children learning (not testing) the core subjects like math, science, engineering, technology and especially English – with a focus on reading and writing.

A favorite whine of the liberal socialist democrat is we need more taxes for infrastructure. We don't need more federal income taxes for local roads and bridges. This is a local and state issue. As I have mentioned elsewhere in this book – why don't we just issue tax-free government guaranteed revenue bonds for all of these roads and bridges, paid for with taxes collected from gasoline and other fuels used for transportation in those geographical areas? More miles driven, more taxes collected from those using the regions' roads and bridges. Is this too simple for the LSD Party to comprehend or does this just remove too much of Washington's power and control? Probably both!

These infrastructure project costs have no business coming out of the "general tax revenue budgets" from federal, state or local governments anyway. Who buys these tax-free bonds? Those evil rich people and corporations that invest their excess capital… Another good thing about this type of financing over using the general tax revenues of the government is that the financing and taxing are temporary (I must be kidding myself to believe it's temporary) and off the general budget.

Companies are not evil – *some* of the individuals who run them are. If individuals with bad character traits are at the head of companies, then the top down culture of those firms will lead to a company full of liars, cheats and thieves. These companies will eventually be put out of business by competitors with integrity. If you have owners, boards, executives and managers who are working toward long-term goals and are fair minded, honest, God-fearing individuals then they will create a great company with great results. There are thousands of companies all across America with these characteristics that are thriving and paying good wages and high taxes.

Payroll taxes are not income taxes, they are contributions to this countries' Social Security retirement system. Only dirty politicians or dirty media co-conspirators would try to get away with this misdirection (lie). For the last 2 years this lie of calling this a tax break to stimulate the economy is a joke. Using this money is just robbing the Social Security fund and the young to pay for more social programs that are full of waste, fraud and abuse. This is just more liberal socialist propaganda from the democrats and their sycophants in the media and most of our republican politicians just let them get away with it.

Getting people who have been out of work or underemployed for more than two (2) years back to work and off the welfare rolls, or long-term unemployment insurance and those on social security disability with marginal physical and behavioral or emotional disabilities can also be accomplished with training and implementing the following:

- Have those described above (2+ years out of work) enter re-training programs or even return to work (with full pay checks) as a sort of re-training period while collecting 75% of full benefits for the first 6 months if returning to work and 12 months for re-training;
- 50% of benefits, plus pay checks, for the next 6 months; and,
- 25% of benefits, plus pay checks, for the last 6 months.

This 2 year transitional process would have the goal of moving a large percentage of over 50 million Americans off of depending on federal tax payers and actually paying taxes themselves. I understand the fear of not being able to return to a productive job. The goal would be to get everyone who can work – back to work. The only reason this should be considered is so many workers have lost their skills during the worst recession since the great depression. Some strict guidelines on who would qualify for this generous program would look like this:

Those who have been on out of work for over 2 years would qualify for the above schedule of work and benefits. Those out of work for 18 to 24 months would qualify for 75% of the above. Those out of work for 12 months to 18 months would qualify for 50% of the above. Those out of work for 6 to 12 months would qualify for 25% of the above.

This would be a one-time "Great Recession" return to work program and therefore could be meaningfully phased out in the future.

Chapter 18

American Energy: Want more jobs, taxes and less Trade Deficits – What are we waiting for?

The short answer is: Environmental socialists have an agenda to: 1. Reduce worldwide carbon consumption; 2. Reduce widespread prosperity from capitalism, and; 3. Increase the number of people dependent on socialist leaders for their welfare. Also, these idiots don't have any idea of how free-enterprise markets work. They think they can force green energy on the world before its time. Green energy will become much cheaper as new technologies are developed with hydrogen being the most promising long term energy source. Hydrogen is practically limitless with zero emissions.

Do you know why the glaciers have been receding for the last million years or so? Prehistoric SUVs… That's how stupid liberal socialist democrats are! Enough said on global warming?

A favorite corporate demon of the left is big oil. Why? This major industry is one of the jewels of American's vast natural resources. How many people are employed by Exxon Mobil Corporation alone – not to mention all the other energy companies? What is the average annual salary paid to its employees? What is the total amount of income taxes paid by all of their employees? What is the total amount of taxes paid by the corporation? How much does a gallon of water or a gallon of milk cost in comparison to a gallon of gas? How much does a gallon of gas cost in Europe, Japan, China, Africa, or even the Middle East. Also, these oil companies can't ship jobs in Texas, Oklahoma, North Dakota or Alaska overseas like Apple or GE can. Again, instead of appreciating Exxon, the left would stone the company to death if it were legal. What are these idiotic liberal socialist democrats thinking?

Why all the focus on Exxon Mobil? What about General Electric? According to a Forbes article by Christopher Helman, dated 4/10/10 General Electric generated $10.3 billion in pretax income but ended up with a tax benefit of $1.1 billion. Let me repeat: GE did not pay taxes on $10.3 billion in income – they got a credit forward on their taxes. Hmm…

I wonder why the head of GE is such a passionate supporter of President Obama.

Here is an American energy economy accelerator that is being promoted by T. Boone Pickens that makes too much sense to ignore. Natural gas is available to just about every urban and suburban home in America. My family had it in our home in Florida in 1965. Here are some excerpts from a T. Boone Pickens interview with Chris Wallace on Sunday June 25, 2012:

> It (natural gas) is the largest natural resource we have and we're now talking about exporting it out of this country; use it here; increase the demand for natural gas; don't send our cheap, clean – it's 30% cheaper than diesel. So don't ship it out to China or where ever else and import dirty OPEC crude. I mean we're going to go down as the dumbest generation in the world, if we do that; I mean we're fools if we do it; because, we have so much natural gas – it's unbelievable. But, we also have a lot of oil too. We're increasing our oil in the United States. And that's all because the industry has done a fabulous job of techniques [fracturing underground oil-rich rock formations] to recover both oil and gas." He went on to say that there have been hundreds of thousands of wells that have used the "fracking" methods within an eight state region from Texas to South Dakota with no known ground water contamination – so the environmental concerns are not valid.
>
> …Chris Wallace mentioned Mr. Pickens idea of converting 8 million heavy trucks from diesel to natural gas and how it will affect pollution and our [US] dependence on foreign oil. Mr. Pickens's response: "There are 250 million vehicles in America; I just want 8 million; …if I had the 8 million; that would be about 3 million barrels of oil a day. We import about 4.4 million barrels of oil a day from OPEC; …We could cut OPEC by about 70%; …With just the 8 million [trucks]. It's like a freebee. Natural gas is a $1.50 to $2 cheaper per gallon than diesel.

Mr. Pickens went on to discuss how the free-market could install the infrastructure around the country in about eight years vs. a federal tax-credit program that would accelerate that to half the time, or about four years. He also revealed how [his] the associated legislation did not pass. The tax-credits associated with his recommend legislation failed to pass the Senate because it required a "super-majority" based on a technicality. He explained that the tax credits would have been paid out of user fees collected by the industry, costing nothing to the treasury and the tax payer. Mr. Pickens went on to say the measure also failed to pass because another multi-billion dollar corporation had too much to lose if the bill passed.

This is why we have Congress – to sort out what's best for the country. I Googled this interview on Fox News and found everything Mr. Pickens said to be very believable. Bottom line is he feels this is going to happen; one way or another and it will be highly beneficial to the economy and the environment.

The Energy Independence and Security Act of 2007 and the Energy Policy Act of 2005 that preceded it have grown the federal government, added new layers of commerce and job strangling rules, regulations and laws, but has done very little to make America more energy independent. These bills have more to do with turning food into fuel, thereby raising food prices, than increasing oil production and decreasing the price of a gallon of gas or fuel oil – which would benefit us all.

It seems all our politicians do is pay lip service to America's need for a new comprehensive energy policy; they never seem to have the guts to take on all the opposing constituents. Imagine that…

Recently, Obama has been taking credit for the huge increase in America's oil production. Is he kidding? He and his administration had nothing to do with the massive increase in oil discoveries and production. All of these increases are on private lands that he has no control over and can't block. His administration has made federal lands off limit; just the opposite of his claims. What a con job!

Chapter 19

Government Safety Net vs. Private Sector, Local, Church and Family Safety Nets

Maslow's "Hierarchy of Needs" is a description or ranking from our most basic human needs to our higher human desires once those basic needs are satisfied. Here they are from our most basic needs to our higher desires:

Physiological – breathing, food and water, excretion, sleep, sex, and homeostasis (the ability to adapt to our environment);

Safety – security of the body, family, health, employment, property, resources and morality;

Love and Belonging – friendship, family and sexual intimacy;

Esteem – self-esteem, confidence, achievement, respect of others and respect by others; and,

Self-Actualization – morality, creativity, spontaneity, problem solving, lack of prejudice and acceptance of facts.

The charitable free-enterprise, free-market capitalist America that God-fearing conservatives and libertarians truly believe in will never abandon the needy. Socialism strips man of much of his self-esteem and self-actualization desires that separate man from the other highly intelligent species on this planet. It's too bad our ignorant fellow Americans aren't taught the above so they would be less likely to fall for the LSD hustlers on the left. Again, the truly needy will always be taken care of by God fearing, constitutional-conservative, republicans. The able bodied crooks that are hustling the welfare system would "have to work" to eat in a fair, honest and accountable society… A Christian culture or society, that is!

During the dust bowl and the great depression of the 1930s people with very little shared food and shelter with people who had nothing.

This is the American charitable culture and behaviors that will never allow the needy to go hungry. The big centralized federal government in Washington has replaced that charity with forced taxes, and local accountability with distance and fraud.

I'm not saying the government should not play a role in helping the needy and the poor – they certainly should. What I'm saying is the greater the distance between the source of charity and the recipient, the greater the opportunity for waste, fraud and abuse. How does the country devise a system of helping the poor? It's not by hiring a bunch of bureaucrats in Washington to dole out money through state bureaucrats! There are so many alternatives that will work much better.

There are charities everywhere, some are religious, and some are not. How much real energy and thought has been invested in closer to home solutions? Radical atheists, secularists and other enemies of family values and morality have done such a good job of breaking down the cultural cement that keeps well-functioning societies from chaos and decay – it's no wonder we have to rely on government.

I experienced a severe accident in 2010 that left me hospitalized for 5 weeks, on my back and in a wheelchair for several more weeks and then on crutches for months. I still must walk with a cane and suffer with swelling and pain constantly. I did not have health insurance because of a loss of employment in the 2008 financial crisis, so I lost everything. If it had not been for close Christian friends, my son and I would have been on the street. I was not at home for months so it was burglarized and we lost everything. Because I had lost my career do to the housing crisis, I lived in a rental home on 5 acres in a very rural area of Texas. I was hospitalized for 5 weeks and burglarized of all my valuables. Those burglars left the back door open so field rats infested my home. You can only imagine the filth and the smell. Cloths, bedding, furniture and everything else not stolen was completely ruined and had to be thrown out.

I was 58 years old, bankrupt and everything I had acquired over the years was gone – furniture, appliances, tools, computers, cloths and everything else. I had more wealth in 1972 when I was just 20 years old and in college. Starting over has been brutally depressing but it has given me the opportunity to appreciate life more and understand the plight of those who fall on hard times and need help. It also allowed me the time to watch the news in depth and closely study the subject of this book from the fall of 2010 to the summer of 2013.

It is burglaries like what happened to me in so many neighborhoods all across America that led to the tragic death of Trayvan Martin by the overzealous watchman, George Zimmerman. Of course, the race hustlers ignore that fact and we never heard anyone speak of the real cause for Zimmerman to be watching the neighborhood for vandals and burglars in the first place. He was simply doing his job when he noticed Trayvon walking about in the neighborhood. I will discuss this tragedy in more detail in Chapter 21.

Getting back to my experience in 2010 with getting hurt, losing everything and needing help to survive. I applied for and received food stamps and was very grateful to have it. What I observed during the 7 or so visits to the Health and Human Services Office caused me to suspect there was some fraud. How much? I have no idea; I was only there for short periods of time. Sure, there was a ton of paperwork, so some form of qualification standards were being met but no one knew me, or my circle of friends, or made surprise visits to check on me and my son <u>to see if the need was legitimate</u>.

How much longer can we afford the waste, fraud and abuse that is a documented part of these bureaucratic big-government social welfare programs? It's not only individuals gaming of the welfare system but even more incredibly the corporate welfare, money center and international banking fraud that amounts to trillions of dollars over decades? It's all got to stop before it's too late! Sure, the "Occupy Wallstreet Hippies" were on to something regarding corporate welfare and banks too big to fail but they have no idea where the problem really lies. It's not free-market capitalism which will sort out fraud and abuse naturally; it is the crony-capitalists, capitalist-socialism and the liberal socialist democrats that live and feed off cronyism; it's also a leviathan federal government – a government way too big and expensive to monitor or control.

One only needs to look at some of the largest churches in America to see how caring and faithful Christians are to the poor, the broken hearted and others suffering from lack or tragedy. Small and medium sized churches also help the poor and needy all over America proportionately as much as the big churches. I point out large the "mega" churches simply because they can be easily Googled. Example: The largest church in Phoenix Arizona is Phoenix First; this church helps thousands every month with the essentials of life, including love and belonging. **Here is what they say about their "Dream Center:"**

> **Serving over 40,000 people each month,** we believe in the incredible potential of the at-risk youth, homeless, and needy within our community. Services at the Phoenix Dream Center include a residential rehabilitation program, shelter and care for victims of human trafficking, affordable housing for single men and women in transition, and distribution of food and clothing throughout various Phoenix neighborhoods where the predominately poor reside.

Here is just one of their many programs that I had never thought about:

> Each year, nearly six hundred Arizona youths in foster care age-out of the system upon reaching eighteen years old. At this time, they are given a black trash back with their belongings and sent into society. Sadly, three hundred of these young adults, each year, will enter unknown and often dangerous situations. We find them in homeless shelters, on the streets, or in other vulnerable living conditions. But there is hope. The Phoenix Dream Center is opening thirty beds for these youths at its Grand Avenue facility, where they receive care, support, and hope for a future in which they become productive and thriving members of our community. See more at: www.phoenixfirst.org

There are Christian churches like this all over America serving those among us who are suffering, especially women and children. Liberal socialist democrats, as a party, are doing everything in their power to undermine Christian churches, which will ultimately hurt the very people they claim to stand for, the poor and the needy. Washington, DC will never be able to care for the needy the way the private sector, churches and families can.

The following Christian New Testament Scripture sums up what Jesus Christ had to say to his believers, the Church, concerning the poor and the needy:

Matthew 25:35-40

35 For I was hungry and you gave me food, I was thirsty and you gave me drink, I was a stranger and you welcomed me, 36 I was naked and you clothed me, I was sick and you visited me, I was in prison and you came to me. 37 Then the righteous will answer him, saying, Lord, when did we see you hungry and feed you, or thirsty and give you drink? 38 And when did we see you a stranger and welcome you, or naked and clothed you? 39 And when did we see you sick or in prison and visit you?' 40 And the King will answer them; Truly, I say to you, as you did it to one of the least of these my brothers, you did it to me.

Look at all the programs the Catholic Church has to help the needy, including hospitals and schools. The Democratic Party is home to the Socialist Party and radical atheism. **It is beyond my understanding how a God fearing Christian can belong to a Democrat Party with factions that are hell bent on removing God from our society. That goes for God fearing Jews and Muslims also…**

I'm illustrating this point for the kind hearted, generous Americans who don't believe in God, but are not radical atheists. I'm not trying to persuade them to suddenly believe in God; I'm trying to persuade them to believe in the good that many God fearing Americans and churches do for our fellow men, women and children.

Chapter 20

"The Rich get Richer and the Poor get Poorer" Liberal Socialist Democrats are you Smarter Than a 5th Grader? Apparently not!

First of all this saying is a pathetic manipulation of the facts. The truth is the rich and the poor have gotten richer in the last 50 years. The poor enjoy air conditioning, cell phones, cable TV, computers, the internet, autos or cheap public transportation and much more than even the super-rich enjoyed a hundred or so years ago. Also, most of the world's 7 billion people don't have these luxuries available to them, and surely the opportunities to move from poverty to financial freedom.

Instead of teaching the proven methods to move from poverty to the middle class, what suggestions do the liberals make? More socialism instead of more a more effective education system and inspirational examples of how to achieve financial independence…

First of all this war cry, *The Rich Get Richer*, is another lie by socialist hustlers – the truth is the poor in this country are also getting richer. It is correct that the difference between the rich and the poor is getting greater. The simple explanation to this is basic math and nothing else! Why the hell republicans don't respond with this simple truth and then ask the person saying this lie: "Why can't you understand simple math – what is your real agenda by making such a stupid statement?"

What the liberal socialist democrat will soon learn is that by punishing the rich with higher taxes and making them poorer, the poor will suffer even more because of a mediocre economy and job market. Just look at the countries that have trended towards socialism in recent decades, like Greece, the rich get poorer along with the poor getting poorer. Studies show that the average poor person in America lives better than most of the world's population. I repeat, poor Americans live better than most of the world's population.

This stupid worn-out liberal socialist democrat phrase, "the rich get richer," is so simple to debunk it should be embarrassing to all you self-professed liberal intellectuals.

This chapter is about how mathematically obtuse liberals are. Now for you *"Dumber than a 5th Grader Socialist Class,"* try to follow the basic math below that proves just how stupid the socialist phrase "The rich get richer and the poor get poorer" is! I'll go slowly for the LSDs…

All of the estimated illustrations below are for a family of four:

Family 1 earns $50,000 before taxes per year and does not have any money left over for savings and investments. Family 2 earns $100,000 per year and has $20,000 left over for investments with an expected return of 4% per year. Family 3 earns $250,000 per year and has $75,000 left over for investments with a return of 4% per year. Family 4 earns $1,000,000 per year and has $300,000 left over for savings and investment with an expected return of 4% per year. I used a very conservative 4% "net" return instead of a 50% larger rate of 6% to approximately account for the Fed tax on the investment earnings.

After 10 years each family has paid approximately the following income taxes and has the following investment totals, which could be deposited in banks to be lent out for credit cards, car loans, student loans, boat loans and home mortgages, or loaned to companies to build plants, buy equipment, and hire more employees, to name just a few possibilities available to them – especially those earning $250,000 plus:

Family	Annual Income	10 Year Savings	Total Fed Taxes
#1	$50,000	Nearly Zero	Nearly Zero
#2	$100,000	$250,000	$200,000 plus
#3	$250,000	$950,000	$600,000 plus
#3	$1,000,000	$3,750,000	$3,000,000 plus

The above table illustrates the simple math of compound interest on savings and investments. The family with the most earnings can save the most. Again, this is simple 5th grade arithmetic; nothing evil, dishonest or greedy about the results. The answer is to learn how to start and run a successful business so your income can grow exponentially.

The secret: work your ass off providing a better product or service to your customers for decades until the business is big enough to practically run itself. You would probably be pretty old by that time but you may also be rich and financially independent. This is being done all over America every day but you'll never hear the democrats promoting these ideas. No, they promote taking that hardworking successful entrepreneur's working and investment capital, and giving it to their constituents – that's how Obama's socialism works in America.

Look at the family above who contributed the most to federal taxes and therefore all the programs that help the poor. Does this family get anything for their far larger contribution to America than the other families? Or even more incredibly, are they given any appreciation? No, they are demonized by the liberal socialist democrats and their stooges in media, on college campuses by the socialist elite professors and liberally ignorant students, labor union leaders and in the halls of congress by the elected blood sucking democrats. Too harsh? Hell No! Brave God fearing conservatives need to be saying this daily.

The socialist con artists are lying daily – trying to program the weak minded. **We have to counter this every day.** Would you allow thieves to take a small amount of your possessions every day? Well that's exactly what liberal socialist democrats are taking from American taxpayers and the wealth of our nation every day! They're killing working capital of small businesses that create the majority of American jobs and are a major part of our economy. Of course, liberal socialist democrats believe that food stamps are a major job and economy creator. That's why they are working over-time trying to get tens of millions more Americans on these programs that really don't need it (in addition to buying votes!).

Instead of demonizing the rich, if they really cared about anything but their own power and wealth, these socialist hustlers would educate, motivate, believe in and encourage the poor on how to get to an income level of $100,000 plus per year. Anyone can – if they have the belief system, the knowledge and the work ethic. How is it that so many people from poor countries in Southeast Asia and all across the planet come to America and within one generation become financially independent? Is it because America is the land of opportunity that they passionately believe in? Of course it is!

The self-made hard working rich small businessman or woman should be admired. Instead, the socialist media and democrats wage class warfare between the rich and the poor. They have made it admirable among socialists to subscribe to the hatred of the rich and super taxation of their income and assets – including death taxes; all this while climbing in bed with the rich LSD fat cats in NYC, Hollywood, Madison Avenue, labor unions and academia. **What hypocrisy!**

In addition to millions of Americans who started with nothing, thousands of immigrants have come to this country with little to nothing, started small businesses, worked their tails off, saved every penny they could and became millionaires. They didn't stop to listen to the liberal socialist democrat con artists – they just got busy!

The rich get richer and **the poor suckers that believe they can't – can't!** Again, it's a pretty simple set of beliefs; a philosophy, a culture and set of actions to follow that are common with most wealth creators. It's called modeling – one doesn't have to reinvent the wheel, just copy it. How many liberal democrats do we see on TV news programs talking about the success stories of the poor over-coming adversity, and working their way up the income ladder to become rich, financially independent or at least middle class? **NONE!** Because it doesn't serve the liberal socialist democrats and their slobbering sycophants in media, labor unions, Hollywood and academia.

Here are some of these success stories that should be heralded, celebrated, studied and emulated: The first story became a bestselling book and an award winning Hollywood movie starring Will Smith who is quite a success story himself. I pray he is a conservative, because of his Christian background, even though being a conservative is unlikely in Hollywood and the culture that goes with it.

Success Story Number 1:

Chris Garner, CEO and Founder of Gardner Rich LLC

> Conquering grave challenges to become a successful entrepreneur, Gardner is an avid motivational and aspirational speaker, addressing the keys to overcoming obstacles and breaking cycles. Gardner is also a passionate philanthropist whose work has been recognized by many esteemed organizations.

The amazing story of Gardner's life was published as an autobiography, *The Pursuit of Happiness*, in May 2006, and became a *New York Times* and *Washington Post* #1 bestseller. In paperback, the book spent over twenty weeks on the New York Times bestseller list and has been translated into more than thirty languages. Gardner was also the inspiration for the movie "The Pursuit of Happiness," released by Columbia Pictures in December 2006. Will Smith starred as Gardner and was nominated for the Best Actor Academy Award, Golden Globe and Screen Actors Guild nominations for his performance. Mr. Smith had my vote; he is a great actor and one of my favorites. Gardner was an associate producer on the film.

In his second New York Times bestselling book, *Start Where You Are: Life Lessons in Getting from Where You Are to Where You Want to Be*, published in May 2009, Gardner shared his philosophies on, and the crucial steps behind, creating a fulfilling, successful life. The book provided a much-needed blueprint for navigating tumultuous times with positivity, courage, tenacity, discipline and common sense. The book was released in paperback in May 2010.

In the fall of 2010, Gardner was named the Ambassador of Pursuit and Happiness for AARP, which has nearly 40 million members worldwide. His mission is to share his hard-won wisdom to encourage the 50+ audience to pursue new challenges, search for fulfillment at any stage of life, or craft the legacy they want to leave behind.

Born February 9, 1954 in Milwaukee, Wisconsin, Christopher Paul Gardner's childhood was marked by poverty, domestic violence, alcoholism, sexual abuse and family illiteracy. Gardner published his autobiography out of a desire to shed light on these universal issues and show they do not have to define you. Gardner never knew his father, and lived with his beloved mother, Bettye Jean Triplett, when not in foster homes. Gardner is indebted to Bettye Jean for his success as she provided him with strong "spiritual genetics" and taught him that in spite of where he came from, he could chart another path and attain whatever goals he set for himself. [Amen – Praise God!]

Gardner joined the Navy out of high school and after discharge moved to San Francisco where he worked as a medical research associate and for a scientific supply distributor. In 1981, as a new father to son, Christopher Gardner, Jr., he was determined to find a career that would be both lucrative and fulfilling. Fascinated by finance, but without connections, an MBA or even a college degree, Gardner applied for training programs at brokerages, willing to live on next to nothing while he learned a new trade. Chris Jr.'s mother left and Gardner, despite his circumstances, fought to keep his son because, as he says, "I made up my mind as a young kid that when I had children they were going to know who their father is, and that he isn't going anywhere." [Brings tears to my eyes – I Praise God for this great man!]

Gardner earned a spot in the Dean Witter Reynolds training program but became homeless when he could not make ends meet on his meager trainee salary. Today, Gardner is involved with homelessness initiatives assisting families to stay intact, and assisting homeless men and women who are employed but still cannot get by. It is estimated that 12% of the homeless population in the United States is employed; in some communities that estimate is as high as 30%.

Dedicated to improving the well-being of children through positive paternal involvement, Gardner is a board member of the National Fatherhood Initiative, and received the group's Father of the Year Award in 2002. He served on the board of the National Education Foundation and sponsors two annual awards: the National Education Association's National Educational Support Personnel Award and the American Federation of Teachers' Paraprofessionals and School-Related Personnel (PSRP) Award. He also serves on the board of the International Rescue Committee, which works to provide access to safety, sanctuary, and sustainable change for millions of people whose lives have been shattered by violence and oppression. Gardner is still very committed to Glide Memorial

> Church in San Francisco, where he and his son received assistance in the early 1980's. He has helped fund a project that creates low-income housing and opportunities for employment in the notoriously poor Tenderloin area of the city. Source: chrisgardnermedia.com

People, if this story doesn't inspire you – you must be dead emotionally!

Story Number 2:

Dr. Benjamin S. Carson, M.D. Pediatric Neurosurgeon

This great American is one of my favorite success stories. Everyone should read his books and see the movie made about his life. They are awe inspiring and motivating. I believe Dr. Carson would make an outstanding president and could lead this country back to greatness and bring Americans of every race together in harmony; just the opposite of what Obama and the race hustlers have created. Here are his words:

> The more stories I read about the success of people who applied themselves to make their lives better, the more motivated I am to be one of them. Knowledge really is power, and when I became a voracious reader, my confidence and grades improved accordingly. I needed little in the way of pep talks by adults, and today it is my strong belief that if you can just get children to believe in themselves and understand that when they achieve academically, they are the ultimate beneficiaries, they will do what is necessary to become a successful contributor rather than a drain on society…
>
> There are few places in the world where people enjoy the level of freedom we have in America. Here you don't have to ask anyone's permission to start a new career or move to a new location. You are free to associate with whomever you please, and **you are free to speak your mind if you decide not to allow yourself to be constrained by political correctness.** If you have a fabulous idea, you are free to put as much time and effort into it as you like, and if that idea results in a financial windfall, you are entitled to spend your money to your heart's desire – after you have paid your taxes, of course. You can worship however you choose without

fear of persecution. **Even the poorest people in our society live like kings compared to billions of desperately poor people throughout the world.**

- Ben Carson, excerpt from *America the Beautiful: Rediscovering What Made This Nation Great*

Success Story Number 3:

Howard Shultz, Starbucks Chairman and CEO

Starbucks Chairman and CEO Howard Schultz was not the founder of Starbucks but he is the man known for transforming the Seattle coffee chain into a global empire. Schultz's humble beginnings have also influenced the way he runs the company. *The Guardian* reports that Schultz was always interested in creating a company that his own father (who worked as a truck driver, factory worker and taxi driver) never got the chance to work for.

When Schultz was 7, his father lost his job working as a diaper service delivery driver after he broke his ankle. Schultz's Starbucks is known for providing healthcare benefits to its employees. According to *Entrepreneur Magazine*, Schultz grew up in the Canarsie Projects of Brooklyn. Schultz lived in a cramped two-bedroom unit in an apartment building that housed about 150 families. He recalled how embarrassed he would be when he found out that the sleepaway camp he went to as a kid one summer was "a subsidized program for underprivileged kids." Schultz eventually went to Northern Michigan University on an athletic scholarship, being the first person in his family to go to college. [Mr. Shultz is a hugely successful and admired CEO.]

Success Story Number 4:

Sam Walton, the Founder of Wal-Mart

Walton's family lived on a farm in Oklahoma during the Great Depression. In order to make ends meet, he helped his family out by milking the cow and driving the milk out to customers. He also delivered newspapers and sold magazine subscriptions. By 26, he was managing a variety store after graduating from the University of Missouri with a B.A. in economics. He used $5,000 from the army and a $20,000 loan from his father-in-law to buy a Ben Franklin variety store in Arkansas. He expanded the chain, and then went on to found Wal-Mart and Sam's Club. His passion was to provide the lowest prices and the most products of any stores anywhere. He died in 1992, leaving the company to his wife and children. He was the richest man in the world when he died.

Success Story Number 5:

Ursula Burns, Xerox CEO

The Xerox CEO grew up on New York City's Lower East Side 'when it was really bad, when the gangs were there and the drug addicts were there,' she recalled to the *NY Times.*

Burns' mother, whom she calls her biggest influence, constantly repeated different sayings to her while she was a child. The mantras included: 'Where you are, is not who you are.'

Her mother ran an at-home daycare center taking care of other children and also ironed shirts for people in order to allow her daughter to afford to go to a Catholic school. Burns is the first African-American woman to run a Fortune 500 company, and has made quite the impressive progression from being a Xerox summer intern in 1980 to the company's CEO. Burns is glad she never took the advice of her teachers who knew she was a good student but predicted she should just pursue a great career as a nun, nurse or teacher."

Success Story Number 6:

John Paul Dejoria, Co-Founder and CEO of Paul Mitchell

"John Paul Dejoria is every budding entrepreneur's dream. His hair care company John Paul Mitchell Systems began as a $700 startup from loans. According to *Entrepreneur,* he started his first job at the age of nine when Dejoria, his mom, and his brother would wake up at 4 a.m. every day to fold and deliver newspapers.

But at one point his mom could not support him anymore, and he was sent to a foster home. He was homeless twice before making his fortune, including when he was 22, working jobs from being a janitor to driving a tow truck. His second bout of homelessness came as a single father. His wife left him and his son and took half of his savings.

Dejoria was left to take care of his 2-year-old son on his own and was so poor he resorted to exchanging soda bottles for change. The turning point came when he got a job working as a salesperson at Redken Hair Company and was influenced to start a hair company with his friend Paul Mitchell. He is now worth $4 billion.

Success Story Number 7:

Oprah Winfrey, Billionaire Media Mogul

Oprah Winfrey was born to unmarried teenage parents. As a child, she split time between her mother Vernita who lived in Milwaukee, and her father Vernon who lived in Nashville, reports *The Biography Channel.* Her mother was never really around much to take care of her, and Winfrey was abused by several family friends and relatives in Milwaukee.

Winfrey's first job? She worked as a "quiet grocery store worker" and was not allowed to talk to customers.

In 1968, she moved permanently to Nashville after becoming pregnant at the age of 14. After her week-old baby died, her father decided to help her turn her life around by instilling strict discipline and making sure that she would get an education, reports *People.*

She eventually became an honors student in high school and attended Tennessee State University on a full scholarship. Winfrey later transitioned into television, and became Nashville's first African-American female news anchor. Oprah Winfrey is likely the richest self-made women in history. She overcame tremendous adversities by sheer determination and talent.

It's a shame she has "conformed" to the race baiters and hustlers. She has now joined the senseless racial division chorus after the Trayvon tragedy instead of joining the brave Black American leaders who can discern that Zimmerman was not a racist. Zimmerman could not retreat when his back was on the ground and Trayvon was on top of him beating the crap out of him. It seems out of character for her and certainly unnecessary for her career advancement – since she is the wealthiest self-made woman in the world. To make an earlier point crystal clear: Where would she be had her ancestors stayed in Africa? I don't mean that to just be about her wealth – I mean that to mostly be about all the good she has done with her TV talk show in the area of race relations in particular, but certainly all relationships in general. I believe her show was so hugely successful because of her wisdom and class. Characteristics the race baiters and hustlers are without.

Success Story Number 8:

Herman Cain, Former CEO and Business Executive, Author, Radio Host, Syndicated Columnist and Candidate for President of the US

> Herman Cain was born in Memphis, Tennessee, to Lenora Davis Cain, a cleaning woman and domestic worker, and Luther Cain, Jr., who was raised on a farm and worked as a barber and janitor, as well as a chauffeur for Coca-Cola Company president Robert W. Woodruff. Cain has said that as he was growing up, his family was "poor but happy." Cain related that his mother taught him about her belief that "success was not a function of what you start out with materially, but what you start out with spiritually." His father worked three jobs to own his own home – something he achieved during Cain's childhood – and to see his two sons graduate.
>
> Cain grew up on the west side of Atlanta, Georgia, attending school and Rev. Cameron M. Alexander's Antioch Baptist Church North in the neighborhood now known as The Bluff. Eventually Cain's father saved enough money and the family moved to a modest brick home on Albert Street in the Collier Heights neighborhood. He attended Archer (public) High School, graduating in 1963.

Cain married Gloria Cain (Etchison), of Atlanta, soon after her graduation from Morris Brown College in 1968. His wife of 43 years is a homemaker, with experience as a teacher and a librarian. The couple has two children and three grandchildren.

Cain ran for president of the US in 2012 and was very popular among the Tea Party Patriot movement.

Success Story Number 9:

Dr. Terry Morris, Ph.D., NASA Engineer

He was four years old the first time his mother beat him. She grabbed the nearest thing she could find, an extension cord, and lashed his legs until blood ran dark on his flesh. When she tired of him, she shoved him out the door, onto the wintry streets of Chicago, and let him fend for himself. He was the scapegoat amongst his five siblings, called worthless and unwanted more often than by his name.

At 13, his parents forced him onto a Greyhound bus headed south, where he landed in Plantersville, just outside of Tupelo. It was a strange new world, but his story was not over. Terry Morris was rescued from the streets and taken to Alpha House Home for Boys in Tupelo. And slowly, the boy became a man. Morris laid bare his life Friday night at the 100 Black Men of Columbus' 15th annual Protégé Banquet, hoping it would inspire the young men seated among their elders.

The local organization is a chapter of 100 Black Men of America, which formed in New York in 1963 as a way for African-American men to improve conditions in their communities through the mentorship, economic advancement and education of black youth. Today, there are 116 chapters nationwide and more than 10,000 members.

The annual banquet in Columbus highlights the young protégés, with benefits going toward scholarships and other programs. Organizers hope people like Morris, who served as guest speaker for the event, will show the young men that no matter what they have faced, they can make something of their lives.

Everywhere Morris goes, he tells his rags to riches story, speaking at a lengthy roster of places which include the White House, the Pentagon, the Department of Justice and the FBI and CIA headquarters. It is a troubled tale of triumph. "I'm still alive." Morris says his childhood is a blurred memory of walking on eggshells, trying not to anger his mother but inevitably failing. I used to lie in bed as a kid and think, "What did I do to deserve this? This is crazy," he recalls.

But Friday night, he stood at the podium in Mississippi University for Women's Hogarth Student Center, telling the assembled crowd of community leaders and up-and-coming high-schoolers that while the road to success is neither quick nor easy, the greatest struggle is conquering oneself.

Now 48, Morris works as an electrical systems engineer at NASA's Langley Research Center in Hampton, Va., specializing in high-speed aerodynamics, solar-pumped lasers, flight simulators and wind tunnel design.

He holds a bachelor's degree in electrical engineering from Mississippi State University, a master's degree in electrical engineering from Old Dominion University, a doctorate in systems engineering from the University of Virginia, a certificate in public leadership from The Brookings Institute and received a fellowship to attend Massachusetts Institute for Technology.

There are no shortcuts, he told the teenagers. Success takes work, but the work is worth it. "It's a miracle I'm still alive today," Morris said. "I overcame that, and I can look back now, because that was not the end of the story. Regardless of where you are, the story ain't over."

He called 100 Black Men a shining example of the way a man should behave. He believes love, trust, faith and hard work are paramount to triumphing over life's worst. But no one can do it by himself, he cautioned. The guidance of good men is critical, and he credits where he is today with men who served as his mentors.

www.cdispatch.com/news/article.asp?aid=16533#ixzz1xMXyY4M0

Again, if this doesn't move you – you can't be moved. Also, why can't the Al Sharpton's and Maxine Waters' of the world get this? Answer that and you may have discovered why American race relations are on the decline!

Success Story Number 10:

Dave Thomas, Founder of Wendy's

Here is a testimony to all that is good about America and the opportunities available here that a friend of mine was able to start out as a short order cook in a Kentucky Fried Chicken restaurant and, from there**, through hard work and carefully observing the values that lead to success, established his own national chain of fast-food restaurants.** As with any good rags-to-riches story, however, his life wasn't always easy.

Born to an unwed mother he never knew, he was adopted after six weeks. His adoptive mother died when he was five, and his father went in search of work around the country. From his family, my friend learned the value of hard work and perseverance, and in his early thirties, this young entrepreneur was given the opportunity to use his restaurant experience to take over four Kentucky Fried Chicken restaurants in need of help in Columbus, Ohio. He was able to completely turn around those restaurants, and four years later he sold them back to KFC, making approximately $1.5 million. That was just the beginning of his success; as he went on to found his own national fast-food chain.

"Only in America," he was once quoted as saying, "would a guy like me, from humble beginnings and without a high school diploma, become successful. America gave me a chance to live the life I want and work to make my dreams come true. We should never take our freedoms for granted, and we should seize every opportunity presented to us." His name of course is Dave Thomas, the founder of Wendy's, and my wife and I were among his first houseguests after he built his dream home in Fort Lauderdale prior to suffering a fatal heart attack. The effect that he has had on America has been overwhelmingly positive. Adopted himself, he went on to found the Dave Thomas Foundation for Adoption. He claims his decision to drop out of high school was his biggest regret, and so not only did he go on to get his GED at around age sixty, he started the Dave Thomas Education Center to help other adults complete their GED.

Dave Thomas's success is not rare in our country because of the freedoms we enjoy, and like him and so many others, I am incredibly thankful to call America home. I have been privileged to travel the world and visit all of its major societies, but to be born in a land of opportunity for anyone willing to work hard is an unfathomable blessing that should never be taken for granted. As I learned growing up, even with all the economic turmoil that surrounds us today, entrepreneurial opportunities still exist for anyone who is willing to work hard and think innovatively.

Readers, there are millions of success stories just like these throughout American history. Why don't we have mandatory high school classes that teach the subjects of entrepreneurialism where success stories like these are studied? THE ANSWER: Because our national public school systems are run by unions which have a socialist bias – a bias that sees business and profits as evil… Again, is anybody getting the point of this book and why I believe I'm doing the Lord's work by writing it? Here are some excellent quotes, by the famous and the wise, regarding the subject of success and hard work:

By working faithfully eight hours a day, you may eventually get to be a boss and work twelve hours a day. – Robert Frost

It is the working man who is the happy man. It is the idle man who is the miserable man. – Benjamin Franklin

Inaction breeds doubt and fear. Action breeds confidence and courage. If you want to conquer fear, do not sit home and think about it. Go out and get busy. – Dale Carnegie

When you cease to make a contribution, you begin to die.
– Eleanor Roosevelt

Our greatest weakness lies in giving up. The most certain way to succeed is always to try just one more time.
– Thomas Edison

It's not that I'm so smart; it's just that I stay with problems longer. – Albert Einstein

The miracle, or the power, that elevates the few is to be found in their industry, application, and perseverance under the prompting of a brave, determined spirit. – Mark Twain

Most people never run far enough on their first wind to find out they've got a second. Give your dreams all you've got and you'll be amazed at the energy that comes out of you. – William James

Chapter 21

Group Hustlers: Race, Gender, Sexual Orientation, the Poor, Senior Citizens, College Students and Environmental Extremists – LSD's goal: Divide and Conquer America!

At the root of all hustles is deception; some hustle for money, some hustle for control, some hustle for power, some hustle for fame and they all use lies, manipulation and deception to get what they crave.

Gender Hustlers: The most significant issue facing America is not the economy, or jobs, or a good education for our kids, or the massive public debt, or the massive annual budget deficits, or the like; No! The most pressing issue facing our Nation is a women's right to free birth control pills and an abortion. Oh! Wait a minute, that's right – they use the term "Women's Reproductive Rights." No one is trying to stop them from using birth control, so why not be honest and call it "Free Abortion on Demand Rights?"

A great many women, especially single women, seem to lack the intelligence or at least the intuition, to see that the Liberal Socialist Democratic Party is deceiving and using them. These women fall prey to the slick con man which in the end will lead them to pain and heartache. The "something-for-nothing promise" is usually the bait that hooks the pawns of the democrats.

Interesting note: I took a quiz that my daughter had to take for a high school assignment at blogthings.com/areyouafeministquiz. She scored 84% feminist and I scored 93% feminist. Imagine that – the author of this book scored 93% feminist on a quiz designed to separate the bigot from the feminist! Again, I believe in total equality but many gender laws are written by lawyers, for lawyers, just to make work for their profession. The main reason I didn't get a 100% feminist was I answered "not sure" on the **"morning after"** pill. I am SO AGAINST the brutal act of abortion that I'm not sure the morning after pill is the same as abortion, **in comparison**. If I had to choose, I choose the pill.

Sexual Orientation Hustlers: I discuss this issue in detail in several places throughout so I'll make this brief. Sin is sin; no matter if it's a lie or slander, or lust, or an extra marital affair. We are "all" guilty of sin in the eyes of God. That's why the Grace of God came to earth in the form of Jesus Christ – so we could be forgiven of our sins and redeemed as a child of God. The problem I have with a radical, or flagrant homosexual, is the same problem I have with a heterosexual flaunting their sexuality. Society and especially our children don't need to see it. I believe there are Gay men and women who are born that way; if they are as discrete as most people are about their sexuality then who am I to be offended, or to judge them. They deserve all the rights that any American deserves.

Youth or College Student Hustlers: I discuss this elsewhere so this will be brief. It is only natural to be impressionable when we are young. Each of us is far more knowledgeable, experienced and wise when we are 50 than when we are 20. Liberal socialist democrats take advantage of this fact and exploit our youth as solders in their insidious and destructive causes.

Poverty Hustlers: Let' face it – the liberal socialist democrats need as many poor people as possible to stay in power. So how do they keep these people poor? By dumbing down the education system and getting as many of them as possible to settle for socialist table scraps and crumbs in exchange for votes. These LSD hustlers don't dare inspire or educate the poor to move from poverty to prosperity and take the chance that they may start voting for God-fearing, conservative, free-market republicans…

Senior Citizen Hustlers: I'm a senior citizen who believes if we don't do something about Social Security and Medicare pretty soon it won't be there for our children and grandchildren. How fare is that? Conservative republicans like Paul Ryan have solutions that will save these programs for the future but the demagogues in the Democrat Party have very successfully suckered many gullible seniors into believing their outrageous lies like throwing grandma over the cliff. Can't you seniors see how ridiculously stupid the democrats think you are?

Environmental Hustlers: Global warming is killing the planet! Really, I guess it was 100,000 year old SUV's that caused the glaciers to recede from Yosemite Valley in the Sierra Nevada Mountains in central California. Can't you environmental morons figure out the planet has been warming and cooling for millions of years before man came along. Global warming is the epitome of the liberal socialist democrats' hustle that I'm writing about in this book. Whoever thought up this money grab is a liberal genius – much smarter that the typical Marxist/socialist/statist, power hungry, money grabbing, control freak, hustler. Why? Because this hustle/con is worth trillions and everyone will have to pay to play – especially the vast majority of the world's poor population. But before everyone else is soaked, these pin heads will focus on middle class Americans. Don't think for a minute that Obama's "Cap and Trade" has been given-up on.

The globe was warming long before mankind existed. Wake up all of you college graduate suckers and stop being so gullible since you will be picking up the majority of this tab in the future! Are there reasons to conserve energy resources and keep the air and water clean – absolutely! Is it the federal government's role to set standards, rules and regulations? Yes, because air and water cross state lines. But, do we need to crush the economy and job creation with an over reaching and tyrannical EPA to ensure we have clean air and water? Hell no! Again, it's just another liberal socialist democrat's reason to grab money and power from a gullible population.

Also, once you give a legislative pencil to a politician or bureaucrat they go crazy. We kicked a money-grabbing tyrannical England out of this country over 225 years ago; so, why do you think the modern day Tea Party movement sprang out of nowhere in the 2010 elections? Is it the same reason King George III got the boot (actually it was the Parliament's fault; the King had little to do with it) – tyranny, statism and unjust taxation...

Education of the poor – especially the inner city poor:

We have all heard of the ridiculous notion of giving reparations to Black Americans for the history of slavery. This idea was so easily debunked that we don't hear about it anymore. I'm going to make a suggestion here "tongue-in-cheek," but with much truth and application.

We should give reparations to the parents of inner city poor children, of all colors, who are suffering from the terrible union infected school systems. Of course, those reparations must be used for Charter Schools that are making great advances in energizing and inspiring these children to learn and excel. These schools are proving to be a "game changer" for the inter-city poor by really teaching the foundations of reading, writing and arithmetic, along with inspiring them to reach for their dreams. Any honest examination of this proves my point.

Race Hustlers: First of all hustling isn't about race or gender or rich white males or any other ginned up group the liberal socialist democrats have concocted to divert attention from their real motive of money, power and fame cravings (their addiction) or their pathological desire to control others. Proof of this statement is that if you're a conservative women, you're a slut or some other disparaging name, and if you're a black conservative, either male or female, you're an Uncle Tom or a sell-out.

Second, what about all of the old rich white male liberal socialist democrats like Joe Biden, John Kerry, Harry Reid, all the Kennedy men and all the many other rich, white, liberal leaders? The best example of these hypocrites was LSD Senate Majority Leader Robert Byrd who served in congress from 1953 to 2010. You have probably heard that he was a member of the Ku Klux Klan in the 1940s and filibustered against the 1964 Civil Right Act. See my point! This isn't about black/white, rich/poor, gay/straight, old/young, it is solely about the "Club" – the Liberal Socialist Democratic Party and their never ending march toward a socialist America where the "Royalty Class" controls every aspect of society and they dole out crumbs to "their" pleasant class to maintain "their" power.

When will the poor, the disadvantaged and other groups learn they are just being used and there are only so many positions at the top in a socialist country? More importantly, the whole notion of the probability of a successful ending to a redistributionist socialist economy is about zero! In other words, the duped democrat groups like the poor, blacks, women, Mexicans and others are going to be screwed in the coming financial collapse. Don't believe it? Look at Greece, Spain and all of the other nations who have ignored the failings of the Soviet bloc nations like Cuba, North Korea and several African nations. Better yet, look at the miserable suffering that the residents of inner-city Detroit are experiencing. It only took 50 years for the liberal socialist democrats, and the public and private sector unions to destroy the city and the auto industry! How long will it take the LSD to destroy America if Republicans can't figure out how to get the points of this book across to the gullible democrat voters?

I believe with certainty that it wasn't because Obama was 50% black that 95% of black voters cast their ballots for him. I believe they voted for him because he is a big-government, social welfare, redistributionist, i.e., a liberal socialist democrat. As an example: If Joe Biden, a rich old white man, were running against a black conservative republican like Dr. Ben Carson, or Herman Cain, or Alan West, or Alan Keyes, or Mia Love, or Tim Scott, or Dr. Walter E. Williams, or Dr. Thomas Sowell, or Condoleezza Rice, or Clarence Thomas, or Michael Steele, or E. W. Jackson, or any other great black conservative – the rich white liberal socialist democrat, Joe Biden, would likely get the black vote. Why? Seriously, why would the old-rich-white-liberal-socialist-democrat-male get the majority of the black votes? Answer that, and you may just have the answer to why this country is doomed to economic poverty.

Third, I am not a racist, and I'm certainly not rich. In fact, I currently live below the poverty level. I don't care if my children marry other races as long as they are God fearing conservative republicans or libertarians. My Christian ancestors came here from England in 1654 to start a new life in America. They were poor shopkeepers and never owned slaves. Over 200 years later several of my ancestors sacrificed their lives fighting Confederate Rebels in the Civil War to free the slaves. Some are buried in the Confederate prison cemetery in Andersonville, Georgia. I am proud that my Christian ancestors not only fought for Black American's freedom in the Civil War but also fought and died for everyone's independence in the American Revolutionary War.

Think about it; the bible says in John 15:13, "There is no greater love than to lay down one's life for one's friends." My ancestors laid down their lives and gave up their children, brothers, husbands and fathers for black slaves they didn't even know; just, so the slaves and their offspring could enjoy their God inspired Constitutional rights to freedom and the "Pursuit of Happiness." My parents weren't racist, I'm not a racist and my teenage kids are not racists. My home is a parade of teenagers, white, black and Hispanic. I have only barred one kid from coming back, and he was white. All of these kids are great and well-mannered; which is a reflection of the character their parents and of my kids for choosing them as friends.

It is human nature to try to get an advantage over another, whether for money, power or privilege. An unjust charge of racism, to gain an advantage, for any reason, is just as evil as racism itself. Reverse racism is also just as evil as racism. Now that George Zimmerman was rightly found "not guilty" for the murder of Trevon Martin, mobs all across America want civil rights charges pressed against him. Some even want him dead. This is certainly racial hatred by any definition, or at least reverse racism. If anyone presses a charge against me of racism because of my criticism of race baiters and race hustlers, just to shut me up, or disqualify my opinions, how is that not racism or at least a violation of my First Amendment rights?

During my childhood in the 1950s and my teenage years in the late 1960s my dad taught me there was no difference between blacks and whites – they were children of God just like every other American. I remember how cool it was when the Civil Rights Act of the 1960s gave blacks the opportunity to go to my school in the seventh grade. It made me sick and angered me when I found out some of my friends' fathers made racist comments about the integration of blacks in my school.

Is there still racism in America? Of course there is, but give me a break, our President is black and if he wasn't a liberal socialist democrat, every conservative I know would be proud to have him as our president! I knew Barack Obama was a socialist and would lead this country further towards socialism, but I was still glad he was black. I don't care if every president in the future is black, as long as they are God-fearing, free-market conservatives. I also look forward to the day we elect a women president – as long as she is also a God-fearing free-market conservative.

Better yet, let's recognize all the black God-fearing free-market conservative women and elect them as presidents in the future.

A hundred years, or even fifty years ago, the average American white male might have been guilty of discrimination – not anymore. Today, most whites have close friends or family ("loved ones") that fit into every minority group the democrats claim to represent. **They just don't want to give in to special regulations and privileges that will enable reverse discrimination, unjust powers and stupid lawsuits.** If you insist on special rules and regulations that lead to reverse discrimination and give special privileges to any group of people, making it easier for unjust lawsuits, then you might be the self-centered money grubbing bigot you pretend to despise, i.e., a hustler…

Kids born the last few decades had to be taught discrimination. They can see every race and "group" represented in movies, on TV, in sports, as athletes and coaches, in business and even in politics… Hmm a black President! If just left alone, these children also could care less about any differences there might be, between each other, because they're too busy playing with one another to notice. It doesn't matter what race, gender, religion or sexual preference they are, they just want to go about the business of being a little kid – playing and having fun!

Liberal socialist democrats need to leave our kids alone and stop polluting their impressionable minds with liberal hatred and their propaganda "bull crap." I believe schools that lead our children in chants about Barrack Obama and other liberal socialist democrat propaganda is patterned after socialist or communist indoctrination and is obviously an evil "means-to-an-end."

SOCIALIST ADULTS – LEAVE OUR KIDS ALONE! At some point the focus on and fight against racism will be counterproductive and will only serve to keep racism alive…

The race hustlers today can't afford to let America forget racism; they certainly can't afford to allow conservative black politicians to succeed. If racism disappears in America the Democrat Party is in big trouble – which is why their "new blacks" are Mexicans!

President Obama had no business going on network TV and injecting himself into the Trayvon Martin tragedy. The words he spoke were highly self-centered and self-serving. Saying, "if he had a son that son would look like Trayvon." How narcissistic can he be? Those statements only served to flame race divisions that democrats so commonly promote. What are all these race baiters/hustlers doing to minimize the deaths of young black men in America? Very little to nothing!

They say stupid things like this from liberal socialist democrat Eliot Spitzer, a former governor of New York, attorney general and prosecutor, on a Sunday news program: "In this case (Zimmerman's not guilty verdict), the justice system has failed, there is a simple reality here. An innocent young man walking down the street was confronted by a man with a gun, and that innocent young man was shot." What a political pandering maggot! Just walking down the street – why didn't he go all the way with the deception and say Zimmerman shot the innocent young man in the back, in cold blood? See my point? Pandering!

Can't everyone see how pathetic that statement is; but statements just like that are being made by race hustlers all over this country every day. Now, this isn't an ordinary legal expert. This is a man who prosecuted people in the prostitution industry and then was caught using prostitutes while the governor of New York. He resigned in disgrace (he is now running for public office again – go figure!). How will this country continue to make race relations progress if we to listen to lies and twisted statements like that? This creep is pandering for votes; plain and simple… Someone in the liberal left community better grow some balls and get the courage to confront their liberal comrades or they will eventually be seen by "everyone" for who they really are: *"race hustlers…"*

If Trayvon Martin made any mistakes in the confrontation with George Zimmerman he paid for it with his life. It appears Trayvon was a good kid from a good Christian family. What a tragedy! I can only imagine the pain and suffering his family has endured. George Zimmerman is paying every day and will continue to pay for the rest of his life for his mistakes in this confrontation. I hear liberals claiming that this was not self-defense because Trayvon was an unarmed teenager. Trayvon hit George hard enough to break his nose, knocked George to the ground and then took complete control of the fight by straddling George like a mixed martial arts (MMA) fighter. George had several cuts to the back of his head from Trayvon slamming his head on a concrete sidewalk. I listen to the stupid ranting's of Bob Beckel on Fox's *The Five* every day

(July 2013) saying "that poor little George just had a few scratches that did not justify shooting Trayvon."

I have a few questions that Bob apparently doesn't have the intelligence to figure out for himself: 1. Was Travon through beating George when George shot Trayvon; 2. Was Trayvon getting up or was he still beating George? Not according to an expert witness and eye witness testimony; 3. Was Trayvon capable of beating George unconscious; 4. Has anyone ever been beaten to death or killed by bare hands? 5. Has a 17 year old ever killed anybody, and did George know that Travon was only 17 years old; 6. Did Trayvon tell George he was going to kill him; 7. Did Trayvon see or feel George's gun on his hip. Remember Trayvon was straddling George and could have discovered and reached for the gun; 8. Was George supposed to wait until he was about to lose consciousness before he pulled the gun; and, 9. Should George have waited until the much stronger and better positioned Trayvon took the gun away and possibly killed George with it? In an MMA cage fight the referee's most important job is to stop the fight if someone is getting beat too badly, especially if one of the fighters is unable to defend himself. George didn't know anything about Trayvon except he was aggressively attacked and getting his ass kicked by Trayvon.

Again, the NUMBER 1 QUESTION IS: WHEN DID THE BEATING STOP? According to the only eye witness, it apparently stopped when he heard the gun shot. He said Trayvon was still on top of and beating George, MMA style, when he went back into the house to call 911 – then he heard the shot. It may have been less than a minute between his last seeing the MMA style beating and the gun shot. If that is not self-defense, there is no such thing as self-defense. Why do the liberal race baiters and race hustlers ignore such over whelming evidence? **Attention, power, money, control, career advancement and most importantly their drug of choice – fame…**

Why is it that so many people choose to blame this tragedy on the Florida "Stand Your Ground Law" when George could not retreat after he was punched hard enough to break his nose; he was knocked to the ground with Trayvon straddling and beating him about the head. How could he retreat with Trayvon on top of him? This was a simple case of self-defense, just like George's attorneys said.

Bob Beckel is a simple minded idiot like most liberal socialist democrats and has no business judging George Zimmerman. He thinks this was like one of his school yard fights and that a "few little scratches" didn't justify self-defense. I'd bet his fat ass would feel differently if he found himself being straddled by an "UNKNOWN" mixed martial arts fighter beating the crap out of him in the dark of night, telling him he was going to die and feeling that if the other guy got a really good punch in, he could lose consciousness at any moment. Who knows maybe Bob Beckel is as brave as he is passionately stupid – I doubt it.

We know George Zimmerman was trying to protect the residents of his neighborhood and their belongings because of previous burglaries. It was his duty within that community. Had there not been a history of vandals, thieves and burglaries in that neighborhood George would have probably been watching TV with his wife instead of driving around the neighborhood streets on a wet and drizzly night. I'm not defending George, maybe he's one of those want-to-be-cops with behavioral pathologies – maybe not! If the stories are correct about him helping poor kids, including black kids, then perhaps he's a great guy that should have completely backed off when the 911 dispatch told him to or at least immediately identified himself to Trayvon as a neighborhood watchman.

If Trayvon confronted and attacked George without provocation then he paid the ultimate price for his aggression. Did Trayvon deserve to die – absolutely not! My point is fighting is risky behavior; so is sky diving, rock climbing and driving too fast. High risk behavior has a greater statistical probability of harm or death – just ask any insurance company. My younger brother died, in 1990, from an accident in a brand new corvette that hydroplaned because of standing water on the highway. Although it wasn't anyone's fault, it was still crushingly painful to our family for years so I can only imagine what Trayvon's parents when through.

What is the lesson here that can be taught to young boys who watch MMA or cage fighting on TV? Fighting is a lose/lose situation. If you win you could suffer civil or criminal charges; if you lose, you could lose your life. Instead of teaching this lesson and telling these young boys to walk away from a fight, the race hustler's lesson is that "white-Hispanics" are "hunting down" and killing black kids and getting away with it because of racism. That's the current state of the race hustler's industry in America – they don't care about anything but dividing America and making a fortune from it. The problem is – everyone in America loses – except the race baiting industry. See the hustle?

Fortunately, America has brave men and women, both white and black that are standing up to these race baiters and intimidators. The loudest and most effective is Bill O'Reilly in the summer of 2013. God bless him for standing at the front-line of this controversial issue and giving brave cover for others, both black and white, which see these high profile race hustlers for who they really are. By God's grace America seems to have someone like Bill O'Reilly every generation who will stand up to the bullies of the world. In the 50's and 60's it was Dr. Martin Luther King and all the white people who stood with him.

Again, even though George was acquitted, he will still pay for his part in this tragedy for the rest of his life. I've been telling my sons since they were very young not to get into fights. They are both tough, but that's not the point. Nothing good can come from fighting if you can walk away. Someone may get hurt and hurt badly. Expensive civil lawsuits or criminal charges are likely, not to mention jail time if you are prosecuted. Why – because of macho testosterone and the threat of being called a chicken? Parents that teach their boys to fight have mental health problems that probably stem from their own insecurities. I'm not talking about organized boxing which is a sport – I'm talking about street fighting where there is no referee to stop the fight.

I can honestly say that if either of my sons died because they did the same thing that Trayvon apparently did and aggressively attacked another man, I would be furious with them for not listening to me; and myself because I had not convinced him of the dangers of fighting strangers. If he's beating the crap out of a guy and the guy pulls a knife or especially a gun – he's screwed! Anything can happen and tragically – it did. If my son died in an auto accident because he was speeding I would feel the same type of anger at him, and me, for the same reasons. When your child dies the crushing pain is always mixed with – if only I could have prevented it somehow…

If the race hustlers and the "drive by media" really cared about a black teenager being killed by a hand gun they would focus more on the thousands killed by other black teenagers with guns every year. They would focus on telling their boys not to fight, to find a way out. How many other parents of 17 year old black kids have felt the crushing pain of losing them to gun violence since this tragedy was made public? Do they feel abandoned by our national leaders because of the energy and focus on just one easily sensationalized "racial" case verses the thousands of black "drive-by" and other gang related murders?

I have to give tremendous credit to the courageous black leaders who are countering the mob mentality of the race hustlers. Here is one that stood up against the mob mentality soon after the acquittal: On the Hannity Show following the weak racist crap put forward by Juan Williams (a black man), Leo Terrell, a black radio talk show host said this: "Let me be very clear, shame on you Juan Williams, you're not a lawyer. Let me be clear as a civil rights lawyer, there was not a race case here, at all, and the jury got it right. This is a wrong case for people like Juan (he then alluded to several others like Juan) to use this as a racial division in this country. It is outrageous! That jury was absolutely correct as a lawyer (he then expanded on the race hustlers and race baiters that are using the Trayvon case). Zimmerman was tried, he was found innocent of these charges and that woman who said God is a racist – it's embarrassing for me as an African American to hear Juan Williams, MSNBC and CNN talk about this case as a race case."

This tragic, but simple case of self-defense has turned out to be a financial and fame bonanza for America's race baiter/hustlers… Let's face it – racial division is an industry that makes multi-millionaires out of people with no other bankable talents and fits right in with the liberal socialist democrat's goals of power, money, control and fame. The Trayvon Martin tragedy is exactly what they are always looking for and once they sink their vampire fangs into the story, they do everything possible to anger the black community and intimidate the white community. FACTS DON'T MATTER – only the ability to increase racial tensions. They succeeded!

The parade of black liberal socialist democrat race hustlers like congress women Maxine Waters was pathetic and inflammatory. My first reaction to race hustlers like Jesse Jackson and Al Sharpton was to condemn them for focusing on this isolated black youth killing, by what seemed early on and now has been judged a justifiable shooting in self-defense. All this clamoring while ignoring the thousands of black youths being killed by each other in drug, gang or other crime related shootings is so predictable. After some research it appears both Jackson and Sharpton do some work within the black community to change the crime and gang culture. For that I applaud them. I still believe they are race hustlers for the way they handled this tragedy and many other high profile race incidents but maybe they also do some good within their communities. In any event, I look forward to the day when race hustlers like Al Sharpton and Maxine Waters are totally inconsequential. Then, and only then, will this country completely heal and move on.

There are thousands of reasons, and solutions, for the high unemployment and crime rates in the African American community. Bill O'Reilly says, and I agree, the primary cause is the breakdown of the black family resulting from a 73% of black babies being born out of wedlock. Additionally, and more importantly, I believe the above was caused first by removing God form the public square and our schools in the 50's and also by the sexual revolution of the 60's (moral breakdown). It is beyond the scope of this book to cover even a small number of the other reasons and solutions for the above so let me focus on just one thing that any individual, black/white, rich/poor, can do to produce a prosperous life for themselves and their family.

Get the best education you can. This is the only solution that an individual has any control over – they don't have to wait for anyone or anything else. Anyone in America can get a free education through 12th grade and then get help from the government to pay for a college education – ANYONE… If a mother or a father or a mentor can convince a young child that they can be anything they dream of by taking advantage of an American education – they are Heroes! Next, get a job and do it better than anyone else; keep that job until you have a better one lined up. Find the right spouse and commit to that person – no matter what! Love can fade – a commitment or a promise is forever… Remember two can live together much cheaper than living alone. Don't spend more than you make, except for a home mortgage and watch that amount too. This one paragraph alone is the simple "proven" formula to go from poverty to the middle class and possibly prosperity. Do you ever hear the liberal socialist democrats or the race hustlers teaching this to our kids? Hell no – it doesn't serve them like poverty does…

Dr. Ben Carson was raised by a great mother that made sure he took advantage of America's educational opportunity even though he had no father at home and lived in intercity poverty. She made him read an abundance of books that opened his mind to the possibilities he could achieve by his own free-will and hard work. Again, once the light goes off in a young mind about the possibilities that exist – there are no limits. Dr. Ben Carson is evidence of that – he is one of America's top brain surgeons developing and performing the first pediatric separation of conjoined brains of twin children joined at the skull. Please study everything that this great, God fearing, conservative American has to say about improving America. His ideas are both brilliant and simple; something lacking in our leadership in Washington, DC today.

In closing, the greatest and most dominate golfer of all time is Tiger Woods. The greatest and most dominate basketball player of all time was Michael Jordan. What are some similarities between these two men?

- Both are black
- Both grew-up <u>with</u> fathers
- Both are super competitive
- Both are self-made billionaires
- Both are practically worshiped by white men

Sure, white men are racists… Get a real job race hustler!

Here are some great Black Americans who have been in the past, and are destined to be to be in the future – instrumental in the success of not only race relations, but America in general. They are some of the bravest, smartest, God fearing conservative black leaders who should be leading this country instead of the current liberal socialist democrat occupying the White House:

<u>Bishop E. W. Jackson:</u> He is currently running for Lieutenant Governor of Virginia (September 2013) and is exactly what this country needs to battle against the forces of evil that are at work destroying the very fabric that has made this nation the greatest in human history. He is highly intelligent, highly articulate, God fearing, spiritual, bold and brave. I believe this man will prove to be one of our "ReFounding Fathers" that God will anoint to return America to its Constitutional foundation.

I discovered him June 2012 running for the US Senate seat from Virginia. Sadly, the democrats made him a major target for defeat. If this man ever became president that would be the end of the Liberal Socialist Democratic Party. I firmly believe God has a plan for Mr. Jackson, if not in politics, then as a national leader for change. He gave a speech on You Tube titled *"E. W. Bishop Message to Black Christians"* that is so powerful that I placed it at the close of this book.

I know very little about this man, but what I know so far is extremely impressive. I was impressed in the same way with Alan Keyes when he ran for president. I pray that men like Mr. Bishop and Mr. Keyes will run for president in the next election cycle. Maybe if one of them wins the presidential nomination of the Republican Party he could select the other as his running mate. If they were running against a white liberal we would then see if the black community really cared about having a black president or if they just want a liberal socialist democrat no matter what…

Alan Keyes: This is one of my favorite American Heroes. When he ran for president in 1996, 2000 and 2008 I was 100% behind him. He is a brilliant Reaganite Conservative and his resume is just as impressive as his speeches. He is more articulate than any conservative I have ever listened to. Take the time to research (Google) this man and see if you agree with me. That said – is it any wonder that he could not win the nomination process that continued to elect moderates like Bob Dole in 96, George Bush in 2000/2004, John McCain in 2008 and Mitt Romney in 2012. When will we learn?

Just because the great American conservative, Barry Goldwater, lost in a landslide to President Johnson in 1964, after beating GOP moderate, Nelson Rockefeller, in the primary, we should never give up. The only other time a conservative won the primary was Ronald Reagan in 1980 and 1984 – look how that turned out. Some say Nixon was a conservative – baloney! He was a disaster domestically with price controls, ending the gold standard and other bad policies. Alan Keyes is the closest candidate we have ever seen to the Great Ronald Reagan. We can thank the "establishment" republicans for missing the best opportunity to launch the American way-of-life well into this millennium, and to give America its first Black president. I have an idea – the GOP establishment should announce their choice of a primary candidate so we all know who not to vote for… You can bet the LSD Party loves our GOP primary selections of "establishment" moderates to run against in the general election. How's that worked out for us?

Allen West: is a former one-term United States Congressman and current contributor to Fox News. After a 22-year military career, this retired Lieutenant Colonial entered politics in the 2008 election, when he ran for U.S. Representative from Florida's 22nd congressional district as a Republican, but lost against Democratic incumbent Ron Klein. In a rematch against Klein in 2010, West won the seat, coinciding with historic Republican gains in the 2010 midterm elections. On January 3, 2011, West took office as the first black Republican Congressman from Florida since Josiah T. Walls left office in 1876. He was also a member of the Tea Party Caucus and has been referred to as one of the champions of the Tea Party movement.

Redistricting due to the 2010 census made his district more Democratic, resulting in West switching to Florida's 18th congressional district for the 2012 House elections. However, he lost by 2,146 votes in a very expensive and contentious election against political newcomer, Democrat Patrick Murphy. Allen's defeat was the result of a national effort and goal of the Democrat Party. They knew to put a full effort into defeating this great conservative else they suffer from his national prominence. I hope he continues to run for Congress and wins in spite of the massive liberal socialist democrat's assaults against him. Praise God that Fox News keeps him in the national spotlight.

Clarence Thomas: is an Associate Justice of the Supreme Court; the second Black American to serve on the Court nominated by President George Bush (41) in 1991. Even though he was black, the liberal socialist democrats went berserk – because he was a black "conservative." Imagine that, liberals' greatest fear – a black conservative. Nothing could be more dangerous, to their deceitful plans and the "hustling" of the entire black race, than a black conservative. They better get used to it because millions more are coming! God bless Clarence Thomas for standing strong against these hate mongering liberal socialist democrats.

Condoleezza Rice: Wow, just saw her interviewed by Greta Van Susteren (June 26, 2012). Greta asked her if she would accept the Vice Presidential candidate selection by Mitt Romney if he asked her. She is so intelligent, knowledgeable and graceful. She would make an excellent VP, and President, but you can tell she would not be able to stomach the politics that would come with either job. You could tell Greta was impressed also. It wasn't just foreign policy, but her comments about so many other problems facing America that gives one a gut feeling just how great a national leader she would be.

She is a great illustration of why we can't find more statesmen like George Washington and Abraham Lincoln. Few people of that caliber and character would be able to stomach the stench of politics.

She is also one of the first, of two, women to be given a membership in the ultra-exclusive Masters Golf Club. Congratulations to her!

Mia Love: It is a shame this articulate conservative lost in her bid, in 2012, to become the first black female Republican to be elected to congress in history. She ran against a six-term incumbent and lost by just 768 votes; quite a feat for anyone! I live on a small fixed income so I didn't have much money available to contribute to the 2012 elections. I only gave to three campaigns; Newt Gingrich, Mia Love and E. W. Jackson. That's how impressive I feel these great Americans are.

She is a God fearing, constitutional conservative, Tea Party Patriot that will become a leader in the Republican Party in the future. Mia's parents emigrated from Haiti two years before she was born. What a great story that we're sure to hear more about in the future. This young lady will be back and will be a member of a new class of Republicans that will lead America back to its moral and economic roots. Google Mia Love and give her your support. America needs her!

Dr. Thomas Sowel, PhD: is an American economist, social theorist, political philosopher, and author. He is currently the Rose and Milton Friedman Senior Fellow on Public Policy at the Hoover Institution of Stanford University. He was born in North Carolina in 1930 and grew up in Harlem, New York. He dropped out of high school and joined the Marine Corps (the "ps" is silent Mr. Obama) during the Korean War. He went on to get his education earning his master's degree in 1958 and his

Doctorate in Economics from the University of Chicago in 1968. He is the author of 30 books and is a National Humanities Medal winner; he advocates laissez-faire economics and writes from a conservative and libertarian perspective.

Dr. Sowel has been a guest-host for the Rush Limbaugh radio talk show for several years and is certainly as impressive as Dr. Walter E. Williams, PhD, another favorite of mine. Both men are brilliant and great assets to this Nation. It's a shame the liberal Keynesian idiot, Paul Krugman, is showcased every Sunday on a liberal News Program instead of Dr. Sowel or Dr. Williams. I know Krugman won a Nobel Prize for Economics but so did Friedrich Hayek and Milton Friedman who have polar opposite beliefs as Paul Krugman. Liberal socialist democrats follow John Maynard Keynes and Paul Krugman economic theories; Drs. Sowel and Williams follow the conservative/libertarian economic theories of Friedrich Hayek and Milton Friedman.

Reagan followed the Hayek/Friedman economic theories to recover from the worst recession since the great depression in 1980 – 82 resulting in one of the most robust economies ever that lasted for over two decades. Obama is following the Keynesian/Krugman economic theories resulting in the worst American economic recover since the Great Depression. Krugman argues that we are not doing enough socialist Keynesian programs. See why I called him an idiot…

Dr. Walter E. Williams, PhD: See Chapter 22 for a complete discussion of this great American and his many contributions to our Nation. Dr. Sowel and Dr. Williams are two brilliant economists that should be considered by the next republican president to "Chair" the Federal Reserve Board.

Rear Admiral Barry C. Black: Retired USN was born November 1, 1948 and is the 62nd Chaplain of the United States Senate. He was elected to this position on June 27, 2003 (during a republican senate), becoming the first Black American and the first Seventh-day Adventist to hold this office. The Senate elected its first chaplain in 1789.

> CBN.com – FROM ADVERSITY TO BLESSING: "As the Chaplain of the U.S. Senate, Chaplain Barry Black is a spiritual

leader to the Senate lawmakers, their families, their staffs, and other people who work on the Senate side – about 6,000 people.

Chaplain Black performs traditional pastoral duties, offers one-on-one counseling, and leads weekly Bible studies in the Capital. His mother, Pearline, loved God and taught him life lessons. When she got baptized, she was pregnant with him. God told her she needed to do something for her unborn child. She kept praying for him throughout his life and kept telling him that God created him for something special.

Pearline worked hard to give him a Christian education and instilled in him early a love for the scriptures. He was raised in poor, inner-city public housing in Baltimore, Maryland where crime and drugs were rampant. Chaplain Black's father was a long distance truck driver and was rarely home. His mother was the spiritual leader of the home. When his father was home he drank excessively and rarely spoke. Later, he spent months in jail for not making court-ordered child support payments. Chaplain says his father felt like a stranger for most of his life. Chaplain and his siblings would pray that their father would stop drinking and become a responsible parent. (Eventually his father did come to the Lord.)

Despite these challenges, God gave Chaplain Black a love for learning, a gift of memorization, and good public-speaking skills. He had good relationships with his siblings and good mentors. He accepted the Lord when he was 10 and can't remember a time when he didn't want to preach. He loved the library and church, reading and worshipping God. These kept him out of trouble and on the right path.

Chaplain Black continued these disciplines through his academic and military careers. He is thankful for his problems. Without problems, he wouldn't have discovered God's infinite capacity to make a way when there is no way and to do exceedingly abundantly above all that he could ask or imagine.

CELEBRATE YOUR TROUBLES: Chaplain Black says that most people see adversity and trouble as something negative and try to avoid it whenever possible. However, if we learn to meet our troubles with joy, our adversity can turn to our advantage and God's purposes will be found in our lives.

This guidance is given by the apostle James: "Consider it pure joy, my brothers, whenever you face trials of many kinds, because you know that the testing of your faith develops perseverance. Perseverance must finish its work so that you may be mature and complete, not lacking anything." (James 1:2-4 NIV)

Chaplain Black says a critical thing with adversity is to celebrate troubles. King David understood this when he wrote, "It is good for me that I was afflicted" (Psalm 119:71, ESV). Joseph also learned this when he told his brothers, "You intended to harm me, but God intended it for good to accomplish what is now being done, the saving of many lives. (Genesis 50:20 NIV).

In Romans 8:28 it says… In all things God works for the good of those who love him, who have been called according to his purpose. God can empower you to find blessings in your troubles. Also if we can praise God through adversity we bring honor to Him.

HOW TO HANDLE ADVERSITY: As a nation, we are facing huge troubles, but we need to recognize how brief our troubles are compared to the light of eternity. Life is not just what we experience in this life. Like Jesus told Martha when her brother Lazarus died, "I am the resurrection and the life. He who believes in me will live, even though he dies; and whoever lives and believes in me will never die…"

The apostle Paul learned to see his afflictions as light compared to Christ's (Colossians 1:24). What Paul went through was nothing compared to what Christ went through. Paul was happy to continue in fellowship of Christ's sufferings. We as Christians should be grateful that we fellowship with Christ's sufferings. We should accept the inevitability of trouble and know that we have a choice in how we respond to adversity.

One thing to do in a time of adversity is to guard your tongue. There is a harvest in the words you speak and you can forfeit God's blessings by what you say. As it says in Proverbs 18:21, "The tongue has the power of life and death, and those who love it will eat its fruit (NIV)." Chaplain Black also says where you can, avoid sources of trouble and adversity, especially in cases where we bring adversity on ourselves."

www.cbn.com/700club/guests/bio/barry_black042711.aspx

I simply don't have the space available to mention the tens of thousands of other great Black Americans; for that, I apologize to all God fearing, constitutional conservative, Black Americans who are working, publically and privately, to restore our Nation to the Founder's roots. These brave and courageous Americans are willing to confront the assaults from the Liberal Socialist Democratic Party and their sycophants, armed mostly with their faith in God and the strength of their convictions. God Bless each and every one of them for their sacrifices…

I want to close this chapter with the transcript of a June 2013 YouTube speech by **Louisiana State Senator Elbert Guillory**:

> Hello, my name is Elbert Lee Guillory, and I'm the senator for the twenty-fourth district right here in beautiful Louisiana. Recently I made what many are referring to as a "bold decision" to switch my party affiliation to the Republican Party. I wanted to take a moment to explain why I chose to became a Republican. And also to explain why I don't think it was a bold decision at all. It is the right decision – not only for me – but for all my brothers and sisters in the black community.
>
> You see, in recent history the Democrat Party has created the illusion that their agenda and their policies are what's best for black people. Somehow it's been forgotten that the Republican Party was founded in 1854 as an abolitionist movement with one simple creed: that slavery is a violation of the rights of man.
>
> Frederick Douglass called Republicans the "Party of freedom and progress," and the first Republican president was Abraham Lincoln, the author of the Emancipation Proclamation. It was the Republicans in Congress who authored the thirteenth, fourteenth, and fifteenth amendments giving former slaves citizenship, voting rights, and due process of law.
>
> The Democrats on the other hand were the Party of Jim Crow. It was Democrats who defended the rights of slave owners. It was the Republican President Dwight Eisenhower who championed

the Civil Rights Act of 1957, but it was Democrats in the Senate who filibustered the bill.

You see, at the heart of liberalism is the idea that only a great and powerful big government can be the benefactor of social justice for all Americans. **But the left is only concerned with one thing – control. And they disguise this control as charity.** Programs such as welfare, food stamps – these programs aren't designed to lift black Americans out of poverty; they were always intended as a mechanism for politicians to control the black community.

The idea that blacks, or anyone for that matter, need the government to get ahead in life is despicable. And even more important, this idea is a failure. Our communities are just as poor as they've always been. Our schools continue to fail children. Our prisons are filled with young black men who should be at home being fathers. Our self-initiative and our self-reliance have been sacrificed in exchange for allegiance to our overseers who control us by making us dependent on them.

Sometimes I wonder if the word freedom is tossed around so frequently in our society that it has become a cliché.

The idea of freedom is complex and it is all-encompassing. It's the idea that the economy must remain free of government persuasion. It's the idea that the press must operate without government intrusion. And it's the idea that the emails and phone records of Americans should remain free from government search and seizure. It's the idea that parents must be the decision makers in regards to their children's education – not some government bureaucrat.

But most importantly, it is the idea that the individual must be free to pursue his or her own happiness free from government dependence and free from government control. Because to be truly free is to be reliant on no one – other than the author of our destiny. These are the ideas at the core of the Republican Party, and it is why I am a Republican.

So my brothers and sisters of the American community, please join with me today in abandoning the government plantation and the Party of disappointment. So that we may all echo the words of

> one Republican leader who famously said, "free at last, free at last, thank God Almighty, we are free at last."

Some say Elbert is only trying to get attention. I seriously doubt it because the words he spoke are the absolute truth and I believe God inspired. The LSD Party is already doing a masterful con job of dismissing Guillory, as they always do to conservatives, but they can't dismiss the words he spoke. His words are true and accurate and apply to the liberal socialist democrats and their insidious quest to take over America and "Fundamentally Transform" it to fit their delusional utopian ideas that never seem to work.

They will never give up, so we can't either!

I realize Black Americans vote predominately for the Democrat Party, but I also believe there is a sweeping change coming to America where ALL of our citizens are becoming aware that the Democratic Party is the party of socialists and radical atheists. The liberal socialist democrats are hell bent on grinding the economy to a halt and removing God completely from America.

I pray we don't let that happen…

Chapter 22

Professor Walter E. Williams' books **"The State Against Blacks"** and **"Race and Economics: How Much Can Be Blamed on Discrimination?"** If you're a typical liberal preaching "The Rich get Richer and the Poor get Poorer…" and you haven't read, and studied, Dr. Williams's brilliant and courageous works about racism and poverty then shut-up on the subject until you have!

Think about it – the title is: "The State Against Blacks," meaning the government against blacks. How appropriate is this title and a primary reason for giving economics professor Williams his own chapter in this book. I apologize to him if this attention causes him any grief of any kind. I think he is a great American Patriot who deserves a place in history for his intelligence, insight and courage. His books should be read by everyone who cares about America and is suspicious of the race baiting and race hustling that goes on every day.

Why do the poor suffer the most under socialism? Because they don't have any power connections and are just voting pawns to keep the elites in control. We don't have to wait for the advancing financial catastrophe to see that the poor will suffer the most. Just look at the inter-city housing projects across the country that have been built since the war on poverty began in the 1960's. It's pathetic – with the crime and drug culture. The money should have been spent on suburban housing support to integrate black families into middle class neighborhoods. Also, it was a big mistake to reward single mothers with greater welfare benefits for having more children.

We should have found some mechanism to reward black fathers to stay home and help raise their children. Of course, hindsight is always 20/20 but what is being done now that our leaders have the advantage of hindsight? More liberal socialist democrat policy failures – that's what! We should also examine how the removal of God from society in the 50's and 60's and societies' moral breakdown from the sexual revolution in the 60's has impacted the family structure! Radical atheists have brilliantly used the courts against America and the religious Christian founding of a nation. We fought a revolution in part to escape the power and tyranny of a state controlled religion in England. That tyranny has now been replaced with a much more destructive tyranny of radical atheism.

The words referring to "Separation of Church and State" have been perverted and used against America by these radical atheists. Once God was "kicked-to-the-curb" in the 50's and the liberal left was successful in the 60's in winning the "sexual revolution," America's course was set. Bill O'Reilly is bravely blaming the plight of poor blacks in America in the areas of poverty and crime on the one parent family and black mothers having babies out of wedlock. I wish he would focus on the "root" causes of having babies out of wedlock as passionately as he has been saying to "just stop it." One of the goals of communism and socialism is to remove God and religion from society. It's working!

The insidious advance of socialism has had a huge cost to the world's per capita income and wealth creation and is leading to the greatest depression and wealth destruction in the history of mankind. America is the economic engine of the world; once America falls, the rest of the world is screwed… Why will the poor suffer the most? Why do the economically freest countries have the best standard of living for the poor? Just compare the free-market economies of South Korea and Texas to the socialist economies of North Korea, California and Illinois! Just these two comparisons should be enough to convince the thick headed voters. Why do I say voters instead of politicians? Because most politicians are crooks and don't care… Our focus must be on educating voters to the massive suffering that is in store for us if we don't return America to its moral and free-market roots by voting for God fearing, constitutional conservative republicans.

Here is great review of Dr. Williams' works, history and life that illustrate just how brilliant and courageous this man is:

> Economist Dr. Walter E. Williams, Ph.D., lends a powerful, eloquent voice to the growing chorus of black leaders and academics determined to upset the intellectual applecart in discussions about civil rights and the plight of minorities in the United States. In

books, journal articles, and newspaper columns, Williams marshals economic data and sociological observations to reach a conclusion about blacks in contemporary society – a conclusion that varies sharply from the one offered by many liberal theorists. Rather than attributing economic hardship, crime, unemployment, and other social ills to racism and bigotry, Williams, a self-described radical who abhors the subjugation of individual rights to abstract notions of a greater good, puts the blame squarely on the shoulders of the U.S. Government, whose programs, in his view, have unquestionably hurt the very people they were designed to help."

Whether discussing minimum wage laws, education, social security reform, or affirmative action, Williams spiritedly waves the conservative banner of a free-market society, arguing that government should embrace a narrow scope of interest. He claims that politicians try to accomplish too much and inadvertently create and perpetuate poverty, immorality, and dependency, qualities which society understandably decries. According to Williams, an astonishingly high percentage of the black population has been conditioned to live on welfare and act as unwitting guinea pigs in government programs that teach them to look to others, rather than to themselves, for the means of pursuing rich and productive lives.

Walter Edward Williams was born March 31, 1936, in Philadelphia, Pennsylvania, and was raised there by his mother, Catherine, a day servant, after his father deserted the family when Walter was three. Following his graduation from Philadelphia public schools, Williams drove a taxi for two years, served in the army, and enrolled at California State College in Los Angeles, where he received his undergraduate degree in 1965.

It was during the final stages of his graduate training at the University of California at Los Angeles – he received his M.A. in 1968 and his Ph.D. in 1972 – that Williams first began to question the role government plays in attempting to help citizens who are both politically and economically disenfranchised. After an eight-year teaching stint at Temple University in Philadelphia, Williams moved to George Mason University in Fairfax, Virginia, where he is currently John M. Olin Distinguished Professor of Economics and a sought-out analyst on a broad variety of issues confronting popular culture.

Studying the standard economic questions concerning minimum wage laws, laws which liberals have championed in the name of the common man and woman, Williams grew to believe that such legislation actually increases unemployment. He sees a definite danger in government's acting to effect economic and social change. Of Williams's four books, two – *America: A Minority Viewpoint* and *All It Takes Is Guts* – are collections of his syndicated columns on social and economic topics, which he began writing in 1978. His 1982 work *The State Against Blacks* was his first book length argument that the government, with its myriad social programs, has not been a good friend to blacks and indeed has been a strident enemy to social and economic black progress. Trumpeting deregulation and hands-off government, Williams revisits the dispute over minimum wage legislation and discusses the state's strangulation of entrepreneurial spirit and economic opportunity. He claims that an uneducated poor person in New York City in the 1920s could buy a used car and turn it into a taxi business, but that a cab license, necessary today, is prohibitively expensive.

Reviewing Williams's treatise in *Commentary* magazine, Michael Novak wrote: "This clear and useful book prompts a general observation. Williams is one of several black scholars who are now enriching the economic profession with fresh inquiries into culture, family, and race. Their work is bound to have an impact on future discussions of differences in 'human capital' both in the United States and in the Third World." Christopher Policano, writing in the *Nation,* also praised the book, but argued that Williams had not adequately addressed the lasting economic and psychological impact of the slave institutions that framed the historical experience of blacks brought to the United States against their will.

Consistent with his quest to debunk traditional, and in his opinion simplistic, ways of viewing the world, Williams's 1989 book *South Africa's War Against Capitalism* probes the historic, economic forces that shaped the internationally reviled and alienated apartheid regime of white minority rule there. Williams argues that contrary to popular perception, apartheid was not created as a means for white-owned businesses to exploit the work of the native black majority. He claims that in the early part of the twentieth century, business owners were inclined to hire blacks, but leaders of the communist and socialist movements decried the loss of white-worker jobs and supported the implementation of apartheid's explicit racial separation. After World War I, when many white South Africans returned home to see that their colorblind employers had hired lower wage black workers, the call for separate worker markets was again issued.

In the larger political context, Williams berates what he views as the knee-jerk, naive, and emotional response of the international community to apartheid. Williams contends that the sanctions implemented by many countries, including the United States, merely hurt black South African workers, and the pullout of American and European corporations has enabled white South Africans to buy the companies at deeply discounted prices and operate them without regard for free-market principles or racial equality. In successfully challenging the view that South Africa's political apparatus was originally driven by greedy capitalists, and pointing out that apartheid is fundamentally a socialist-tainted system, Williams is positioned to make a larger, more theoretical point, a point which echoes throughout his writings: that capitalism and free-market forces, without the intervention of government, will engender the freest and least prejudicial society.

The principal intellectual enemy that Williams fights is the belief that all the ills suffered by blacks are rooted in racism. He does not deny the existence of discrimination, only its prevalence and power in spawning so many contemporary social and economic disasters. He contends that the problems in the black community – high unemployment, crime, illiteracy, high illegitimate birth rate – are exacerbated or, at worst created, by social programs that, though well-intentioned, have not been effective.

Some economic experts believe that many leaders – both black and white – view society through the lens of bias, thereby unintentionally provoking discrimination in situations where it did not exist before. Williams contends that affirmative action programs set up by the U.S. government in the 1970s to provide minorities with educational and employment opportunities are one glaring example of this thesis. He attributes the disproportionately few blacks at institutions of higher learning not to discrimination, but to the fact that blacks have historically underperformed against other groups on standardized testing. Many college administrators, in an effort to bolster black presence on campus, have compromised their academic standards of admission for blacks, Williams claims.

The result, he maintains, is not only a misguided policy, but a counterproductive one. "Whatever justification may be given for such a practice, it cannot help but build resentment, bitterness, and a sense of unfair play among whites, as it has already in matters of hiring, promotions, and layoffs," Williams wrote in *National Review* in 1989. "Official policy calling for unequal treatment by race is morally offensive whether it is applied to favor blacks or applied to favor whites."

For Williams, the underlying reason for blacks' poor test performance and for other problems many blacks encounter as adults is the substandard education offered in many secondary public schools, particularly inner-city schools. Again, this is an arena in which the government has woefully failed, he argues. Concurring with conservative doctrine, Williams believes that inadequate funding is not the core impediment to successful public education. The problem, as he sees it, lies in the fact that government has a monopoly on most children's education, and where a monopoly exists, the quality of the product drops. "At the heart of the problem in public education is a system of educational delivery which creates a perverse set of incentives for all parties involved," Williams wrote in *American Education* magazine in 1982. "At the core of the perverse incentives is the fact that the teachers get paid and receive raises whether or not children can read and write; administrators receive their pay whether or not children can read and write. Children (particularly minority children) receive grade promotions and diplomas whether or not they can read and write."

Also contributing to the deterioration of black youth, according to Williams, is the breakdown of the black family – another condition fostered by well-meaning government programs, such as welfare. He argues that state handouts and unearned benefits subsidize behavior that society finds deplorable. He criticizes, for example, the provision of entitlements to women who give birth out of wedlock, claiming that the government is implicitly sanctioning an activity that contributes to the collapse of the black community.

In general, Williams claims the welfare state stymies the development of values that are essential if parents are to properly rear moral, law abiding children who can succeed in school and ultimately, as adults, contribute meaningfully to society. "We don't have the decency to treat poor people the right way," Williams was quoted as saying in the *Christian Science Monitor* in 1991. "We do to them what we would never do to someone that we loved. We want to give the poor money without demanding responsibility. Would you do that to your children? If we love our children, we teach them responsibility."

Leery of the "politically correct" movement, which emphasizes racial and gender sensitivity, Williams goes against the liberal grain on a broad variety of issues. He argues, for instance, against the term "African American" for blacks, claiming that the term is really meaningless. "Africa[n] refers neither to a civilization, a culture, or even a specific country," he wrote in *Society.* "Instead, Africa is a continent consisting of many countries, cultures, ethnic groups, and races. Referring to Africa as a culture reflects near inexcusable ignorance." He claims that American blacks have an ancestral but not a cultural tie to Africa, and, if they are serious in adopting a new name, should look to terms such as Nigerian-American, Ugandan-American, Senegalese-American, etc.

In questioning the far-reaching effects of discrimination, Williams wonders why contemporary black society is in tatters, while the same group of people 30 or 40 years ago, when prejudice was perhaps more widespread, succeeded in building a more cohesive, safe, and morally intact community. His answer lies in government, which, he believes, has strayed from its more legitimate function of law enforcement and entered the arena of social activism.

He argues that black Americans, the supposed beneficiaries of this shift in policy direction, have not fully realized the damage that has been done to them and have been blinded to the cause of many of their most disabling troubles. Black people have bought the "siren song of promises," he said on the television program *Wall Street Week* in 1991. "All Americans in general, but black Americans in particular, have to recognize that government has always been the enemy; that is, blacks were enslaved because government did not do its job."

The Works and Writings of Professor Walter E. Williams, Ph.D.:

- *America: A Minority Viewpoint,* 1982.
- *The State Against Blacks,* New Press, 1982.
- *All It Takes Is Guts,* 1986.
- *South Africa's War Against Capitalism,* Greenwood, 1990.
- Author of articles and columns for various newspapers and journals.

Source: — *Isaac Rosen*
www.answers.com/topic/walter-e-williams#ixzz22cRrOetM

Another third party quote from Wikipedia 4/12/13

Walter Edward Williams (born March 31, 1936) is an American economist, commentator, and academic. He is the John M. Olin Distinguished Professor of Economics at George Mason University, as well as a syndicated columnist and author known for his libertarian views.

Williams family during childhood consisted of himself, his mother, and his sister. His father played no role in raising either child. He grew up in Philadelphia. The family initially lived in West Philadelphia, moving to North Philadelphia and the Richard Allen housing projects when Williams was ten. His neighbors included a young Bill Cosby. Williams knew many of the individuals that Cosby speaks of from his childhood, including Weird Harold and Fat Albert.

Williams was a talented high school student who displayed a very inconsistent performance in his studies. Following high school he came out to stay with his father in California, and attended one semester at Los Angeles City College, in regard to which he would later state that he was not ready yet to be a serious student. In 1959 he was drafted into the military, and served as a Private in the United States Army. While stationed in the south, he waged a one man battle against Jim Crow from inside the army. He challenged the racial order with provocative statements to his fellow soldiers. This resulted in an overseeing officer filing a court-martial proceeding against Williams. Williams argued his own case, and was found not guilty. While considering filing countercharges against the officer that had brought him up for court martial, Williams found himself transferred to Korea. Upon arriving there, Williams marked "Caucasian" for race on his personnel form. When challenged on this, Williams replied wryly if he had marked "Black", he would end up getting all the worst jobs. From Korea Williams wrote a letter to President John F. Kennedy denouncing the pervasive racism in the American government and military, and questioning the actions black Americans should take given the state of affairs, writing:

"Should Negroes be relieved of their service obligation or continue defending and dying for empty promises of freedom and equality? Or should we demand human rights as our Founding Fathers did at the risk of being called extremists. I contend that we relieve ourselves of oppression in a manner that is in keeping with the great heritage of our nation."

He received a reply from the Deputy Assistant Secretary of Defense, Alfred B. Fitt, a response which he termed "the most reasonable response that I received from any official."

Following his military service, he re-entered college as a far more motivated student. Williams earned a Bachelor's Degree (1965) in economics from California State University, Los Angeles. He earned both his Masters Degree (1967) and his Ph.D. (1972) in economics from the University of California, Los Angeles. Speaking of his early college days, Williams says "I was more than anything a radical. I was more sympathetic to Malcolm X than Martin Luther King because Malcolm X was more of a radical who was willing to confront discrimination in ways that I thought it should be confronted, including perhaps the use of violence. But I really just wanted to be left alone. I thought some laws, like minimum-wage laws, helped poor people and poor black people and protected workers from exploitation. I thought they were a good thing until I was pressed by professors to look at the evidence." While at UCLA Williams came into contact with economists such as Armen Alchian, James M. Buchanan, and Axel Leijonhufvud who challenged his assumptions. Never one to be over-awed by others, Williams regularly challenged his professors as well. But on examining the evidence of actual outcomes he came to believe such programs were abject failures. "I learned that you have to evaluate the effects of public policy as opposed to intentions."

While at UCLA, Thomas Sowell arrived on campus in 1969 as a visiting professor. Though he never took a class from Dr. Sowell, the two met and began a friendship that has lasted to this day. In the summer of 1972 Sowell was hired as director of the Urban Institutes Ethnic Minorities Project, which Williams joined shortly thereafter; correspondence between Sowell and Williams appears in the 2007 "A Man of Letters" by Sowell.

Williams has written eight books and hundreds of articles. His syndicated column is published weekly in approximately 140 newspapers across the United States, as well as on several web sites by Creators Syndicate. He also wrote and hosted documentaries for PBS in 1985. The "Good Intentions" documentary was based on his book *The State Against Blacks.*

As an economist, Williams is a proponent of free-market economics and opposes socialist systems of government intervention. "I praise laissez-faire capitalism as being the most moral and most productive system man has ever devised. Capitalism is relatively new in human history. Prior to capitalism, the way people amassed great wealth was by looting, plundering and enslaving their fellow man. Capitalism made it possible to become wealthy by serving your fellow man." In advancing these theories, Williams has said "That's a challenge I love: making economics fun and understandable."

In the mid-to-late 1970s Williams conducted research into the Davis-Bacon Act of 1931 and on the impact of minimum wage laws on minority employment. His research led him to conclude the government's interventional programs were harmful. Among those state programs Williams was critical of were minimum wage and affirmative action laws, stating both practices inhibit liberty and are detrimental to the blacks they are intended to help. He published his results in his 1982 book *The State Against Blacks*, where he argued that laws regulating economic activity are far greater obstacles to economic progress for blacks than racial bigotry and discrimination. Subsequently Williams has spoken on the topic and penned a number of articles detailing his view that increases in the minimum wage price low skill workers out of the market, eliminating their opportunities for employment. Williams believes that racism and the legacy of slavery in the United States are overemphasized as problems faced by the black community today. He points to the crippling effects of a welfare state and the disintegration of the black family as more pressing concerns. "The welfare state has done to black Americans what slavery couldn't do, and that is to destroy the black family" Though in favor of equal access to government institutions such as court houses, city halls and libraries, Williams opposes anti-discrimination laws directed at the private sector on the grounds that such laws infringe upon the people's right of freedom of association.

Williams views gun control laws as a governmental infringement upon the rights of individuals, and argues that they end up endangering the innocent while failing to reduce crime. Williams also makes the argument that the true proof of whether or not an individual owns something is whether or not they have the right to sell it. Taking this argument to its conclusion, he supports legalization of selling one's own bodily organs. He argues that government prohibiting the selling of one's bodily organs is an infringement upon one's property rights, asking "If I don't own my organs, please tell me who does?"

Regarding Federalism, Williams is in favor of power being in the hands of the states, with limited powers being held by the Federal government. He notes this was the design of the nation's founding documents, which were largely undermined by the events of the civil war.

The War between the States settled by force whether states could secede. Once it was established that states cannot secede; the federal government, abetted by a Supreme Court unwilling to hold it to its constitutional restraints, was able to run amok over states' rights, so much so that the protections of the Ninth and Tenth Amendments mean little to nothing today. Not only did the war lay the foundation for eventual nullification or weakening of basic constitutional protections against central government abuses, but it also laid to rest the great principle enunciated in the Declaration of Independence that "Governments are instituted among Men, deriving their just powers from the consent of the governed."

In light of the founding documents, Williams concludes it is the right of U.S. states to secede from the union if they so wish, as several states attempted to do during the Civil War. He has gone on record as advocating the Free State Project in at least two columns and once on television. The Williams endorsement correlated with the largest single membership jump in the first 5000 phase of the project, a jump even higher than the results of the project being Slashdotted.

Williams believes programs such as affirmative action and minimum wage laws set up to aide minorities have, in fact, been harmful to them and stifled their ability to advance in society. "Affirmative action has led to, I believe, many Black people expecting favors from the system and not working as hard as they otherwise would. That is, if you know that you can get into college because of affirmative action – or some people call it diversity nowadays – well then why work as hard in high school? So it might undermine some of the spirit of people. And I think that the basic premise of those who advocate affirmative action is that the problems that Black Americans face today are the result of racial discrimination." In reaction to what he viewed as inappropriate racial sensitivity that he saw hurting blacks in higher education, Williams began in the 1970s to offer colleagues a "certificate of amnesty and pardon" to all white people for Western Civilization's sins against blacks – and "thus obliged them not to act like damn fools in their relationships with Americans of African ancestry." He still offers it to anyone. The certificate can be obtained at his website.

Williams is opposed to the Federal Reserve System. He has also compared U.S. monetary policy to "counterfeiting:" Knowing the dangers posed by central banks, we might ask whether our country needs the Federal Reserve Bank. Whenever I'm told that we need this or that government program, I always ask what we did before. It turns out that we did without a central bank from 1836, when President Andrew Jackson closed the Second Bank of the United States, to 1913 when Federal Reserve Act was written. During that interval, we prospered and became one of the world's major economic powers.

In his work, Williams builds on the economic theories of F. A. Hayek, Ludwig von Mises, Henry Hazlitt, and Milton Friedman, as well as the previously mentioned Thomas Sowell, and he has said of Ayn Rand's 1967 work *Capitalism: The Unknown Ideal* that it is "one of the best defenses and explanations of capitalism one is likely to read."

Besides his weekly columns, Williams has become known nationally as a highly popular guest host before the twenty million listeners of the Rush Limbaugh radio program when Limbaugh is away traveling. *Reason* has called Williams "one of the country's leading libertarian voices." In 2009, Greg Ransom, a writer for the Ludwig von Mises Institute, ranked Williams as the third-most important "Hayekian" Public Intellectual in America, behind only Thomas Sowell and John Stossel.

We may have all come on different ships, but we're in the same boat now. – Martin Luther King, Jr.

Whatever your life's work is, do it well. A man should do his job so well that the living, the dead, and the unborn could do it no better. – Martin Luther King, Jr.

Darkness cannot drive out darkness; only light can do that. Hate cannot drive out hate; only love can do that. – MLK

I have decided to stick with love. Hate is too great a burden to bear. – Martin Luther King, Jr.

Nothing in the world is more dangerous than sincere ignorance and conscientious stupidity. – Martin Luther King, Jr.

Rarely do we find men who willingly engage in hard, solid thinking. There is an almost universal quest for easy answers and half-baked solutions. Nothing pains some people more than having to think. – Martin Luther King, Jr.

An individual has not started living until he can rise above the narrow confines of his individualistic concerns to the broader concerns of all humanity. – Martin Luther King, Jr.

We must learn to live together as brothers or perish together as fools. – Martin Luther King, Jr.

I have a dream that my four little children will one day live in a nation where they will not be judged by the color of their skin, but by the content of their character. – Martin Luther King, Jr.

Chapter 23

Immigration Reform – Let's process Mexican Immigrants and even Mexican Unlawful Permanent Residents separately from other Immigrants!

We should simultaneously start building a massive border fence from the Gulf of Mexico to the Pacific Ocean and establishing each undocumented immigrant; those that came to America before 1/1/11 can stay under certain conditions. If they have no proof or if they came here after that date they will be deported. Give them 6 months to register and after that they will be deported. No more anchor baby citizens. If a Mexican mother crosses the border illegally and immediately has a baby, that baby would get a non-citizen birth certificate. This is an in-your-face sneaky way to circumvent the intent of the law so it's got to stop. They would be deported along with their parents. If the parents are here legally, the child would automatically become a US citizen.

Deportation is an element of our immigration laws so why is it such an ugly term? We are a nation of laws so how can we ignore the law – how can we reward breaking the law. It's got to stop and now is the time. The LSD importation of more democrats (illegal immigrants) is the total purpose of all their whining about fairness. They could care less otherwise. If Hispanic immigrants were more likely to vote for republicans, the LSDs would turn 180 degrees and would do everything in their power to stop Hispanic immigration. Even if Hispanics voted for republicans I believe republican attitudes and beliefs would change very little, if at all. Why? Because the rule of law is a foundation of America and republicans have far more honesty and integrity than the LSD. It's as simple as that…

First, the most recent Immigration legislation (June 2013) passed by the senate and likely rejected by the house is just another liberal socialist hustle of the American public. The total purpose of this senate LSD law is to increase the population of the poor in America, enhancing the likelihood that democrats will be in permanent control of the federal government forever. Liberal socialist democrats don't care about the poor that live here today. They know that bringing another 10+ million Mexicans here, mostly poor Mexicans who will cross the border illegally, will hurt the chances of current Americans (even the unlawful permanent residents here now) to get jobs. Again, liberal socialist democrats don't care; they just want more voters who will believe their socialist propaganda and perpetually vote for democrats.

Other than my suggestions below, our current focus should be solely on completely securing the border and identifying "all" unlawful permanent residents ("UPR") who have been here since 1/1/11. Give these UPRs 6 months to register which will give them the right to remain here legally. This group, some 10 to 30 million, would be given lawful permanent resident ("LPR") status but would never be allowed to become citizens, with voting rights, because they broke our laws and came here illegally. To account for the children who were brought here by their parents we could verify those children who attended elementary school in America and give them the right to apply for citizenship if they graduate from high school. If it could not be verified that they attended school and graduated they could not become citizens but they could have legal status. We have to draw the line somewhere or we might as well have open borders and fire everyone in the federal U.S. Citizenship and Immigration Services Department and kiss the Republican Party and America goodbye.

Here are my suggestions that will likely upset many hard lined believers in much more closed borders:

I believe we need to double size of the United States Department of Citizenship and Immigration Services and create a section that deals solely with Mexican immigrants. According to the US Census Bureau the Hispanic population in America today is over 52 million (expected to grow to 138 million by 2050) with nearly 12 million illegal Mexican immigrants. Why would a self-confessed small government advocate like me make such an expansionary suggestion? The answer is quite simple – because border security and immigration, along with the Department of Defense are two of the primary responsibilities of the federal government. Border and port security are paramount to keep weapons of mass destruction away from our cities and killing Americans in mass.

Our neighbor to the south accounts for the vast majority of immigrants, both legally and illegally, so new resources should be obvious. Additionally, this new department, for Mexicans, should have two sections: The first department would be for those who are already here and a second department for those waiting and wanting to come here from Mexico. By having these separate sections, specialists would be trained and could focus on the unique circumstances of each "class" of Mexican immigrant. It is paramount that we build the "great wall/fence of America" from the Gulf of Mexico to the Pacific Ocean. If a dirty nuclear bomb is set off in a major American city that is brought here through our porous border to the south this suggestion will not seem so absurd, or costly…

All other immigrants, even from Canada and South America, would be processed by the current department. By creating a duplicate Immigration Department just for Mexicans, all other immigrants would receive more attention also. Why am I suggesting this when I am a confessed Tea Party Conservative that believes in limited government and cutting the federal budget? Immigration is the role of the federal government, not education, commerce, energy, housing or several of the other federal departments that would be better handled by the states. Plus it's the right thing to do – the Christian way.

The vast majority of Mexicans are hardworking religious people that have helped to build our nation's economy. By focusing our resources on lawful permanent resident status for the above identified 10 million plus unlawful residents, and a legal path to citizenship for those who qualify, we will all benefit. Republicans should never pander to any group, especially Hispanics; they should focus on what every group wants, which is to experience the freedom and the opportunity to achieve financial independence and to raise their families in a safe environment.

Only free-market constitutional conservative republicans can provide a society where this is possible. We call it the American way; not the French way or the Mexican way or the European way – for a reason. It is the only proven socioeconomic means that has provided the real opportunity for millions of poor immigrants to achieve financial freedom in the history of the world. Socialism does just the opposite – it traps people in poverty and tyranny. Get that point across to every minority, especially Mexican and other Hispanic immigrants, and they will gladly vote for conservative republicans every time. How do you get that point across and distinguish the differences between liberals and conservatives – that's the primary purpose of my writing this book!

Sound bites about the destructive consequences of socialism…

Back to Mexican immigration policy – we should immediately build an American "Great Wall" from the Gulf of Mexico to the Pacific Ocean to completely close off any illegal crossings from the southern border. The LSD party is always crying for federally funded infrastructure jobs building roads and bridges. Why should the people of California, Arizona, New Mexico and Texas pay for rebuilding the roads and bridges in the Northeast and the Great Lakes states? Here is a too simple solution for the brainiacs in DC to think of for themselves: Finance those road and bridge repairs with gas taxes in those regions and allow "scarce" federal dollars be used for National Defense and border security. The "Great Wall" is the responsibility of the federal government, not roads and bridges in different areas of the country.

We are a nation of laws and the first act of coming to America should not be an illegal one. Additionally, a porous border invites drug smugglers, criminals and even terrorists to cross our southern border. Border security is as important to America as a strong national defense. Until an American "Great Wall" is built we should station returning military soldiers on our southern border.

Here are some additional points and suggestions to consider:

- The southwestern states from Texas to California used to be part of Mexico and enjoys a uniquely Mexican culture and heritage;
- Mexico is by far the largest immigrant nation of origin accounting for 27% of the legal immigrants in 1996. 2011 has a similar percentage;
- Mexican Americans make up 10.3% or over 31 million of the US population – nearly the entire population of Canada;
- In October 2008, the illegal immigrant population stood at 11.9 million according to the Pew Hispanic Center;

- We have to confront the fact that we have a significant complex problem with no easy answers, but doing less must be replaced with doing more;
- The drug cartels in Northern Mexico are one of the greatest threats to America's safety and security;
- We need to process those Mexicans wanting to come to America alongside those who are already here; and,
- Once we reform our welfare, Medicare and Social Security systems we can benefit from more consumers creating more business and more workers paying more taxes.

Newt Gingrich was criticized in the 2012 presidential republican debates for his "compassionate" stance on dealing with the illegals that are now in this country. I though he was courageous and right then and now we see all these Johnny-come-lately republicans agreeing with much of what he said. Again, Gingrich was the smartest guy in the room. How can we remove someone who has lived here for decades and has raised a family here? They should go to the head of the new line created especially for them; but they should never obtain US citizenship unless they go to back to Mexico and get in the "legal" line.

Now, after Mitt Romney lost the election, along with the majority of Hispanic voters, the pundits on both sides are blaming and clamoring for answers. It's as simple as what Newt Gingrich said in the debates and what I am illustrating throughout this book. Everyone wants a better life – especially the poor and disenfranchised. Professor Walter E. Williams, Ph.D. is a brilliant economist and an expert on the failings of government sponsored welfare programs designed by liberal socialist democrats. If Mexicans knew what Dr. Williams knows they would never vote for another democrat. We're not teaching this in every school, grades 1 through 12, because the democrats control the public schools and university systems!

Conservative Republican Arizona's US Senator Jeff Flake's website:

> One of the primary functions of the federal government is to provide national security, which includes border security. With a

southern border so porous, and increasingly dangerous, the federal government continues to fail in this most basic function.

In the past, I have supported a broad approach to immigration reform – increased border security coupled with a temporary worker program. I no longer do. I've been down that road, and it is a dead end. The political realities in Washington are such that a comprehensive solution is not possible, or even desirable given the current leadership. Border security must be addressed before other reforms are tackled.

Most importantly, the situation along the border has changed significantly. In years past, groups of illegal aliens crossing the southern border tied to drug or smuggling cartels were the exception to the rule. Today, such ties are the rule. The lawless situation in northern Mexico largely driven by drug cartels is fueling lawlessness north of the border. Such a situation calls for an exclusive focus on border security.

Once we've secured the border we still face considerable immigration challenges, like the fact that nearly half of the illegal aliens residing in the United States didn't sneak across the border – they came legally and have overstayed their visas. But we have to focus on border security first.

The great American war hero and Senior US Senator from Arizona, John S. McCain should have been our 44th president. I was so impressed with his selection of Sarah Palin as his running mate and his moral honor and character in how he handled his presidential campaign, especially his defense of Sarah when the LSD and their slobbering sycophants attacked her. He has been a major force in America's efforts to solve our immigration issues and should be a central figure in future solutions, but I feel he is too aligned with the liberals on immigration and I no longer trust him to do the right thing for our future. I agree much more with Senator Flake.

My suggestions above may differ from these two senators views, and I acknowledge their superior knowledge and experience, but my idea of significantly expanding the United States Department of Citizenship and Immigration Services and create a separate department with two distinct sections that deals solely with Mexican immigrants may have merit.

Chapter 24

A Nation of Codependent Socialist Enablers!

Socialist leaders are a pathetic group of narcissists, control freaks, pathological liars; and power, money and fame addicts... The democrat voters, like all codependent enablers, are either: too lazy, ignorant, stupid or naïve to see they're being hustled.

Codependency is defined as a psychological condition or a relationship in which a person is controlled or manipulated by another who is affected with a pathological condition (typically narcissism or drug addiction); and in broader terms, it refers to the dependence on the needs of or control of another. Codependency can occur in any type of relationship, including family, work, friendship, and also romantic, peer or community relationships. Codependency may also be characterized by denial, low self-esteem, excessive compliance, or control patterns. Narcissists are considered to be natural magnets for the codependent.

Historically, the concept of codependence "comes directly out of Alcoholics Anonymous, part of a dawning realization that the problem was not solely the addict, but also the family and friends who constitute a network for the alcoholic." It was subsequently broadened to cover the way "that the codependent person is fixated on another person for approval, sustenance, and so on."

Codependent Enabler is defined by one who lies or makes excuses for an addict or control-freak. Enablers make it easier for the addict or control-freak to continue their destructive behaviors, and are reinforced by a person's need to be needed or belong. Why is enabling so destructive to all parties – because it delays or circumvents any healing that might occur if the addict did not have the codependent relationship.

Narcissism is a generalized personality trait characterized by egotism, vanity, conceit, or selfishness. However, *narcissism* has subsequently included particular meanings in specific fields, including:

- A central concept of psychoanalytic theory
- A mental illness
- A social or cultural problem
- A personality trait

Except in the sense of primary narcissism or healthy self-love, narcissism is usually considered a problem in a person or group's relationships with self and others.

I was so impressed with New Jersey Governor Chris Christie when he first came on the national scene. Before the Republican National Convention in 2012, I considered him to be an exciting contender for a future nomination. I no longer do, and here's why: he was the key note speaker at Mitt Romney's nomination and his speech was a narcissistic narrative about how great he was and how other republicans should be like him. Then came his love affair with President Barrack Obama on the Jersey Shore after hurricane Sandy. Sure, I don't blame him for schmoozing the President for as much federal funds as he could get. No, what I can't understand is his naive belief that once the photo op was over that he would get any special treatment. Those photo ops along with not promoting Mitt Romney, which is the "only" purpose of the key note speaker, hurt this country's chances to stop Obama's liberal socialist agenda at four years. Instead look at the mess we are now (February 2013) in and we're only one month into his second term.

Governor Christy has done a great job and certainly is a conservative, but tonight, February 27, 2013, Fox showed him in a news conference talking to a little girl in the audience. She asked him what the most fun thing he does as governor was. He gave a serious answer, and a fun answer – the fun answer was the most telling. He told the little girl (and everyone in the room and on TV) that the most fun thing he does is go to NY City, with his wife, because they close down the tunnel just for him. He also gave the impression that he had a police escort down one way streets (the wrong way). I don't care if he's the most conservative guy in America and can win any election. He's an inconsiderate narcissist that thinks it is fun, and his privilege, to inconvenience thousands of citizens in New Jersey and New York. How many of them think it's cool and fun to be tied up in traffic because of another self-centered politician. We have thousands of politicians everywhere with this kind of attitude. It's pathetic! Also, how much money does each of his trips cost the tax payers?

Let's see, Senator Rand Paul saved hundreds of thousands of his annual office budget and turned the money back to the Treasury. We need a thousand less Chris Christie(s) in government and a thousand more Rand Paul(s). I don't give a crap if they're republicans or democrats; let's throw all of the self-centered money wasting bums out of office. See the review of Peter Schweizer's book: "Throw Them All Out" in Chapter 30. If we don't learn about the candidates and get rid of those that are helping to bankrupt America, we have nobody to blame but ourselves.

> **Control Freaks** are often perfectionists defending themselves against their own inner vulnerabilities in the belief that if they are not in total control they risk exposing themselves once more to childhood angst. Such persons manipulate and pressure others to change so as to avoid having to change themselves, and use power over others to escape an inner emptiness. When a control freak's pattern is broken, "the Controller is left with a terrible feeling of powerlessness... But feeling their pain and fear brings them back to themselves.
>
> In terms of personality-type theory, control freaks are very much the Type A personality, driven by the need to dominate and control. An obsessive need to control others is also associated with antisocial personality disorder.
>
> Wikipedia.org/wiki/Control_freak
>
> **Pathological Liars** are far different from the casual liar trying to avoid problems. Lying is the act of both knowingly and intentionally/willfully making a false statement. Most people do so out of fear. Pathological lying is considered a mental illness, because it

takes over rational judgment and progresses into the fantasy world and back.

Excessive lying is a common symptom of several mental illnesses. For instance people who suffer from antisocial personality disorder use lying to benefit from others. Some individuals with borderline personality disorder lie for attention by claiming they've been treated poorly (though it is not diagnostic). **Pathological lying, on the other hand, can be described as an addiction to lying.** It is when an individual consistently lies for no personal gain. The lies are commonly transparent and often seem rather pointless.

There are many consequences of being a pathological liar. Due to lack of trust, most pathological liars' relationships and friendships fail. If the disease continues to progress, lying could become so severe as to cause legal problems, including but not limited to fraud.

Psychotherapy appears to be one of the only methods to treat a person suffering from pathological lying. No research has been performed regarding the use of pharmaceutical medication to treat pathological liars. Some research suggests that certain people may have a predisposition to lying.

Wikipedia.org Pathological Liars

I watch FOX News daily (imagine that) and I have come to the conclusion that most of the liberal socialist democrat guests have their PhDs in not answering any direct question. They are masters of not answering questions that would lead to the truth and a better understanding of the topic being discussed. In other words they distort, deflect and just outright lie; all part of the planned deception or hustle. It doesn't matter how many times the question is pleaded to be answered; the guests will deflect and say "so – blah, blah, blah…" It is as truly amazing as it is frustrating to watch them get away with it. If I were interviewing these twits I would ask the question and then before they can answer I would tell the audience that "they are not allowed, by their leaders, to answer the question directly or truthfully and will likely say: So – blah, blah, blah… or they will lose their liberal socialist democrat club membership."

In other words I would make fun of them if they deflected answering the question again.

Here is the pathetic part – roughly 40% of the American population can't tell these guests are manipulating the interview for their liberal socialist propaganda and in most cases are lying with such boldness that it would make Bill Clinton proud. Don't believe me? The next time you see a liberal socialist democrat being asked a question they don't want to answer you will them start their verbal deflection with the word "So" – and then began their babbling propaganda.

Dumb ass republicans that also use this routine need to be called out and learn to clearly and honestly answer questions and then dissect the topic in the most articulate conservative and straight forward way possible. If the interviewer is leading you into a "gotcha trap" be straight forward (like Newt did with Chris Wallace in the 2012 republican presidential primary debates) and call them out on it. If they don't want to have an honest debate of ideas then shame them into looking like the liberal hacks they are.

Below is a website that I discovered while researching the subjects of this chapter. It is one of the most interesting and "telling" concepts that describe liberal socialist democrats and their slobbering sycophants in mainstream media, Hollywood and Madison Avenue…

> **Power/Money/Esteem** addicts are, by far, the most destructive of all addicts because they will do anything to protect and trigger dopamine flow (the natural high drug like chemical produced in the brain). They abhor truth and ruthlessly lie, cheat, steal, bribe, corrupt, demean, persecute, attack, destroy, and/or crush. To make matters worse, their addictions provide them with the resources that make it possible to ignore, obfuscate, or eliminate any and all threats to their dopamine flow. It doesn't help that insatiable dopamine cravings keep power, money, esteem addicts scrambling for the degrees, positions, and power that allow them to define what are and aren't addictions. Which is why you aren't reading this on thousands of, or any, other sites.
>
> Power/money/esteem addictions are the reason our species is flirting with self-annihilation.

Source: "Why Power/Money/Esteem Addicts are more Dangerous than Junkies," by Charles Lyell 1/19/13, dopamineproject.org

Wow… That short paragraph, plus the word "arrogant," succinctly and completely describes the pathologies of the LSD Party and their sycophants in the news media, Hollywood and Madison Avenue.

Chapter 25

The Author's "Dream Team" of God fearing Constitutional and Tea Party Conservatives with the "Right Stuff" to lead our Nation and restore America's global reputation…

I pray that Dr. Ben Carson, MD will run for president in 2016. I realize he has no experience in politics but I see that as a plus, not a minus. He is highly intelligent and has the same Godly characteristics of George Washington and Abraham Lincoln, which is what America desperately needs. Like any good chief executive he would be able to put together a team of experts in their respective fields that share his core beliefs and values. I don't know if he could stomach the slander and hate from the left that would be assailed against him, but I know America would benefit from his candidacy and certainly his presidency… In any event, here are my recommendations of the likely GOP candidates. The first one might sound like a crazy combination but bear me out and give it serious thought:

- 2016 US President Dr. Ben Carson, MD (then age 65), running mate South Carolina Governor Nikki Haley (then age 44) or Texas Governor Rick Perry (then age 66). Think about it Dr. Carson would be like the Chairman/CEO promoting the "new" culture of our government and Nikki Haley or Rick Perry would be like the President/Chief Operating Officer of a large corporation. Rick has been the Governor of the second largest state, and best economy, in America. He has been a highly successful and passionate advocate of growing the highly successful economy of Texas. He also knows how many states we have in America, how to pronounce corpsman and which ports are on the Gulf of Mexico! Forget his "forgot" moment – he handled it with grace and humility – something lacking in most politicians today where arrogance and narcissism are the typical characteristics…

- 2024 President Rand Paul (then age 62) in a landslide with Vice President Paul Ryan (then age 55) because America would be enjoying a robust economy with more jobs than ever. We would have returned to "fiscal" responsibility along with beginning the dismantling of big government and the leviathan of tens of millions of overlapping and strangling laws, rules and regulations;
- 2028 GOP Ticket of Paul Ryan (then age 59) and Ted Cruz (then 53) or Marco Rubio (then age 57) in another landslide victory because America would be enjoying unprecedented freedom and prosperity for every American especially the poorest class; and,

Here is President Obama's 2013 State of the Union address with my brief comments in **[bold]**, followed by GOP Senator Rand Paul's Tea Party alternative rebuttal speech. I did not include Senator Marco Rubio's GOP rebuttal speech because of space limitations and my impression that Senator Paul's speech was a better representation of the conservative Tea Party movement's issues and solutions. If we could elect both of these two great Americans as President and Vice President in 2016 – 2024 along with a conservative Tea Party movement majority in both houses of Congress we will, in all likelihood, return American to a path of widespread freedom and prosperity. This chapter closes with an outstanding speech by an outstanding American who, if he had been elected America's first Black President in 2008 this country would now be back on track to freedom and prosperity for everyone, especially the poorest among us. I added my **[comments]** in bold brackets at the end of dubious paragraphs.

The President's 2013 State of the Union Address:

Mr. Speaker, Mr. Vice President, Members of Congress, fellow citizens:

Fifty-one years ago, John F. Kennedy declared to this Chamber that "the Constitution makes us not rivals for power but partners for progress"… "It is my task," he said, "to report the State of the Union – to improve it is the task of us all."

Tonight, thanks to the grit and determination of the American people, there is much progress to report. After a decade of grinding war, our brave men and women in uniform are coming home. After years of grueling recession, our businesses have created over six million new jobs. **[Part-time?]** We buy more American cars than we have in five years, and less foreign oil than we have in twenty.

Our housing market is healing, our stock market is rebounding, and consumers, patients, and homeowners enjoy stronger protections than ever before. Together, we have cleared away the rubble of crisis, and can say with renewed confidence that the state of our union is stronger. **[Than when?]** But we gather here knowing that there are millions of Americans whose hard work and dedication have not yet been rewarded. Our economy is adding jobs – but too many people still can't find full-time employment. Corporate profits have rocketed to all-time highs – but for more than a decade, wages and incomes have barely budged. **[Many studies show they have fallen.]**

It is our generation's task, then, to reignite the true engine of America's economic growth – a rising, thriving middle class. It is our unfinished task to restore the basic bargain that built this country – the idea that if you work hard and meet your responsibilities, you can get ahead, no matter where you come from, what you look like, or who you love.

It is our unfinished task to make sure that this government works on behalf of the many, and not just the few; that it encourages free enterprise, rewards individual initiative, and opens the doors of opportunity to every child across this great nation.

The American people don't expect government to solve every problem. They don't expect those of us in this chamber to agree on every issue. But they do expect us to put the nation's interests before party. They do expect us to forge reasonable compromise where we can. For they know that America moves forward only when we do so together; and that the responsibility of improving this union remains the task of us all. Our work must begin by making some basic decisions about our budget – decisions that will have a huge impact on the strength of our recovery.

Over the last few years, both parties have worked together to reduce the deficit by more than $2.5 trillion – mostly through spending cuts, but also by raising tax rates on the wealthiest 1 percent of Americans. As a result, we are more than halfway towards the goal of $4 trillion in deficit reduction that economists say we need to stabilize our finances. **[Here comes the case for socialism]**

Now we need to finish the job. And the question is, how?

In 2011, Congress passed a law saying that if both parties couldn't agree on a plan to reach our deficit goal, about a trillion dollars' worth of budget cuts would automatically go into effect this year. These sudden, harsh, arbitrary cuts would jeopardize our military readiness. They'd devastate priorities like education, energy, and medical research. They would certainly slow our recovery, and cost us hundreds of thousands of jobs. That's why Democrats, Republicans, business leaders, and economists have already said that these cuts, known here in Washington as "the sequester," are a really bad idea.

Now, some in this Congress have proposed preventing only the defense cuts by making even bigger cuts to things like education and job training; Medicare and Social Security benefits.

That idea is even worse. Yes, the biggest driver of our long-term debt is the rising cost of health care for an aging population. And those of us who care deeply about programs like Medicare must embrace the need for modest reforms – otherwise, our retirement programs will crowd out the investments we need for our children, and jeopardize the promise of a secure retirement for future generations **[What the hell is he talking about? It is an LSD government monopoly unionized education industry that has dumbed down our poor kids]**.

But we can't ask senior citizens and working families to shoulder the entire burden of deficit reduction while asking nothing more from the wealthiest and most powerful. We won't grow the middle class simply by shifting the cost of health care or college onto families that are already struggling, or by forcing communities to lay off more teachers, cops, and firefighters. Most Americans – Democrats, Republicans, and Independents – understand that we can't just cut our way to prosperity. They know that broad-based economic growth requires a balanced approach to deficit reduction, with spending cuts and revenue, and with everybody doing their fair share. And that's the approach I offer tonight. **[That's right – take the investment and working capital of the millions of small businesses, the job generators, and redistribute it to your cronies and your voters… The hell with jobs!]**

On Medicare, I'm prepared to enact reforms that will achieve the same amount of health care savings by the beginning of the next decade as the reforms proposed by the bipartisan Simpson-Bowles commission. Already, the Affordable Care Act is helping to slow the growth of health care costs. **[Truth is unavoidable]** The reforms I'm proposing go even further. We'll reduce taxpayer subsidies to prescription drug companies and ask more from the wealthiest seniors. We'll bring down costs by changing the way our government pays for Medicare, because our medical bills shouldn't be based on the number of tests ordered or days spent in the hospital – they should be based on the quality of care that our seniors receive. And I am open to additional reforms from both parties, so long as they don't violate the guarantee of a secure retirement. Our government shouldn't make promises we cannot keep – but we must keep the promises we've already made. **[Wow!]**

To hit the rest of our deficit reduction target, we should do what leaders in both parties have already suggested, and save hundreds of billions of dollars by getting rid of tax loopholes and deductions for the well-off and well-connected. After all, why would we choose to make deeper cuts to education and Medicare just to protect special interest tax breaks? How is that fair? How does that promote growth?

Now is our best chance for bipartisan, comprehensive tax reform that encourages job creation and helps bring down the deficit. The American people deserve a tax code that helps small businesses spend less time filling out complicated forms, and more time expanding and hiring; a tax code that ensures billionaires with high-powered accountants can't pay a lower rate than their hard-working secretaries; a tax code that lowers incentives to move jobs overseas, and lowers tax rates for businesses and manufacturers that create jobs right here in America. That's what tax reform can deliver. That's what we can do together. **[Did Paul Ryan write this paragraph?]**

I realize that tax reform and entitlement reform won't be easy. The politics will be hard for both sides. None of us will get 100 percent of what we want. But the alternative will cost us jobs, hurt our economy, and visit hardship on millions of hardworking Americans. So let's set party interests aside, and work to pass a budget that replaces reckless cuts with smart savings and wise investments in our future. And let's do it without the brinksmanship that stresses consumers and scares off investors. The greatest nation on Earth cannot keep conducting its business by drifting from one manufactured crisis to the next. Let's agree, right here, right now, to keep the people's government open, pay our bills on time, and always uphold the full faith and credit of the United States of America. The American people have worked too hard, for too long, rebuilding from one crisis to see their elected officials cause another. **[Sounds too good to be true – what's he up to?]**

Now, most of us agree that a plan to reduce the deficit must be part of our agenda. But let's be clear: deficit reduction alone is not an economic plan. A growing economy that creates good, middle-class jobs – that must be the North Star that guides our efforts. Every day, we should ask ourselves three questions as a nation: How do we attract more jobs to our shores? How do we equip our people with the skills needed to do those jobs? And how do we make sure that hard work leads to a decent living? **[Who is his republican speech writer?]**

A year and a half ago, I put forward an American Jobs Act that independent economists said would create more than one million new jobs. I thank the last Congress for passing some of that agenda, and I urge this Congress to pass the rest. Tonight, I'll lay out additional proposals that are fully paid for and fully consistent with the budget framework both parties agreed to just 18 months ago. Let me repeat – nothing I'm proposing tonight should increase our deficit by a single dime. It's not a bigger government we need, but a smarter government that sets priorities and invests in broad-based growth. **[Amazing!]**

Our first priority is making America a magnet for new jobs and manufacturing. After shedding jobs for more than 10 years, our manufacturers have added about 500,000 jobs over the past three. Caterpillar is bringing jobs back from Japan. Ford is bringing jobs back from Mexico. After locating plants in other countries like China, Intel is opening its most advanced plant right here at home. And this year, Apple will start making Macs in America again. **[Thank you business.]**

There are things we can do, right now, to accelerate this trend. Last year, we created our first manufacturing innovation institute in Youngstown, Ohio. A once-shuttered warehouse is now a state-of-the art lab where new workers are mastering the 3D printing that has the potential to revolutionize the way we make almost everything. There's no reason this can't happen in other towns. So tonight, I'm announcing the launch of three more of these manufacturing hubs, where businesses will partner with the Departments of Defense and Energy to turn regions left behind by globalization into global centers of high-tech jobs. And I ask this Congress to help create a network of fifteen of these hubs and guarantee that the next revolution in manufacturing is Made in America. **[Sounds good on the surface – let's see the details.]**

If we want to make the best products, we also have to invest in the best ideas. Every dollar we invested to map the human genome returned $140 to our economy. Today, our scientists are mapping the human brain to unlock the answers to Alzheimer's; developing drugs to regenerate damaged organs; devising new material to make batteries ten times more powerful. Now is not the time to gut these job-creating investments in science and innovation. Now is the time to reach a level of research and development not seen since the height of the Space Race. And today, no area holds more promise than our investments in American energy. **[Excellent, our businesses are the best!]**

After years of talking about it, we are finally poised to control our own energy future. We produce more oil at home than we have in 15 years. We have doubled the distance our cars will go on a gallon of gas, and the amount of renewable energy we generate from sources like wind and solar – with tens of thousands of good, American jobs to show for it. We produce more natural gas than ever before – and nearly everyone's energy bill is lower because of it. And over the last four years, our emissions of the dangerous carbon pollution that threatens our planet have actually fallen. **[Energy production in spite of you.]**

But for the sake of our children and our future, we must do more to combat climate change. Yes, it's true that no single event makes a trend. But the fact is, the 12 hottest years on record have all come in the last 15. Heat waves, droughts, wildfires, and floods – all are now more frequent and intense. We can choose to believe that Superstorm Sandy, and the most severe drought in decades, and the worst wildfires some states have ever seen were all just a freak coincidence. Or we can choose to believe in the overwhelming judgment of science – and act before it's too late. **[Just an excuse to funnel billions to cronies.]**

The good news is, we can make meaningful progress on this issue while driving strong economic growth. I urge this Congress to pursue a bipartisan, market-based solution to climate change, like the one John McCain and Joe Lieberman worked on together a few years ago. But if Congress won't act soon to protect future generations, I will. I will direct my Cabinet to come up with executive actions we can take, now and in the future, to reduce pollution, prepare our communities for the consequences of climate change, and speed the transition to more sustainable sources of energy. **[Who cares about the constitution?]**

Four years ago, other countries dominated the clean energy market and the jobs that came with it. We've begun to change that. Last year, wind energy added nearly half of all new power capacity in America. So let's generate even more. Solar energy gets cheaper by the year – so let's drive costs down even further. As long as countries like China keep going all-in on clean energy, so must we. **[$$$ to his cronies!]**

In the meantime, the natural gas boom has led to cleaner power and greater energy independence. That's why my Administration will keep cutting red tape and speeding up new oil and gas permits. But I also want to work with this Congress to encourage the research and technology that helps natural gas burn even cleaner and protects our air and water. **[Words are worthless without actions to back them…]**

Indeed, much of our new-found energy is drawn from lands and waters that we, the public, own together. So tonight, I propose we use some of our oil and gas revenues to fund an Energy Security Trust that will drive new research and technology to shift our cars and trucks off oil for good. If a non-partisan coalition of CEOs and retired generals and admirals can get behind this idea, then so can we. Let's take their advice and free our families and businesses from the painful spikes in gas prices we've put up with for far too long. I'm also issuing a new goal for America: let's cut in half the energy wasted by our homes and businesses over the next twenty years. The states with the best ideas to create jobs and lower energy bills by constructing more efficient buildings will receive federal support to help make it happen. **[Agreed.]**

America's energy sector is just one part of an aging infrastructure badly in need of repair. Ask any CEO where they'd rather locate and hire: a country with deteriorating roads and bridges, or one with high-speed rail and internet; high-tech schools and self-healing power grids. The CEO of Siemens America – a company that brought hundreds of new jobs to North Carolina – has said that if we upgrade our infrastructure, they'll bring even more jobs. And I know that you want these job-creating projects in your districts. I've seen you all at the ribbon-cuttings. **[State and local tax-free revenues bonds – please.]**

Tonight, I propose a "Fix-It-First" program to put people to work as soon as possible on our most urgent repairs, like the nearly 70,000 structurally deficient bridges across the country. And to make sure taxpayers don't shoulder the whole burden, I'm also proposing a Partnership to Rebuild America that attracts private capital to upgrade what our businesses need most: modern ports to move our goods; modern pipelines to withstand a storm; modern schools worthy of our children. Let's prove that there is no better place to do business than the United States of America. And let's start right away. **[Some good, some bad.]**

Part of our rebuilding effort must also involve our housing sector. Today, our housing market is finally healing from the collapse of 2007. Home prices are rising at the fastest pace in six years, home purchases are up nearly 50 percent, and construction is expanding again.

But even with mortgage rates near a 50-year low, too many families with solid credit who want to buy a home are being rejected. Too many families who have never missed a payment and want to refinance are being told no. That's holding our entire economy back, and we need to fix it. Right now, there's a bill in this Congress that would give every responsible homeowner in America the chance to save $3,000 a year by refinancing at today's rates. Democrats and Republicans have supported it before. What are we waiting for? Take a vote, and send me that bill. Right now, overlapping regulations keep responsible young families from buying their first home. What's holding us back? Let's streamline the process, and help our economy grow. **[Government meddling!]**

These initiatives in manufacturing, energy, infrastructure, and housing will help entrepreneurs and small business owners expand and create new jobs. But none of it will matter unless we also equip our citizens with the skills and training to fill those jobs. And that has to start at the earliest possible age. **[Then end the government/union monopoly that has restricted new innovations and successes – such as Charter Schools, especially for the inter-city poor!]**

Study after study shows that the sooner a child begins learning, the better he or she does down the road. But today, fewer than 3 in 10 four year-olds are enrolled in a high-quality preschool program. Most middle-class parents can't afford a few hundred bucks a week for private preschool. And for poor kids who need help the most, this lack of access to preschool education can shadow them for the rest of their lives.

Tonight, I propose working with states to make high-quality preschool available to every child in America. Every dollar we invest in high-quality early education can save more than seven dollars later on – by boosting graduation rates, reducing teen pregnancy, even reducing violent crime. In states that make it a priority to educate our youngest children, like Georgia or Oklahoma, studies show students grow up more likely to read and do math at grade level, graduate high school, hold a job, and form more stable families of their own. So let's do what works, and make sure none of our children start the race of life already behind. Let's give our kids that chance. **[More government deficits!]**

Let's also make sure that a high school diploma puts our kids on a path to a good job. Right now, countries like Germany focus on graduating their high school students with the equivalent of a technical degree from one of our community colleges, so that they're ready for a job. At schools like P-Tech in Brooklyn, a collaboration between New York Public Schools, the City University of New York, and IBM, students will graduate with a high school diploma and an associate degree in computers or engineering. **[Then get rid of teachers' unions!]**

We need to give every American student opportunities like this. Four years ago, we started Race to the Top – a competition that convinced almost every state to develop smarter curricula and higher standards, for about 1 percent of what we spend on education each year. Tonight, I'm announcing a new challenge to redesign America's high schools so they better equip graduates for the demands of a high-tech economy. We'll reward schools that develop new partnerships with colleges and employers, and create classes that focus on science, technology, engineering, and math – the skills today's employers are looking for to fill jobs right now and in the future. **[Just privatize and get!]**

Now, even with better high schools, most young people will need some higher education. It's a simple fact: the more education you have, the more likely you are to have a job and work your way into the middle class. But today, skyrocketing costs price way too many young people out of a higher education, or saddle them with unsustainable debt.

Through tax credits, grants, and better loans, we have made college more affordable for millions of students and families over the last few years. But taxpayers cannot continue to subsidize the soaring cost of higher education. Colleges must do their part to keep costs down, and it's our job to make sure they do. Tonight, I ask Congress to change the Higher Education Act, so that affordability and value are included in determining which colleges receive certain types of federal aid. And tomorrow, my Administration will release a new "College Scorecard" that parents and students can use to compare schools based on a simple criteria: where you can get the most bang for your educational buck. **[I love his conservative republican/libertarian speech writer that is writing "some" of this speech; if he puts words to action.]**

To grow our middle class, our citizens must have access to the education and training that today's jobs require. But we also have to make sure that America remains a place where everyone who's willing to work hard has the chance to get ahead.

Our economy is stronger when we harness the talents and ingenuity of striving, hopeful immigrants. And right now, leaders from the business, labor, law enforcement, and faith communities all agree that the time has come to pass comprehensive immigration reform. Real reform means strong border security, and we can build on the progress my Administration has already made – putting more boots on the southern border than at any time in our history, and reducing illegal crossings to their lowest levels in 40 years. **[Just build the fence and enforce our existing laws before you try to import more democrats…]**

Real reform means establishing a responsible pathway to earned citizenship – a path that includes passing a background check, paying taxes and a meaningful penalty, learning English, and going to the back of the line behind the folks trying to come here legally. And real reform means fixing the legal immigration system to cut waiting periods, reduce bureaucracy, and attract the highly-skilled entrepreneurs and engineers that will help create jobs and grow our economy. In other words, we know what needs to be done. As we speak, bipartisan groups in both chambers are working diligently to draft a bill, and I applaud their efforts. Now let's get this done. Send me a comprehensive immigration reform bill in the next few months, and I will sign it right away.

But we can't stop there. We know our economy is stronger when our wives, mothers, and daughters can live their lives free from discrimination in the workplace, and free from the fear of domestic violence. Today, the Senate passed the Violence Against Women Act that Joe Biden originally wrote almost 20 years ago. I urge the House to do the same. And I ask this Congress to declare that women should earn a living equal to their efforts, and finally pass the Paycheck Fairness Act this year. We know our economy is stronger when we reward an honest day's work with honest wages. But today, a full-time worker making the minimum wage earns $14,500 a year. Even with the tax relief we've put in place, a family with two kids that earns the minimum wage still lives below the poverty line. That's wrong. That's why, since the last time this Congress raised the minimum wage, nineteen states have chosen to bump theirs even higher. **[More laws, more lawyers, less jobs, less wealth, less freedom, more tyranny – just what we need…]**

Tonight, let's declare that in the wealthiest nation on Earth, no one who works full-time should have to live in poverty, and raise the federal minimum wage to $9.00 an hour. This single step would raise the incomes of millions of working families. It could mean the difference between groceries or the food bank; rent or eviction; scraping by or finally getting ahead. For businesses across the country, it would mean customers with more money in their pockets. In fact, working folks shouldn't have to wait year after year for the minimum wage to go up while CEO pay has never been higher. So here's an idea that Governor Romney and I actually agreed on last year: let's tie the minimum wage to the cost of living, so that it finally becomes a wage you can live on. **[Someone please buy the president the brilliant book by world renowned Professor Walter E. Williams titled: *The State Against Blacks.* That's right the state (government) against blacks so that he can comprehend this destructive socialist job killing policy.]**

Tonight, let's also recognize that there are communities in this country where no matter how hard you work, it's virtually impossible to get ahead. Factory towns decimated from years of plants packing up. Inescapable pockets of poverty, urban and rural, where young adults are still fighting for their first job. America is not a place where chance of birth or circumstance should decide our destiny. And that is why we need to build new ladders of opportunity into the middle class for all who are willing to climb them. **[Wow, Marx would be proud.]**

Let's offer incentives to companies that hire Americans who've got what it takes to fill that job opening, but have been out of work so long that no one will give them a chance. Let's put people back to work rebuilding vacant homes in run-down neighborhoods. And this year, my Administration will begin to partner with 20 of the hardest-hit towns in America to get these communities back on their feet. We'll work with local leaders to target resources at public safety, education, and housing. We'll give new tax credits to businesses that hire and invest. And we'll work to strengthen families by removing the financial deterrents to marriage for low-income couples, and doing more to encourage fatherhood – because what makes you a man isn't the ability to conceive a child; it's having the courage to raise one. **[It's the atheistic culture.]**

Stronger families. Stronger communities. A stronger America. It is this kind of prosperity – broad, shared, and built on a thriving middle class – that has always been the source of our progress at home. It is also the foundation of our power and influence throughout the world. **[You're right – so how do we return to a Godly culture?]**

Tonight, we stand united in saluting the troops and civilians who sacrifice every day to protect us. Because of them, we can say with confidence that America will complete its mission in Afghanistan, and achieve our objective of defeating the core of al Qaeda. Already, we have brought home 33,000 of our brave servicemen and women. This spring, our forces will move into a support role, while Afghan security forces take the lead. Tonight, I can announce that over the next year, another 34,000 American troops will come home from Afghanistan. This drawdown will continue. And by the end of next year, our war in Afghanistan will be over. **[Answer this: why do we still have troops in Germany? Because WWII followed WWI – get it? We need a presence around the world to promote peace and stability. Why not Iraq and Afghanistan? They would benefit greatly from both a security and a financial stand point. Just like Europe and Germany has over the last 68 years…]**

Beyond 2014, America's commitment to a unified and sovereign Afghanistan will endure, but the nature of our commitment will change. We are negotiating an agreement with the Afghan government that focuses on two missions: training and equipping Afghan forces so that the country does not again slip into chaos, and counter-terrorism efforts that allow us to pursue the remnants of al Qaeda and their affiliates. Today, the organization that attacked us on 9/11 is a shadow of its former self. Different al Qaeda affiliates and extremist groups have emerged – from the

Arabian Peninsula to Africa. The threat these groups pose is evolving. But to meet this threat, we don't need to send tens of thousands of our sons and daughters abroad, or occupy other nations. Instead, we will need to help countries like Yemen, Libya, and Somalia provide for their own security, and help allies who take the fight to terrorists, as we have in Mali. And, where necessary, through a range of capabilities, we will continue to take direct action against those terrorists who pose the gravest threat to Americans.

As we do, we must enlist our values in the fight. That is why my Administration has worked tirelessly to forge a durable legal and policy framework to guide our counterterrorism operations. Throughout, we have kept Congress fully informed of our efforts. I recognize that in our democracy, no one should just take my word that we're doing things the right way. So, in the months ahead, I will continue to engage with Congress to ensure not only that our targeting, detention, and prosecution of terrorists remains consistent with our laws and system of checks and balances, but that our efforts are even more transparent to the American people and to the world.

Of course, our challenges don't end with al Qaeda. America will continue to lead the effort to prevent the spread of the world's most dangerous weapons. The regime in North Korea must know that they will only achieve security and prosperity by meeting their international obligations. Provocations of the sort we saw last night will only isolate them further, as we stand by our allies, strengthen our own missile defense, and lead the world in taking firm action in response to these threats. **[Words to actions – please!]**

Likewise, the leaders of Iran must recognize that now is the time for a diplomatic solution, because a coalition stands united in demanding that they meet their obligations, and we will do what is necessary to prevent them from getting a nuclear weapon. At the same time, we will engage Russia to seek further reductions in our nuclear arsenals, and continue leading the global effort to secure nuclear materials that could fall into the wrong hands – because our ability to influence others depends on our willingness to lead. **[Don't undermine our strength?]**

America must also face the rapidly growing threat from cyber-attacks. We know hackers steal people's identities and infiltrate private e-mail. We know foreign countries and companies swipe our corporate secrets. Now our enemies are also seeking the ability to sabotage our power grid, our financial institutions, and our air traffic control systems. We cannot look back years from now and wonder why we did nothing in the face of real threats to our security and our economy.

That's why, earlier today, I signed a new executive order that will strengthen our cyber defenses by increasing information sharing, and developing standards to protect our national security, our jobs, and our privacy. Now, Congress must act as well, by passing legislation to give our government a greater capacity to secure our networks and deter attacks. Even as we protect our people, we should remember that today's world presents not only dangers, but opportunities. To boost American exports, support American jobs, and level the playing field in the growing markets of Asia, we intend to complete negotiations on a Trans-Pacific Partnership. And tonight, I am announcing that we will launch talks on a comprehensive Transatlantic Trade and Investment Partnership with the European Union – because trade that is free and fair across the Atlantic supports millions of good-paying American jobs.

We also know that progress in the most impoverished parts of our world enriches us all. In many places, people live on little more than a dollar a day. So the United States will join with our allies to eradicate such extreme poverty in the next two decades: by connecting more people to the global economy and empowering women; by giving our young and brightest minds new opportunities to serve and helping communities to feed, power, and educate themselves; by saving the world's children from preventable deaths; and by realizing the promise of an AIDS-free generation. **[A super robust American economy is the turbo-charged engine of the world's economy. So learn what will turn it loose and then get out of the way and watch generous, kind-hearted Godly Americans do the rest.]**

Above all, America must remain a beacon to all who seek freedom during this period of historic change. I saw the power of hope last year in Rangoon – when Aung San Suu Kyi welcomed an American President into the home where she had been imprisoned for years; when thousands of Burmese lined the streets, waving American flags, including a man who said, "There is justice and law in the United States. I want our country to be like that." **[Amen!]**

In defense of freedom, we will remain the anchor of strong alliances from the Americas to Africa; from Europe to Asia. In the Middle East, we will stand with citizens as they demand their universal rights, and support stable transitions to democracy. The process will be messy, and we cannot presume to dictate the course of change in countries like Egypt; but we can – and will – insist on respect for the fundamental rights of all people. We will keep the pressure on a Syrian regime that has murdered its own people, and support opposition leaders that respect the rights of every Syrian. And we will stand steadfast with Israel in pursuit of security and a lasting peace. These are the messages I will deliver when I travel to the Middle East next month.

All this work depends on the courage and sacrifice of those who serve in dangerous places at great personal risk – our diplomats, our intelligence officers, and the men and women of the United States Armed Forces. As long as I'm Commander-in-Chief, we will do whatever we must to protect those who serve their country abroad, and we will maintain the best military in the world. We will invest in new capabilities, even as we reduce waste and wartime spending. We will ensure equal treatment for all service members, and equal benefits for their families – gay and straight. We will draw upon the courage and skills of our sisters and daughters, because women have proven under fire that they are ready for combat. We will keep faith with our veterans – investing in world-class care, including mental health care, for our wounded warriors; supporting our military families; and giving our veterans the benefits, education, and job opportunities they have earned. And I want to thank my wife Michelle and Dr. Jill Biden for their continued dedication to serving our military families as well as they serve us. **[Sounds good to me.]**

But defending our freedom is not the job of our military alone. We must all do our part to make sure our God-given rights are protected here at home. That includes our most fundamental right as citizens: the right to vote. When any Americans – no matter where they live or what their party – are denied that right simply because they can't wait for five, six, seven hours just to cast their ballot, we are betraying our ideals. That's why, tonight, I'm announcing a non-partisan commission to improve the voting experience in America. And I'm asking two long-time experts in the field, who've recently served as the top attorneys for my campaign and for Governor Romney's campaign, to lead it. We can fix this, and we will. The American people demand it. And so does our democracy. **[ACORN anyone? How can we possibly trust the ex-attorney of this Chicago organized criminal socialist organization? We can't and shouldn't – voter fraud is their hallmark!]**

Of course, what I've said tonight matters little if we don't come together to protect our most precious resource – our children.

It has been two months since Newtown. I know this is not the first time this country has debated how to reduce gun violence. But this time is different. Overwhelming majorities of Americans – Americans who believe in the Second Amendment – have come together around commonsense reform – like background checks that will make it harder for criminals to get their hands on a gun. Senators of both parties are working together on tough new laws to prevent anyone from buying guns for resale to criminals. Police chiefs are asking our help to get weapons of war and massive ammunition magazines off our streets, because they are tired of being outgunned. **[Blah, blah gun control.]**

Each of these proposals deserves a vote in Congress. If you want to vote no, that's your choice. But these proposals deserve a vote. Because in the two months since Newtown, more than a thousand birthdays, graduations, and anniversaries have been stolen from our lives by a bullet from a gun. One of those we lost was a young girl named Hadiya Pendleton. She was 15 years old. She loved Fig Newtons and lip gloss. She was a majorette. She was so good to her friends, they all thought they were her best friend. Just three weeks ago, she was here, in Washington, with her classmates, performing for her country at my inauguration. And a week later, she was shot and killed in a Chicago park after school, just a mile away from my house.

Hadiya's parents, Nate and Cleo, are in this chamber tonight, along with more than two dozen Americans whose lives have been torn apart by gun violence. They deserve a vote.

Gabby Giffords deserves a vote.

The families of Newtown deserve a vote.

The families of Aurora deserve a vote.

The families of Oak Creek, and Tucson, and Blacksburg, and the countless other communities ripped open by gun violence – they deserve a simple vote.

Our actions will not prevent every senseless act of violence in this country. Indeed, no laws, no initiatives, no administrative acts will perfectly solve all the challenges I've outlined tonight. But we were never sent here to be perfect. We were sent here to make what difference we can, to secure this nation, expand opportunity, and uphold our ideals through the hard, often frustrating, but absolutely necessary work of self-government. **[When will the liberal socialist democrats get it – guns in the hands of the crazy and the criminal are what kills innocent people. If we disarm law abiding citizens, they are at the mercy of the crazy and the criminals, and they are not merciful. Almost all of these tragedies occurred in no gun zones. Get it! When will these liberal idiots learn their lessons?]**

We were sent here to look out for our fellow Americans the same way they look out for one another, every single day, usually without fanfare, all across this country. We should follow their example. We should follow the example of a New York City nurse named Menchu Sanchez. When Hurricane Sandy plunged her hospital into darkness, her thoughts were not with how her own home was faring – they were with the twenty precious newborns in her care and the rescue plan she devised that kept them all safe. **[Hmm, no government mandate.]**

We should follow the example of a North Miami woman named Desiline Victor. When she arrived at her polling place, she was told the wait to vote might be six hours. And as time ticked by, her concern was not with her tired body or aching feet, but whether folks like her would get to have their say. Hour after hour, a throng of people stayed in line in support of her. Because Desiline is 102 years old. And they erupted in cheers when she finally put on a sticker that read "I Voted."

We should follow the example of a police officer named Brian Murphy. When a gunman opened fire on a Sikh temple in Wisconsin, and Brian was the first to arrive, he did not consider his own safety. He fought back until help arrived, and ordered his fellow officers to protect the safety of the Americans worshiping inside – even as he lay bleeding from twelve bullet wounds. **[God bless him!]**

When asked how he did that, Brian said, "That's just the way we're made." We may do different jobs, and wear different uniforms, and hold different views than the person beside us. But as Americans, we all share the same proud title: We are citizens. It's a word that doesn't just describe our nationality or legal status. It describes the way we're made. It describes what we believe. It captures the enduring idea that this country only works when we accept certain obligations to one another and to future generations; that our rights are wrapped up in the rights of others; and that well into our third century as a nation, it remains the task of us all, as citizens of these United States, to be the authors of the next great chapter in our American story.

Thank you, God bless you, and God bless the United States of America.

The Author's additional comments: Just about everything President Obama said positive about America is attributable to conservative principles and just about everything he said negatively about America is attributable to 100 plus years of liberal socialist democrat policies. More of these socialist policies crammed down our throats by unconstitutional "executive orders," or legislation passed in the middle of the night, that nobody has read, will only lead to more suffering. An Example: They want to raise the minimum wage to a "livable family wage" which is noble, but will have the unintended consequences of fewer jobs for students and entry level employees. Higher minimum wages forced on employers will allow them to be more selective in the area of experience, leaving the inexperienced out of luck. Higher wages come from free-market forces like supply and demand. Why is it that the McDonald's fast-food restaurants in the boom-towns of oil rich North Dakota pay double, even triple, the minimum wages of the rest of the Country? Hmm… See my point?

Here is Senator Rand Paul's excellent Constitutional Conservative Tea Party movement response that provides a clear distinction between his free-market beliefs and Obama's socialist beliefs.

US Senator Rand Paul, M.D., Ophthalmologist

Feb. 12, 2013, 10:22 p.m.

Kentucky GOP Senator, Rand Paul, gave an alternative response to Obama's speech. Florida GOP Senator Marco Rubio's official Republican response was good but, I chose to use Rand's response over Marco's because I feel it is a "little" better and Dr. Rand Paul has/is the "prescription" America needs today.

Senator Rand Paul's following video speech can be found on several internet sites:

> Good evening. I speak to you tonight from Washington, D.C. The state of our economy is tenuous but our people remain the greatest example of freedom and prosperity the world has ever known. People say America is exceptional. I agree, but it's not the complexion of our skin or the twists in our DNA that make us unique. America is exceptional because we were founded upon the notion that anyone, in fact everyone, should be free to pursue life, liberty, and happiness.
>
> You know, for the first time in history, men and women were guaranteed in America a chance to succeed based NOT on who your parents were but on your own initiative and your desire to work. We are in danger, though, of forgetting what made us great. The President seems to think the country can continue to borrow $50,000 every second. The President believes that if we can just squeeze more money out of those who are working. I don't think it will work.

The path we are on is not sustainable, but few in Congress or in this Administration seem to recognize that their actions are endangering the prosperity of this great nation.

Ronald Reagan said, "Government is not the answer to the problem, government is the problem."

Tonight, the President told the nation he disagrees. President Obama believes the government is the solution: More government, more taxes and more debt. What the President fails to grasp is that the American system that rewards hard work is what made America so prosperous.

What America needs is not Robin Hood but Adam Smith [a 1776 free-market economics genius and the author of *"The Wealth of Nations"*]. In the year we won our independence, Adam Smith described what creates the Wealth of Nations. He described a limited government that largely did not interfere with individuals and their pursuit of happiness.

All that we are, all that we wish to be, is now threatened by the notion that you can have something for nothing, that you can have your cake and eat it too, that you can spend a trillion dollars every year that you don't have.

I was elected to the Senate in 2010 by people who were worried about their country, worried about their kids and worried about their future. I thought I knew how bad it was until I got here [in Washington]. But it is worse than I ever imagined.

Congress is debating the wrong things. Every debate in Washington is about how much to increase spending – a little or a lot. About how much to increase taxes – a little or a lot.

The President does a big "oh woe is me" over the $1.2 trillion sequester, cuts in spending, that he endorsed and he signed into law. Some Republicans are now joining him. Few people understand that the sequester doesn't even cut any spending. It just slows the rate of growth. Even with the sequester, if it goes through, government will grow over $7 trillion over the next decade. Only in Washington could an increase of $7 trillion in spending over a decade be called a cut.

So, what is the President's answer? Over the past four years he has added over $6 trillion in new debt and may well do the same in a second term. What solutions does he offer? He takes entitlement reform off the table and seeks to squeeze more money out of the private sector.

He says he wants a balanced approach. What the country really needs is a balanced budget. Washington acts in a way that your family never could – they spend money they don't have, they borrow from future generations, and then they blame each other for never fixing the problem.

Tonight I urge you to demand a new course. Demand Washington change their ways, or be sent home.

To begin with, we absolutely must pass a Balanced Budget Amendment to the Constitution! The amendment must include strict tax and spending limitations.

Liberals complain that the budget can't be balanced, but if you cut just one penny from each dollar we currently spend, the budget would balance within six or seven years. The Penny Plan has been crafted into a bill that millions of conservatives across the country support.

It is often said that there is not enough bipartisanship up here. That's not true. In fact, there is plenty of bipartisanship. Both parties have been guilty of spending too much, of protecting their sacred cows, of backroom deals in which everyone up here wins, but every taxpayer loses.

It is time for a new bipartisan consensus. It is time Democrats admit that not every dollar spent on domestic programs is sacred. And it is time Republicans realize, myself included, that military spending is not immune to waste and fraud.

Where would we cut spending; um well, let's start with ending all foreign aid to countries that are burning our flag and chanting death to America. In addition, the President could begin by stopping selling or giving F-16s and Abrams tanks to Islamic radicals in Egypt.

Not only should the sequester stand, many pundits say the sequester [is] far short, that we need $4 trillion in cuts. If you were to freeze spending, it would actually be called [a] $9 trillion [cut] in Washington. If we don't, we're in danger of having our credit rating downgraded.

Now the parties will have to agree to cut; we have to work together or we will never fix our fiscal mess. Bipartisanship is not what is missing in Washington. Common sense is. Trillion-dollar deficits hurt us all. Printing more money just feeds the never-ending appetite for spending and it hurts us all. We pay higher prices every time we go to the supermarket or the gas pump. The value of the dollar shrinks with each new day.

Contrary to what the President claims, big government and debt are not a friend to the poor and the elderly. Big government debt keeps the poor – poor, and saps the savings of the elderly. This massive expansion of the debt destroys savings and steals the value of your wages. Big government makes it more expensive to put food on the table. Big government is not your friend. The President offers you free stuff but his policies keep you poor.

Under President Obama, the ranks of America's poor have swelled to almost 1 in 6 people; we are now at an all-time high in long-term unemployment. Millions of Americans are struggling and out of work. The cycle must be broken. The willpower to do this will not come from Congress. I've seen how they act. It must come from the American people.

Next month, I will propose a five-year balanced budget, a budget that last year was endorsed by taxpayer groups across the country for its boldness, and for actually solving the problem. I will work with anyone on either side of the aisle who wants to cut spending. But in recent years, there has been nobody to work with.

The President's past massive tax hikes and spending increases; and, you know how many people he gets to vote for his budget? ZERO… Nobody voted for his budget. Not a single Democrat voted for the President's budget! How's that for leadership? But at least he tried. Senate Democrats have not even produced a budget in the entire time I that have been in office. This is shameful. It's a display of incompetence that illustrates their lack of seriousness. This year, they say they will have a budget, but after just recently raising taxes by hundreds of billions, they now say that their budget [is] going to include more tax hikes. The President tonight said; "He wants to squeeze more money out of folks."

We must stand firm. We must say NO to any MORE tax hikes! Only through lower taxes, less regulation and more freedom will the economy begin to grow again. Our party is the party of growth, jobs and prosperity, and we will boldly lead on these issues.

Under the Obama economy, 12 million people are out of work. During the President's first term 800,000 construction workers lost their jobs and another 800,000 simply gave up looking for work. With my five-year budget, millions of jobs would be created by cutting the corporate tax, cutting the corporate income tax in half, by creating a flat personal income tax of 17%, and by cutting the regulations that are strangling American businesses.

The only stimulus ever proven to work is leaving more money in the hands of those who earned it! For those who are struggling we want you to have something infinitely more valuable than a free phone, we want you to have a job and pathway to success.

We are the party that embraces hard work and ingenuity; therefore we must be the party that embraces the immigrant who wants to come to America for a better future. We must be the party who sees immigrants as assets, not liabilities. We must be the party that says, "If you want to work, if you want to become an American, we welcome you."

For those striving to climb the ladder of success we must fix our schools. America's educational system is leaving behind anyone who starts with disadvantages. We've cut classrooms size in half and tripled spending on education and still we lag behind much of the world. A great education needs to be available for everyone, whether you live on Country Club Lane or in government housing.

This will only happen when we allow school choice for everyone, rich or poor, white, brown, or black… Everyone!

Let the taxes you pay for education follow each and every student to the school of their choice. Competition has made America the richest nation in history. Competition can make our educational system the envy of the world. The status quo traps poor kids in a crumbling system of hopelessness. When every child can, like the President's kids, go to the school of their choice, then the dreams of our children will come true!

Washington could also use a good dose of transparency, which is why we should fight back against middle of the night deals that end with massive bills that no one has read. We must continue to fight for legislation that forces Congress to read the bills! For goodness sake, at least read the bills!

We must continue to object when Congress sticks special interest riders on bills in the middle of the night! And if Congress refuses to obey its own rules, if Congress refuses to pass a budget, if Congress refuses to read the bills, then I say: Sweep the place clean. Limit their terms and send them home!

I have seen the inner sanctum of Congress and believe me there is no monopoly on knowledge there. If they won't listen, if they will not balance the budget, then we should limit their terms.

We are the party that adheres to the Constitution. And so we won't let the liberals tread on the Second Amendment! We will fight to defend the entire Bill of Rights from the right to trial by jury to the right to be free from unlawful searches. We will stand up against excessive government power wherever we see it. We cannot and will not allow any President to act as if he were a king. We will not let any President use executive orders to impinge on the Second Amendment. We will not tolerate secret lists of American citizens who can be killed without trial.

Montesquieu wrote "that there can be no liberty when the executive branch and the legislative branch are combined." Separation of powers is a bedrock principle of our Constitution. We took the President to court over his unconstitutional recess appointments and won. If necessary, we will take him to court again if he attempts to legislate by executive order. Congress must reassert its authority as the protector of these rights, stand up for them, no matter which party is in power. Whether it's a republican or a democrat I will oppose abuses of power by the executive. Congress must stand as a check to the power of the executive, and it must stand as it was intended, as the voice of the people.

The people are crying out for change. They are asking for us to hear their voices, to fix our broken system, to work together, to right our economy and to restore their liberty.

Let us tonight let them know that we hear their voices. That we can and must work together, that we can and must re-chart our course toward a better future.

America has much greatness left in her. We will begin to thrive again when we begin to believe in ourselves again, when we regain our respect for our founding documents, when we balance our budget, when we understand that capitalism and free-markets and free individuals are what creates our nation's prosperity.

Thank you and God Bless America.

The following is a brilliant speech by a God fearing free-market constitutional conservative who would make an excellent President of the United States and may have the courage to actually run in the future. I certainly hope so! At the very least he would help form the national debate that usually occurs during presidential campaigns. I hope Godly Americans will pray for this courageous man daily. He is anointed by God to make a profound difference in the future of America and therefore the entire world…

<u>Dr. Benjamin "Ben" Solomon Carson, Sr.</u> is a neurosurgeon and the Director of Pediatric Neurosurgery at Johns Hopkins Hospital, an author of several books, a philanthropist, winner of several awards too numerous to list here and the Founder of Carson Scholars Fund which has awarded over 5,000 college scholarships for students who have embraced high levels of academic excellence and community service. An equally significant initiative is the Ben Carson Reading Rooms, which are warm, inviting rooms where children can discover the joy of independent leisure reading. It is very apparent from Dr. Carson's story that his tremendous success in medicine and life is a direct result of his mother's demands that he and his brother read daily instead of watching TV – when he was young. He is encouraging that same positive behavior to children today.

Here is Dr. Carson's amazing speech at the National Prayer Breakfast February 13, 2013 with several prominent leaders, including the President:

Thank you so much. Mr. President, Mr. Vice President, Mrs. Obama, distinguished guests – which includes everybody. Thank you so much for this wonderful honor to be at this stage again. I was here 16 years ago, and the fact that they invited me back means that I didn't offend too many people [Laughter], so that was great.

I want to start by reading four texts which will put into context what I'm going to say.

Proverbs 11:9 With his mouth the Godless destroys his neighbor, but through knowledge the righteous escape.

Proverbs 11:12 A man who lacks judgment derides his neighbor, but a man of understanding holds his tongue

Proverbs 11:25 A generous man will prosper. He who refreshes others will himself, be refreshed.

And, 2nd Chronicles 7:14 If my people who are called by my name will humble themselves and pray and seek my face and turn from their wicked ways, then will I hear from heaven and will forgive their sins and heal their land.

You know, I have an opportunity to speak in a lot of venues. This is my fourth speech this week and uh I have an opportunity to talk to a lot of people. And I've been asking people what concerns you? What are you most concerned about in terms of the spirituality and the direction of our nation and our world? And, I've talked to very prominent democrats, very prominent republicans. And I was surprised by the uniformity of their answers. And those have informed my comments this morning. Now, it's not my intention to offend anyone. I have discovered, however, in recent years that it's very difficult to speak to a large group of people these days and not offend someone. [Laughter]

And, people walk away with their feelings on their shoulders waiting for you to say something, ah, did you hear that? And they can't hear anything else you say. The PC [Political correctness] police are out in force at all times. I remember once I was talking to a group about the difference between a human brain and a dog's brain, and a man got offended. You can't talk about dogs like that. [Laughter] But uh, people focus in on that; completely miss the point of what you're saying. [Laughter] And we've reached the point where people are afraid to actually talk about what they want to say because somebody might be offended. People are afraid to say Merry Christmas at Christmas time. Doesn't matter whether the person you're talking to is Jewish or, you know, whether they're any religion. That's a salutation, a greeting of goodwill. We've got to get over this sensitivity. You know, and it keeps people from saying what they really believe.

You know, I'm reminded of a very successful young businessman, and uh he loved to buy his mother these exotic gifts for mother's day. And he ran out of ideas, and then he ran across these birds. These birds were cool, you know? They cost $5,000 apiece. They could dance, they could sing, they could talk. He was so excited, he bought two of them. Sent them to his mother, couldn't wait to call her up on mother's day, mother, mother, what'd you think of those birds? And she said, they was good. [Laughter] He said, no, no, no! Mother, you didn't eat those birds? Those birds cost $5,000 apiece!

They could dance, they could sing, they could talk! And, she said, well, they should have said something. [Laughter] And, you know, that's where we end up, too, if we don't speak up for what we believe. [Laughter & applause] And, uh you know, what we need to do in this PC world is forget about unanimity of speech and unanimity of thought, and we need to concentrate on being respectful to those people with whom we disagree.

And that's when I think we begin to make real progress. And, one last thing about political correctness, which I think is a horrible thing, by the way. I'm very, very uh compassionate, and I'm not never out to offend anyone. But PC is dangerous. Because, you see, this country, one of the founding principles, was freedom of thought and freedom of expression, and it muffles people. It puts a muzzle on them. And at the same time, keeps people from discussing important issues while the fabric of this society is being changed. And we cannot fall for that trick. And what we need to do is start talking about things, talking about things that are important; things that were important in the development of our nation.

One of those things was education. I'm very passionate about education because it's made such a big difference in my life. But here we are at a time in the world, the information age, the age of technology, and yet 30% of people who enter high school in this country do not graduate. 44% of people who start a four-year college program do not finish it in four years. What is that about? Think back to a darker time in this our history. Two hundred years ago when slavery was going on – it was illegal to educate a slave, particularly to teach them to read. Why do you think that was? Because when you educate a man, you liberate a man. And there I was as a youngster placing myself in the same situation that a horrible institution did because I wasn't taking advantage of the education. I was a horrible student. Most of my classmates thought I was the stupidest person in the world. They called me dummy. I was the butt of all the jokes. Now, admittedly, it was a bad environment; single-parent home, you know, my mother and father had gotten divorced early on.

My mother got married when she was 13. She was one of 24 children – had a horrible life – discovered that her husband was a bigamist, had another family. And she only had a third grade education. She had to take care of us – dire poverty. I had a horrible temper, poor self-esteem. All the things that you think would preclude success. But I had something very important, I had a mother who believed in me, and I had a mother who would never allow herself to be a victim no matter what happened.

Never made excuses, and she never accepted an excuse from us. And if we ever came up with an excuse, she always said do you have a brain? And if the answer was, yes, then she said then you could have thought your way out of it. It doesn't matter what John or Susan or Mary or anybody else did or said. And it was the most important thing she did for my brother and myself. Because if you don't accept excuses, pretty soon people stop giving them, and they start looking for solutions. And that is a critical issue when it comes to success.

Well, you know, we did live in dire poverty, and one of the things that I hated was poverty. You know, some people hate spiders, some people hate snakes, I hated poverty. I couldn't stand it… And uh but, you know, my mother couldn't stand the fact that we were doing poorly in school, and she prayed and she asked God to give her wisdom, what could she do to get her young sons understand the importance of developing their minds – so that they could control their own lives. And you know what; God gave her wisdom – at least in her opinion. My brother and I didn't think it was that wise – cause it was to turn off the TV, let us watch only two or three TV programs during the week, and with all that spare time read two books apiece from the Detroit Public Library and submit to her written book reports which she couldn't read, but we didn't know that. You know and uh… [Laughter] She put check marks and highlights and stuff… [Laughter] But, you know, I just hated this.

And my friends were out having a good time. Her friends would criticize her. They would say you can't make boys stay in the house reading books, they'll grow up, they'll hate you, and I would overhear them and I would say, you know, mother, they're right. But she didn't care you know and uh… [Laughter] And but after a while, I actually began to enjoy reading those books. Because we were very poor, but between the covers of those books I could go anywhere, I could be anybody, I could do anything. I began to read about people of great accomplishment, and as I read those stories, I began to see a connecting thread. I began to see that the person who has the most to do with you and what happens to you in life is you.

You make decisions. You decide how much energy you want to put behind that decision. And I came to understand that I had control of my own destiny. And at that point I didn't hate poverty anymore, because I knew it was only temporary. I knew I could change that – it was incredibly liberating for me, made all the difference.

And, to continue on that theme of education, in 1831 Alexis de Tocqueville came to America to study this country. The Europeans were fascinated. How could a fledgling Nation, barely 50 years old already be competing with them on virtually every level? This was impossible. De Tocqueville was going to sort it out and he looked at our government and he was duly impressed by the three branches of government – four now because now we have special interest groups – but it was only three back in those days... [Laughter] He said, WOW, this is really something, and then he said, but let me look at their educational system and he was blown away. See, anybody who had finished the second grade was completely literate. He could find a mountain man on the outskirts of society who could read the newspaper and have a political discussion, could tell him how the government worked.

If you really want to be impressed, take a look at the chapter on education in my latest book, *America the Beautiful*, which I wrote with my wife – it came out last year, and in that education chapter you will see questions extracted from a sixth grade exit exam from the 1800's – a test you had to pass to get your sixth grade certificate. I doubt most college graduates today could pass that test.

We have dumbed things down to that level and the reason that is so dangerous is because the people who founded this Nation said that our system of government was designed for a well-informed and educated populace, and when they become less informed, they become vulnerable. Think about that – our system of government and that is why the education is so vitally important.

Now some people say, ah you're over blowing it, things aren't that bad, and you're a doctor, a neurosurgeon. Why are you concerned about these things? Got news for you. Five doctors signed the Declaration of Independence. Doctors were involved in the framing of the Constitution, the Bill of Rights, in a whole bunch of things. It's only been since recent decades that we've extracted ourselves, which I think is a big mistake.

We need doctors, we needs scientists, engineers. We need all those people involved in government, not just lawyers... I don't have anything against lawyers, but you know, here's the thing about lawyers... I'm sorry, but I got to be truthful... got to be truthful – what do lawyers learn in law school? To win, by hook or by crook. You gotta win, so you got all these democrat lawyers, and you got all these republican lawyers and their sides want to win. We need to get rid of that. What we need to start thinking about is, how do we solve problems? [Much applause]

Now, before I get shot, let me finish here [Laughter]. I don't like to bring up problems without coming up with solutions. My wife and I started the Carson Scholars Fund 16 years ago after we heard about an international survey looking at the ability of eight graders in 22 countries to solve math and science problems, and we came out No. 21 out of 22. We only barely beat out Number 22 – very concerning.

We'd go to these schools and we'd see all these trophies: All-state Basketball, Allstate Wrestling, this, that and the other. The Quarterback was the Big Man on Campus. What about the intellectual Superstar? What did they get - a National Honor Society pin – a pat on the head, there, there little Nerd. [Laughter] Nobody cared about them. And, is it any wonder that sometimes the smart kids try to hide? They don't want anybody to know they are smart? This is not helping us or our Nation, so we started giving out scholarships to students from all backgrounds for superior academic performance and demonstration of humanitarian qualities. Unless you cared about other people, it didn't matter how smart you were. We've got plenty of people like that. We don't need smart people who don't care about other people.

We would give them money. The money would go into a Trust. They would get interest on it. When they would go to college they would get the money, but also the school gets a trophy, every bit as impressive as a sports trophy – right out there with the others. They get a medal. They get to go a banquet. We try to put them on the same kind of pedestal as we do the All-State athletes. I have nothing against athletics or entertainment. Please believe me. I'm from Baltimore. The Ravens won. This is great – okay [Laughter]. But, but – what will maintain our position in the world; the ability to shoot a 25 foot jump shot or the ability to solve a quadratic equation? And we need to put the things into proper perspective. [Applause]

And you know, many teachers have told us that when we put a Carson Scholar in their classroom, the GPA of the whole classroom goes up over the next year. And, it's been very gratifying. We started 16 years ago with 25 scholarships in Maryland, now we've given out more than 5,000 and we are in all 50 states, but we've also put in Reading Rooms. These are fascinating places that no little kid could possibly pass up. And uh, they get points for the amount of time they spend reading, and the number of books they read. They can trade the points for prizes. In the beginning they do it for the prizes, but it doesn't take long before their academic performance begins to improve.

And we particularly target Title One schools where the kids come from homes with no books and they go to schools with no libraries. Those are the ones who drop out. We need to truncate that process early on because we can't afford to waste any of those young people. You know, for every one of those people we keep from going down that path [Applause] – that path of self-destruction and mediocrity, that's one less person you have to protect yourself and your family from; one less person you have to pay for in the penal or welfare system; one more taxpaying productive member of society who may invent a new energy source or come up with a cure for cancer. They are all important to us and we need every single one of them; it makes a difference [More applause]. And when you go home tonight read about it, Carson Scholars Fund – carsonscholars.org

But, why is it so important that we educate our people; because we don't want to go down the same pathway as so many pinnacle nations that have preceded us. I think particularly about ancient Rome. Very powerful. Nobody could even challenge them militarily, but what happened to them? They destroyed themselves from within; moral decay, fiscal irresponsibility. They destroyed themselves. If you don't think that can happen to America, you get out your books and you start reading; but you know, we can fix it.

Why can we fix it – because we're smart. We have some of the most intellectually gifted people leading our Nation. All we need to do is remember what our real responsibilities are so that we can solve the problems. I think about these problems all the time, and you know my role model was Jesus. He used parables to help people understand things. And, one of our big problems right now, and like I said, I'm not politically correct, so I'm sorry, but you know – our deficit is a big problem. Think about it. And our National Debt – $16.5 Trillion dollars – you think that's not a lot of money?

I'll tell you what! Count one number per second, which you can't even do because once you get to a thousand it will take you longer than a second, but number per second. You know how long it would take you to count to 16 Trillion? 507,000 years – more than a half a million years to get there. We have to deal with this.

Here's a parable: A family falls on hard times. Dad loses his job or is demoted to part time work. He has 5 children. He comes to the 5 children; he says we're going to have to reduce your allowance. Well, they're not happy about it but – he says, except for John and Susan. They're, they're special. They get to keep their allowance. In fact, we'll give them more. How do you think that's going to go down? Not too well. Same thing happens. Enough said.

What about our taxation system? So complex there is no one who can possibly comply with every jot and tittle of our tax system. If I wanted to get you, I could get you on a tax issue. That doesn't make any sense. What we need to do is come up with something that is simple.

When I pick up my Bible, you know what I see? I see the fairest individual in the Universe, God, and he's given us a system. It's called tithe. Now we don't necessarily have to do it 10% but it's [a] principle. He didn't say, if your crops fail, don't give me any tithes. He didn't say, if you have a bumper crop, give me triple tithes. So there must be something inherently fair about proportionality. You make $10 Billion dollars you put in a Billion. You make $10 you put in $1 – of course, you gotta get rid of the loopholes [Applause and cheers], but now – now some people say, that's not fair because it doesn't hurt the guy who made $10 Billion dollars as much as the guy who made $10. Where does it say you have to hurt the guy? He's just put in a billion in the pot. We don't need to hurt him. [Applause]

It's that kind of thinking – it's that kind of thinking that has resulted in 602 banks in the Cayman Islands. That money needs to be back here, building our infrastructure and creating jobs – and we're smart enough [Applause] – we're smart enough to figure out how to do that.

We've already started down the path to solving one of the other big problems, health care. We need to have good health care for everybody. It's the most important thing that a person can have. Money means nothing, titles mean nothing when you don't have your health, but we've got to figure out efficient ways to do it. We spend a lot of money on health care, twice as much per capita as anybody in else in the world, and yet not very efficient. What can we do?

Here's my solution. When a person is born, give him a birth certificate, an electronic medical record and a health savings account [HSA], to which money can be contributed, pre-tax from the time you are born, to the time you die. When you die, you can pass it on to your family members so that when you're 85 years old and you've got 6 diseases, you're not trying to spend up everything. You're happy to pass it on and nobody is talking about death panels. That's number one.

And, also – for the people who are indigent, who don't have any money, we can make contributions to their HSA each month because we already have this huge pot of money instead of sending it to bureaucracy – let's put it into HSAs. Now they have some control over their own health care and what do you think they're going to do? They're going to learn very quickly how to be responsible. When Mr. Jones gets that diabetic foot ulcer, he's not going to the Emergency Room and blowing a big chunk of it. He's going to go to the clinic. He learns that very quickly – gets the same treatment. In the Emergency Room they send him out. In the Clinic they say, now let's get your diabetes under control so that you're not back here in three weeks with another problem. That's how we begin to solve these kinds of problems. It's much more complex than that [Applause], and I don't have time to go into it all, but we can do all these things because we are smart people.

And, let me begin to close here by another parable: Sea Captain, and he's out on the sea near the area where the Titanic went down. And, they look ahead and there's a bright light right there – another ship he figures. He tells his signaler to signal that ship: deviate 10 degrees to the South. Back comes the message, no you deviate 10 degrees to the North. Well, he's a little bit incensed, you know. He says, send a message, this is Captain Johnson, deviate 10 degrees to the South. Back comes the message, this is Ensign 4th Class

Reilly, deviate 10 degrees to the North. Now Captain Johnson is really upset. He says send him a message, this is a Naval Destroyer. Back comes the message, this is a Lighthouse. Enough said.

Now, what about the symbol of our Nation? The Eagle – the Bald Eagle. It's an interesting story how we chose that but a lot of people think we call it the bald eagle because it looks like it has a bald head. That's not the reason it comes from the Old English word Piebald, which means crowned with white – and we just shortened it to bald. Now, use that the next time you see somebody who thinks they know everything. You'll get'em on that one. But, why is that eagle able to fly, high, forward? Because it has two wings: a left wing and a right wing. Enough said.

And I wanna close with this story: two hundred years ago this Nation was involved in a war, the war of 1812. The British, who are now our good friends, thought that we were young whipper-snappers. It was time for us to become a colony again. They were winning that war and marching up the Eastern Seaboard, destroying city after city, destroying Washington D.C., burned down the White House. Next stop Baltimore. As they came into the Chesapeake Bay, there were armadas of war ships as far as the eye could see. It was looking grim. Fort McHenry standing right there. General Armistead, who was in charge of Fort McHenry, had a large American flag commissioned to fly in front of the Fort. The Admiral in charge of the British Fleet was offended, said take that flag down. You have until dusk to take that Flag down. If you don't take it down, we will reduce you to ashes.

There was a young amateur poet on board by the name of Francis Scott Key, sent by President Madison to try to obtain the release of an American physician who was being held captive. He overheard the British plans. They were not going to let him off the ship. He mourned. As dusk approached he mourned for his fledgling young Nation, and as the sun fell, the bombardment started. Bombs bursting in air – missiles, so much debris. He strained, trying to see, was the flag still there? Couldn't see a thing. All night long it continued. At the crack of dawn he ran out to the bannister. He looked straining his eyes all he could only see dust and debris.

> Then there was a clearing and he beheld the most beautiful sight he had ever seen – the torn and tattered Stars and Stripes still waving. And many historians say that was the turning point in the war of 1812. We went on to win that war and to retain our freedom and if you had gone onto the grounds of Fort McHenry that day, you would have seen at the base of that flag, the bodies of soldiers who took turns; propping up that flag, they would not let that flag go down because they believed in what that flag symbolized. And what did it symbolize? One Nation, under God [Applause], indivisible, with liberty and justice for all.
>
> Thank you. God Bless.[More applause and a standing ovation]

Everyone should Google and watch Dr. Ben Carson's 2013 speech on YouTube for the full benefit of his speech (2013 National Prayer Breakfast in Washington, DC). The reaction alone from Obama sitting three feet away is priceless. I want to repeat maybe the most important words of Dr. Carson's speech in the area of overcoming the grinding poverty that the liberal socialist democrats have cast so many of our Nation's citizens into:

> I began to read [when he was young] about people of great accomplishment, and as I read those stories, I began to see a connecting thread. I began to see that the person who has the most to do with you and what happens to you in life is you.

I want to close this chapter with an admonition to the republican presidential candidates in the 2016 primaries. DO NOT ATTACK EACH OTHER. Newt Gingrich tried as long as he could to maintain a positive campaign in 2012 to no avail. This is the one thing I hated about Mitt's campaign – his trashing of the far more qualified Newt Gingrich.

This negative infighting is nothing more than an indication of arrogance and narcissism on the part of a candidate and their stupid "handlers." America's future is far more important than your "legacy." Work together to deliver the White House…

November 8, 2015 update: An email to Dr. Ben Carson because he is under attack by the main street media.

Dear Dr. Ben Carson,

Please know that God fearing conservative Americans are praying for you and supporting you for president.

CONSIDER THIS: The main street media are soldiers for the **L**iberal **S**ocialist **D**emocratic (the "LSD") Party. They're weapons are their mouths and their bullets are words. They use a relentless barrage of armor piercing bullets against conservatives and a few marshmallow bullets against the LSD candidates (just to say they are fair). "No weapon formed against you will prosper;" and, "greater is He that is in you than he that is in the world."

BEWARE of the Rodham wing of the LSD propaganda machine; they will produce 12 bold faced lairs connected to your past to destroy you personally and politically. Prepare for them...

THE LSD media's GOAL IS TO KILL CONSERVATIVES POLITICALLY. Don't ever be discouraged – God is with you and millions are praying for you.

God Bless you Dr. Carson,

Chapter 26

John Stossel's "Stupid in America" – Do Libertarians have the answers to some of our problems? Sure looks like it!

Remember, a criminal's chosen profession is crime. You've heard "crime doesn't pay," don't believe it. Crime pays big! It doesn't matter if it's theft, fraud, dealing drugs, forgery, embezzlement, or insider trading. What the saying means is that the risk of getting caught and going to prison isn't worth the potential reward (penalty) the crime might result in. Of course, this doesn't consider that a good percentage of the population that has the moral characteristics of honesty, integrity and fairness would never think of engaging in these criminal activities.

The modern libertarian's proposition that drugs and prostitution should be legalized makes perfect sense from the point of view that the cost of the war on drugs has been a total failure. It took me a long time to come to this realization. I've had close friends and relatives that became addicts to drugs and alcohol. I saw firsthand how lives are ruined from drug and alcohol addiction. Luckily, they were never charged with a crime but drug addiction ruined not only their own lives but put tremendous hardships on everyone around them, including me. I hated drugs and alcohol because of the devastation I saw it had on families' lives and broken dreams.

Although I did not see firsthand the effects of the criminal consequences of these addictions, I know millions of lives are ruined and will never be the same. Add to that the billions spent in law enforcement, the court system with prosecutors and defense teams, and finally the tremendous cost of the prison system.

Modern libertarians believe drugs and prostitution are a person's private business – that adults should have the freedom to make their own choices. To them, "freedom means that we put whatever we want in our bodies as long as we refrain from aggression or harm to others." I used to disagree on the basis that drug and alcohol addictions ruined the innocent lives around them. But has any of these laws worked or changed anything? Did prohibition of the 1920s change anything? **HELL YES!**

It gave us organized crime. What has the war on drugs and prostitution brought us? More organized crime, gangs, murders, drug related burglaries (probably resulting in the death of Travon Martin?), trillions of dollars of lost productivity and taxes, and millions of wasted and ruined lives. **It has been a total failure!**

Why don't we repeal these laws like we repealed Prohibition? The same reason we allow the socialist to continue making progress each and every decade. We are stupid and gullible! ***We believe the idea that human behavior can be controlled with rules, regulations and laws instead of understanding that natural consequences are the only reliable agent of change. How naive…***

Although this book isn't meant to be an endorsement of the libertarian party or a thorough examination of pros and cons of drug and prostitution legalization we do want to point out a few more obvious benefits to society.

Drug Legalization: I believe some drugs, especially marijuana, are much safer for both the public at large and the individual than the six pack of beer or the bottle of wine sold at the corner convenience store. I have seen many people become addicted to beer, wine and hard liquor and some even died of alcohol poisoning or cirrhosis of the liver. I used marijuana when I was in high school (1969-1970) and never drove fast or recklessly while high. I mostly stayed inside with friends, laughed, ate munchies and had incredible sex. I didn't bother anyone and it didn't seem to affect my brain. I made all A's, one B and one C in college engineering classes before starting a small manufacturing and construction sub-contracting company. Keeping marijuana sales in the hands of the drug dealer assures our kids of entering the gate(way) to harder drugs these dealers are "pushing." Can't you conservatives, which are holding on to your prohibition line of thinking, see that the prisoners of war on marijuana are our kids? Again, I haven't smoked pot for decades and would not even think of breathing that crap into my lungs again so don't get the idea I have a personal agenda here.

Legalized Prostitution: Let's see – a women can kill her baby but she will go to jail for charging for sex. Go figure! Each state has the power to determine the legality of prostitution in that state. So far Nevada is the only state which allows some forms of prostitution. It allows licensed brothels only in some rural counties. John Stossel did a special on Fox News about one of these brothels. Some of us have never been with and will never be with a prostitute, but I was convinced.

These girls viewed this licensed profession the same way a licensed masseuse might look at theirs. They choose this profession, unlike the many of girls that criminal pimps enslave. This Nevada brothel is a service industry that provides a safe and marketable service to their clientele. Just like an in-house masseuse, the girls didn't have to spend time running a business and marketing their services. The company provides security, collects the fees and everyone pays taxes.

Give me a break on the sexually transmitted disease argument. Free casual sex is happening all the time and everywhere anyway. What's the difference? A well-managed brothel policy for these women would help them to protect themselves and get regular checkups. If a brothel gets a reputation for poor cleanliness then it suffers the natural consequences of lost business. Underage girls are a big target for criminals today so this would allow the criminal justice system to focus all of its efforts on protecting the young and keeping organized crime out of this industry. Notice to my Christian brothers: I have never been with a prostitute and never will. I don't go to strip clubs because of my Christian beliefs. I believe both of these activities are sin and we should teach that to our kids and discourage prostitution and striping. Some girls would never think of striping even if they can make $1,000 a night so I doubt legalizing prostitution would be any different.

If you don't agree with legalizing prostitution and especially marijuana then you're naïve, or ignorant, or a trial lawyer, or a criminal that doesn't want legal competition to end their monopoly! I predict that society will come to its senses within this decade and legalize marijuana and prostitution. Let's see… Legalization would lead to <u>more</u> business <u>taxes</u>, <u>more</u> employees paying <u>taxes</u> and <u>less</u> government <u>expenditures</u> on the law enforcement, criminal justice and prison systems. Wait a minute – that might help America balance its budget deficit. Getting it yet? You didn't know you were being "Hustled" by the trial lawyers and criminals – did you? Well you are! Ignorance is no excuse. Look up John Stossel's work in this area. It's simple to do, just Google John Stossel and go from there.

I am a very conservative Christian and would not smoke pot or use the services of a prostitute even if they were legalized, but over time I have come to the conclusion that these laws are just giving criminals an exclusive franchise that is costing lives and needless suffering – not to mention enriching criminals instead of collecting taxes. America gave birth to organized crime with our religious creation of prohibition. We are just continuing the insanity by not repealing these two laws the same way we repealed the prohibition laws. The multiplier fiscal benefits are: we spend less tax revenues on law enforcement, courts and prisons, and we collect more tax revenues from newly regulated businesses. Wow… Can we find any other losers to turn into winners?

Don't give me that stupid and so easily debunked line that pot is a gateway drug to more dangerous drugs. Think about how stupid that is before you repeat it again. Let me walk you guys through it so you don't hurt yourself. If marijuana were sold in registered and regulated "pot shops" it would help because they don't have the harder drugs that the dealer on the street corner has – so your son or daughter would avoid that dangerous encounter with the criminal "pusher." Now, was that so hard to understand?

How long are we going to keep protecting the careers of pimps and drug dealers? Do you think any of these outstanding businessmen are paying their taxes? Are you guys in Washington, DC on the take from organized crime or are you just thick headed? Why don't you order some multi-billion dollar studies for this ever-so-complicated problem? Isn't that what you do best – order expensive studies from your friends on the left? Let's all puke together!

Sean, I know you, Bill and Rush are much smarter than me, but please wake up soon on this subject! America needs your help…

Chapter 27

Gun Control – No easy answers to this 2nd Amendment Constitutional "Right to Bear Arms"

The only reason for Diane Feinstein's law requiring a national registry is so the federal government can confiscate guns from law abiding citizens sometime in the next 200 years. Liberal socialist democrats long-term goal is to remove all guns from the public, and don't ever doubt it! Criminals will not register their guns and they certainly won't give them up if guns are outlawed by an LSD controlled federal government in the distant future. Remember liberal socialist democrats think in terms of decades or generations to enact their goals of undermining our Constitutional rights, removing God and morality from the public square and creating a totalitarian state that they are in control of.

For several days after the Sandy Hood tragedy I threw in the towel on semi-automatic assault weapons. Here's why – I've had 2 relatives that were killed in gun accidents but I don't personally know anyone that has been killed by criminals, or even anyone that has had to use their weapons to protect themselves or their family. Now don't have a cow, I'm 100% behind the Second Amendment. But, for the sake of argument consider the current laws which prevent us from having machine guns; to illustrate my point more plainly we can't have a pick-up truck mounted 50mm machine gun. Why, these weapons would come in handy if we are attacked by Russia or China. And, if the federal government failed and we had anarchy in the streets those machine guns would also come in handy. See my point? We already accept limits on the Second Amendment. Why do we need semi-automatic assault weapons? If Russia attacked or an insurrection occurred we will have many more pressing issues than hiding in our homes armed with assault rifles. Just a thought – you can have the cow now…

The Founding Fathers Second Amendment purpose is obvious, but will we really be attacked by some future nation that will land an army on our shores where we will need to defend ourselves with these military assault weapons? Not going to happen! Will we have to defend ourselves from our own tyrannical government and its military? Also, not likely, and if that happened assault weapons would be impotent against our military. What if almost all governments collapse in the future and food and other life resources become so scarce that gangs are formed to take whatever they want from those who have stored up these resources for their families' survival until society solves its problems. Again, not likely – **but possible**! In that case, you better be in a bunker in a very rural area if you want to avoid a relentless assault by well-armed criminal bands. Remember the movie, "The Magnificent Seven?" The only way to stop these killers from killing and raping the villagers was to kill the killers. If, in the future our society collapses and banded criminals have assault weapons with high bullet magazine clips law abiding citizens better have them also – if they want to survive. Again, not likely – **but, it is certainly the best reason for allowing law abiding citizens to own these weapons.**

Don't get me wrong – I don't have any more than two weeks of groceries and just one 9mm pistol for home protection so I'm not a survivalist. I not suggesting millions of Americans shouldn't be a survivalist – only time will tell…

Big-government control-freak liberal socialist democrats always think they can solve the mass killing tragedies by psychos with more gun control legislation. They can't. It's about as stupid as them enacting new legislation outlawing sociopath's brains. Wait a minute… maybe that just might work! Find all of the sick brains with sociopathic thoughts and put these people in jail. No… that won't work. What was I thinking? I must have had some previously dormant liberal brain cells kick in! See how this works – outlawing everything, even thoughts!

Actually the above sarcasm has some truthful direction to it. What I mean is this – we need to develop ways and means to detect the mental health identification triggers which will reveal psychopathic tendencies. A free society can't outlaw guns, knives, fires, bombs, poison, cars ramming into crowds and any other means to killing as many innocent strangers as possible, so why not focus on what we can do.

We need to look at everything that may be causing these tragedies like:

- **Reasonable gun purchasing and ownership laws.** What I mean is no more guns purchased at gun shows without background checks. Even a background check for private selling is reasonable. I only own one hand gun. If I sold it to an individual I would want some assurance that this person is not a criminal or have mental health problems that would lead to a crime using the gun I sold them. This would also serve to protect me from any lawsuit if the gun was used to hurt someone. When I sell my car to someone I go with them to the DMV to get the car out of my name and register it to the new owner. That is an aggravation I'm willing to go through to limit my liability. Why not do the same thing with a gun. It's registered in my name – I want my name off of it and registered in the name of the new owner.

  I know some survivalist will say the government will know all of the names of the gun owners and how many they own. Do you really think the government can't figure out who all of the gun owners are if it came to confiscating legal guns and disarming the public at large? What was I thinking? Strike that last statement. I forgot how the liberal socialist democrats work. They are insidiously patient and determined in their long term goals – one of which is to outlaw all gun ownership. Again, some of these intentions may be for noble reasons like "no more guns so no more gun killings."

  Of course, they also naively believe criminals will be willing to part with their guns also. What they can't seem to get into their delusional brains is that only law abiding citizens will be disarmed so criminals can enter homes at will to do whatever they want. I think there is also a possibility that <u>some</u> liberal socialist democrats want to disarm Americans so they can have a completely tyrannical country to rule over?
- **If the control freak LSD club really wants to weld their powers then we need to outlaw the media culture of violence and the murder of innocent people in entertainment.** Everywhere you look in movies, video games or on TV today we see "The Walking Dead" of zombies and vampires. Killings, blood and violence are making fortunes for Hollywood and TV actors, directors, producers, writers and video game companies. It

doesn't have to be this way. Some of the best entertainment today is wholesome comedy, dramas or suspense with no bloody killings.

The culture of violence in America can't help but to further the fantasies of the sick brain described in the next bullet. The primary reason this suggestion will never come to reality is the entertainment industry is controlled by liberal socialist democrats who make fortunes off this type of "entertainment." **The culture of violence in America is just fine with these maggots as long as they are getting paid...** Expect more empty discussions, intentions and hand ringing but nothing that will change their "Culture of Violence" packaged under the entertainment label.

- **Brain disorders are at the heart of all these mass killing tragedies.** How can we identify these people without infringing on everyone else's liberties? This could be the paramount solution to many of society's ills. It's not just these highly politicized tragedies but all of the rapes, murders, stalking, wife and child beatings and abuse, and other serial criminal activities that harm individuals and our society that <u>must</u> be at the center of our focus. I realize much has been done in this area – but an all-out effort is needed to educate each and every one of us to the findings and solutions. This is not a police or government solution. Everyone must be vigilant and involved.

  First, we must be educated, starting at the earliest acceptable age (I don't know when that would be!) and surely on TV specials run every so often. Remember, if a psychopath wants to kill a bunch of people and we have rid America of all guns he could poison Tylenol bottles or water systems, or drive a car into a crowd, burn apartment buildings down in the middle of the night, or make a hugely devastating bomb out fertilizer and fuel oil. Remember the Oklahoma City domestic terrorist bombing? **My point is: it's not the weapon; it's the person that uses the weapon that must be the focus of our efforts to stop the killings...**

How about the 2012 scandal of the justice department and US Attorney General Eric Holder concerning the Fast and Furious sting by the Tobacco and Fire Arms Department. What in the world were they thinking – selling assault weapons to drug cartels in Mexico. We know one Border Patrol agent was murdered with one of these weapons. God only knows how many other Americans have been murdered, and certainly how many Mexicans have been murdered that we don't know about. Probably hundreds! Some conclude the purpose was the liberal agenda of gun control legislation by democrats. They just can't stop trying to take guns from law abiding citizens knowing full well that only criminals would have guns if they got their way.

Right now a criminal in rural Texas knows he would be taking his life in his own hands if breaks into someone's home unless they are gone. What if two or three people with concealed weapons permits were armed in the crowd when the crazy nut, Jared Loughner, started shooting Congresswoman Gabriel Giffords and the crowd gathered to meet her? Lives likely would have been saved as these armed citizens could have shot Jared Loughner before he was finished. The same applies to the movie theater in Colorado or the Sandy Hook elementary school tragedy. Who did the liberal socialist democrats and their slobbering sycophants in the liberal media blame for the Congresswomen Gifford shooting? Sarah Palin, gun toting conservatives and the Republican Party. Really! It turns out he is more of a crazy leftist than anything else. Truth never matters to an LSD control freak…

But self-protection is only one reason for the Bill of Rights Second Amendment to the Constitution. Early American settlers viewed this *"Right to Bear Arms"* as the Second right behind the First Amendment *"Right to Free Speech."* Another "Right" the liberal socialist democrats want to change for their benefit. In no particular order the authors of the Second Amendment felt it was necessary for:

- Facilitating a natural right of self-defense;
- Participating in law enforcement;
- Suppressing insurrection;
- Repelling an invasion;
- Enabling people to organize a militia system; and,
- Deterring a tyrannical government.

Which of these considerations they thought were most important, which of these considerations they were most alarmed about, and the extent to which each of these considerations ultimately found expression in the Second Amendment is disputed.

None of these reasons matter to the liberal socialist democratic control-freaks. They naively believe criminals will give up their guns and ammo if laws are passed. No, only law abiding citizens could be forced to give up their protection, giving armed criminals a clear advantage in any confrontation. It's amazing how liberal socialist democrats' actions always protect criminals at the expense of law abiding citizens.

Here's some absurdity to chuckle about: Let's outlaw Bush masters (assault rifles) and high capacity clips above so many rounds… Wait a minute… I've got a better idea that is sure to work – let's make it illegal for criminals to have possession of "any" firearms! And, let's outlaw fire so arsonists can't kill… And, let's outlaw fertilizer and fuel oil because of the Oklahoma City bombing… And, let's outlaw alcohol because of drunk drivers… And, we should outlaw poison – remember the poison tainted Tylenol deaths. Do you know how many people including kids are poisoned each year – of course you don't, it's not sensational enough for the news media to bother with…

The liberal socialist control-freak's Gun Control's purpose is to disarm the 77 million Americans to pave the way for tyranny a hundred years from now. What is tyranny – total control over a country's population and a police state… We have been moving in that direction over the last one hundred years so it may take another hundred years to finish the job! Sandy Hook nearly changed my mind on assault weapons ban because my heart was broken and I cried for hours for the parents of these precious little kids.

The real problem is mental health or more specifically brain disorders – usually from birth but also from an acute or prolonged stressful environment. Gun control will never end till the liberals confiscate all of the guns from law abiding Americans – leaving us defenseless from criminals or rioting crowds (anarchy) arising from a bankrupt nation. Remember, America's unfunded liabilities are estimated to be in excess of 120 trillion dollars and the liberal socialist democrats could care less!

Surveillance cameras: One item I support that will probably upset my conservative and libertarian brethren is the use of surveillance cameras. In fact, I believe we should have surveillance cameras everywhere outside the home. Why? We have to catch criminals and catch them quickly, especially in the event of a child or woman abduction. If we have cameras everywhere we might be able to catch these psychopaths before they kill or rape our women and children. Surveillance cameras are also an important deterrent to crime which would help offset the cost of a national camera system. I could care less if cameras record me driving down the street, turning at corners and getting into and out of my car at the grocery store. So what! Small price to pay to protect our kids…

Also, law abiding citizens would have nothing to fear from "big brother" watching because there is no way "all" these cameras could be monitored. They would only be reviewed immediately after a kidnaping or a crime is reported in a particular area. This is how we eventually caught the Boston marathon bombers – surveillance cameras on the side of a retail building. Think of the thousands of kids and women we might be able save over time along with solving so many other crimes!

Chapter 28

LET'S BREAK IT DOWN! Ridiculous quotes from famous liberal "Hustlers" broken down to reveal their con and just how stupid they think their gullible suckers are…

Quote number 1: This moronic quote gets the top billing because it epitomizes just how stupid these people are; or, how stupid they think everyone else is. *Chris Matthews April 2012 TV commercial where he said:* "The next time you're driving around in the country, think about the fact that tens of thousands of those bridges you're crossing are below safety code, and we've got millions of people out there looking for work. The corporations aren't going to put those people to work fixing those bridges. We the people have to do it."

LET'S BREAK IT DOWN:

Who are "we the people?" Is Chris a structural engineer, or an iron worker, or a welder, or a concrete specialist, or a construction bid specialist, or all the other trade specialists and professionals required to determine the repairs and associated costs to bring these tens of thousands of bridges up to safety code? And how would he organize the company who would hire all of these engineers, supervisors and workers?

Who is he kidding? Would it be a partnership, or a sole proprietorship, or a corporation? Get real – most of the companies that will be fixing these bridges will be corporations. And, they are going to hire "We the People" to do all of the work? So what is this LSD Party "SCREWBALL," Chris Matthews', agenda here? It's probably to demonize corporations and get weak minded people to distrust corporations and the free-market enterprise system. **That's the Hustle!** Who are the suckers? You are, if you believe this screwball con artist and the rest of his liberal media friends and vote for democrats or moderate republicans. Hard work, investment, ever increasing commerce and production is what made this country great. Not socialism!

If we would simply get rid of most of the millions of overlapping rules, regulations and controls that is strangling our economy, turn loose the energy sector and simplify the tax code by lowering the tax rates and getting rid of "all" tax deductions, loopholes and tax credits, we could put everyone that wants to work, back to work. Do this along with getting rid of all waste, fraud and abuse in government at all levels and freezing non-discretionary spending at current levels for 5 years and we could also start paying off our 18 trillion dollar national debt.

I suggest elsewhere in this book that we simply issue *municipal revenue bonds* to fix and repair all these roads and bridges; paid for out of gasoline and roadway diesel fuel taxes collected in those regions where the roads and bridges are located. Why should retired folks in the western states pay for road and bridge repairs in the Northeast and Midwest cities? If you don't drive in those regions, you don't pay anything to fix them. If you don't drive much, you don't pay much. Is this too simple for the (self-professed intellectual) liberal socialist democrat to understand? Either that or it's part of their broader socialist con…

Here is another point I need make on the subject of putting the millions of construction workers back to work repairing these roads and bridges. How many out of work (because of the housing crisis) constructions workers in the following trades will be needed for these road and bridge repairs: plumbers, painters, carpet and tile subs, kitchen and bath cabinet subs, A/C and heating subs, window subs, roofers, drywall subs, electricians and, door and trim carpenter subs? NONE…

This is why we're in such trouble – Obama and his slobbering sycophants, like screwball Chris Matthews, think they can con everyone! And, I guess he can get enough dupes to believe anything he says without even thinking about how stupid it is.

Quote number 2: This next one proves that any lie, no matter how easily debunked, slanderous or just plain moronic, is not beyond the most powerful liberal socialist democrat in the senate, Senator "Dingy" Harry Reid is… *"Dingy" Harry on the floor of the US Senate chambers, August 2, 2012 on national TV said:* "The GOP nominee for president of the United States, Mitt Romney, did not pay any taxes for 10 years." He originally told the Huffington Post that a person who had invested with Bain Capital had called his office and told him this. Then, he told reporters in Nevada that "I have had a number of people tell me that."

LET'S BREAK IT DOWN:

This puke of a little man refused to identify his sources (of course) and stood firm in repeating the claim every chance he got. I can understand him not revealing his sources but did he get any proof before making such a stupid claim. Of course not! Think about it – Mitt Romney was Governor of the state of Massachusetts during this time and is a hugely successful financial genius, deeply religious and a model family man. He has served his fellow man, his church and his community with great energy and complete compassion. Also, it appears he gave away millions to charities ever year. "Dingy" Harry is a member of Mitt's worldwide church organization, the Mormon Church, and knows this is a slanderous lie. He knows Mitt would not cheat on his taxes. Why in the world would he cheat and risk losing everything, including his freedom, just to keep more of his earnings. Sure, that's a man that wants the IRS on his tail…

The only reason "Dingy" Harry would make up such a ridiculous story is because he would probably do it himself if he thought he could get away with it. Maybe he has! The real reason for doing this is the underlying pathology of all liberal socialist democrats – control. "Dingy" Harry was trying to force Mitt into revealing as many of his tax returns as possible to gin-up resentment of this "rich-white-man," and to manipulate Mitt into providing more data to turn against him. Class warfare is the primary weapon of these sick politicians; ironically, so they can get rich too. That's right – "Dingy" Harry is rich and enjoys living like American royalty because he's the Senate Majority Leader. How did he get his wealth? That's a story for another chapter! Again, hypocrisy reigns supreme among these sleazy politicians in the Democrat Party. Do you think my harsh language about Senate Majority Leader, "Dingy" Harry Reid, is appropriate? Me too!

Quote number 3: This is another pathetic implication of the liberal socialist democrats' slobbering sycophants in the mainstream media. *Andrea Mitchell said on NBC News on December 13, 2012 in response to UN*

Ambassador Susan Rice's withdrawal of her name for consideration for Secretary of State: Andrea Mitchell said: "I think that this had become uh sort of an impossible challenge for her to be confirmed that she realized that; the White House realized it as well. I think they know they are on good political solid ground that you were just pointing out [she was speaking to another news genius]. This is not going to be; this is not going to help republicans at all. The fact that a woman; and a woman of color has been forced out of a confirmation process. Even before she was nominated." [She was implying republicans are racist and feminist because they were intending to block Rice's nomination to Secretary of State.]

LET'S BREAK IT DOWN:

I thought Andrea Mitchell was bright. How bright could she be if she is unaware of, or forgot that Condoleezza Rice, a black woman, was President George W. Bush's Secretary of State? Or that Condoleezza's immediate predecessor, Colin Powell, the 65th Secretary of State for President George W. Bush, was also black.

I really don't think she's that stupid, but I do believe she thinks a portion of her audience is either that stupid, or too ignorant of the facts, or too lazy to question her statements, or just pathologically inclined to chase the racist rabbit the liberal socialist democrats send the dogs after…

Wake up America – can't you see the liberal socialist democrats and their sycophants in the news media are "Hustling" you?

As far as to why Susan Rice withdrew her name – could it be that her misleading of the American public about the real cause of the terrorist killing of our Ambassador to Libya, Christopher Stevens, along with those heroes coming to his aid; Glen Doherty, Tyrone Woods and Sean Smith was the reason. If I were the White house I would prefer that this issue just go away also! A lengthy battle during Susan Rice's Senate confirmation process could prove to be very damaging to the legacy of Barrack Obama.

It now looks as though the White House's excuse for the pre-election Libyan terrorist cover-up is itself a cover up. Former CIA Chief, David Petraeus, testified that within a day he knew the assault on our consulate in Benghazi was a premeditated terrorist attack committed by a Libyan militia with ties to al-Qaeda. The bottom line, then, is that during her Sunday show appearances, Rice knew the information she was spreading was a false narrative that the killings were due to some stupid YouTube video. Remember, Obama and his reelection campaign had been spiking the proverbial "football" about killing Osama and devastating al-Qaeda. This occurred on September 11th 2012 just before the November elections. This major news story had the potential to devastate Obama's reelection bid so it would make sense to keep this as quite as possible until after November 4th. And that's exactly what happened – with the help of Andrea Mitchell and the other liberal socialist democrat propaganda machine sycophants.

DNI spokesman Shawn Turner told CBS News, "The intelligence community assessed from the very beginning that what happened in Benghazi was a terrorist attack." He added that this classified information was shared with the White House. CBS News then quite correctly concludes that, as a member of Obama's cabinet, Susan Rice would've known this. All cabinet members are given classified briefings.

Good job Shawn!
Case closed Andrea!

Quote Number 4: I'm so glad that I was watching CNBC December 27, 2012 so I could see another episode of the hysterical hypocrisy of Senator "Dingy" Harry: I'll make this one very short. This hypocritical pathological liar called Speaker John Boehner a dictator because he would not bring to the floor a vote on avoiding the "fiscal Cliff."

LET'S BREAK IT DOWN:

I don't really know what to say. This little creep must live in his own fantasy world. You would think his friends would tell him what a fool he is making of himself. The reason I refer to Dingy as a "hypocritical pathological" liar is because he is the epitome of a congressional dictator and has the audacity to call the speaker a dictator. Dingy's Senate had not brought an annual federal budget to a vote on the Senate floor in nearly four years and refuses, consistently, to bring any republican legislation to a vote. This little squirt's hypocrisy is unbelievable. Do you like/dislike my juvenile name calling? I do it when it's appropriate – and it's always appropriate with Senate Majority Leader Hairy Slug…

I saved the most important "Let's Break It Down" quote for last. Please forgive the length of this quote and my comments but this is the essence of socialism in America today and an indication of the power of persuasion and the skill level of the most powerful liberal socialist democrat "hustler" ever…

Quote number 5: Obama's press conference 1/14/13; His first in a long time.

> PRESIDENT OBAMA: "Please have a seat everybody. Good morning."
>
> "I thought it might make sense to take some questions this week, as my first term comes to an end. It's been a busy and productive four years, and I expect the same for the next four years. I intend to carry out the agenda that I campaigned on – an agenda for new jobs, new opportunity, and new security for the middle class."

AUTHOR'S RESPONSE: The worst economy since the Great Depression and he's following the same liberal socialist democrat big government meddling as imposed on America by FDR during the Great Depression. It took nearly 20 years for us to recover back then and we may never fully recover from this LSD and moderate republican imposed Great Recession if we don't stop electing these hustlers to political office…

> OBAMA: "Right now, our economy is growing and our businesses are creating new jobs. So, we are poised for a good year if we make smart decisions and sound investments, and as long as Washington politics don't get in the way of America's progress."

AUTHOR'S RESPONSE: Very cunning on his part. "If we make smart decisions and sound investments." CODE for more spending and taxes, which got us here in the first place! And, "As long as Washington politics don't get in the way." Really, you are the greatest political soldier of all time and you have the gall to say that!

> OBAMA: "As I said on the campaign, one component to growing our economy and broadening opportunity for the middle class is shrinking our deficits in a balanced and responsible way. And for nearly two years now, I've been fighting for such a plan, one that would reduce our deficits by $4 trillion over the next decade, which would stabilize our debt and our deficit in a sustainable way for the next decade."

AUTHOR'S RESPONSE: Is he hallucinating? More taxes and spending is the balanced and responsible way to solve the massive taxes and spending problems of the past that has slowed the economy along with job killing regulations and the hugely expensive takeover of the health care industry? Your labeling this as "balanced and responsible" is exactly what a hypocritical hustler would say… Hustlers always say how much money you're going to make just before they rip your head off!

> OBAMA: "That would be enough not only to stop the growth of our debt relative to the size of our economy, but it would make it manageable so it doesn't crowd out the investments we need to make in people and education and job training and scientist and medical research, all the things that help us grow."

AUTHOR'S RESPONSE: Please stop repeating the same old socialist con that got us in trouble in the first place! Want to improve job training and education – get rid of teachers unions and over-lapping, wasteful, bureaucratic jobs programs and turn them over to the free-market. It's the free-market economy stupid…

> OBAMA: "Now, step by step, we've made progress towards that goal. Over the past two years, I've signed into law about $1.4 trillion in spending cuts. Two weeks ago, I signed into law more than $600 billion in new revenue, by making sure the wealthiest Americans begin to pay their fair share."

AUTHOR'S RESPONSE: Please, spending cuts never happen and "fair share" is a political hustler's code for soak the producers out of more "investment and working capital" to pay for the socialist agenda! Exactly the opposite of what we need to do. John F. Kennedy knew this 60 years ago – can't you read history?

> OBAMA: "When you add the money that we'll save in interest payments on the debt, altogether that adds up to a total of about $2.5 trillion in deficit reduction over the past two years, not counting the $400 billion already saved from winding down the wars in Iraq and Afghanistan."

AUTHOR'S RESPONSE: Please, do you have no shame at all? There is no savings in future interest payments. The future annual deficits that the LSD Party will give us are never ending. And, the savings of $400 billion from stopping the wars would have happened without you. This guy is even slicker than the great slickster, Clinton!

> OBAMA: "So we've made progress. We are moving towards our ultimate goal of getting to a $4 trillion reduction. And there will be more deficit reduction when Congress decides what to do about the $1.2 trillion in automatic spending cuts that have been pushed off until next month."

AUTHOR'S RESPONSE: "Next month" has already happened and as expected, you are demagoguing the republicans for these automatic "sequester" cuts and fighting them tooth and nail. Can't have it both ways Mr. President, can you? What did I just say? Of course you can have it both ways – you're the smartest and most cunning hustler in the history of the world! Just ask all your slobbering sycophants…

> OBAMA: "The fact is, though, we can't finish the job of deficit reduction through spending cuts alone. The cuts we've already made to priorities other than Medicare, Medicaid, Social Security and defense mean that we spend on everything from education to public safety less as a share of our economy than it has; than has been true for a generation. And that's not a recipe for growth. So we've got to do more both to stabilize our finances over the medium and long term, but also spur more growth in the short term."

AUTHOR'S RESPONSE: Want to spur growth – get rid of the leviathan socialist program, ObamaCare, and the other unnecessary overlapping million rules and regulation that are strangling our economy and "real" job creation, unleash the oil industry to create new jobs, new tax revenues and reduce trade deficits. Liberal socialist democrats only care about creating government jobs and loath free-market capitalism which is the real creator of jobs and national wealth…

> OBAMA: "Now, I've said I'm open to making modest adjustments to programs like Medicare to protect them for future generations. And, I've also said that we need more revenue through tax reform, by closing loopholes in our tax code for the wealthiest Americans. If we combine a balanced package of savings from spending on health care and revenues from closing loopholes, we can solve the deficit issue without sacrificing our investments in things like education that are going to help us grow."

AUTHOR'S RESPONSE: More revenue, more revenue, more revenue… You guys sound like a broken record. We already spend more than any other nation on a dumbed-downed, union-poisoned, bureaucratic-strangled, liberal education system that can't even teach reading, writing and arithmetic to elementary school students, which is the foundation to higher learning. Also, they are rewriting the history books to fill our children's' heads with socialist propaganda.

> OBAMA: "It turns out the American people agree with me. They listened to an entire year's debate over this issue. And, they made a clear decision about the approach they prefer. They don't think it's fair, for example, to ask a senior to pay more for his or her health care or a scientist to shut down life-saving research so that a multimillionaire investor can pay less in tax rates than a secretary. They don't think it's smart to protect endless corporate loopholes and tax breaks for the wealthiest Americans rather than rebuild our roads and our schools, invest in our workers' skills, or help manufacturers bring jobs back to America."

AUTHOR'S RESPONSE: Wow! Is anyone better at socialist propaganda rhetoric than Obama? Are you implying that America chose you over Mitt Romney because they agree with you on the rest of your above babbling? Here is the reason you were elected and don't forget it:

"A democracy cannot exist as a permanent form of government. It can only exist until the voters discover that they can vote themselves largesse from the public treasury. From that moment on, the majority always votes for the candidates promising the most benefits from the public treasury with the result that a democracy always collapses over loose fiscal policy, always followed by a dictatorship. The average age of the world's greatest civilizations has been 200 years. – Alexander Tytler [We're there now!]

The dupes that vote for these highly skilled liberal socialist democrat "Hustlers," like Barack Hussein Obama or Hillary Rodham Clinton, are destroying the future of America. You, along with the rest of us, will lose everything we have because you are too gullible for words. The Liberal Socialist Democratic Party is made up of two groups – the hustlers and the hustled… Which one are you (if you're a democrat)?

OBAMA: "So they want us to get our books in order in a balanced way, where everybody pulls their weight, everyone does their part. That's what I want, as well. That's what I've proposed. And we can get it done, but we're going to have to make sure that people are looking at this in a responsible way, rather than just through the lens of politics."

AUTHOR'S RESPONSE: "So they want (republicans)… That's what I (Obama) want, as well. That's what I've (Obama) proposed as well. …people are looking at this in a responsible way, rather than through the lens of politics." Can't any of you stupid gullible democrat voters see the con that this master hustler is feeding you?

OBAMA: "These are bills that have already been racked up, and we need to pay them. So, while I'm willing to compromise and find common ground over how to reduce our deficits, America cannot afford another debate with this Congress about whether or not they should pay the bills they've already racked up. If congressional Republicans refuse to pay America's bills on time, Social Security checks, and veterans benefits will be delayed.

We might not be able to pay our troops, or honor our contracts with small business owners. Food inspectors, air traffic controllers,

> specialist who track down loose nuclear materials wouldn't get their paychecks. Investors around the world will ask if the United States of America is in fact a safe bet. Markets could go haywire, interest rates would spike for anybody who borrows money. Every homeowner with a mortgage, every student with a college loan, every small business owner who wants to grow and hire.
>
> It would be a self-inflicted wound on the economy. It would slow down our growth, might tip us into recession. And ironically it would probably increase our deficit. So, to even entertain the idea of this happening, of the United States of America not paying its bills, is irresponsible. It's absurd. As the speaker said two years ago, it would be, and I'm quoting Speaker Boehner now, "a financial disaster, not only for us, but for the worldwide economy."

AUTHOR'S RESPONSE: The sky is falling, the sky is falling, and it's those dastardly republicans fault. Scare tactics of the liberal socialist democrats are so predictable it's pathetic. BUT: Obama is right! The bills that Congress allowed/approved must be paid – so pay them. You want to balance the budget? Then freeze non-discretionary spending and do the heavy lifting that will balance the budget. You don't need to focus on cuts; just freeze and allow new "improved economy" tax revenues to overtake deficit spending.

Here's how: 1. Start drilling on federal lands and collect royalties on top of new taxes. 2. Completely reform and simplify the tax code to get rid of "every" non-business expense tax deduction, tax credits, etc. **(offset by lower tax rates).** 3. Completely reform the billion pages of rules, regulations and bureaucratic layers to turn loose the economy. 4. Get rid of many of the Federal Departments and Agencies that are either worthless or can better be handled at the state level. Replace them with a new independent agency called the "Department of Waste, Fraud and Abuse" and give them the power necessary to clean house with subpoena powers and structured with independence like the Federal Judiciary and the Federal Reserve. NOTE: Just before publication of this book, October 2013, we are going through the same stupid Debt Limit battle, except this time the president and his sycophants have polished name calling and slander of the republicans to a mirror finish. They are calling the republicans and the Tea Party a "faction regime;" also, terrorists, suicide bombers, ransom and hostage holders "with guns to government heads," extortionists, arsonist, anarchists and other vitriolic language to cast the most hatred they can towards these God fearing constitutional conservatives. No, we are just trying to save America from a financial and moral bankrupting big-government, redistributionist, and socialist state. Wow, now I'm doing it… Except I'm not calling them psychopathic terrorists, arsonist, suicide bombers – just Liberal Socialist Democrats! Much kinder and gentler – don't you think?

> OBAMA: "So we've got to pay our bills. And, Republicans in Congress have two choices here. They can act responsibly, and pay America's bills, or they can act irresponsibly and put America through another economic crisis. But they will not collect a ransom in exchange for not crashing the American economy. The financial wellbeing of the American people is not leverage to be used. The full faith and credit of the United States of America is not a bargaining chip. And they better choose quickly, because time is running short.
>
> The last time republicans in Congress even flirted with this idea, our AAA credit rating was downgraded for the first time in our history. Our businesses created the fewest jobs of any month in nearly the past three years, and ironically, the whole fiasco actually added to the deficit.
>
> So it shouldn't be surprising, given all this talk, that the American people think that Washington is hurting rather than helping the country at the moment. They see their representatives consumed with partisan brinkmanship over paying our bills while they overwhelmingly want us to focus on growing the economy and creating more jobs."

AUTHOR'S RESPONSE: Again, pay the damn bills, but do we really need to be preached to by the biggest political hypocrite on planet earth. The only time he seems to be fiscally responsible is when it's part of the bigger socialist "hustle." Also, "it takes two to tango" or to shut down the government – see who the hypocritical hustler is…

OBAMA: "So let's finish this debate. Let's give our businesses and the world the certainty that our economy and our reputation are still second to none. We pay our bills, we handle our business, and then we can move on because America has a lot to do.

We have got to create more jobs. We have got to boost the wages of those who have worked. We've got to reach for energy independence. We have got to reform our immigration system. We've got to give our children the best education possible. And we've got to do everything we can to protect them from the horrors of gun violence.

And let me say, I'm grateful to vice president – Vice President Biden for his work on this issue of – of gun violence, and for his proposals which I'm going to be reviewing today and I will address in the next few days and I intend to vigorously pursue.

With that I am going to take some questions and I am going to start with Julie Pace of the AP. And I want to congratulate Julie for this new, important job."

AUTHOR'S RESPONSE: In other words; give me everything I want or I will demonize you to death every day through my slobbering sycophants in the mainstream media and there's nothing you can do to prevent it! Either way – I win, and you lose…

President Obama now opens the "show" up to questions.

QUESTION: Thank you very much.

OBAMA: Yes?

QUESTION: "I wanted to ask about gun violence. Today marks the one-year – or one-month anniversary of the shooting in Newtown, which seemed to generate some momentum for reinstating the assault weapons ban. But there's been fresh opposition to that ban from the NRA, and even Harry Reid has said that he questions whether it could pass Congress.

Given that, how hard will you push for an assault weapons ban? And if one cannot pass Congress, whatever measures would need to be included in a broad package in order to curb gun violence successfully?"

OBAMA: "Well, as I said, the vice president and a number of members of my cabinet went through a very thorough process over the last month, meeting with a lot of stakeholders in this, including the NRA; [We] listened to proposals from all quarters. And they've presented me now with a list of sensible, common sense steps that can be taken to make sure that the kind of violence we saw at Newtown doesn't happen again."

AUTHOR'S RESPONSE: Nobody can responsibly say they can stop future psychopaths from mass murder. To imply he can, shows how pathetically ignorant the president is, or how pathetically ignorant he thinks the audience is! Be honest for a change... Psychopaths and serial killers use knives, bombs and strangulation more often than assault weapons. Can you make sure mass murders or serial killers, using these weapons "doesn't happen again." This red herring is, and always has been, about taking the "guns and bibles" away from rural Americans who "cling to them" – to use Obama's words! Rural America, the heartland and conservatives better wake up soon – he's targeting you...

OBAMA: "I'm going to be meeting with the vice president today. I expect to have a – a fuller presentation later in the week to give people some specifics about what I think we need to do. My starting point is not to worry about the politics. My starting point is to focus on what makes sense, what works, what should we be doing to make sure that our children are safe and that we're reducing the incidence of gun violence.

And I think we can do that in a sensible way that comports with the Second Amendment. And then members of Congress, I think, are going to have to have a debate and examine their own conscience. Because, you know, if in fact – and I believe this is true – everybody across party lines was as deeply moved and – and saddened as I was by what happened in Newtown, then we're going to have to vote based on what we think is best. We're going to have to come up with answers that set politics aside. And that's what I expect Congress to do.

But – but I want you can count on is, is that the things that I've said in the past – the belief that we have to have stronger background checks, that we can do a much better job in terms of keeping these magazine clips with high capacity out of the hands of folks who shouldn't have them, an assault weapons ban that is meaningful, that those are things I continue to believe make sense.

Will all of them get through this Congress? I don't know. But what's uppermost in my mind is making sure that I'm honest with the American people and with members of Congress about what I think will work, what I think is something that will make a difference and – to repeat what I've said earlier – if there is a step we can take that will save even one child from what happened in Newtown, we should take that step."

AUTHOR'S RESPONSE: I wish humans were not evil. Unfortunately, some of them are. I also wish some Americans were not hard core socialists and even communists – but some of them are. If America is either taken over by socialists or communists that want totalitarian control leading to tyranny, or we experience anarchy due to a financial meltdown in the future we may need our Second Amendment rights. If neither of these possibilities existed and if we could disarm criminals then maybe the Second Amendment would not be necessary. But there can be no assurances that our government will never become tyrannical or criminals will ever be disarmed – so we're stuck with guns for self-defense… Let's focus on protecting our kids and schools with armed guards and finding the psychopaths before they act out their sick plans. Again, remember most of these sickos use knives, strangulation and bombs to cause suffering and death. I have deleted several pages of the transcript of this press conference because it was just more political psychobabble and I'm getting nauseated.

QUESTION: Blah, blah, blah debt ceiling whining…

OBAMA: Blah, blah, blah I completely agree with you slobbering sycophants…

AUTHOR'S RESPONSE: I'm so sick and tired of all this political masturbation. **The republicans will never beat the democrats at manipulation and lying so give it up.** The only way America can get out of this mess is with a robust national (and international) economy and fiscal responsibility. Republicans better figure out how to educate the voters, especially the democrat voters, on the benefits of free-markets vs. the suffering caused by socialism – even socialist-capitalism. If America can return to "pure" free-market capitalism combined with fiscal responsibility it will dominate the world economy and lead other countries to do the same. If that happens there will be an explosion of worldwide wealth that will lift poor people everywhere out of their suffering and into the middle class. Only "pure" free-market capitalism is capable of doing this! Just compare North Korea to South Korea or China with their relatively new capitalist elements… Also, start teaching, motivating and inspiring our kids the formulas of wealth building and investment compounding; it's not that complicated if it's built on a solid reading, writing and math foundation. Something the socialist teachers' unions are incapable of!

Jon Karl?

QUESTION: Thank you, Mr. President. "On the issue of guns, given how difficult it will be, some would say, impossible, to get any gun control measure passed through this Congress, what are you willing or able to do using the powers of your presidency to act without Congress?

And – and I'd also like to know, what do you make of these long lines we're seeing at gun shows and gun stores all around the country? I mean, even in Connecticut, applications for guns are up since the shooting in Newtown."

AUTHOR'S RESPONSE <u>to the question</u>: To reporters repeating the same questions over and over again: Do you morons just want to hear yourself talk or do you think if you keep asking the same questions over and over again the speaker will slip and you will get that career advancing slip of the tongue? No wonder newspaper reporters are the lowest paid jobs in America!

> OBAMA: "Well, my understanding is the vice president's going to provide a range of steps we can take to reduce gun violence. Some of them will require legislation, some of them I can accomplish through executive action. And so I'll be reviewing those today, and as I said, I'll speak in more detail to what we're going to go ahead and propose later in the week.
>
> But I'm confident that there are some steps that we can take that don't require legislation and that are within my authority as president. And where you get a step that has the opportunity to reduce the possibility of gun violence, then I want to go ahead and take it."

AUTHOR'S RESPONSE: Sure, executive actions on the Second Amendment will really sit well with Americans and help your political legacy! President Barack Hussein Obama IS keeping one of his original campaign promises – that's right, you guessed it – "To Fundamentally Transform America." To what? You're right again! A socialist-capitalist state with very limited freedoms and opportunity where friends of of the LSD Party can make billions off the backs of the countries' producers… I have to stop now – I'm getting nauseated!

Chapter 29

What we have here is "Failure to Communicate!"

This Cool Hand Luke quote is so applicable to conservatives' failure to fight back the progressively greater Liberal Socialist Democratic Party's march towards a tyrannical federal government. A government where controls of everything from the sugar content of our beverages to the economy are common place. Failure to communicate is the essence of what I'm trying to get across to the Republican Party.

You will not get more votes from women, Blacks, Mexicans, Gays, seniors, young adults or any other minority group who vote mostly for democrats by promising anything other than the truth about socialism and the day of reckoning that awaits America because of the ***"Something for Nothing Hustle."*** We must communicate the disastrous consequences of socialist strongholds like the City of Detroit or the State of California or the Nation of North Korea and the resultant massive suffering of their poorest citizens…

Everyone, and I mean everyone, must get on board and warn about the crushing poverty created by socialism and crony-capitalism at every opportunity. Look at how well a relentless narrative, like "the Rich Get Richer and the Poor Get Poorer," has worked for the democrats. Some people actually believe republicans want dirty air, dirty water and we want grandma to live off cat food or we want to throw her over the cliff. If that narrative style will work for lying democrats think how well it will work for us when we can prove that socialism causes massive suffering with really simple, and honest, examples.

Are any of you moderate or establishment republicans getting this point? Are you part of the problem or part of the solution? Sounds like something the great Ronald Reagan would have said…

Democrats and especially Obama say the only reason their socialist programs are not more widely received is because they have done a poor job of explaining them. I contend the reason liberal socialist democrats even exist as a major party is because liberal socialist democrats are masters at hiding their true intentions and also republicans haven't explained the democrats' long-term insidious plan to "Fundamentally Transform" America into a European style socialist nation, or a corporatist-socialist nation. Remember a liberal socialist democrat's goal is power; how do they get it with ease? Promise of benefits to the many living off the labor of the industrious! I'm not talking about legitimate welfare recipients; I'm talking about the able-bodied welfare recipients or all of the political crony-connected blood suckers in Washington, DC whose career and wealth depend on dirty connections and secret deals at America's expense.

President Obama and his sycophants are always saying; "We just haven't explained our policies and programs well enough," as if the economy or their proposed legislation would succeed if only they had explained them better. Give me a break! They have most every news outlet carrying their water and acting like their own propaganda machine. The elitist media routinely sucks up to liberal socialist democrats and gladly spins, or even creates, the political news of the day. Contrast this with the elitist media's enthusiastic demonization of conservatives and conservatives' ideas and policies.

What they really have is "failure to sufficiently con and hustle the American public" to finally push America past the tipping point of no return. Wait till ObamaCare is fully implemented. How are they going to explain that monumental failure? I only hope constitutional conservatives can take control of both houses of congress and the white house before too much damage is done to the American health care industry and ObamaCare becomes too entrenched to correct.

The next immigration reform legislation better not allow the 10 to 30 million illegal immigrants a path to citizenship without educating them to the truth of the LSD Party or this country is finished. That's why liberal socialist democrats want to import millions of impoverished Mexicans and give them citizenship so they can deliver the LSD Party permanent power and control. There is nothing too dirty for democrats to say and then the media elite propaganda machine gladly spreads the lies for them. Here are a few examples of just how dirty these democrats and their slobbering sycophants in the news media are:

- August 2012 – A new low for sleazy political TV ads run by the pro-Obama group Priorities USA Action. It essentially leads the viewers to believe that Mitt Romney was responsible for the death of a man's wife because he and his firm, Bain Capital, closed the man's company after buying it thereby causing him to lose his health insurance. The ad leads the viewer to believe his wife got sick and died 20 days after the doctors discovered she had cancer. The truth is: They discovered the cancer and she died many years <u>after</u> the steel company was closed down. Further investigations have showed she had her own insurance. The point is the pro-Obama group completely lied about everything in this despicable ad. If they can be so stupid as to lie about Mitt Romney "killing" this woman when it is so easy to disprove, what else will they lie about. How could any self-respecting person vote for President Obama knowing this is what they do ALL the time?
- July 2012 – Senate Majority Leader, "Hairy Slug," launched a dirty rumor about republican presidential candidate, Mitt Romney, that Mitt had not paid income taxes for the previous decade. Hairy Slug said that someone within Mitt's former firm, Bain Capital, had told him. That is a new low, even for this little maggot. He wins no matter if it's true or not. The purpose of the relentless campaign to force Mitt to disclose his tax returns was to provide democrats and their media partners with a plethora of information to attack Mitt. Can you imagine how much information 10 years' worth of tax returns they could use to create more false innuendos and diversions from the economic failures of the liberal socialist democrats? Also, where is Obama's IRS if Romney illegally avoided taxes? And, if he legally did not pay taxes, whose fault is that? Congress… Romney researched the 10 years and reported he had paid an average of 13+ percent per year. This was probably more than $20 million and was probably matched with an additional $20 million in charitable contributions. It's a total shame that we have a political hack like "Hairy Slug" demonize a generous great American like Mitt Romney who probably contributed over $40 million to the tax collector and charities in a 10 year period. What does that say about the 50% of voters who elect these liberal socialist con men/women?

The point is: liberal socialist democrats are hustling America into believing they care about the poor and the middle class when there is such a tremendous amount of data proving their actions and policies are enriching those “royal elites" at the top of the Democrat Party while ruining the chances of the poor and the middle class to become prosperous. “Crumbs for votes…” How pathetic are these people?

Teachers, as a whole, are now becoming aware of the fact that their union leaders are making 10 times what they are making while ruining America’s education of our children (especially the intercity poor). Union leaders, just like liberal socialist democrat politicians and bureaucrats, only care about themselves. They hustle teachers and the poor into believing the Democrat Party is looking out for them. There is so much data available proving teachers are being duped and have become pawns and leverage for the benefit of the union bosses.

Chapter 30

Book Digest – Americans arm yourself in the war to save "America the Beautiful" from the insidious Socialist & Radical Atheist take-over! Here are your weapons: The words, knowledge and the courage of brilliant authors who are willing to shine the light of truth on Tyranny…

The following books and other publications are recommended to educate and equip those of us who wish to save America from declining further into the European socialism that is destroying the living standards of billions of people worldwide. These books make the heads of liberals explode and their mouths foam. It is a joy to witness! Liberal socialist democrats don't even need to read conservative books, their leaders just tell them what to think and what to say. And, like all sycophant drones these mobs follow their leaders!

The rank is in no particular order and is followed with reviews from non-affiliated third parties. These third party reviews, mostly from Amazon.com, are so good at summarizing the books I couldn't resist making this chapter one of the longest in the book:

Newt Gingrich: *"To Save America" Stopping Obama's Secular-Socialist Machine*

Regardless of how controversial Newt is among conservatives (who cares what liberals think!) he is one of the most brilliant people in America and certainly in politics. He has written so many books and tirelessly leads so many conservative causes that liberal socialist democrats fear and despise him. He should wear their distain like a badge of honor. Look at how America responded to his putting the network "gotcha" debate questioners (including Fox News who he had worked for – vintage Newt!) in their place during the Republican Presidential Candidate debates.

There were standing ovations in the debate halls and in living rooms all across America. Why can't we all have that kind of righteous indignation and retorts in the face of liberal hustlers' lies, criticisms and gotcha set-ups? He would have made a great President. A different kind, yes – but maybe as great as Ronald Reagan! I'm not sure, but I suspect, the republican establishment was against Reagan's candidacy as much as Newt's candidacy.

Newt was the architect of the republican takeover of congress in the 90s', after the democrats' control for over 40 years, and then welfare reform. His Speakership led to the only time we had a balanced budget in modern history. This book about *"Stopping Obama's Secular Socialist Machine"* is a brilliant revelation of the liberal socialist democrats' con of America and an inspiration for my book.

Newt's book should be required reading in every high school in America to balance the liberal left's lies about history, the environment, energy resources, taxes, business and free-market capitalism. I'm so tired of conservatives cowering from calling liberal democrats exactly what they are – socialists. The left is so ugly in their name calling of conservatives, why shouldn't we take the gloves off. They fight dirty and we just take it! **Wake up republicans…**

Third party review by Craig Matteson: **Clear and relevant to our present national discussion.** May 27, 2010:

> Gingrich's title for this book has two meanings. The first is "To Save America" from the current reckless and destructive set of policies the Obama administration is cramming through Congress. Our national spending is out of control, the private sector is withering, the public sector (and all its bureaucratic costs) is exploding, and our national sovereignty is being weakened as we are becoming more subject to unelected and undemocratic international agreements and regulatory bodies.
>
> The second meaning flows from the direction Obama is taking to *"fundamentally transform"* the nation. Obama and Congress cannot make these transformations constitutionally, so they simply wave their arms and ignore our nation's history, the basis of our government, and push through their Leftist agenda with wild and ridiculous claims about this or that clause in the Constitution without

any regard to what was actually meant by the founders and framers of our government.

They torture the words until they confess that the Feds can now make each of us buy a health insurance policy they deem proper for us. What's next? Telling us what groceries we can or can't buy so we will not incur extra health care costs? What cars we can own and when we can drive them to avoid health care costs from accidents?

Gingrich lays out his arguments in 24 short and clearly written chapters. This book is the most explicit and direct argument I have seen him make about what is wrong about the Obama agenda and the direction the Progressives are moving the country. He lays out an argument about what America has been and who we are as a people and compares that to what he calls the "Secular-Socialist Machine" (and what he means by that term – don't let others define it for you – read the chapter). He also uses their clear words about what they told us and, by comparing them to the actions Obama has taken, shows them to be liars.

He takes us through the disaster of ObamaCare and ACORN supported voter fraud. I especially appreciated the chapter showing why BIG BUSINESS and the Secular-Socialist Machine are natural allies rather than the enemies the Progressive rhetoric makes them out to be. Big business wants to be protected from competition and be guaranteed revenues, and that can only happen when the government is used to distort the market in their favor. You can be sure that you and I, as consumers, lose big time the stronger this unholy alliance becomes.

Gingrich also takes on the way climate "science" is used to foster the agenda of the secular-socialist machine and how the corruption at the United Nations also fosters this usurpation of our liberties and national sovereignty.

But this book is not just about the threat. Gingrich provides a program for turning this back. The first step is demanding an honest national conversation and using the facts to speak the truth and electing the right people who can implement the tough decisions we have to make as a nation. Merely tweaking the present system will do nothing. We need to replace it and tear out whole bureaucracies and junk vast amounts of regulation.

We must refashion the American economy so we can compete well in the world rather than continue the hollowing out of American manufacturing and the diminishing of American prosperity. We must support the founding of new enterprises and the growth of small companies. Through them our economy can be revitalized and develop the new technologies that will enable America to compete with and lead the entire world. Gingrich wisely calls for replacing the "entitlement state" with the "empowerment society." Amen and it is about time!

He spends two chapters dealing with lowering the cost of healthcare and ending the massive fraud that ALWAYS follows massive government programs. Gingrich also shows that there is a way for conservatives to be "green" and compares that to the phony environmentalism of the Left, which uses massive government regulation as a means of political control more than it seeks true environmental protection and economic growth.

I also appreciated his chapter on religious freedom. You can also read the book he and his wife wrote: "Re-discovering God in America," which I think is terrific. Gingrich also lays out the major threats facing America in the 21st Century.

He also talks about why the Tea Party movement is GOOD for America and closes with three chapters on solutions that are deeply rooted in American history and flow from our historical values as a nation. Terrific, clear, and I hope we have a national discussion around the things Gingrich discusses in this book.

Additional great books by Newt: *"Winning the Future," "God in America," In God We Trust," "Valley Forge"* and many more…

Dr. Walter E Williams: *"The State Against Blacks"*

I read this book several years ago after seeing a documentary on TV on the same subject. I was fascinated that so little of his work had made a difference in public policy changes. He so expertly documents the unintended consequences of laws passed by liberal democrats and moderate republicans. This started my thinking that liberal do-gooders might be either ignorant, stupid or have other motives when they make laws to help the poor that ultimately hurt the poor more than any other group of Americans. Motives that fall under cronyism, pandering and buying votes, and the power to control just about everything in American... Hustlers always focus on how much you will make right up until they rip your head off and leave you completely broke. Individual hustlers ruin individuals and families; LSD hustlers ruin entire nations...

This is a must read for everyone who cares about saving America before it's too late! I hope you realize just how pathetic the race hustlers are in 2012 when they could have studied Dr. Williams' many books and essays since this original book was written in 1984. Do they really care about helping blacks and/or the poor – or do they have another agenda that I suggest throughout *"America You've Been Hustled?"*

Third party review by Tommy Carr: **A well-researched look at good intentions gone awry**, November 28, 1998:

> This book goes into meticulous detail how government programs, ostensibly meant to help the common American worker, actually exacts a tremendous toll on all of American society. However, as Williams so well documents, the costs of these programs fall disproportionately on blacks and other minorities.
>
> One example from the book is the taxi licensing in New York City. Licensing was implemented in the 1930's, and, due to the political pull of existing license holders, not one additional license (medallion) has been issued in more than 60 years. To handle the increased demand for taxi service (there are, after all, a few more people in NYC today than in the '30s) a black market fleet of thousands of illegal taxi drivers has "plagued" the city from almost the very beginning. These "Gypsy" taxis handle the perpetual overflow caused by too many passengers trying to catch too few taxis. They are often the only service to and from the poorer New York neighborhoods that the licensed taxis will not enter.
>
> No one knows exactly how many Gypsy taxis there are at any one time traveling the streets of New York. But the Gypsy taxi driver is almost invariably a poor black or Puerto Rican man who

is just trying to eke out an honest living despite the best intentions of the city government.

If you are of the opinion that government programs have aided minorities, and helped them on the way to realizing the American dream, you need to read this book.

Third party review by Jeanmarie Todd: **One of the most eye-opening, well-reasoned books I've read**, December 28, 1999:

I have a copy of this stored somewhere and am looking for another "loaner"' copy. This book had a huge impact on my thinking when I first read it in my mid-20s. Walter Williams has a gift for making economics clear and nonthreatening to the average reader. The video based on the book is also excellent if you can find it. Exposes the terrible toll America's myriad laws constraining working people, including the minimum wage, have taken on blacks among others. Raises important issues related to the unintended consequences of laws and regulations – or, in many cases, intended but hidden consequences. Taxi medallions, licenses, benefit not riders or would-be drivers but the few who can get their hands on one, to cite one example. You owe it to yourself to read this if you care at all about public policy, freedom, or society.

Dr. Walter E. Williams: *"Liberty Versus the Tyranny of Socialism: Controversial Essays"*

Another excellent example of a Dr. Williams' controversial push-back of the liberal democrats' agenda to remake America into a European socialist state where political connections are paramount and economic competitive excellence is something to be ignored, even distained. Here is what is said on the back cover of his book:

"In Unyielding Defense of Personal Liberty"

In this selected collection of his syndicated newspaper columns, Walter E. Williams once again takes on the left wing's most sacred cows with provocative insights and brutal honesty. He offers his sometimes controversial views on education, health, the environment, government, law and society, race, and a range of other topics, always with uncompromising reverence for personal liberty and the principles laid out in our Declaration of Independence and Constitution.

Do we want socialized medicine? Do peace treaties produce peace? What's discrimination? Do we really care about children? Is this the America we want? Williams answers these and other provocative questions with his unusual unflinching candor. Although many of these thoughtful, hard hitting essays focus on the growth of government and our loss of liberty, many others demonstrate how the tools of free-market economics can be used to improve our lives in ways ordinary people can understand – not just in the realm of trade and the cost of goods and services but in such diverse areas as racial discrimination, national defense, and even marriage.

Third party review by kaabee "kabe:" **A nice selection of logical, well-reasoned, columns,** December 31, 2008:

Once again, Mr. Williams has put together an excellent collection of some of his recent weekly columns. Mr. Williams has a way, by using layman's language and simple explanations, to get across to his reader the basic principles that tie liberty with the free-market. In many instances he takes the "feel good, politically correct, ain't I a saint for believing in this" attitudes and points of view, and quickly and logically shows the fallacies and problems with these "good intentions." He is also good at illustrating the harm and, in some cases, the pure evil that emanates from those sanctimonious attitudes and the subsequent policies/laws that inevitably follow.

I know Mr. Williams doesn't consider himself a libertarian (or at least he claims that, at most, he's a libertarian with a small "l"), but I can find no one better who, on a weekly basis, can impart the libertarian point of view in such a logical and easy to comprehend manner as well as Walter Williams. In addition he uses some level of humor, occasionally, to make his point – always a plus in my book.

He's a true defender of liberty and the free-market. His arguments have a firm foundation based in logic and reason – not feelings. Keep up the good work, Mr. Williams, and continue the on-going battle to defend liberty.

Another third party review by Hanie E. Cole III "HC3:" **Great Book**, July 16, 2009:

Government allocation of resources enhances the potential for human conflict, while free-market allocation reduces it. I'm afraid most Americans view such liberty-oriented solution with hostility. They believe they have a right to enlist the brute forces of government to impose their preferences on others.

Thomas Sowel: *"Intellectuals and Society: Revised and Expanded Edition"*

Thomas Sowel, along with Walter Williams, is among a group of brilliant Black conservatives that, in my opinion, would make great presidents. They are so much more qualified to be the leader of America and the free-world than Barack Hussein Obama – it's pathetic. This country was aching to elect a black man as president and the best we could do was to elect a freshman senator with two years (of absentee) experience and a clouded history of socialist activism. What in the world were the voters thinking? There are thousands of qualified conservative God fearing black men and women in this country that could do a far better job that President Obama. When are we going to stop electing celebrity politicians that the "intellectuals" in the liberal socialist democrat strongholds of California and New York propagandize we should elect?

Third party review by Ravenwings24: **Very Helpful to Students,** January 14, 2010:

This book is a must have for undergrad and graduate students. It will give insight into your own professors' biases and help you understand where they are coming from. From there you can start to take what they tell you, weigh it, and come to your own conclusions. Word of advice to students, especially undergrads: as a graduate student and former teaching assistant, always remember that your professors are only human and they have their own biases, formed by their experiences and what they have been exposed to during their own lives.

This book really helps give you invaluable insight into how intellectuals see themselves, their biases, and beliefs. It will also help you to understand the "Ivory Tower." I too have struggled in the "Ivory Tower" because I fear that not having the "correct" opinion or a "politically correct" thesis will keep me from getting a job later in my career. Like Sowell explains, the "Ivory Tower" does not allow for outside opinions or opinions that differ from the status quo. Being conservative is something you keep to yourself and I have met quite a few conservative professors who have told me they fear being found out as conservatives.

The book helps you see all this. Even conservative scholars have to tow the line or face not getting a job at a college in a very competitive line of work. Only 40% of those who graduate with a PhD get hired and your dissertation can make or break your career. It almost forces you to write as a liberal to get a job – meaning scholarships always trends liberal. In my department even the older conservative liberals on the faculty hate conservative leaning historian Amity Shlaes and her book, "The Forgotten Man" and it may be why she does not work at a college.

David Horowitz: ***"Barack Obama's Rules for Revolution"***

This 56 page work by David Horowitz is a must read for everyone who cares about the survival of the America that was founded some 200 years ago. It is a summation of Alinsky's influence on two of the most powerful, and destructive, leaders of our time – Barack Hussein Obama and Hillary Rodham Clinton. His work is based on the book by Saul Alinsky: ***"Rules for Radicals"*** and Hillary D. Rodham's 1969 thesis: ***"There is Only The Fight… An Analysis of the Alinsky Model."*** As I outline in Chapter 3, in my opinion, the most important weapon in these "radicals" warfare arsenal is DECEPTION. The second is "the-means-justify-the-ends." Deception and the-means-justify- the-ends;

sounds like a "Hustle" to me – a massive multi-trillion dollar hustle, and the end of America as we knew it! The revolution may take generations. If liberal socialist democrats and moderate republicans are not replaced soon by God fearing, constitutional conservatives we will witness the permanent decline of the Great American experiment given birth over two hundred years ago by our founders; they fought, as we are, to separate from a tyrannical, control freak, over-taxing government. One word best describes this LSD crowd: **ARROGANT…**

If you care about America's future please Google the following PDF documents:

- David Horowitz's ***"Barack Obama's Rules for Radicals"***
- Saul Alinsky's ***"Rules for Radicals"***
- Hillary Rodham Clinton's 1969 Thesis ***"THERE IS ONLY THE FIGHT…" An Analysis of the Alinsky Model***

Read them in that order and be frightened – there are millions of these Alinsky disciples and their sycophants in public and private labor unions, academia, News Media, Madison Avenue, Hollywood and other liberal socialist strongholds across America. I would venture to say that 70 to 90 percent of those voting for democrats and moderate republicans would change their minds if they really understood the suffering waiting for themselves, and America, at the end of Saul Alinsky's road.

David Horowitz and Jacob Laksin: *"The New Leviathan: How the Left-Wing Money-Machine Shapes American Politics and Threatens America's Future"*

A deeply informed expose of the powerful, very wealthy network of liberal foundations… Read this and be afraid." – Karl Rove.

Founder of the Freedom Center and *New York Times* bestselling author David Horowitz reveals the damning truth behind the left-wing agenda and its ties to the Obama White House." – FrontPageMag.com

Horowitz and Laksin delve deep into the arteries, nerves, and heart of the Left's deep-pocketed donors to give us this hidden history for the first time. A necessary, important, and troubling read." – Peter Schweizer, author of *"Throw Them All Out."*

The LSDs and their sycophants in the news media, NYC, Hollywood, Madison Avenue and other strongholds always lose their minds, and scream about the billionaires who support conservatives on the right; why in the hell aren't we countering with the liberal socialist democrat billionaires who support the socialist agenda on the left. On March 4, 2013 Forbes identified the world's richest people. Four of the top ten billionaires are from America and three of those four are democratic supporters; they are: Bill Gates, Warren Buffet and Larry Ellison. All the LSDs want to talk about are the free-market conservative Koch brothers. Read this book, arm yourself, and be ready to go on the offensive starting with the international ultra-leftist George Soros!

I haven't finished this book yet but here is an interesting couple of paragraphs on page 21 worth repeating:

> "American Marxists Richard Cloward and Frances Fox Piven had become famous among the Socialist Scholars Conference leftists, for example, by advancing a strategy of "breaking the bank" by overloading its welfare rolls. In a seminal 1966 article in the *Nation* titled "The Weight of the Poor: A Strategy to End Poverty," Cloward and Piven advocated a series of massive "welfare drives" in large cities that would swell the welfare rolls, cause widespread disruption in welfare agencies, and sow financial chaos in local and state governments.
>
> This deliberately engineered "political crisis" would create a political environment more favorable toward socialist policies. This strategy formed the mission of Cloward and Piven's National Welfare Rights Organization, whose leaders later created ACORN, an organization in which Obama played a major role, and which in turn it would play a major role in his rise to the presidency. Both organizations could trace their ideological origins to another proponent of the strategy of undermining capitalism internally, American leftist Saul Alinsky.
>
> A self-identified "professional radical," Alinsky had written an indispensable guide for community organizers based on how to

conduct a war against the free-market system by working inside it. His 1971 book, *"Rules for Radicals,"* would become a bible for left-wing activists (and is a manual to this day recommended on the official website of the National Education Association* as a guide for the nation's unionized teachers). Obama formally trained in the Alinsky principles at Alinsky-created institutions and went on to join a network of organizations dedicated to Alinsky-style radicalism, which became his political base in Chicago."

*Although I couldn't find the link to Alinsky's book at NEA.org, here is a comment quote from the NEA.org website blog by Catherine on September 15, 2010:

"I was stunned when I read the preface on the NEA website page titled Recommended Reading: Saul Alinsky's, The American Organizer. I thought this was just a rumor, it could not be true that the Union organization that most public school teachers belong to would recommend the America hating, violent and communist Alinsky, (who dedicates Rules for Radicals to Lucifer) and cloak his books in a warm and fuzzy preface 'mother's milk of the left.'

I own a copy and have read Rules for Radicals and it is pure nasty communism for losers that can't accomplish anything in life, except what they can steal, agitate and coerce from society. And you people are educating America's children? This is why my child is in PRIVATE SCHOOL. I vow to inform as many people as possible about the vile nature of the NEA, which is best illustrated by the pages I have just easily Googled and printed about this issue."

Third party review of "The New Leviathan" by James R Holland author of "Boston's Notable Addresses:" **Modern Day Mythical Sea Monster Swallowing America's Freedom,** June 12, 2012:

Wikipedia defines "Leviathan" as a sea monster referred to in the Bible. In Demonology, the Leviathan is one of the seven princes of Hell and its gatekeeper.

In this new book of insights, *The New Leviathan* is a network of billion-dollar tax-exempt foundations and advocacy think tanks that work in concert with government unions and grassroots radical groups to make up the organizational core of the political left. The New Leviathan is a political force in the narrow sense of directly influencing electoral outcomes through the support of candidates and parties.

This many legged or tentacled Monster Octopus is completely invisible to most voters because it works under the camouflaged umbrella of tax-free entitles with charters claiming a goal of improving the public good. They mostly operate as a major force in pushing progressive liberal agendas.

One of the most important points detailed in this short book is the myth of the democrats as the 99% and the Republicans as the 1%. It's a continuation of the falsehood that the Republicans are the party of the rich, while progressives speak for the powerless and the poor. The book proves that this folk lore is exactly the opposite of reality. Of the twelve richest lawmakers, Democrats outnumber Republicans three to one.

A New York Times article by Christopher Caldwell, *The Democratic Party is the party to which elites belong.* It is the party of Harvard (and most of the Ivy League), of Microsoft and Apple (and most of Silicon Valley), of Hollywood and Manhattan (and most of the media)... of Goldman Sachs (and most of the investment banking profession)... The Democrats have the support of more, and more active, billionaires. Of the twenty richest ZIP codes in America, 19 gave the bulk of their money to the Democrats in the last election, in most cases the vast bulk, 86 percent in 10024 on the Upper West Side.

George Soros put together a group of billionaires and Democratic political operatives and created a network of 527's, so powerful the Washington Post described it as a "Shadow Party." Its agenda was to seize control of the Democratic election campaign from a party apparatus it felt was in inept hands. The network that Soros put together consisted of progressive billionaires, government unions (SEIU, AFCSME), grassroots radical organizations like ACORN, and other political operatives. Soros, more than any other individual, is thus responsible for the Democratic Party's radical shift to the left.

In nine chapters with titles such as, The Making of a President, The Progressive Money Machine, Deconstructing the American Identity, Redefining National Security, Socialism by Stealth, Controlled Environments, One Nation Under Unions, and the conclusion, A Disturbing Prospect, the authors do a great job of pointing out the Shadow Part's agenda without making the reader glassy eyed with all the supporting numbers, stats and charts. The meat of the explanations of the constantly expanding political Octopus is explained in the first 182 pages of the book. There are plenty of those stats and figures in the Appendices, Notes and Index that may make the reader's eyes glaze over.

By the time the reader has reached the appendices, they will have had their eyes opened about what in the world is going on in America. If nothing else, the readers will become very wary of university professors and large tax-exempt foundations with names that suggest all kinds of worthy goals. Solid American names like Ford, Carnegie, and Rockefeller Foundations no longer represent the ideas of the men who set up the Foundations. Those great conservative businessmen's charity foundations are now run by liberal progressives and are mixed in with other progressive organizations like the "Fannie Mae Foundation." What exactly does that last foundation do and how are they funded when Fannie Mae is one of the economic disasters of the Twenty-first Century?

There is so, so much totally surprising information included in this volume that most readers will suddenly see a spot light focused on "The Shadow Party" and much that has been hidden will be revealed.

Dr. Arthur Brooks: *"The Road to Freedom"*

Third party review by Frances Fiman Pickens: **The Moral Case for Free Enterprise**, May 8, 2012:

Reading *The Road to Freedom* is an incredible experience from start to finish. For some time, I have looked for a way to teach my children and my friends abroad about what makes America unique and why our free enterprise system is so important. Arthur Brooks answers this challenge; he clearly articulates the case for free enterprise, why it is fair, why it is the best system for the poor and the sick, and why it is the system in which we can become truly happy. It is wonderful, as you read the book, to rediscover truths about what makes America such a special place. Our system rewards hard work and offers the most opportunity for every citizen, and I am so glad that Brooks explains how earned success – not money, makes free enterprise a truly moral way of life.

I am not a Republican, and it was refreshing to read a book that really is about defending free enterprise, not a Republican or right-wing political platform. Brooks explains that government does have a role in our society in protecting us from monopolies, corporate cronyism, and of course in protecting our civil liberties and our security. At the same time, by understanding what drives our free enterprise system, I feel Brooks teaches us how to find the right balance between government and our private lives.

Perhaps the best part of the book comes in the second half, in which Brooks switches from explaining the morality of free enterprise to applying this concept to policy issues, ranging from health care reform to taxes. Brooks gives so many policy suggestions that both embrace the free enterprise system and reject partisan labels; I hope every American reads this book and learns about the moral way to help our poor and sick and to maintain our right to the pursuit of happiness.

Third party review by LSP86: Dr. Brooks lays out the path for success in two parts. Part 1 of *The Road to Freedom* is a manifesto on the moral superiority of the free enterprise system. Only free enterprise encourages human flourishing by allowing each individual to define and pursue his success. Only free enterprise creates real opportunity and true fairness based on merit. And only free enterprise lifts up the poor by the billions and encourages a charitable community. While big government may want to do these things, it is incapable, as every government benefit turns into something to aid the well-connected or something that causes learned helplessness.

The book then takes a practical turn. Dr. Brooks provides a better role for government in today's society: providing a minimum safety net for the truly poor and vulnerable, and correcting for market failure where it can be done successfully and efficiently. He lays out the winning formula for any political discussion and applies it to today's most pressing domestic policy issues: tax reform, entitlements, national debt, economic growth, and job creation.

Ann Coulter: *"Demonic" How the Liberal Mob is Endangering America*

This is another Ann Coulter classic. As she always does, she puts liberals in their place and calls them for what they really are, a bullying mob of control freaks doing their best to stop freedom in its tracks.

Third party review by Bitter old guy "Lance:" ***"Great ammunition against drones!"*** June 14, 2011:

I just finished Ann Coulter's Demonic, and thought I'd write a quick review. Ann uses psychologist Gustave Le Bon's 1896 book, *The Crowd: A Study of the Popular Mind* as a backbone to compare the mob mentality to the liberal mind. The book is broken down into four parts, and as other readers stated, the second part has two excellent chapters on the French Revolution. She uses Le Bon's behavioral studies throughout the book comparing and contrasting conservatives and liberals all with her great sense of humor. I think she does a fantastic job connecting mob group think to liberals and democrats. As usual, she also cites each source (but will still be called a liar).

I think this is some of Ann's best work. I know I'm biased: I'm conservative and I have all of her other books. I love when she is on Red Eye, and look forward to her new column every Wednesday. I had to write this after reading some of the 1 star reviews. Unlike those drones, I actually read the book. Bad reviews, full of name calling and outright hatred, written by an uninformed group of people feeding off one another… Hmmm, Spot on Ann! Read everything Ann writes. She's my hero!

Dinesh D'Souza: *"The Roots of Obama's Rage"*

It's too bad this book didn't hit the bookstores before 2007. This is easily one of the best political books of the year and is followed by an even more popular book about President Obama titled, *The Amateur "Barack Obama in the White House"*

Third party review by Joseph A. Klein: ***A Brilliant Analysis of the Real Barack Obama,*** September 30, 2010:

Dinesh D'Souza provides a compelling case that much of Barack Obama's counter-intuitive actions since his inauguration are a direct result of his 'anti-colonialist' victimhood worldview.

For example, when President Obama defensively apologized to the Muslim world during his speech in Cairo last year for America's supposed sins, we can better understand why, as a result of Mr. D'Souza's analysis. Obama did so because he sees the "arrogant" U.S. foreign policy and the exploitative capitalist system as emblematic of the oppressor class and the Muslim world as part of the victim class.

When Obama stood on the White House lawn with the president of Mexico and joined him in denouncing the American citizens of Arizona who passed an anti-illegal immigration law to protect their lives and property from alien criminals freely crossing Arizona's border with Mexico, Obama sided with the "victims" of "gringo" neo-colonialist oppression.

When Obama told the United Nations General Assembly last year that he wants to re-engage with the United Nations and that not following the United Nations' demands would make all people less safe, he was acting like the self-proclaimed global citizen looking out for the victims of imperialism rather than as a United States President proud of America's exceptionalism and protective of its sovereignty.

And, imbued with the anti-colonialist victim mentality that D'Souza so ably traces back to Obama's idealized image of his father, it is no wonder that Obama so willingly accepted from Venezuelan President Hugo Chavez the gift of a Spanish-language book entitled *The Open Veins of Latin America: Five Centuries of the Pillage of a Continent."*

Dinesh D'Souza has connected the dots in Barack Obama's presidency in a clear, well-researched manner and has explained the source of Obama's disturbing pattern of conduct that is taking us down a lethal path. It is no wonder D'Souza hit such a nerve at the White House that it decided to send the white House press secretary to lodge a protest with Forbes, which had published a preview of Mr. D'Souza's book.

Peter Schweizer: – *"Throw Them All Out: How Politicians and Their Friends Get Rich Off Insider Stock Tips, Land Deals, and Cronyism That Would Send the Rest of us to Prison"*

In my book *"America You've Been Hustled"* I am equally critical and disgusted with both democrats and moderate republicans. I don't care if a Tea Party Conservative is guilty of these types of crony-capitalism dealings – throw him/her out along with the other government crooks. We need to stop electing career politicians and start electing short-term statesmen. I am all for reducing the size of government but we need a DOJ special division that is independent of the executive and legislative branches to monitor crony-capitalism of our elected leaders, their staffs and even more importantly the unelected bureaucrats.

Remember the greatest commodities trader of all time, Hillary Rodham Clinton. She wasn't even a politician at the time of her extraordinarily brilliant commodities trading career – her husband was the Attorney General of Arkansas and soon to be governor. I've traded futures and option contracts from time-to-time since 1983, so I know a little about it. No one in the history of non-corrupt commodity trading has turned $1,000 into $100,000 in just 10 months – a single once-in-a-lifetime option trade maybe – but not commodity futures. My guess is that her advisor, a friend and outside counsel to Tyson Foods, Arkansas' largest employer, may have entered some of the buy and sell orders simultaneously and kept the losing side while giving Hillary the winning position. Then again, my guess could be wrong and she and her *"connected"* advisor are the greatest, most brilliant traders of all time. What do you think?

The back cover of ***"Throw Them All Out"*** – "THE BOOK WASHINGTON DOES NOT WANT YOU TO READ

How is it that politicians often enter office with relatively modest assets, but then, as investors, regularly beat the stock market and sometimes beat the most rapacious hedge funds? How did some members of Congress know to dump their stock holdings just in time to escape the effects of the 2008 financial meltdown? And how is it that billionaires and hedge fund managers often make well-timed investment decisions that anticipate events in Washington? How did they get this inside-Washington information before the public had it?

In this powerfully argued book, Peter Schweizer blows the lid off Washington's epidemic of "honest graft." He exposes a secret world where members of Congress insert earmarks into bills to improve their own real-estate holdings, and campaign contributors receive billions in federal grants. Nobody goes to jail. *"Throw Them All Out"* casts light into the darkest corners of the political system – and offers ways to clean house.

Third party review by George Chabot: **Get rid of them all!** November 21, 2011:

Saying the phenomenon is a scandal is an understatement as Schweitzer lists transaction after transaction by named politicians that would be deemed insider trading if anyone but a congressman did it. The book lists politicians of both parties enriching themselves through insider trading that would be illegal for a Wall Street banker but congressmen have thoughtfully exempted themselves from ethical and criminal considerations that the rest of us citizens are subject to.

Not only politicians but their friends are also enriching themselves, even Warren Buffett, who looks like a grandfatherly old figure played with two administrations and profited by the Bank failure and resurgence as the lawmakers changed laws to suit his suggestions. John Kerry, Nancy Pelosi, Spencer Bacchus, Dick Durbin, Hank Paulson, Tim Geithner, John Boehner, Al Gore, Jr., Rahm Emmanuel, and many more individuals are implicated in the insider trading that is a perk of office of the permanent political class but a crime to any other US citizen."

Kate Obenshain: "*Divider in Chief" The Fraud of Hope and Change*

Third party review by Alice Baland: **More than hope and change is a fraud!** January 25, 2013:

"Divider-in-Chief" is shocking in detail about how liberal leaders have misled the American people, those they say they are helping. The truth is that they are leading us into destruction while they grab power, control and money. But don't just take my word. Read the grisly facts about how Barack and the dems are slashing away at our freedom, liberty, money, family and – truth, justice and the American way. It's sickening. Couldn't put it down. Now I am more determined than ever to NOT compromise my core values and dreams. We need more people to stand up and tell the truth to these bullies. Excellent book and fast read – based on what the democrats themselves have said. Do your own research and start here

L. Brent Bozell: "*Collusion:" How the Media Stole the 2012 Election and How to Stop Them From Doing it in 2016*

Third party review by Steve T.: **Almost Makes the Connections,** July 11, 2013:

"Collusion" smartly documents the myriad of examples of media bias and manipulation that happened in 2012. Obama may indeed owe Candy Crowley a $300-Million "energy subsidy." That said, it misses what worked for Obama – technology, and the 30,000+ voter profiles into which the Obama machine categorized every voter, with pre-prepared messaging.

How the GOP consultants fall for these Lucy-pulls-the-football tactics every election cycle just boggles the mind; perhaps if a campaign is "that" clueless, they deserve to lose; but, it's at the expense of the American people.

Mark Levin, Sean Hannity and Rush Limbaugh are, in my opinion, the three greatest influential conservatives of our time. Each are brilliant talk radio superstars with uniquely difference styles. I wish Mark and Rush had daily Fox cable TV shows, like Hannity – maybe during the day for just an hour. They would dominate. I have to say my favorite is Mark because of his passionate ability to exhibit anger and disgust with moronic liberals. I have read all of their books and especially like Mark's latest: *"The Liberty Amendments."* Here are a few of their books:

Sean Hannity: *"Conservative Victory" Defeating Obama's Radical Agenda*

Here is the book description on Amazon's site that provides the essence of Sean's excellent work:

> Barack Obama and his radical team of self-professed socialists, fringe activists, and others are trying to remake the American way of life. They have used their new Democratic majority to launch an alarming assault on our capitalist system – while abandoning the war on terror, undermining our national security, and weakening our position in the eyes of our enemies. The "candidate of change" is threatening to change our country irreparably, and for the worse – if we don't act to stop him now.
>
> Sean Hannity has been sounding the alarms about Obama and his agenda from the start. Now, in his first new book in six years he issues a stirring call to action. Hannity surveys all the major Obama players, from the president's affiliation with radical theology to his advisers' history of Marxist activism, repression of the media, support for leftist dictators, and worse. He exposes their resulting campaign to dismantle the American free-market system

and forfeit our national sovereignty. But he draws on the examples of Ronald Reagan and the GOP's Contract with America to show how conservatives can unite behind this country's most cherished principles and act now to get America back on the right track, while we still can.

Mark R. Levin: "*Liberty and Tyranny" A Conservative Manifesto*

Third party review by Robert F. Schwagerl: **America Needs to Wake Up real Fast…** March 24, 2009

"Mark Levin has hit a grand slam home run with his latest book. Every God fearing law abiding American who still cares about the founding principles of this country must go out and read it now and take action against the knuckleheads in Washington, DC. Mark lays out in great detail how the "statists," the Nancy Pelosi's, Barney Frank's, and Harry Reid's of the world are undermining the founding principles that made the United States of America the greatest country in the world. Mark Levin is not only a constitutional attorney but he is also an intellectual genius who has fought these very people while working in the Justice Department during the Reagan administration."

Mark R. Levin: *"The Liberty Amendments:" Restoring the American Republic*

Although my book, *America You've Been Hustled,* focuses mainly on describing America's enemy within our own citizenry and how we must elect constitutional-conservatives before we reach the "tipping point" or crash; Mark's book describes an alternative route to return America to its foundations. If we could only elect someone with his conservative genius and constitutional focus to be our President instead of the celebrity liberals that the masses worship – our future would be assured Liberty, Justice and "The Pursuit of Happiness."

Third party review by Kenneth Ahearn: **Take Back Our Country…** August 13, 2013

Mark Levin is a former member of the Reagan Administration, who worked in the Department of Justice. He is now the President of Landmark Legal Services, which has defended the U.S. Constitution in courtrooms. At the same time, he is host of The Mark Levin Radio Show, where he has educated his audience about the Constitution.

He has seen the Federal Government take more power for itself, and in the process it is making citizens nearly slaves with no concern about our opinions and future. Although this has occurred over several Administrations, President Obama is taking it to a new level using obvious lawlessness knowing nobody will stop him. Plus, the Congress has no concern about our climbing debt, gives legal making authority to Government agencies via regulations, and the Supreme Court has begun rewriting law (e.g. Justice Roberts) to make Obamacare constitutional. These people are all part of the Washington inner circle, who are only concerned about how to ingratiate themselves and make money with no concern for the public or country.

Mark Levin has outlined a way to take back our country with a long-term lasting approach, and it is almost like one of the Founding Fathers came back to lead us out of the darkness, where we had no hope except to get out of the way of the Federal leviathan. God bless Mark for his contribution, and now it is up to the states and their population to grab this tool and reclaim our country for our future and our children.

Every American who cares about our future should take the time each night to listen to Mark's recorded shows. Go to www.marklevinshow.com and follow the "Audio Rewind" of his taped shows. This great American is, in my opinion, the greatest source of God fearing constitutional conservative information we have in this country today. Listen to him daily and you will be informed and motivated to the take the most important actions we need to save America from the Liberal Socialist Democrats plan to enslave the average American to the socialist agenda. If there is anyway Mark would run for national office he

would crush the LSD agenda and in my opinion make more progress than even the great Ronald Reagan.

Additional books by Mark: *"The Liberty Amendments: Restoring The American Republic," "Ameritopia: The Unmaking of America," "Men in Black: How the Supreme Court is Destroying America,"* and *"Abraham Lincoln's Gettysburg Address Illustrated."*

Rush Limbaugh: ***"The Way Things Ought to Be"*** and ***"See I Told You So"*** were written in the early 90s but, of course, are still appropriate in today's political environment. Again, he is the Superstar on the radio analyzing the day's events, cutting through the liberal "HUSTLE" and advancing constitutional conservative principles.

God Bless all of these great conservative authors…

I apologize to the many authors that I haven't cited in this book, "*America You've Been Hustled.*" There just isn't enough room. By searching any of these books on Amazon, anyone can find a tremendous source of conservative works which will equip readers with the tools to help us return America to its moral and economic roots.

Chapter 31

The "Separation of Church and State" – Why have Liberal Socialist Democrats redefined this "Free Exercise Clause" to mean freedom "from" religion? We have gone from blessings to curses in just 50 years! Expect it to get much worse if we don't reverse the Radical Atheist and Socialist movements…

Children aren't born knowing how to live life with integrity, work ethic, confidence and respect; yet their future depends on it. – D. W. Burdick

I'm making a prediction at the beginning of this chapter – there will be a major push of the liberal socialist democrats in the near future that serves two of their long term goals. Those goals are to finish removing God from America and collect more income taxes from producers for wealth redistribution to their friends and supporters.

Here is the prediction: Charitable deductions to churches will be slowly phased out and then completely disallowed because of the left's perversion of the meaning of the "Separation of Church and State." This is a battle they will lose for a long time but remember, they have very long-term socialist goals and so far it looks like they are winning. Again, I believe they are winning because conservative republicans play fair in a dirty fight while liberal socialist democrats hit below the belt, use brass knuckles and even gouge conservatives' eyes in full view of the public. Stupid republicans think they are in a fair fight with some kind of proper and dignified rules. **When will we learn to publically call these LSD bold faced pathological liars out?**

This is a war for the survival of America that the Founding Fathers created to be the light of the world for all future generations. Instead, liberal socialist democrats want to return America to tyrannical rulers who will take from those they don't like and give to those they do like – crony capitalism anyone? Sure, they do everything in the name of "fairness" for the poor, but the poor are just pawns they use to gain and keep their membership in the ruling class "Club" of royals.

These self-professed intellectuals gather in "Martha's Vineyard" every year and laugh at the rest of the nation that "eats cake."

The separation of church and state was born out of the excessive power that the Church of England welded over the people of England. Initially prompted by a dispute over the annulment of the marriage of Henry VIII to Catherine of Aragon, the Church of England separated from the Roman Catholic Church in 1534 and became the established church by an Act of Parliament in the Act of Supremacy. The King wanted the additional powers of a Pope.

Liberal socialist democrats are heavily infiltrated with secularist and radical atheists who just want God gone from America. Some hate God and some think that anyone who believes in God is simple minded. Their lack of any spiritual discernment would be really sad if they weren't destroying the moral fabric of America and the future of this great country.

The "First Amendment" of the "Bill of Rights" to the "Constitution" of the United States:

> Congress shall make no law respecting an establishment of religion, or prohibiting the free exercise thereof; or abridging the freedom of speech, or of the press; or the right of the people peaceably to assemble, and to petition the Government for a redress of grievances.

One does not need a pointy headed lawyer to understand what it says and we all know that secular God hating liberal socialist democrats have completely perverted this constitutional right (liberty) to attack Christian values and public expressions. Political correctness (PC) was invented to club to death freedom loving conservatives!

"Or prohibiting the free exercise thereof" means exactly what it says no matter how many secular leaning judges twist the meaning to align with their own personal agendas. "We the People" are protected by the United States Constitution to express our Christian beliefs and values anywhere we want within reason; this includes government property. That means crosses and Christmas trees cannot be prohibited under the First Amendment from public property. If space allows – crosses, Christmas trees and nativity scenes stay!

How in the world have Christian leaders let secular democrats get away with this crime against our Founders, the Constitution and the rest of us Christian believers is beyond my understanding!

It's long overdue for the silent majority to be resoundingly heard…

The principles of Christian beliefs are tolerance, charity, turn the other cheek, forgiveness and many other loving actions that no one should have a problem with. It's not the principles that the LSD has a problem with – it's God. I believe if we fight for righteousness, God will bless our cause and give us victory over these God haters. If we don't – we're doomed… We believe this mortal life is temporary, but the next life is eternal. An Atheist believes this life is all they will ever have, which is why they will do anything to get all they can before they die. Too bad for them in the next life! I pray their minds will get out of the way of their spirits and souls – before it's too late.

Agnostics and mild atheism is not corrosive to society, it is the militant radical atheist that is at war with Christianity – the moral fabric that this country is built upon…

Conservatives should detail the near riots within the DNC at the 2012 Democratic National Convention in Charlotte, North Carolina when the leadership wanted God and Israel put back in the party planks at the near riot vocal objections of the atheists in the convention. This is just more evidence that the party of radical atheists is the Democrat Party. I don't have a problem with atheists unless they push their anti-God, anti-Jesus, anti-Jewish, anti-Israel public agenda on the United States of America.

Congress must pass legislation reversing the Supreme Court's mis-interpretation of the "Free Exercise" and the resulting "Separation of Church and State." Hopefully we will have a conservative God fearing president by then to pass it…

Chapter 32

A World full of Religious Hustlers: Man perverts the Word of God and then uses Him for power, money, control, fame and sex… They are as addicted as any drug addict but none of them every go to rehab!

It's not my intention to slander any religion in this chapter. It is my intention to slander men who have used God for their own personal gain. I am a born-again Christian. Like all true Christians, I worship the God of Abraham, Ismael and Isaac. The same God worshiped by the Jews and Muslims. Jews and Muslims accept the historical evidence of Jesus as a great prophet or teacher. The difference between them and me is that I believe every word Jesus Christ said and that He is the Messiah, the Son of God and the Savior of our souls.

Some say the Jews believe the Jewish messiah will be a leader anointed by God, physically descended from the Davidic line, and will rule the united tribes of Israel and herald the Messianic Age of global peace also known as the World to Come. Christians believe Jesus is that Man and will return at the appointed time to accomplish his kingdom and the global peace for all who believe in him. My scripture says "every" knee will bow and "every" tongue will confess that Jesus is Lord.

History is filled with the manipulation of multitudes in the name of God. Many religious leaders have manipulated the word of God or religious history to gain power, money, control, fame and even sex. Isn't that one of the primary reasons people have risked their lives over the centuries to come to America – to escape these religious control freaks. Some of these psychopaths have murdered millions in the name of God; others have killed their followers or even convinced them to commit mass suicide in the name of God. How pathetic is it that people are so gullible that they allow these religious hustlers to control their minds to the point of mass murder, suicide and death of innocent humans? Is it any wonder that gullible democrats in America allow their socialist leaders control their minds and beliefs, and allow themselves to be used as pawns to vote these "hustlers" into office?

Instead of worshiping just God, men worship other men, places and things. The word of God is sacred – not the book it is written in. Men have killed and are still killing other men, who were created by God, in His Image, because they disgraced another man or a book. Who in the world believes God would approve such a thing.

Weak minded men and women have followed these religious leaders to their ultimate death throughout history. It is even more pathetic that they have killed hundreds of millions of innocent humans following these psychopathic religious leaders. The crusades of the middle ages are beyond the scope of this book but can be summarized as: A series of wars taking place in and around the Middle East and Asia Minor between 1100 and 1600. European nations and religious leaders like Pope Urban II and Pope Gregory VII used propaganda to justify these religious expeditionary wars.

How sick was it that European religious, and non-religious, leaders justified the persecution of Jews and Muslims. Innocent people around the world may be suffering today because of those past sins. Conversely, I firmly believe that America's war on terrorism and tyrannical leaders like Saddam Hussein and Osama bin Laden were completely justified along with bringing freedom to the people of Iraq and Afghanistan. America can't just ignore terrorism in the world today or it will spread like cancer… to eventually destroy us here, in our homes and cities.

We should have maintained a large military presence in those countries to ensure the peace that our blood and treasure won. We did that in Europe after World War II in our long term resistance to communism and it worked. Why in the world wouldn't we do the same in these equally important nations? We fought and died to bring freedom to the Middle East, which includes democracy. Why would we just waste all of those military lives and trillions of dollars to just leave those freed people behind to be brutalized again by their psychopathic religious leaders? History will prove that this was a big LSD mistake and Obama is to blame.

Christian denominations are creations of men, not God. Many of these men throughout history and even today have perverted scriptures for their own personal gain whether it is for money, power or control of the weak minded. Reasonable people around these men in power will simply look the other way and enable them to engage in sick behaviors. One only needs to look at the Catholic Church and the homosexual pedophile priests that have abused innocent children for who knows how long? I joined a very large church in Orlando Florida in 1984. Soon afterwards the head pastor was dismissed because he had adulteress affairs with dozens of women – both married and unmarried. There will always be con men like these who prey off weak-willed people.

I believe God fearing people should avoid <u>worshiping</u> anyone or anything except God the Father, God the Son and God the Holy Spirit. To justify harming or killing a fellow human being in the name of religious belief for dishonoring anyone or anything is not from God, it is from a religious hustler, a con man! We should avoid worshiping or praying to any historical or current man/women such as:

- Pastors, Preachers or Evangelists
- Jewish Rabbis
- The Pope
- Catholic Priests, Bishops or Cardinals
- The mother of Jesus Christ
- The twelve Apostles or Disciples of Jesus Christ
- Messengers of God including Angels, Moses and Muhammad
- The prophets of the Torah, the New Testament and the Qur'an
- Any historical person elevated to the category of Sainthood
- Islamic clerics or Muslim religious leaders

The Word of God also condemns worshiping any material item or thing which is idolatry – including:

- Images or religious symbols
- Pictures of God or Christ
- Medals, medallions or images of religious leaders or saints
- Crosses
- Bibles, including the Torah, the New Testament and the Qur'an

One can hold any of the above in high esteem and with great reverence and respect, but God's word is very clear that anyone worshiping them and surely killing anyone that is disrespecting them, such as the Qur'an, has no fear of the living God and has become a puppet of a radical religious leader.

Again, I am a God fearing Christian believer and have a great deal of respect for peace loving Jews and Muslims. My only problem is with men that are nothing more than slick talking "hustlers" with religious pathologies that con their fellow man/woman into their narcissistic schemes, i.e., "extremists." Why is it that they always get gullible young men to "sacrifice" their lives for the "cause" but these con men never sacrifice their own lives? Is it because they feel privileged and too important – meaning their lives are more important than those they are sending to their deaths? I suspect God has a special punishment waiting for these hustlers because of their evil arrogance, and the murder of not only innocent children of their enemies, but the young men, or children, of their own people. I just can't understand how so many people can fall for all of these religious scams.

Radical Muslims do not represent Islam, the vast majority of Muslims or the words of Muhammad written in the Qur'an, any more than Jim Jones of Jamestown, Guyana or David Koresh of Waco, Texas represents Jesus Christ or the Christian church. The hustled young men, of these radical religious control freaks, are no different than other gullible dupes everywhere when they blindly, without question or investigation, follow slick talking con men's directions.

Again, the vast majority of Muslims worldwide want the same thing peace loving Jews and Christians want – to live in peace, to prosper from their work and investments, to raise families, to own property and to enjoy life, "The Pursuit of Happiness." The only thing getting in the way of their happiness is a religious con man.

The only thing getting in the way of "all" Americans experiencing "The Pursuit of Happiness" today are the political control freak hustlers in the Liberal Socialist Democratic Party, of which some are the radical atheists discussed in Chapter 34.

Chapter 33

Religious Jews, Christians and Muslims all worship and serve the same God… The God of Abraham – the Israeli Jews' and Arab Muslims' genetic Forefather! So why do "Radical" Muslims want to kill Jews and Christians?

Three of the great religions on earth all have the same origins and are related by birth or choice from the same Patriarch, Abraham. Abraham's first born son, Ismael, is the "Father" of Islam and Arab Muslims. Ismael's mother, Hagar, was Abraham's second wife or his first wife's maidservant. Some accounts say she was an Egyptian Princess, the daughter of a Pharaoh. Abraham's second son, Isaac, was born 14 years later and is the "Father" of the Israeli Jews. Sarah was Abraham's first wife and the mother of Isaac. Why then do Arab Muslim leaders want to exterminate Jews if they have the same ancestral father, Abraham, and are half-brothers by birth with Jews? The easy answer is because some men are inherently evil, especially when given power. It was the powerful Jewish leaders that had Jesus killed because they felt he threatened their leadership and powerbase. Today, we read about religious Muslim leaders who want to "wipe" the Jews off the face of the earth and destroy America and other "Western" Christian nations.

Jews, Christians and Muslims all worship the same God, the God of Abraham. Abraham's God is described first by Moses in the Old Testament writings of the Torah, then by Jesus and authors of the New Testament, and finally by Mohammad in the Qur'an. The Jewish Torah and the Christian New Testament make up the complete Christian Bible. I believe the strong a divergence describing attributes of the God of the Bible, the Lord God, and the God of the Qur'an, Allah, is that the Bible uniquely reveals that in his essence the ***Lord God is love.*** Is this divergence the reason radical Islam wants Jews and Christians dead? What I mean by that is if the Muslim God, Allah, is not a God of love, where humans are his children, then that difference alone may account for Radical Muslims hating Jews and Christians.

The vast majority of Muslims want the same thing Jews and Christians want – to live in peace, to prosper from their work and investments, to raise families, to own property, to enjoy life and to "Pursue Happiness." But throughout the ages men with hardened hearts and lust for riches and power have waged war against neighbors and even their own people to take what they wanted by brute force. You would think in the year 2013 that the world would have matured beyond this insanity. Apparently not!

The title of this book, ***"America You've Been Hustled"*** also applies to those leaders around the world that are feeding off their weak minded countrymen to gain power and control. The "Arab Spring" of 2012 almost brought about a power shift in the region by those wanting the freedoms and personal wealth that is enjoyed in the West but it slipped away at the hands of the tyrannical leaders. History may point the finger at Obama for missing the opportunity to influence the outcome but who really knows for sure if America could have made a difference.

Here is something to think about if you believe in God and especially if you are a bible believing Christian: Jesus said, **"I would rather you are hot or cold – if you're lukewarm I will vomit you!"** Sorry, but the future of America is at stake – pick a side… Don't believe in Jesus? Even Jews and Muslims believe in Jesus – they just believe he was one of the great Prophets in history.

Really? He said, "He was the son of God and was the Word of God that created heaven and earth. He said He was the Savior of mankind and that whoever believed in Him would be with Him in heaven for eternity." Either he was who he said he was or he was crazy; it can't be both. If he was [is] who he said he is; you better read what he taught in the New Testament and get right with God before you take your last breath! Too intelligent to believe all this spiritual nonsense but you believe in "the big bang theory" and evolution? Consider this: Many believe it's mathematically impossible for the hummingbird and the giant blue whale to have evolved from the same single cell organism. It's far more likely that in the vastness of our unlimited universe there is a supreme being capable of creating earth and everything in it. Does this God exist in a spiritual dimension? I believe so…

If there is such a being, has he [or she, for you PC freaks] ever made contact with man? **Many believe** he has made contact numerous times such as: He or his spokesmen [Angles] spoke to Job, Noah, Abraham and others several thousand years ago, to the Jews through Moses some 3,400 years ago, he spoke to Christians through His Son, Jesus Christ, some 2,040 years ago, he spoke to Muslims through Muhammad some 1,400 years ago, and he spoke to Mormons through Joseph Smith some 190 years ago. There are millions, even billions, who believe in one or more of the above. I'm not going to validate all of them except to say I'm a passionate Christian.

For you intellectuals that just dismiss any notion of God's existence, or at least his historical relevance, without a "personal" and thorough study of these religions is just lazy and moronic.

Morality doesn't originate from government or man's dictates, it comes from the God of Abraham, Ismael, Isaac, Jacob and Jesus Christ. Liberal socialist democrats and other secular strongholds have been successful in removing God from the "public square" and killing 55+ million American babies over the last 50 or 60 years. Maybe our curse is now complete! Maybe we are at the dawn of our destruction. Only time will tell...

I could go on for several more pages on the subject of God and State, but what's the use, either you have spiritual curiosity and discernment, or you don't. If you have known hypocrites that claim to be religious but are liars, cheaters and otherwise crooks and they are keeping you from discovering God, you're in good company. That's the excuse of most people avoiding God. More words on these pages probably will not make any difference.

One more thought: We are spiritual beings. Our flesh is temporal but our spirits are eternal. My bible says: "God is Spirit, and we must worship Him in Spirit and in truth." Please don't allow your physical brain to block your spirit's search for Truth...

I hope and pray you search for and discover God before it's too late for your eternal soul/spirit!

Chapter 34

Why are so many Jews atheists? Even atheists benefit from a Godly society so why do radical atheists hate anything God and put so much effort in using our biblically based court system to restrict public Christian expressions?

Christians don't force their beliefs on atheists so why do radical atheists and other radical non-Christian faiths force their beliefs on Christians. Why are so many Jews atheists? Is it because God's chosen people descended from the Jews that built the golden calf to worship and pray to during the Exodus of Egypt instead of listening to Moses' instructions and believing in the God of Abraham, Isaac and Jacob? These people were eye witnesses to the great supernatural miracles that God preformed through Moses and Aaron in Egypt and later in the desert. These miracles are written in Jewish and Egyptian history and caused the Pharaoh to let millions of Jewish slaves leave Egypt. Talk about a stiff necked people!

Many of the decedents of those spiritually blind Jews are now running most of the world's central and money center banks, college campuses, news media, television networks, Madison Avenue and Hollywood. And there're removing God and morality from the American culture and building modern day "Golden Calves" to worship! What a huge mistake! Don't they realize even they are doomed to suffer from a Godless society in the future if their efforts continue to succeed?

Let me make this perfectly clear after the opening statements above. I'm not anti-Semitic, I'm not anti-Muslim and I'm not even anti-atheist. Everyone is entitled to their opinions and beliefs. The vast majority of atheists are not radical activists trying to restrict religious or Christian freedoms or expressions, whether private or public; so I have no issues with them. What Americans shouldn't tolerate is any group restricting our Christian religious freedom to express our beliefs anywhere we want. Again, I'm not anti-Semitic – my bible says those who bless Israel will be blessed and those who curse Israel will be cursed. I'm a

Christian who believes the Jews are God's chosen people and that Jesus and his early followers were Jews. I have met several Jews who believe Jesus was exactly who he said he was – the Messiah, the Son of God, and the Savior of his people along with the rest of the world who confess and believe what he said in the New Testament. I have met many orthodox Jews that pray daily and follow their religion to the letter. I have also met many Christian Jews that pray daily and follow their religion to the letter and the "Spirit." I admire each.

Other than atheistic Jews, will someone explain to me why the majority of Jews vote for democrats? Jews as a culture teach their children the requirements to become financially successful. Why in the world would they align themselves with the failed financial policies of leftist socialism, i.e., democrat policies? Is it because they love the connections that "give" them an edge to success and attaining power?

Probably…

Through-out modern history Jews have proven to be some of the most brilliant, creative people in science, medicine, banking and investments, and certainly in entertainment and movies. Why do they need any crony connections to gain an edge that the rest of us don't have? They talk about fairness and balance only when they want more tax money or regulations that will benefit them, i.e., crony-capitalism.

I also believe some Jews are very tribal and group together to the benefit of their "tribe," to use their term. "Club" connections anyone? That is not necessarily a bad thing – it's a good thing as long as they are a God fearing, religious people who believe in the Ten Commandments given to Moses during the Exodus. In case you don't know, or have forgotten the Ten Commandments I include them below from my bible:

> And God spoke these words, saying: "I am the Lord your God, who brought you out of Egypt, out of the house of bondage."

1. You shall have no other gods before me.

2. You shall not make for yourself any carved image, or any likeness of anything that is in heaven above, or that is in the earth

beneath, or that is in the water under the earth; you shall not bow down to them nor serve them. For I, the Lord your God, am a jealous God, visiting the iniquity of the fathers on the children to the third and fourth generations of those who hate me, but showing mercy to thousands, to those who love Me and keep My commandments.

3. You shall not take the name of the Lord your God in vain, for the Lord will not hold him guiltless who takes His name in vain.

4. Remember the Sabbath day, to keep it holy. Six days you shall labor and do all your work, but the seventh day is the Sabbath of the Lord your God. In it you shall do no work: you, nor your son, nor your daughter, nor your manservant, nor your maidservant, nor your cattle, nor your stranger who is within your gates. For in six days the Lord made the heavens and the earth, the sea, and all that is in them, and rested the seventh day. Therefore the Lord blessed the Sabbath day and hallowed it.

5. Honor your father and your mother, that your days may be long upon the land which the Lord your God is giving you.

6. You shall not murder.

7. You shall not commit adultery.

8. You shall not steal.

9. You shall not bear false witness against your neighbor.

10. You shall not covet your neighbor's house; you shall not covet your neighbor's wife, nor his manservant, nor his maidservant, nor his ox, nor his donkey, nor anything that is your neighbor's."

Nearly One-thousand four-hundred years after God gave Moses the Ten Commandments Jesus was asked, "Which is the greatest commandment in the Law?" Jesus replied,

11. "Love the Lord your God with all your heart and with all your soul and with all your mind. This is the greatest commandment."
12. "And the second is like it: Love your neighbor as yourself. All the Law and the Prophets hang on these two commandments." "The golden rule!"

Can anyone explain to me why a radical atheist has a problem with these commandments, laws or rules, especially number 12? Do they want to be murdered, or have their wives or possessions taken from them? Or do they just hate God and want to control others to gain power, money and fame? I love and pray for Israel and all of Gods' people and even those who are spiritually challenged and have no inner spiritual sense of God. I pity the spiritually challenged and believe they will eventually see the "Light."

One of my favorite movies was *The Bucket List* staring Jack Nicholson and Morgan Freeman. I have one that everyone should consider adding to their "bucket list" and experience before they die. The experience I'm referring to is a deep Spiritual awakening. I'm not talking about the knowledge of God – I'm talking about the Spirit of God. My bible says God is Spirit and must be worshiped in "Spirit and in Truth." How do you do this? Most people experience this simply by humbling themselves before God and asking Him to help them know Him [better]. Maybe it happens in the privacy of your own room by yourself or perhaps in church with others surrounding you. Maybe it happens the first time you try and maybe it takes years of study and meditation.

For me it happened when I was very young and my grandmother, who was very spiritual, shared the story of Jesus with me. Like any very young child I truly believed everything she told me. I even experienced a physiological miracle that no one could deny or take from me. I had about 7 big warts that just went away, after we prayed, over a few days but left smooth spots for years. Everyone in my family witnessed this and I shared this miracle for years (now for 50 plus years.) The problem was she lived 1,500 hundred miles away and I only saw her one more time before she died. I only remember a few more "religious" encounters in churches when I was young but never anything that had an impact on me.

My parents were very good people who taught me and my siblings right from wrong, the 10 Commandments and certainly the Golden Rule. I never saw my parents "sin" and never even noticed them argue. That's not what I'm talking about. Being "good" and not sinning is not experiencing God, although being bad and sinning will separate us from Him.

My adult Spiritual awakening occurred after I had ruined my first marriage with the young women that God led to me when I was 18 years old and married 5 years later. I had always prided myself on my integrity and never even flirted with another woman – until our 10th year together. To make a long story short I broke her heart and I fell into a deep state of guilt and depression. It was during this time that God led some high school Christian friends back into my life. I knew I was a Christian but humbled myself before them and God by confessing my sins and restating my belief in Jesus Christ and turning my life over to him.

It was not then that I had the deeply Spiritual awakening, although I did feel very different and "reborn." It was later, when I was all alone and experiencing a deep sense worthlessness that I literally cried out to Jesus to help me with my emotional pain and help me turn my life around. Not only did I experience something deep inside my being that I had never even come close to experiencing before, but my request to help me turn my life around was answered very quickly.

I owned three pieces of real estate, one with my ex-wife, all of which I had been trying to sell for over a year. I also wanted to change careers and move out of the area I grew up and disgraced myself in. Within 30 days I sold all three properties and was hired by Dean Witter Reynolds as a stock broker trainee and moved to another city. I saw this as another miracle because everything happened so fast. This was in 1983 with interest rates historically high and real estate moving very slowly. Sure, it could have been coincidental, but when combined with my deeply moving "Spiritual" experience that broke my depression I considered it a sign from God – no one can ever take those miracles away from me either.

I have had several more similar Spiritual experiences, some during sad times when I felt the "Holy Spirit" comforting me, but mostly during prayer and worship. I'm not trying to "convert" anyone to be a follower of Jesus Christ. That's the Holy Spirit's job. I'm only trying to share the experiences I have had with God the Father, his Son Jesus Christ and the Holy Spirit! I believe God will direct anyone who wants to know Him to me or others who believe as I do. I don't preach – I share!

I also pray for America and Israel to be blessed. Not only blessed with health, safety and prosperity – but to know and serve Him better. I pray for our leaders, even the liberal socialist democrats I severally criticize throughout this book. That's what my bible says we should do. Anyone can pray for and bless their friends and family – Jesus prayed for and blessed those who persecuted and even crucified him.

I don't know any "true" Christian that believes any differently. If they do, I suspect they are not "true" Christians or at least they are misguided. The admonitions in this book are meant to educate, enlighten, wake-up and quicken the open minded. If spiritual curiosity or voting behaviors are changed – I will consider this endeavor hugely successful and a Blessing from God…

- It is incredibly puzzling to me how a God fearing Christian who should be sensitive to the promptings of the Holy Spirit can belong to the Democrat Party; an organization hell bent on removing God from America and the Party most responsible for the government approved murder of more than 55 million American babies. The Democrat Party is home to the American Socialist Party and those who are the enemies of God the Father, God the Son (Jesus Christ) and God the Holy Spirit. If anyone who claims to be a God fearing Christian can explain this rationalization to me please let me know…
- It's amazing that so many scientists believe in the big bang theory of the creation – the creation of "something out of nothing," but can't comprehend the possibility of a Creator. And, if they do consider the possibility, then has the Creator ever made contact with Mankind? And if the Creator has made contact then to whom? Was it Abraham, Moses, David or the bible Prophets? Was Jesus who he said he was – GOD entering our world, as a baby, to PERSONALLY teach us about God the Father, Himself and the Holy Spirit, and how to live and

thrive with each other? Have you read the red letters of the Christian New Testament (Jesus' words)? Maybe you should…

- Did the giant redwood sequoia, an orange tree, the bald eagle, the killer whale, the elephant and your house cat or dog come from the same primordial soup? Some super genius mathematicians don't think it's possible. Can't get over the weird stories of the bible and the hypocrites in churches? Don't let those two reasons, or any reason for that matter, keep you from experiencing something you were created to experience. You will be physically dead someday, don't be "Spiritually" dead until then…

So many questions, so little interest, by so many people…

Chapter 35

Abortion: What would a God fearing conservative's provocative book about the destruction of America by liberal socialist democrats be without this discussion?

First, when does human life begin? Is it at conception or when the baby takes its first breath? Is it when the baby can survive without the mother? Is it totally arbitrary and up to the mother alone? This is what this country needs to decide and if it's not on religious grounds it should be on scientific grounds. How would a scientist determine the answers to the above questions?

I remember having a similar discussion decades ago with my older brother. He was a church going Christian but he believed, like most pro-choice people believe, that as long as the baby was inside the mother she was the only one who could decide if the baby would be allowed to live. He simply didn't believe abortion was killing. A few years later my brother also had a "Spiritual Awakening." I sensed he was a different person so I asked him again what he believed about the abortion issue. He had a total change of heart and absolutely believed abortion was taking a human life and that it was totally wrong. What was different? Why did he have such a change of heart? I pray everyone will learn, or better yet, experience the answer to that question. I prefer the term experience instead of learn because I believe a Spiritual Awakening cannot be taught. It is a gift to those who earnestly seek it…

I believe a man and a woman genetically create a human, but God creates the spirit that goes with that child – the soul… The next time you look in the mirror thank your mother for giving birth to you and allowing you to live. Then try to contemplate the 55+ million aborted souls that never had the chance to look in the mirror.

A minority, not a majority, of Americans believe the Supreme Court was justified in allowing a woman to terminate that "thing" growing inside her. They believe it's her reproductive right to put a stop to the baby's heart beat and that no one should be able to tell her what she can or can't do with her own body. "It's her right to privacy." Really, she can't have sex for money but she can kill her baby if she wants to. Shock! I used the word kill instead of abort. What kind of insensitive hate monger am I?

The logic goes – if she has no use for the child and doesn't want to be bothered by the nine month pregnancy ordeal or doesn't like/love the father enough to bring that particular child into the world or wants a boy instead of a girl; then it's her decision – not societies'.

Not much difference from that line of reasoning and the lynching of black slaves 200 years ago. Remember the slave was the property of the owner. The owner could do anything he wanted to do with the slave. The mindset back then was the same as the mindset of the pro-choice believers today – there is no real difference. I wonder if it will take another 100 years for us to come to our senses and realize abortion is just government approved murder. Too harsh? Not as harsh as what the baby suffers…

When I was young and before I became spiritually awake I would have approved of my girlfriend having an abortion. Looking back when I was 19 and my girlfriend was 17 and she was still in high school, we thought she was pregnant so we tried everything to cause a miscarriage. That was 1971 before abortion was legal.

I also remember 24 years later when my first child, Natalie, was born. It was the happiest day of my life. I was right there watching her take her first breath and I was overcome with joy, tears and awe. After my third child was born I did not think it was a good idea to have any more children so I got fixed. Strange term for getting a vasectomy! I had several reasons: 1. I was over 45 and felt it is best for children to have a younger father instead of a father old enough to be their grandfather; 2. Due to the possibility of over population of the world, I felt three children were plenty; 3. It cost a lot of money to raise a child and I was not sure their mother and I could provide for another; and, 4. If I died before the child was out of college it would be unfair to her/him.

First, liberals like to pretend they represent the weak and the disadvantaged. They don't… It's just another lying con job! The weakest group there is – is the unborn baby human. The liberal socialist democrats are the ones most responsible for over 55 million abortions since Roe vs. Wade legalized abortion in 1973. **That Supreme Court was insane! It said to the world that America was so self-absorbed that**

we could now dispose of un-wanted babies. Any young adult knows that the "thing" growing inside the mother will become a baby if left alone. Has this led to a further breakdown of morality and a high rate of inner city gang murders? **We need God's leadership NOW…**

That The Republican Party has been working to over-turn this horrible mistake for nearly 40 years. Since approximately 50 percent of these unborn babies would grow up to be women if they weren't terminated – then over 28 million women are dead today because of liberal socialist democrats. Let me repeat – the unborn female would grow up to be a women if she were not *"terminated."* She is not a tumor or an appendix, she is an unborn female, and if left alone and given the opportunity of birth she would become a beautiful baby girl and probably grow up to be someone's girlfriend or wife. Sure, the LSD Party is the party for women's rights! What self-centered lying hypocrites!

Secondly, a much higher percentage of black babies are aborted each year than white babies. Surely democrats know they are approving the abortion of more blacks proportionally than whites. If not, just how smart and are they? Democrats are the ultimate racists. **Now compare the Republican Party to the secular liberal socialist democrats!** Abortion in America is a racist hate crime because poor blacks are aborted much more disproportionately to middle and upper class whites. If you are a middle or upper class white democrat (or republican) and you believe abortion is a woman's right then you better search your heart. You may be a racist! Population control anybody? Sure, why not? Liberals love mother earth and baby seals, but hate mankind.

Thirdly, it's amazing that God fearing republicans are trying to save that poor black baby girl from being torn out of her mother and thrown into the garbage, but they are the ones being demonized as racist, against women's rights and against the poor by liberal socialist democrats. ***Again, hypocrisy reigns supreme!***

Lastly, let's compromise – make a law that only rich white baby boys can be aborted. Or all baby boys since this is a women's issue. BUT, after the second abortion the man and the woman have to be sterilized. Two dead babies should be enough – even for liberal socialist democrats! Does this absurdity make any sense to you intellectual liberal socialist democrats? ***Not Likely!***

I met a man while I was writing this chapter. The subject of God came up and we discovered how similar our spiritual beliefs were. The subject of abortion naturally came up because it is a passion of mine. He emotionally shared with me that he and his wife had recently adopted a new born baby girl that was to be aborted until members of his church persuaded the mother to let the baby live and be adopted. The mother was black and was a drug addict. My tears fell as he related his story! God bless those two wonderful parents for saving this baby and giving her a home and a future. Another great couple, and close friends of mine, at my church did exactly the same thing for a little black boy. Why did these Christian couples rescue these children from death or at least a life with few prospects? UNCONDITIONAL LOVE... Some would even say Godly Love!

Fellow Americans, what will be the legacy of our nation in 2100; what will be your legacy? That's just 85 year from now. Will America become just another fallen great civilization that could not survive its own success or will we overcome the predicable obstacles that have brought down every other great civilization before us? I refer you to the quote of Alexander Tytler on the opening chapter of this book. It won't be easy, but we can change the current direction we're heading in. It will take hard work and great courage – something that Americans have in abundance...

There is a conservative/libertarian movement gaining momentum in this country within the very groups that vote predominately for liberal socialist democrats. I'm talking about college students and other youths, Hispanic and Black Americans, seniors and many other groups. I believe it's because these brave people can see the truth, the "Hustle" and the con, that liberal socialist democrats have been feeding them for generations. They are no longer following the liberal herds!

I hope and pray that America comes to its senses before it's too late. I'm amazed God hasn't cursed America by now – maybe it's too late, maybe not, maybe we're in the middle of our nation's curse. Pray that God forgives us for our arrogance and the evil we have inflected on each other – especially the 55+ million babies we have killed by "choice" and in the name of convenience....

Don't believe in God? YOU WILL...

Chapter 36

THE OBAMA DOCTRINE

Consider this: Is his plan to use local (community), State, Federal and Global chaos to accelerate the socialist tipping point and bringing down the big trophy – America? Is he causing the chaos?

Is Obama the most incompetent president ever or the most cunning? If everything in the world today is going according to his plan, he's not incompetent, he's is the most cunning world leader ever…

What every conservative is calling incompetence Obama and his minions may be laughing at behind closed doors because conservatives are too stupid to connect the dots. Here are some of the dots, starting with the mentors of young Barrack and those he met after college:

- Obama's anti-colonialist, anti-American/anti-British father – Obama, Sr.
- Communist Party propagandist and anti-Christian – Frank Marshal
- American anarchist, bomber and accused cop killer – Bill Ayers
- 20-year church pastor, anti-American and hate peddler – Jeremiah Wright
- Socialist, communist, anarchist and Satin admirer – Saul Alinsky
- He negotiates with republicans with a flame thrower, and
- He negotiates with communist Putin and anti-Christian Iran with his pants around his ankles
- He talks anti-police and is systematically weakening our military
- He pits as many Americans against each other as possible using group propaganda, envy and racism that promotes hatred
- He said he would "Fundamentally Transform the United States of America" – what did he really mean/plan?

The best case for him being incompetent over evil cleverness is he has two girls that will inherit a poorer and more dangerous world. This idea doesn't apply if he feels he can protect them from harm or if he has an idealistic derangement and therefore believes the world will be better under fascist socialism, especially if he in control.

He is the leader of the **L**iberal **S**ocialist **D**emocratic (the **LSD**) Party where idealistic hallucinations and ignoring conservative free-market wealth building empirical evidence is common place.

Power, money, control and fame is the drug of choice for these political maniacs.

Is the Obama Doctrine derived from Saul Alinsky's "Rules for Radicals" book that was dedicated to Satin?

Only President Obama or possibly his closest advisors know if the erosion and decline of America and worldwide chaos is their plan or simply the result of massive and unrepentant incompetence. Remember what his minion said, **"Never let a crisis go to waste."**

The future and its historians will reveal the answers to the above questions. Of course, some combination of incompetence and his plan to "Fundamentally Transform the United States of America" could be a more accurate truth.

If we follow a Barrack Hussein presidency with a Hillary Rodham presidency we may never recover and the LSD Party's liberal fascism will replace the freedom and liberty derived from true free-market capitalism and a **"Republic"** that the founders created.

Currently we are a country where anyone of any race can go from poverty to prosperity. There is no longer such a thing as "white privilege" because there are so many people of color that are self-made millionaires, even billionaires. It is education (applied) that brings privilege, not skin color.

We had better elect a small-government, God-fearing, Reagan-like conservative in 2016 because the mess Obama will leave will be measurably worse than what President Jimmy Carter left Ronald Reagan.

I believe that person is Dr. Ben Carson and with God's help, and the prayers of millions, he will be elected.

Chapter 37

Wake up America – before it's too late! If we can put men on the moon – we can surely fix these problems!

America has a bigger problem with organized crime in Washington, DC than in LA, Chicago, Miami and NYC combined. I'm referring to politicians and bureaucrats, not the mob. The level of corruption in our federal government is killing the American dream. If we don't do something about it soon, we will have nobody to blame but ourselves. Look at how divisive our president has become – his assault on free-enterprise capitalism and small business entrepreneurs only proves this books' implications. And, the liberal Senate Majority Leader, Harry Reid, did not even allow an annual budget (as required by law) or any jobs programs passed by the House to come to a vote in the senate in four years – Obama's entire first term in office. Do you think there's any coincidence there? I wonder…

And, how dirty can they get with their slanderous accusations of our republican 2012 presidential candidate, Mitt Romney? A felon, tax cheat and a murderer! This man is an Eagle Scout, a deeply religious model of a family man and citizen. He may be a little too moderate for me and I didn't like the way his pro-Romney PACs treated Newt Gingrich and Rick Santorum, but he certainly has all the qualifications to turn this country around. He did it with his hugely successful turn-around private equity investment company, Bain Capital, and as the turn-around specialist who was credited with saving the 2002 Salt Lake City Olympics.

And, finally he was successful as Governor of the State of Massachusetts while working with huge democrat majorities. Wikipedia is a good start to becoming familiar with this great man of God and his qualifications. Those Christians who have a problem with Mormonism better study the scripture on "a house divided will not stand." I'm not an expert on Mormonism but their stated Christian beliefs are the same as any other Christian except for their "Another Testament of Jesus Christ." I'm in no position to judge the validity of this Testament but I know that every <u>devoted</u> Mormon I have ever met was an excellent moral family person, an asset to their community and very Godly in their behavior – Harry Reid being an exception.

I believe Mitt's moderate republican political leanings are more a result of his running for governor of a massively liberal state, Massachusetts, and then working with their liberal democrat house and senate of that state for four years as its governor. I'm stunned America chose Obama over this highly qualified man. I believe Mitt Romney would have made an excellent president, especially if we had also elected a conservative majority in the Senate. We'll never know how good he would have been for America, but we will surely know how bad Obama will be for America's future. That is unless this wizard of a politician is as good at blaming in the future as he has been in his first four years.

In the next election don't just vote for Conservative Republicans, vote God-fearing, Tea Party Patriot, Constitutional Conservative Republicans and/or Libertarians. Why in the world republicans have allowed the liberal socialist propaganda machine to demonize the Conservative Tea Party Movement is a political crime and a national disgrace. The Tea Party Movement is the greatest thing to happen to our country since the Republicans freed the slaves during Reconstruction. These people are Middle America Patriots and you can bet their numbers will grow in the future. They will not stand by and let the LSD Party destroy America without doing everything they can to stop them. Have the Tea Party politicians made some strategic or tactical political mistakes, especially with debt ceiling battles, probably, but their motives were absolutely right.

You, your children's and grandchildren's future depends on your votes, not just now but forever because socialist hustlers will never stop their insidious lust for more power, control, fame and fortune. Satin's big-government liberal socialist democrats either serve him willingly or out of ignorance and stupidity (co-dependent enabling). It doesn't really matter – freedom and prosperity are being replaced by tyranny and financial bankruptcy. If we don't sound the alarm for all who love the American way of life and a better standard of living for everyone, especially the poor, than by default, we are to blame for our destruction.

Are rich people, corporations and their managers responsible for keeping the rest of America down? If they are colluding with politicians and bureaucrats (crony capitalism) to get an unethical edge on everyone else – the answer is yes. But most rich people and corporations i.e., small business owners, don't have any political connections with cronies in government. Small business owners are the largest group of rich people and are the real targets of liberal socialist democrats call for more rules, regulations, controls and taxes.

The "Occupy Wall Street" morons were on the right tract – they just don't have the requisite intelligence or knowledge to distinguish the non-connected good rich from the crony-connected bad rich. Here is the bait and switch (hustle) that stupid Americans (or those not paying close attention) believe: "The rich are not paying their fair share." This lie is a misdirection trick by rich politicians and their connected rich cronies in the elite bastions of America.

The truth is; ***"rich liberals must use their connections to further enrich themselves."*** They need the poor to keep them in power to maintain those connections. Remember, liberals don't believe in competition, they believe: "If you have a successful business, you didn't build that business without roads, bridges and/or someone else's help," i.e., connections. Therefore, they need as many poor people in America as possible. Why do you think these crooks want to open the borders with Mexico and then give another 20 million poor Mexicans voting rights? Don't believe it – just keep your eyes and ears open…

Simply put – they're lying and they know it. Everyone has the same roads, bridges, education and someone else's help but only a few entrepreneurs made the right choices, were willing to work extraordinarily long hours, and likely risked all their wealth to start a new business. Every month they must stay alive to pay the bills and meet payroll. Some of these entrepreneurs become rich, but the vast majority does not. In fact, most don't make nearly as much money as they could if they worked for someone else – especially the government. They don't work for the government or run for office because they can't stomach the unethical crap that must be endured to succeed.

But again, democrats believe in and value connections to get ahead and Tea Party Conservatives believe in and value hard work, ethics and competitive excellence to get ahead. LSD's are naturally drawn to the government leviathan and its promise of the easy life. I'm not talking about the majority of government workers who are honest and hardworking. I'm referring to the leeches – and they know who they are. They make much more than the average American with an MBA degree and that's not enough – they want more.

I repeat and emphasize: the Democrat Party is a cesspool of dirty con artist politicians and deceitful elites that can't make it without connections and dirty dealings. Does that mean every democrat politician is dirty? Absolutely not! But ask yourself this question: How can any self-respecting democrat watch what their leadership and their leadership's slobbering sycophants in the media say and do to America and stay a democrat? These guys/girls enter politics with average means and before they retire they're worth millions. Democrats are the party of: "It's not what you know – it's who you know." Just look at Obama's resume and all his multi-millionaire and billionaire supporters…

Wake up America – can't you see "You've Been Hustled?"

Are some republicans, especially moderates and the republican establishment, dirty? Yes, some of them. Why do you think the Tea Party movement grew spontaneously after the 2008 elections and before the 2010 elections? Because we're sick of the usual politics with moderate "establishment" republicans that are also dirty; or the weak, go-along republicans that just sit by while the liberal socialist democrats push them around and inch America closer and closer toward a European style socialist society. I suspect, but I don't know for sure, that the republican establishment is as big a problem as the liberal socialist democrats. They fought against Ronald Reagan and Newt Gingrich, and they always seem to back the most moderate republican candidates for president. They better back the most conservative republican candidates in the next cycles or we're done as a nation.

This country doesn't need another "pretty boy celebrity president" that plays the saxophone or sings the blues. Let's elect an ugly statesman with the moral and ethical characteristics of George Washington or Abraham Lincoln (Honest Abe was pretty ugly!).

WE ARE RUNNING OUT OF TIME VOTERS!

Get busy replacing all of these arrogant crooks. America is like the Titanic traveling through an iceberg riddled ocean and Captain Barrack

Hussein Obama is saying "full Steam ahead – this ship is unsinkable." He is more concerned with the seating assignments of the banquet hall than the safety and survival of the passengers. He is just as naive today about our economic future as the owners, builders and Captain were of the great Titanic in 1912. I'm giving him the benefit of the doubt that he is not bankrupting America on purpose, although I suspect he is not the kind of Captain that will go down with the ship. I'm pretty sure he will be on one of the life boats!

How is it that Greece is wreaking havoc with world markets when they are the economic equivalent of just one or two of our small states? Greece's financial problems are nothing compared to America's. We are the financial, economic and commerce engine of the world. Remember, if California was a country, it would be the 8th largest economy in the world – which is declining rapidly because of <u>their</u> socialist policies. When America gets a runny nose the rest of the world gets the flu. When the debt bomb goes off in America, the entire world will suffer the worst depression imaginable. Unlike Greece, the United States can print its way out of bankruptcy. It's called inflating our way out of our debts. As a result, inflation will eat up the current value of our money. (Note: the economy could go in just the opposite direction and enter a deflationary period or much worse – a depression. The extremely low interest rates around the world may be signaling a depression…)

Here is how sovereign currency governments inflate their way out of enormous public debts: Assets like real estate might go up a tenfold but not US Treasury Bonds. Compare the current value of a $100,000 piece of real estate, or even a shipping container of groceries worth $100,000, to a $100,000 US Government Treasury bond. Ten years later, if we experience hyperinflation, that piece of real estate and a shipping container of groceries might cost 10 times the original $100,000, or $1,000,000. It has happened to an even greater degree in South American and other banana republic nations before; it's not likely, but it could happen to America also!

Because the US Treasury Bond is an obligation to return only the original $100,000 to the owner of that bond, the future relative value of that bond will have been reduced to a current relative equivalent value of $10,000, or 1/10th of its original value (when compared to the $100,000 real estate or container of groceries). That's how governments inflate their way out of massive debts. If hyperinflation begins it is almost impossible to stop. Our Federal Reserve has made so many devastating mistakes in steering the economy they should be replaced and possibly abolished entirely – I'm not sure!

I made this illustration very simplistic and narrow to avoid as much confusion as possible for the average non-economics reader. It's much more complicated, but the road from year 1 to year 10 is paved with great heart ache and suffering – that is for the poor and the middle class, not the elites in Washington, NYC and California.

Let me ask you a question: When your grocery bill goes from $700 a month to $7,000 a month, will you and your family go hungry? Will the grocery stores get robbed and burglarized so often they go out of business? Will your company be able raise prices fast enough to stay in business? What about crime – do you think you'll be safe in your car or in your home? Will the police get paid? Maybe we should take all the guns away from law abiding citizens so only criminals have the guns! Second Amendment anyone? See why we don't trust liberal socialist democrats' agenda to disarm law abiding Americas? Ask the residents of poor neighborhoods in Detroit how long it takes for the police to come to their rescue. The answer is "after" the criminal is long gone!

Look around – municipalities are failing all over America and we haven't even begun to pay the final consequences of trillion dollar annual deficits and projected unfunded liabilities of 120+ trillion dollars. That number and especially the annual interest on it is unthinkable. Who's to blame? It should be obvious – the LSD Party!

The blame for America's future massive suffering will be laid at the feet of the liberal socialist democrats' agenda. Sure, you're not a socialist – you're just a caring liberal democrat or a compromising, go-along, caring moderate republican. Problem is you are incapable of seeing the truth and are being suckered into believing the big-government liberal socialist democrats' – *"SOMETHING FOR NOTHING CON."*

How is this going to end? I believe, just like most destructive addictions end, we will end up losing everything and find ourselves in the preverbal gutter. Then, after we finally realize socialism, in any form simply will never work, no matter who's in charge, we will do whatever is necessary to cleanse socialism from America. We will return to free-market capitalism and the basic laws, rules and regulations that protect the weak from common crooks and the powerful, politically connected cronies. They are the destructive forces who feed off the masses settling for crumbs and hand-outs. We don't need a million laws to do this; and, we don't need more lawyers and accountants than all the rest of the world combined. What we need is what the Tea Party Movement stands for – liberty, honesty, integrity, fairness, free-market enterprise, the rule of law, the American Constitution, and much more freedom!

We can hit the reset button after we experience the gutter or we can elect conservative free-enterprise God fearing statesmen instead of politicians.

It's our choice! It's not too late voters! We have very brave people like Senators Tom Colburn, Rand Paul, Ron Johnson, Pat Toomey, Marco Rubio, Tim Scott and many more honest, hardworking, courageous Congressmen like Paul Ryan and many other Conservative Republicans. These conservative and libertarian leaders have worked their butts off developing solutions that will turn America around financially and not only save America but help the rest of the world reach financial solvency. The liberal socialist democrats and their slobbering sycophants in the media, academia, unions and other liberal strongholds have masterfully demonized the Tea Party Movement to the point that reluctant republicans have distanced themselves from association with the Movement. Don't fall for this political warfare tactic, stand strong and boldly proclaim your support to the Constitutional Conservative and Libertarian Tea Party Movement beliefs. History will prove your bravery will be "right."

It's a shame the left has been so successful in their relentless negative campaign, because the Movement will certainly continue even without its appropriately named banner. The Tea Party Movement is not a party – it's an idea or a passion that was rooted in the birth of the greatest nation in history. It's a damn shame we are allowing the liberal socialist democrats to take the title of this conservative Movement away from us. Citizens who are passionate about saving America will not be defeated even if we have set backs. We will be heard…

Who is standing in the way of the brave conservative leaders passing the necessary legislation to "right" American from its current destructive course? **President Barrack Hussein Obama, Senator "Dingy" Harry Reid, "Let's pass it first before we read it" Nancy Pelosi, the**

liberal media, union leaders and, nearly 50% of all voters who are either being too stupid to figure out how this hustle is going to end, or too weak, or too lazy to do anything about it! Don't buy into their liberal socialist democrat scams anymore – don't allow them to hustle your friends, neighbors, kids and parents anymore. Vote all of these big-government liberal socialist democrat and moderate republican control freaks out of office and boycott the liberal media and Hollywood elites!

I mean that! Don't watch their movies, tune into their TV programs or read their print. Put all out of these liberal socialist businesses out of business – before they put America out of business! They believe profits are evil – that's great; don't give them any…

Elect national conservative Tea Party Movement leaders who will do the following at the federal level in Washington, DC. American patriots, here is your mission, if you chose to accept it:

1. Study the early history of America and try your best to understand why George Washington, most of our other Founding Fathers and Abraham Lincoln were so deeply grounded in their faith in God, Jesus Christ, prayer and Christian Scriptures;
2. Following number 1, return the American culture back to a God fearing society where morality, integrity, industry, performance, achievement and charity are paramount – where success is rewarded with admiration instead of demonization. Get rid of the socialist tenants of political correctness, labor unions, sexual immorality and the big-government leviathan which strangles the private sector free-market economy;
3. Passionately educate the poor and the disenfranchised that conservative, free-enterprise, limited government philosophies are the only way to increase the standard of living for all citizens, especially the poor, no matter what race they are. And replace the current corrupt and waste riddled welfare system with a more accountable local system to help the temporary and permanently disadvantaged among us. Wherever there is a river of money flowing there must be absolute checks and balances with severe consequences for cheating;

4. Completely overhaul and double the size of the US Immigration and Customs Enforcement Service to focus 50% of the entire department on Mexican legal and illegal immigrants. This should be a primary focus of the federal government to protect our citizens from imported criminals and provide a better path for all immigration to the US. We are a nation of immigrants and Mexican Americans have too much to offer our nation's future. We just need to accomplish this legally and fairly, and we simply can't add to our social welfare debts;
5. Protect our borders and this country from terrorist attacks with a massive fence/"Great Wall" from the Gulf of Mexico to the Pacific Ocean, a strong military, sufficient border guards and strong port security. This is one of the few responsibilities of our federal government;
6. Unleash America's vast energy resources. Instead of sending money to buy oil from foreign countries, some of whom want us dead, sell our newly discovered excess oil to Japan, China and other countries to help offset our enormous trade deficits with these same countries. This will also significantly increase our tax collections that help pay for all of the "worthy" social programs to benefit the poorest among us (inspirational and targeted educational programs will produce the most benefits). Green energy will increase, in time, through innovation and free-enterprise, not through tax credits or deductions and the force of taxation. More efficient future solar and wind will provide much more electricity, and hydrogen and natural gas will power most autos and trucks in the distance future. Until then, clean burning carbon fuel technology should be used because they work and are the cheapest to keep us warm and fuel our progress;
7. Completely overhaul the massively complex IRS tax code to simplify and remove "all" loopholes and subsidies of every kind. This could be accomplished over a 10 year period so the pain of losing deductions could be reduced over time. We should be making financial decisions based on anything other than saving or avoiding taxes. Otherwise we will be controlled by the powerfully connected and unelected parasitic lobbyist;

8. Unleash the American economy by getting rid of all stupid laws, rules and regulations that end up favoring some "crony" industries and businesses over others. The economy simply can't become robust and thrive with "millions" of overlapping and strangling laws, rules and regulations. Tort reform must be part of this formula. Follow the lead of Texas, which is part of their success story. Numbers 6, 7 and 8 will turn the economy loose leading to much higher tax collections and allow us to do the spending cuts necessary to balance the budget and eventually pay off our enormous federal debts. The national savings and wealth creation for everyone will be exponential;
9. Find equitable solutions to save Welfare, Social Security and Medicare from the runaway spending levels that is currently bankrupting these programs. Study what Gingrich & Co. did in 1990's and reform these programs to get rid of runaway spending, waste, fraud and abuse;
10. Get rid of all unnecessary federal departments (most of them) or send them to the states if the Constitution says it is the states' responsibility. Sending rivers of money to DC to be divvied up by these political and bureaucratic HUSTLERS; then they send fractions of our money back to us in states and localities. It is an enormous waste of precious resources;
11. Cut all other spending to the bone until we have paid off the federal debt and are running surpluses. This can be spread out over a few years so as not to shock the economy. The Republican sponsored Penny Plan or something like it may be the solution. Congressman Paul Ryan's 2013 budget plan is also a solution to our future train-wreck (he is another conservative that would make a great President). If all of these ideas are enacted the economy will explode to the up-side, offsetting these spending cuts over the near term. Again, look at what Gingrich & Co. did in the 90's that resulted in balancing the budget and growing the economy. Remember, Clinton was dragged kicking and screaming against republican ideas and reforms;
12. Legislate a constitutional amendment to balance the federal budget each year. We have come close to doing this in the past

but maybe, like an addict, we have to experience so much pain before we submit to rehab;

13. Begin the long process of changing the congressional and presidential election cycles to minimize the ratio of sleazy campaigning to governing. Change congressional terms to 4 years with 1/2 up for reelection every 2 years and presidential term to one 5 year term. Senator's terms would remain at 6 years with 1/3rd of the senators up for reelection every 2 years. Also, to ensure we have leaders with a citizen's mentality instead of a "royalty" mentality we should limit the terms of congressmen/women to 16 years, senators to 18 years and the president to one 6 year term. We should restrict the president from campaigning of any kind during his 6 year term. As it is now we are getting a president whose major focus is campaigning for himself and his party. We need a president whose "only" focus should be on increasing the safety, freedoms and prosperity of our citizens – not on sleazy political campaigns; and,
14. Last – start celebrating free-enterprise exceptionalism and teach how success and financial freedom is achieved. Teach this to every student, every year just like math, science and English from 1st grade through seniors in high school and give real life examples along with guest speakers. Why this hasn't been a focus of our educational curriculum for the last 50 years is a national crime or at least a disgrace. Can you imagine several generations of students being taught the lessons of entrepreneurship, hard work, achievement, compound savings and investment plans and other wealth building strategies instead of the liberal socialist democrats' steady diet of dependence on a trillion dollar wasteful and corrupt government?

Our children must be educated on the principles and history of free-enterprise, free-market capitalism, instead of the "indoctrination" of liberal socialist democrat propaganda that was so commonly used by communist and socialist countries like North Korea, China and the Soviet Bloc. Compare the nightmare of anti-capitalist, communist North Korean or Cuban regimes to the huge success of capitalist, free-market South Koreans and the recent success of communist China with their move towards a capitalist economy. Can you stupid liberal socialist democrats see the difference between North Korea and South Korea or Detroit and Dallas? Of course you can, but you don't care – do you? You only care about how much power, control, fame and fortune you can hustle from us…

How do democrats boil a live frog? They put it in cool water and turn the heat on high – the gradual change in temperature will not alarm the frog until it's too late. That is what has happened to the world, and America, over the last 150 years! Americans, when are you going to stop acting like those frogs?

Wake up and fight the spread of socialism by the liberal democrats and moderate republicans…

Let's get busy turning this country around and again becoming the freedom loving, free-enterprise, wealth building, exceptional nation that was, and still could be, the model for the rest of the world. Isn't this the reason we are the "melting-pot" nation and why poor people around the planet have risked their lives over the centuries to come to America? Or, have they come here for the crumbs being doled out by the liberal socialist democrats and their sycophants in DC, NYC, California, Chicago, Detroit and other socialist states and cities around the country.

I don't think so…

In other words: Stop being hustled by the liberal socialist democrat con artist. Do your research! Bulk up.
0! Get busy!

Look behind the curtain and see who is really pulling the strings. It's not who you think it is. America is the envy of the world because of liberty and opportunity – not because of socialism! Vote for constitutional conservative, God fearing, Tea Party "Movement" Republicans and Libertarians. Even if you don't believe in God you surely know or feel you will benefit from what I'm suggesting. If our elected leaders don't follow the above principles and our Constitution while in office replace them with others that will. Democrats love zero tolerance – well it's time we gave them a big dose of zero tolerance…

We are going to return to our Founding Fathers' ideals – either soon or after much more needless suffering. If we could rebuild this country after the devastation of our Civil War in the 1860's we can rebuild it today. Our two greatest presidents were George Washington and Abraham Lincoln who by God's will were also two of our most religious, God-fearing, Christian presidents. Their lives and actions were dedicated to prayer and the scriptures of the Christian New Testament. There are God loving Americans all over this country that are diligently praying every day that He will have mercy on us and send us leaders that will change the hearts of voters who are blinded by the liberal socialist democrats' sound bite propaganda; i.e., "the Hustle." Notice I didn't say that God will change their hearts, I said send America leaders that will change their hearts. These leaders MUST be God fearing and anointed by God to accomplish the greatest and most important social change in History. Don't believe in God but you believe in and back these principles? There are scriptures in the Christian bible that honor that kind of deed. I thank you profoundly…

The God of Abraham, Ishmael, Isaac, Jacob and Jesus must be central in America or we will continue our decline as a Nation. Jesus Christ was not just a great Prophet or teacher written about in Jewish history or the Muslim Qur'an – he is exactly who he said he was and his words to us must be our guide in all we do individually and as a Nation. Then and only then will this country return to her exceptional place in history and our "Pursuit of Happiness" is further fulfilled. Our past doesn't have to equal our future! We can create any future we want – as long as we elect leaders with the moral courage, integrity and the character traits of our Founding Fathers.

If we do these things, and I Pray we will, America will once again be the envy of the world and the desired destination of every poor or abused human that yearns for a better life and the "Pursuit of Happiness" for themselves and their family.

I am closing this book with the transcript of a powerfully anointed 4 minute YouTube video by Bishop E. W. Jackson titled: ***"Message to Christians in the Black Community"*** dated September 18, 2012:

My name is Bishop E.W. Jackson, Chairman of Ministers Taking A Stand, with a message to Christians in the black community.

It is time to end the slavish devotion to the Democrat Party. They have insulted us, used us and manipulated us. They have saturated the black community with the ridiculous lie: Unless we support the Democrat Party, we will be returned to slavery, we will be robbed of voting rights, the Martin Luther King holiday will be repealed."

They think we're stupid and that these lies will hold us captive while they violate everything we believe as Christians. The Democrat Party has created an unholy alliance between certain so-called civil rights leaders and Planned Parenthood, which has killed unborn black babies by the tens of millions. Planned Parenthood has been far more lethal to black lives than the KKK ever was. And the Democrat Party and their black civil rights allies are partners in this genocide.

The Democrat Party has equated homosexuality with being black, which is another outrageous lie. They can keep their homosexuality private; you and I cannot hide being black. I need not recount to you the painful history of slavery, Jim Crow, lynching and sterilizations – all because of skin color. Anyone who dares equate the so called gay rights movement with the history of black Americans is exploiting the black community.

They say opposition to same-sex marriage is the same as opposition to interracial marriage. That is an insult to human intelligence. It is a lie. No Christian should support this. Yet the Democrat Party has now declared same-sex marriage an official part of its platform and black Christians remain in that party?

The civil rights establishment has embraced the lies and betrayed the black community and God Almighty for 30 pieces of silver from the Democrat Party. We, as Christians, ought to know better. Shame on us for allowing ourselves to be sold to the highest bidder! We belong to God. Our ancestors were sold against their will centuries ago, but we're going to the slave market voluntarily today. Yes, it's just that ugly.

> What do you call it when Jesus Christ died on the cross for your sins and my sins and paid the price for our freedom and you join in covenant with a political party that doesn't even want God mentioned in their platform? And gets offended at the very mention of Jesus' name?
>
> If your pastor tells you to vote for a party that disrespects Jesus, you need to leave that church. Black pastors are also going to have to answer whether they serve Jesus or the Democrat Party. The black community will never prosper by betraying God and following leadership that curries the favor of the Democrat Party. It is time for Christians to have the faith and courage to refuse to associate with a political party that has over the years become anti-Christian, anti-church, anti-Bible, anti-life, anti-family and anti-God. The Democrat Party is also becoming increasingly anti-Israel and God said, "I will curse those that curse Israel." Do you want to be cursed with them?
>
> It is time to come out of the Democrat Party and to refuse to support its candidates in their rebellion against God. It's not about party, but principle. It's not about race, but righteousness. And you will stand before God to give an account for your choices and motives. We don't need the Democrat Party or any party. We need God. God will take care of us. It's been a long time coming, but the time has come to take a stand. Come out from among them… Exodus now!

Wow! It is brilliant, courageous, God fearing men like Bishop E. W. Jackson that gives me so much hope for the future of America…

I believe this message is vital for ALL Christians everywhere as the future of the World depends greatly on the future of America, and the future of America depends greatly on Godly government stewards and especially leaders like Bishop E. W. Jackson… We simply must elect these leaders – soon!

Who is D. W. Burdick? He is just an average American single father trying to raise three teenagers, and wants desperately to help make a difference in the future of this great Country. If I can be the catalyst to save just one baby's life from being aborted or add to the Tea Party Movement's success in electing God fearing, constitutional conservatives to public office, I will consider this 18 month long endeavor a success. In any event, it has kept a recently disabled 62 year old senior citizen who lost everything from becoming too depressed to function.

Again, if this book is successful and gets the attention of those in power on the left, we will see if I have lost my First Amendment right to free speech (especially political speech) without retribution. Please pray that God gives me the strength to withstand the probable onslaught of attacks from the liberal socialist democrats, their sycophants in the news media and other liberal strongholds if this book is successful!

The great president, Ronald Reagan, once said: "Freedom is never more than one generation away from extinction."

I pray we are not that generation…

> **One day your life will flash before your eyes. Make sure it's worth watching. – Unknown source**

www.ingramcontent.com/pod-product-compliance
Lightning Source LLC
Chambersburg PA
CBHW060834280326
41934CB00007B/775

* 9 7 8 0 9 9 1 0 8 9 6 0 4 *